Winning Ways

Best Practices in Work-Based Learning

Edited by
Albert J. Pautler, Jr.,
and Deborah M. Buffamanti

Tech Directions Books
Prakken Publications, Inc.

Library of Congress Catalog Card Number: 97-66548
ISBN: 0-911168-94-X

Permissions

Permission to use "Apprenticeships and Community Colleges: Linkages in America's Defense" by Jeffrey A. Cantor granted by *Journal of Industrial Teacher Education*. The work first appeared in *Journal of Industrial Teacher Education*, Vol. 31, No. 3, Spring 1994.

Permission to use "Basic Academic and Vocational Skills Required of Employees with Only a High School Diploma" by Kenneth S. Volk and Henry A. Peel granted by the authors. The work first appeared as a report sponsored by the Eastern North Carolina Consortium for Assistance and Research in Education.

Permission to use "Education and Work: The Choices We Face" by Arthur G. Wirth granted by *Phi Delta Kappan*. The work first appeared in *Phi Delta Kappan*, Vol. 74, No. 5, January 1993.

Permission to use "An Emerging Perspective on Policies for American Work and Education for the Year 2000: Choices We Face" by Arthur G. Wirth granted by *Journal of Industrial Teacher Education*. The work first appeared in *Journal of Industrial Teacher Education*, Vol. 31, No. 4, Summer 1994.

Permission to use "Growth Patterns in Workplace Training" by Anthony P. Carnevale and Ellen S. Carnevale granted by American Society for Training and Development. The work first appeared in *Training and Development*, May 1994.

Permission to use "How We Will Learn in the Year 2000: Reengineering Schools for the High Performance Economy" by Deborah M. Buffamanti and Albert J. Pautler, Jr., granted by *Journal of Industrial Teacher Education*. The work first appeared in *Journal of Industrial Teacher Education*, Vol. 31, No. 4, Summer 1994.

Permission to use "Improving the School-to-Work Transition of American Adolescents" by Robert W. Glover and Ray Marshall granted by Teachers College Press. The work first appeared in Ruby Takanashi's *Adolescence in the 1990s: Risk and Opportunity*, Teachers College, Columbia University, 1993.

Permission to use "Postsecondary Technical Education: The Proprietary Sector" by Albert Pautler, Sterne Roufa, and John Thompson granted by *Journal of Studies in Technical Careers*, Vol. X, No. 1, Winter 1988.

Permission to use "Youth Apprenticeship in the United States: Transmission or Transformation of the German Apprenticeship System" by Nevin R. Frantz, Jr., granted by *Journal of Industrial Teacher Education*. The work first appeared in *Journal of Industrial Teacher Education*, Vol. 31, No. 3, Spring 1994.

To Don, with much love. *–D. B.*

To Marilyn, Mark, Ann, Mary, and Mike–I love you all. *–A. P.*

Contents

Introduction

This book arose from a series of conversations held between George Kennedy, publisher of Prakken Publications' Tech Directions Books, and Al Pautler. A few years ago, George and Al began to mull over the notion of a book that would include material on apprenticeships, on the school-to-work transition, and on the corporate training programs that affect people once they've entered the working world. The dialog continued on and off for a time, and it ultimately evolved to include work-based learning, school-based learning, and the exploration of connecting activities between the two. Eventually, we arrived at a substantial idea of what a book on this subject could (and should) include. At that time, we began planning a strategy to compile a volume that would lead the reader to explore some of the basic tenets surrounding the complex world of school to work and, more recently, school *at* work. At this juncture, *Winning Ways: Best Practices in Work-Based Learning* was born.

The materials included within this publication naturally lent themselves to be divided into three major sections—the first concentrating on the background issues of work-based education; the second emphasizing the depth, breadth, and range of corporate training efforts; and the final section dealing with the pragmatic issue of school-based practices and procedures. While all reprinted articles and original contributions can be read as separate works, the attentive reader will find a variety of linkages between articles, between sections, and between organizational structures.

Organization of the Material

The first section of the book addresses some philosophical issues and provides background information on current topics for those interested in work-based education. This first section contains five chapters designed to illuminate for the reader a variety of underlying assumptions, implied or explicit, on which many of our educational and career systems are founded. Articles in this section include an excellent examination of the issue of choice by Arthur Wirth, as well as a substantive article on the nature of skill improvement and training today by Carnevale and Carnevale—two preeminent writers in their field. This section also includes a historical overview on the issue of "human capital"—a topic currently in vogue and of future interest, as well.

The book's second section concentrates on issues surrounding the field of corporate training and its impact on the world of work and the changing workforce. Contained in its seven chapters are a variety of original submissions from such corporations as Hewlett-Packard, JCPenney, the Bank of Montreal, and Rich Products. While each corporate entity presents a different view of its organizational ability to manage and manipulate change, readers will discover that some training issues cut across time, place, and industry. Other issues, like the "new employment contract" are only now becoming widely recognized and have some far-ranging implications for the American labor market.

The third section has nine chapters on school-based practices. The focus here is on the educational constructs in middle, secondary, or proprietary schools, or community colleges that impact directly either on the school-to-work transition or some other learning system in America. This section also includes a number of pieces on the current state of American apprenticeship programs. Articles by Frantz, Glover and Marshall, and Melnik and Doty all provide a fresh, broad perspective on one of America's more persistent problems—how people move from school to work.

Work-Based Learning Identified

What is *work-based learning*? The major focus of work-based learning is preparing people for meaningful, gainful employment, based on individual abilities, knowledge, and skill level. It may include work experience, mentoring, and industry-specific skill training, as well as classroom instruction and on-the-job (OJT) training. Frequently, this type of training is combined into a sequential program of skill attainment that ultimately results in skill mastery and measurably enhanced productivity back on the job. Work-based education is not a substitute for vocational preparation, although it does include both vocational and academic preparation. The phrase *work-based learning* was chosen for this book since it aptly describes the current American mission of preparing the workforce for both the near future and the long-term "unknowable" future.

The process of work-based learning typically starts in the schools, sometimes as early as the middle-school level. It increases in importance and duration during the secondary and community college years. Once an individual finds gainful employment, employers engage in further training. Since not everyone can manage to become em-

ployed easily today, or maintain his or her employability, we've included one chapter that deals with the *second-chance system*. This particular learning system, under the sponsorship of the United States Department of Labor, covers remedial measures to assist those who need retraining or skill upgrading.

Frameworks for Analysis

One framework for analysis of the material presented here is the recent (1994) School-to-Work Opportunities Act. The act defines a *school-to-work system* as a network of key players that combines three central elements: (a) work-based learning systems, (b) school-based learning systems, and (c) connecting activities. The wording of the act, and the elements identified, are most suitable within the context of academic public schooling, but they apply to other learning systems—such as corporate training—as well.

The attentive reader can also identify a second framework for analysis by considering pre- and postemployment preparation programs. Preemployment work-based programs occur before employment and normally aim to assist a person's progress toward employment. Postemployment experiences occur as part of employment or at a person's own expense. Generally, postemployment programs enhance an employee's professional development and at the same time benefit his or her employer. Both types of preparation program are widely used and both can work at various stages of an employee's professional development.

A third paradigm for analysis revolves around the nature of "best practices." This slippery topic is difficult to quantify, changes frequently, and is rather amorphous in nature. Everyone engaged in both formal education and the training and development fields realizes that practices change over time—as does instructional technology. Hence, what is widely in favor one year may seem of little use the next. One of our goals has been to identify some of the best practices as currently identified by various scholars in both the education and the training and development fields.

Content Selection

We have tried to select a broad range of topics and materials that will appeal to a wide audience. Those interested in the nature or future of work, the linkages between school and work, the linkages between government and work, and the ongoing development of the American workforce should all find something interesting here. Our overall objective in selecting contributions was to make sure that they present stimulating factual material. With some very hard work, we also uncovered some "gems."

At this point, we would like to take the opportunity to thank those who contributed to this work—the corporate authors, the academic authors, and those who allowed us to use previously published material. In addition, we would like to thank the staff of our publisher, the Tech Directions Books division of Prakken Publications, for their time, effort, and assistance. We hope that you will find the book valuable—in both your personal and professional development.

Deborah M. Buffamanti
Albert J. Pautler, Jr.

Contributors

DIANE BLAIR is manager of meta learning at the Bank of Montreal's Institute for Learning. She has responsibility for ensuring that both facilitators and learners fully benefit from the institute's rich environment. Ms. Blair has had a career-long interest in education, adult learning, and managing centers of learning. She holds a B.A. from University of Western Ontario; a B.E. from Queen's University, Kingston; an M.S. in education from Northern Illinois University; and a master's of management in hotel administration from Cornell University. She has many years of experience in residential education and leadership development, including serving as founder and director of Wildwood Outdoor Leisure Center, an adult adventure-based learning and conference center; working in strategic planning, operations, and marketing at a conference center; and serving as program director at the government of Ontario's Bark Lake Leadership Center.

DEBORAH M. BUFFAMANTI is the director of the Geographic Information and Analysis Laboratory at the State University of New York at Buffalo. She received her B.A. (1982) in political science from the University of Toronto and her Ed.M. (1994) in higher education administration from the State University of New York at Buffalo. She has held a variety of positions in the computing industry, is an active member of the National Association of Female Executives and of the university's Departmental Computing Consultants Committee. Ms. Buffamanti has published in the *Journal of Industrial Teacher Education*. Her expertise in the corporate training field began in the mid-1980s, when she worked as a training manager at Centennial College's management training center in Scarborough, Ontario, Canada. She plans to pursue a doctorate.

JEFFREY A. CANTOR is director of technical education, Virginia Community College System, Richmond, Virginia. He is responsible for systemwide planning and guidance, budgetary administration, and evaluation of technical studies programs. He was previously associate professor of adult and business education at Lehman College of the City University of New York. There, he instructed courses in human resource development and training. His principal research interests are in issues of policy related to employment and training, apprenticeship program development, and training program design and evaluation. He has published extensively in those areas. Dr. Cantor has held positions in business and industry and in community colleges in Maryland and Florida. He holds a Ph.D. in educational leadership and instructional systems from Florida State University.

ANTHONY CARNEVALE is chief economist of the American Society for Training and Development, Alexandria, Virginia.

ELLEN S. CARNEVALE is editor of *Technical and Skills Training* magazine. The magazine is published by the American Society for Training and Development, Alexandria, Virginia.

MARY BETH DEBUS has worked in the training and development fields for more than 10 years. She is currently the training manager at Rich Products Corporation, Buffalo, New York. Before working at Rich Products, Ms. Debus held key training positions with Mount Carmel East Hospital, Columbus, Ohio, and at Graphic Controls Corporation, Buffalo, New York. She received her B.A. (1984) and M.A. (1986) in communication, both from the State University of New York at Buffalo. After pursuing additional graduate work, she taught at the Ohio State University and at Canisius College. Ms. Debus has led a variety of seminars for professionals in health care, industry, and education. She has presented many academic papers, co-authored a journal article, and has a strong background in the volunteer movement. She has also worked with the boards of Alcohol and Drug Dependency Services of Western New York and Western New York United Against Drug and Alcohol Abuse.

CHARLES R. DOTY is associate professor of career and technical education, Rutgers University, New Brunswick, New Jersey. He has written a variety of publications related to community colleges: *National Conference on Postsecondary Staff Development* (1976); *Review and Synthesis of Research in Technical Education 1968-82* (1980, 1982); *Handbook of Skills for Industrial Trainers and Occupational Educators* (1984); *Preparing for High Technology: Model Programs in the U.S.A. and Resources for Automated Manufacturing Technologies Programs* (national surveys, 1985); *Technical Upgrading* (1985); *Robotics/Automated Systems Technicians* (1985); *Longitudinal Evaluation of Technical Programs* (1985); *General Education for Technical Education* (1985); and *Developing Occupational Programs* (1987).

GALE DUFF-BLOOM is senior executive vice president and director of personnel and company communications at the J. C. Penney Company, Inc., headquartered in Plano, Texas. After beginning her career with J. C. Penney as a management trainee in 1969, she advanced through company ranks, holding a variety of management positions including district merchandiser, regional fashion merchandiser, and women's fashion merchandise specialist. She continued to make major career advances with J. C. Penney and by 1988 was appointed manager of investor relations. The same year, Ms. Duff-Bloom was elected vice president and director. In 1990, she was promoted to senior vice president and associate director of merchandising. In 1993, she was elected to executive vice president and director of administration, and by in 1994 she assumed her current position. Ms. Duff-Bloom is also an active community member, maintaining memberships in a variety of professional organizations, including the Dallas Forum, the Fashion Group International, the National Association of Female Executives, and the International Women's Forum. She also serves as director of the Geon Company, The National Alliance of Business, the Texas Commerce Bank, and several other business and community groups.

NEVIN R. FRANTZ, JR., is professor of vocational and technical education at Virginia Polytechnic Institute and State University, Blacksburg, Virginia. He holds a baccalaureate degree from Millersville State Teachers College and received his master's and doctorate degrees from the University of Maryland. In more than 30 years of experience in vocational teacher education, he has served on the faculties of Northern Illinois University, the University of Georgia, and the University of Delaware. His international experience includes being a visiting lecturer in Finland, Norway, and Sweden. He spent several weeks in the Federal Republic of Germany observing the dual system of vocational education in that country. He has served as a representative for the People to

People program in the People's Republic of China and was awarded a Fulbright fellowship to study at the University of Jyvaskyla in Finland in 1994. Dr. Frantz is a recognized leader in the field of vocational and technical education and has many publications. He also has served as consultant to many organizations and agencies in the vocational education field.

JIM FULLER is manager of learning and performance technology at the Hewlett-Packard Company, headquartered in Palo Alto, California. His area has specific responsibility for performance improvement processes, instructional design methods, education evaluation systems, and the application of technology to accelerate learning. Mr. Fuller has worked at Hewlett-Packard for 17 years, holding management positions in research and development, manufacturing, marketing, sales, support, and education. He has an M.S. in instructional and performance technology from Boise State University, where he teaches graduate courses in performance technology. He is author of the book *Managing Performance Improvement Projects* and is a frequent speaker at conferences of such organizations as the International Society for Performance Improvement and the American Society for Training and Development. He has spoken on implementing performance technology, evaluation strategies, the use of technology in training delivery, the use of metacognition in learning, and gender-based-communications in the workplace.

KATHERINE M. GERSTLE is administrative director of the M.B.A. program at the State University of New York at Buffalo. She received her B.S. (1987) in accounting from Boston College and became a CPA while working for KPMG Peat Marwick. Dr. Gerstle earned an M.B.A. (1989) with a concentration in human resources management and a Ph.D. (1992) in higher education administration from the State University of New York at Buffalo. Before joining the staff of the School of Management, she worked in several other offices at the University of Buffalo, including undergraduate admissions, student life, and the office of the vice president for student affairs. Dr. Gerstle contributed to *Higher Education in Crisis: New York in National Perspective*, published by Garland Publishing in 1995. In addition, she is involved in a number of community and professional organizations, including the Food Shuttle of WNY and the Association for the Study of Higher Education.

ROBERT W. GLOVER is a research scientist at the Center for the Study of Human Resources, University of Texas, Austin.

MICHAEL P. LILLIS is assistant professor of management at Medaille College in Buffalo, New York. He received his Ph.D. in organizational behavior from the State University of New York at Buffalo in 1994. Dr. Lillis received the Decision Sciences Institute's 1994 Theoretical/Empirical Research Paper Award. In 1994 and 1995, he received certificates for significant contributions in research, teaching, and service at Medaille College. Dr. Lillis has consulted for a number of organizations, including E. I. du Pont de Nemours and Company, Inc., and the Medina Memorial Hospital. His research focuses on organizational justice and on the micro-level processes of individual choice behavior.

RAY MARSHALL is professor, LBJ School of Public Affairs, University of Texas, Austin.

LEE MELNIK began her career in education as a secondary teacher of English and reading. After 6 years of teaching she joined the cooperative education staff at Brookdale Community College, Lincroft, New Jersey. She has been affiliated with the program for 16 years and has served as its director for 8 years. During that time, she has also been a field reader for Title VIII cooperative education federal funding program, a trainer for the Atlantic Cooperative Education Training and Resource Center, and a consultant to the Monmouth County Vocational School District, where she developed assessment instruments for school-to-work programs. Ms. Melnik is an active member of the Cooperative Education Association, the New Jersey Cooperative Education Association, and the National Commission for Cooperative Education. She is a frequent presenter on cooperative education, work-based learning, and school to work. She earned her B.A. from Rutgers University and her M.E. from the Graduate School of Education, Rutgers University.

JERRY M. NEWMAN is director of the Center for Team Performance in the School of Management at SUNY-Buffalo. He is co-author of the book *Compensation* (Irwin Publishing, 1996) and author of more than 60 articles on compensation, performance management, training, and employment discrimination. He has consulted with such firms as Hewlett-Packard, RJR Nabisco, AT & T, and Cummins Engine.

ALBERT J. PAUTLER, JR., is professor of education, Graduate School of Education, University of Buffalo. Earlier, he was a faculty member at Rutgers University, Brunswick, New Jersey, and a high school teacher of electronics in New York state. He is the author or editor of several books, including *Vocational Education in the 1990s: Major Issues* (1990) and *High School to Employment Transition: Contemporary Issues* (1994). He has written more than 50 articles on topics dealing with vocational education, curriculum planning, and school-to-work transition. He has served as a consultant to many organizations including the U.S. Department of Education, the U.S. Department of Labor, General Motors, DuPont, and the New York State Education Department.

HENRY A. PEEL is associate professor in the Department of Educational Leadership and associate dean in the School of Education, East Carolina University, Greenville, North Carolina. He has 15 years of experience in teaching, counseling, and adminis-

tration in public schools and higher education. His doctoral dissertation at the University of North Carolina at Chapel Hill examined business leaders' perceptions of the superintendent's role in economic development. His current research interests include school improvement and facilitative leadership.

PAUL J. POLEDINK is internal education and training consultant, UAW-GM Center for Human Resources (CHR). During his 11-year career with the United Auto Workers and General Motors, he has supported the design of training programs, facilitated discussions and meetings, provided research data on proposed CHR joint initiatives, and coordinated relationships between the CHR and public education agencies. Mr. Poledink's background in education as teacher and administrator, his formal education, and his professional activities in the field of adult education, including the presidency of the Michigan Association for Adult and Continuing Education, have enabled him to assist the UAW and GM in carrying out their mutually agreed on services to UAW-represented GM employees.

STERNE A. ROUFA holds a Ph.D. in educational administration from State University New York at Buffalo, where he served as program director of the Micro Computer Labs and Center for Apple Labs Operation. Before that, he had a 21-year military career, during which he earned both B.A. and M.A. degrees in human resource management. He now lives in Machesney Park, Illinois, and works with marketing and development of computer systems.

SCOTT R. SWEETLAND is an associate of the Department of Educational Organization, Administration and Policy and the Center for Educational Resources and Technologies, State University of New York at Buffalo. He earned B.B.A. and M.B.A. degrees from Saint Bonaventure University and served in various managerial and administrative capacities for a large commercial banking institution. Since 1990, he has held professorial appointments, worked as a business consultant, and completed doctoral coursework. Mr. Sweetland is working on a doctoral dissertation on human capital theory.

JOHN THOMPSON is a school superintendent and former chief training officer for the state of Georgia. He has also served as executive director of another state training organization, as vice president of an international training company, director of a university computer training facility, and as president of his own training firms. Mr. Thompson has taught at the community college and university levels in both credit and noncredit courses. He has presented workshops on various topics. Mr. Thompson earned his B.A. from the State University of New York at Binghamton and his M.A. from the University of Rochester. He is a doctoral candidate in Education Administration at the State University of New York at Buffalo.

CONRAD R. TOEPFER, JR., is professor in the Department of Learning and Instruction, State University of New York at Buffalo. A past president of the National Middle School Association, he is on the Advisory Council for the National Resource Center for Middle Grades Education. Dr. Toepfer works with middle level schools throughout the U.S. and abroad. He has addressed several European Middle School League conferences and works with middle level schools in Austria, Belgium, Germany, the Netherlands, and Switzerland. Dr. Toepfer is author of the section on junior high and middle school education in the last edition of the *Encyclopedia of Educational Research*. He has also written 35 books and monographs and published more than 150 articles in major professional journals in the general curriculum and middle level educational literature. He edits *Transescence: The Journal on Emerging Adolescent Education* and is a contributing editor to the *Journal of Early Adolescence*.

KENNETH S. VOLK is a senior lecturer in the Department of Engineering and Technology Studies, Hong Kong Institute of Education. He has 18 years of teaching experience in secondary education, industrial training, and teacher education. His doctoral dissertation at the University of Maryland examined technology education curriculum guidelines for developing countries. He also writes on political and social issues related to technology.

ARTHUR G. WIRTH was a professor in the Department of Education and in the Interdisciplinary Human Resource Management Program (1975-1985) at Washington University, St. Louis. He holds a Ph.D. in education from Ohio State University. He has received grants from the John Dewey Foundation, which supported studies of changes in workplaces toward more democratic participation at work research institutes in Norway and Sweden, as well as at various industrial sites in the U.S. On the basis of these experiences, Dr. Wirth wrote *Productive Work in Industry and Schools* (University Press of America, 1983) and *Education and Work for the Year 2000* (Jossey-Bass, 1992).

Part I

Background and Philosophy

Education and Work: The Choices We Face

By Arthur G. Wirth

Reprinted with permission from *Phi Delta Kappan,* Vol. 74, No. 5, January 1993.

IN 1916, John Dewey considered the awesome impact of early industrialism and said, "Democracy has to be born anew in each generation, and education is its midwife'" (Dewey, 1916, pp. 409-414). I wrote *Education and Work for the Year 2000* out of a sense that, as we entered the 1990s, changes were occurring in work and education that could give us another chance at democratic renewal. At the same time, strong forces of resistance were at work that could cause us to miss the opportunity. By looking at both possibilities, I hope to improve the chances for the kind of renewal that Dewey sought.

We are well into the beginning of the new postindustrialism, which is marked by three momentous developments: (1) the electronic computer revolution, (2) the emergence of a competitive global market, and (3) the prospect of serious ecological damage. As we struggle to cope with these developments in work and education, I believe that the choices we make will be determined by the way we choose to resolve the tension between two major value orientations in American culture. On the one hand, our national culture reflects the rational model of bureaucratic control that we mastered so effectively in factory-based industrialism; on the other hand, certain key values of the democratic tradition have strong roots in the culture as well—among them, respect for the dignity of individuals, chances for participative involvement, and opportunities to be active and inquiring learners.

In American work and education there has been a partial turn toward the democratic tradition—primarily for functional reasons related to our survival. The tradition of centralized control has proved to be dysfunctional for coping with the turbulent change of the postindustrial era.

To gain some much-needed perspective, I wish to reflect first on events in work and education in the 1980s. There was considerable alarm about productivity problems in both work and schooling in the face of powerful new challenges from Japanese and German competition. Both industry and education were under pressure to "reform"—and there was a surprising range of responses from policy makers in both institutions.

Creative leaders in industry and labor began to see the long-standing tradition of top-down, expert-controlled, scientific management as the source of problems, rather than as the solution to problems. They were probing various forms of workplace democracy or democratic sociotechnical theory as alternatives.

At the same time, policy makers in American education, under the leadership of Secretary of Education William Bennett, were rushing in the opposite direction. The linchpin of education reform, Bennett argued, was measurable accountability–expert-designed, centrally monitored instruction and testing.

But by the early 1990s new factors had emerged that were making the centralized, bureaucratic model of control as dysfunctional in American schooling as it was in American industry. Efforts at democratic renewal were becoming necessary for coping with the fast pace of change. First, I will offer some comments about changes in industry and work, and then I will take up some key issues in education.

Changes in Work: "Automating" or "Informating"

The great transformer of work in this generation is computer technology, and it must be acknowledged up front that it can be used either to de-skill or to upgrade jobs. However, some important studies show that the trend is toward upgrading. In my latest book, I cite examples in textiles, apparel, banking, business services (Bailey, 1991), the military, and the General Motors Corporation's Saturn plant. Leading this trend are events in high-tech industry, described by Shoshanna Zuboff and Robert Reich.

In her book *In the Age of the Smart Machine: The Future of Work and Power*, Zuboff argues that powerful new computer technologies confront us with two very different possibilities of what can happen to both the quality of production and the quality of life at work (Zuboff, 1988). The first option she calls "automating," in which computer intelligence is located in "the electronic smart machine." As in Taylorism, management retains exclusive control over the knowledge base and organizes the system in a way that preserves and increases its power, with mechanical work turned over to computer-directed management. Using the automating model, management can de-skill work, create electronic surveillance, or move the entire system overseas to take advantage of cheaper labor. The ideal form of automating is the robotized factory, in which robots make robots–no need for pension funds, health insurance, or alcohol rehabilitation programs.

The second possibility Zuboff calls the "informating" option. It grows out of the recognition that the centrally controlled automated choice is not flexible enough–intelligent enough, if you will–to cope with the new order of change and complexity. In the informating choice, computer technology becomes a source for designing innovative methods of sharing information with the work force–informating them. New types of skills and knowledge that depend on the understanding and manipulation of information are needed to tap the potential of an intelligent technology. As the work force is given access to data from an information-rich environment, hierarchical distinctions begin to blur. Managers and workers fashion new roles that permit them to invent creative ways to add value to products and services.

Zuboff gives detailed examples of how work "in the age of the smart machine" gets transformed by the emergence of an "electronic text." The change is from the action-centered skills of physical production that characterized the industrial era to work marked by abstract intellective skills.

Action-centered skills require a detailed understanding of the physical medium in which work is done. With computerization, this personal understanding is abstracted and transferred to the electronic text, which incorporates the whole range of skills and processes that constitute the production system. Physical responses are replaced by symbols and abstract thought processes as control of production is incorporated into "the smart machine." One worker said, "I used to listen to the sounds the boiler makes and know just how it was running. I could look at the fire in the furnace and tell by its color what kinds of adjustment were needed. Now I only have numbers to go by." (Zuboff, 1988, p. 63)

When hammers and wrenches are displaced by numbers and buttons, a whole new kind of learning must begin, and it can be scary. After being introduced to the electronic text, operators must know how the data contained in that text correspond to actual processes and relations in the system. To do that, operators must understand the information system itself.

To understand the information system requires a kind of learning that demands the constructing of meaning from a symbolic medium. When people confront the electronic text and ask, "What is happening? What does that mean?" the answers frequently require a sharing of hypotheses to secure the best interpretation of the text. Thus, both managers and workers see the need to bring together people who are involved in the production process to discuss what they see, what they understand, and what should be done.

Learning becomes a top priority. Managers begin to see that all workers in the system need access to data so that they can understand the system in order to troubleshoot and innovate. As one operator said, "If I can control my own access to data, I can control my own learning." (Zuboff, 1988, p. 357) Beyond the need for access to data, the organizational climate must support the essential conditions of a learning environment—freedom to play with ideas, to experiment, and to enter into dialogue. Such an environment enhances competitive effectiveness, but at a cost that can be threatening to management. When the information of the electronic text is made accessible to the workforce, the knowledge that was once extracted from workers and given to the managers is returned to the workers.

There is knowledge in the electronic text that all must grapple with. The boundaries that used to define managerial knowledge begin to blur, and as they do so lines of authority are redrawn. Zuboff describes the fascinating choice faced by American management. If managers make the automating choice, they retain the classical power of hierarchical management—but at the cost of losing the flexibility required to be effective in the global market. If they choose to informate, they bring workers into active participation by data sharing and shift considerable learning and power to people at work. This makes them more competitive in the global market—but at the cost of losing traditional prerogatives of management.

Faced with this choice, some organizations flinch and stay with the automating option—retaining control but risking vulnerability to competition. The trend, however, is toward the informating option. The manager who wondered whether we were all going to end up working for a smart machine or whether there would be smart people around the machine clearly expressed the critical choice faced by management (Zuboff, 1988, 285).

In *The Work of Nations: Preparing Ourselves for 21st Century Capitalism,* Robert Reich (1991) describes another dimension of the transformation of work that explains the need for new qualities of learning in the emerging workplace. His point is that the model of industrial mass production of the 1950s is moving toward dinosaur-type obsolescence.

American corporations that can no longer generate large earnings from the high-volume production of standard commodities are gradually turning toward serving the diverse special needs of customers dispersed around the globe. They are surviving by shifting from high-volume to high-value production. National corporations are being transformed into international corporations with offices and personnel located all over the world. Their products are international composites made with components from worldwide networks of production, research, finance, and marketing.

Global communication networks of computers, facsimile machines, satellites, and modems link engineers, designers, contractors, and dealers worldwide and have made daily work a transnational affair for ever-increasing numbers of people. This global system, which is in a constant state of change and refinement, is made possible not only by evolving technology but also by four key human skills that drive high-value enterprises. Reich says that these are the skills of "symbolic analysis":

● abstraction—the capacity to order and make meaning of the massive flow of information, to shape raw data into workable patterns;

● system thinking—the capacity to see the parts in relation to the whole, to see why problems arise;

● experimental inquiry—the capacity to set up procedures to test and evaluate alternative ideas; and

● collaboration—the capacity to engage in active communication and dialog to get a variety of perspectives and to create consensus when that is necessary.

Postindustrial work, centered on these skills, requires a radical shift in the way we approach the world. The shift is from a world view founded on notions of mass production, which were linear, atomistic, hierarchical, manipulative, and dualistic, to a perspective based on symbolic analysis, which is interactive, decentralized, contextual/intellective, nonhierarchical, and participative.

Leaders of American industry and labor must plot strategies for survival in the turbulent world of high technology and international competition. By their choices, they will be deciding the quality of life and learning that Americans will experience in their daily work. The style and content of learning in American schools are as directly involved in these choices as are the features of the American workplace. What was going on in education while changes like these were taking place in work?

The Choices in Education

Under Secretary Bennett's banner of "back to basics" and test score accountability, the 1980s produced the hyperrationalization that Arthur Wise warned us about

in *Legislated Learning: The Bureaucratization of the American Classroom*. For example, an action by the Texas legislature made Texas teachers subject to a $50 fine if they were caught teaching reading without an approved textbook, and legislators in Florida passed a law making basal materials "the only legal means to provide reading instruction" (Goodman, 1988, p.33). With regard to role models, we were given Joe Clark, the New Jersey principal who got improved performance with a bullhorn, a baseball bat, and school expulsions.

The *Report Card on Basal Readers,* funded by the National Council of Teachers of English, said that the style of the 1980s was based, more than anything else, on control: "to control reading, to control language, to control learners, to control teachers. And this control becomes essential to tight organization and sequence. Any relaxation of the control in any of these elements would appear to undermine the whole system" (Goodman, 1988, p. 125). What was being described was, in short, the centralized model of bureaucratic control.

Just as so many of the corporate giants in industry had eventually discarded this model, the movement to adopt it in education faltered. At the end of the 1980s, Lauro Cavazos, Bennett's successor, acknowledged, "We tried to improve education by imposing regulations from the top down, while leaving the basic structure of the school untouched. Obviously, this hasn't worked" (Cooper, 1989, p. 1).

The time was ripe for school restructuring—with at least 40 definitions of what it was about. Mary Anne Raywid helped cut through the restructuring fog by identifying two salient aspects: (1) local school autonomy and (2) public schools of choice. While American schools were not functioning with the kind of high technology available to informating workplaces, the school restructuring movement was incorporating more democratic, participative ways of attempting to solve problems. Educational work structures were created that respected the capacity of teachers, parents, students, and administrators to take creative action for change at the local level. These work structures were often linked to more active and constructivist styles of learning for students. Some of the most effective restructuring attempts are being made in schools that confront our most intractable problems—the inner-city schools in impoverished, blighted neighborhoods.

One example is Manhattan's District 4 (which includes Deborah Meier's Central Park East schools). In the borough's most impoverished district, empowered teachers and parents generated ideas for change. They challenged the factory model of schooling by creating 44 different schools in 20 buildings. Parents and children may now choose from a variety of school themes: a health and biomedical studies school, a human services school, a maritime school, and so on. There have been striking positive results in attendance and academic growth. Such success shows that a democratic framework can tap unused creative resources to generate high-quality education in an urban area blighted by severe poverty.

James Comer has also challenged the factory school in his work in inner-city New Haven. His plan for school governance means that the principal shares power with parents, teachers, mental health workers, students, and staff.

Finally, the Accelerated Schools Program, launched by Henry Levin in the San Francisco Bay Area, works from the outrageously sensible principle that, to help at-risk students catch up with their more advantaged peers, you ought to scrap "dumbed down" instruction and provide them with enriched resources and opportunities for active learning similar to those made available to "gifted" students.

Beyond these renewal efforts for impoverished children, educators in the early 1990s were seeking alternatives to centralized control in two other areas that are crucially important for a postindustrial society: science education and the use of computers.

With regard to science education, Bill Aldridge, the executive director of the National Science Teachers Association identified the culprit for the sorry state of science education in the U.S. as the counterproductive reform effort of the 1980s. It assumed, he said, that standards could be raised by increasing the amount of material to be covered. "What's happening from grade school to graduate school," he said, "is the suffocation of curiosity under an avalanche of fact." Much of the pressure to cover material, he argued, derives from the epidemic of testing. "Testers break science up into small objects. What you get is an unassembling of the most fantastic features of science—its stories, its patterns." This approach assumes that covering science by the teacher results in learning science by the students. The result is millions of students "wasting their time learning virtually nothing of value," coming to hate science, and avoiding it in the future." (Cole, 1990, p.18)

One important response to the kind of science education that was pushed by the reforms of the 1980s is Project 2061, which requires that all students study science, technology, and mathematics in grades K through 12—working in groups instead of as competitors, using new technologies, and making their own discoveries instead of learning correct answers from a book. The kind of learning envisioned by Project 2061 requires following what Piaget called the pedagogical inspiration from the history of science itself: "to understand is to discover, or reconstruct by rediscovery, and such conditions must be complied with if in the future individuals are to be formed who are capable of production and creativity not simply repetition" (Piaget, 1973, p. 20).

Where computers are concerned, there are estimates that 85 percent to 90 percent of school use of computers has been devoted to drill and practice, far from the participative interaction with computer technology that is found in informated workplaces. But there are important exceptions. One that I have followed is the Apple Classrooms of Tomorrow (ACOT) Project. Its aim is to provide five very different schools in different parts of the country with the kind of computer-enriched environment that might exist in the year 2000. All students and teachers in ACOT classrooms are given personal computers and software to use at school and at home.

Instead of having expert advisors prescribe correct usage for teachers and students, the decision was made to give active support to teachers who wanted to innovate in their own chosen ways. At the same time, ACOT advisors, with years of classroom experience behind them, got discussion going about two concepts of learning. One sees knowledge as an accumulation of facts and principles that can be communicated to the learner. The other sees knowledge as personal, as something that must be constructed or discovered by learners.

The first concept of learning supports the notion that instruction can be an orderly science; the second leads to the more idiosyncratic views of teaching that the ACOT setting encourages. For example, students simulate a newspaper company, assuming such group tasks as art, business, graphics, article writing, and editing. In a related project, an electronic news-wire network connects students from California, Alaska, Hawaii, Israel, and Mexico. Students at each site write and edit articles that are sent to all participating sites. They then combine their own articles with ones written elsewhere to produce their own local newspaper (Sarason, 1990). We don't have to work very hard to see the connection between the style of learning of these ACOT students and the way a computer programmer described his view of his work:

> Anyone who works as a computer programmer and wants to advance is always learning in everything he does. . . . Either you are learning from someone or you are teaching someone else because they want to learn from you. (Light, 1992)

This is the style of work and learning that we found Zuboff describing in her book. In the ACOT program, we glimpse how an inquiring, collaborative style of learning can be combined with the power of computer technology to produce an education appropriate for our time.

These brief examples of trends in school restructuring illustrate the fact that educators as well as industrial designers are seeking to break out of the habits of mind of the industrial era. The shift is from top-down manipulation of people and programs to what Philip Murray, president of the steelworkers' union in the 1940s, called "tapping the brains of people at work"—tapping the potential for creative learning and troubleshooting that is essential for coping with a complex, fast-changing postindustrial reality.

The Societal Choice

Finally, even if our best hopes for restructuring materialize, we will still face another crucial choice—a societal choice. In the 1990s, America is at a crossroads and must decide how it will organize itself for engagement in the electronic global market and how it will define itself as a democracy under postindustrialism.

For survival and success in the global market, a critical ingredient, for *individuals* and *societies,* is access to the kind of education that, to use Reich's term, teaches the skills of "symbolic analysis": abstraction, systems thinking, experimental inquiry, and collaboration.

In the past 15 years, the individuals who have these skills have prospered; those lacking them have increasingly fallen behind. By 1990, the richest 20 percent received over half of the nation's income, and the top 5 percent received 26 percent—an all-time high in both cases. The poorest fifth received only 3.7 percent of total income, down from 5.5 percent in 1970. Between 1973 and 1987, the income of high school graduates declined by 12 percent, while during the 1980s the number of full-time workers falling below the poverty line rose by 43 percent (Harrison & Bluestone, 1988, p. 164).

This deepening social division is, in part, a product of the impact of technology on work. The level of workers' incomes depends increasingly on the value placed on the skills needed in the world market. There is more demand for some skills and less for others. As Reich puts it, those with the skills in symbolic analysis are rising; those with routine production skills are sinking, and those with lower interpersonal skills involved in many service jobs are also sinking but at a slower pace (Reich, 1991, p. 206). A similar division holds true for *societies* that want to have world-class economies.

How are American schools doing? The social divisions of the society are paralleled, of course, by similar divisions in the quality of schooling. Children from families with incomes in the top 20 percent do well. They attend private schools or privileged suburban public schools with well-equipped classrooms and low teacher/student ratios, and they are taught by teachers who are not hobbled by bureaucratic prescriptions.

On the other hand, by the end of the 1980s one-fourth of all American children under age 3 (and 44 percent of black children under age 3) lived in families below the poverty level. Recent estimates suggest that as many as 30 percent of children in elementary and secondary schools are "disadvantaged" (*Beyond Rhetoric, p.24*). Deborah Meier (1991, p. 331) sketches a picture of what schooling is like for these children. "The physical condition in New York City schools is simply an outrage. . . . Classes are being held in hallways and gyms, where the bathrooms don't work and the ceilings are falling in. It's a delusion to think . . . that you can teach well in any setting."

There is no more dramatic example of the class-riven society than the physical features of American work and schooling in the heart of the U. S. financial capital—Manhattan. The sumptuous corporate towers, embellished with bubbling fountains and loaded with ever-changing electronics that connect their inhabitants with their counterparts anywhere in the world, shout the message that America has a world-class economy. Compare this vision of corporate America with the conditions of the public schools on the same island.

In the face of such polarization, we confront a choice of two futures. The first, our present path, is to maintain a society wounded by class divisions and unequal access to learning. For the near future, this approach might be made to work. The upper echelons may see the society handicapped by an impoverished nonwhite sector that is largely "out of it" and by many workers with only mediocre education and training. But for the moment they can keep America in the competitive race by choosing the high-tech, centrally administered "automating" option. They can either ship the technology overseas to low-wage labor markets, or they can automate at home under centralized managerial control. They can avoid the informating choice, which reduces hierarchy and increases effectiveness but requires a major re-visioning of American work and education. This option is based on the bet that the middle and lower-middle classes can be kept in line by the diversions of consumption and by playing on racial fears.

But social divisiveness could become increasingly troublesome. By the year 2020, the top fifth may well earn more than 60 percent of American income, while the bottom fifth may drop to 2 percent (Reich, 1991, p. 302). Well-educated elites will withdraw further into their secure enclaves, living a life with excellent health care, challenging work, effective schools, global travel, and international electronic linkages. The urban and rural poor will live largely out of sight in their decaying communities. The despair and hopelessness of their children will be facts of life—as will be the human waste of warehousing thousands of youths of color in prisons. A stepped-up security apparatus may be required to contain them.

But this is not our only choice. We could choose what Lynn White (1968, p. 25) in *Dynamo and Virgin Reconsidered* referred to as a "high democratic culture." It would require the recognition that the best bet for American social well-being is a population equipped with symbolic analysis skills, tempered by ecological awareness and a deep appreciation for the values and traditions of democracy.

The indispensable condition for creating a world-class economy in a democratic society is the creation of world-class schools. To be serious about that would require an investment in education comparable to what has been spent on building a high-tech military machine. Instead of evading reality by continually offering failed proposals—such as accountability based on test scores or vouchers for private schools—we need to get down to real work. I mean such real work as razing the decayed shells of inner-city schools and replacing them with physical plants comparable to those of American corporations—with readily available computer facilities for all students and teachers, fine laboratories for the sciences and studios for the arts, and even air conditioning. Such schools would attract to the teaching profession some of our most able and imaginative young adults.

If we make the informating choice for schools, the appropriate measure of accountability will be to count how many American schools have been turned into world-class learning communities by the year 2000. If this seems like a foolish dream, it shows how far we usually are from asking what is really required to create world-class schools. Such a goal certainly would be in competition with other urgent priorities. The question is, How important are world-class schools to our national well-being?

Looking to the Future

I began by arguing that in the 1990s we have a chance to get on with democratic renewal in American work and schooling because the bureaucratic centralism of the industrial era has proved itself counterproductive for coping with the complexity of the electronic era. On the frontiers of high-tech work, we saw that work styles had to be created that incorporated such democratic values as respect for personal initiative and participative problem solving. The

breakdown of bureaucratic controls in schooling led to restructuring that embraced similar practices and values. Cultural changes of this dimension inevitably trigger resistance, and the matter of which cultural pattern will prevail becomes moot.

Even if we find the will and resources to support the informating choice, we will face another daunting facet of postindustrialism: the imponderables of the competitive global market. It seems clear that expansion of the design of work along the lines that Zuboff and Reich describe will increase our viability in the competitive world market. But that can happen only if American education turns out workers equipped with the required collaborative and symbolic analysis skills. When more workers of this type are available, entrepreneurs will be more likely to invest in creating the type of work that will employ them. If more democratic practices are successful on the frontiers of work and learning, their influence may spread by example.

But huge questions remain. What share of the world market will be required to support rewarding jobs for the American work force? The answer depends considerably on the size and character of the emerging global market. For example, much depends on whether "left out" sectors—such as the former Soviet Union, the newly independent nations of Eastern Europe, and vast areas of the Southern Hemisphere in Asia, Africa, and Latin America—can be brought in as healthy participants in a vigorous world economy.

Even if that goes well and a growing high-tech American economy emerges, we will still face the quandary of what to do with a lost generation of inner-city minority youths and adults. We do not know how many of these individuals might respond well to retraining or how many might be absorbed in massive publicly financed work projects to revitalize the American infrastructure (railroads, highways, bridges, housing, national parks, and so on). Certainly imaginative approaches will be required. Apart from the moral costs of neglecting so large a portion of our people, the economic costs associated with closing our eyes to the problem or proceeding in a conventional manner will be enormous and will handicap us in global competition.

Where schooling is concerned, it is now clear that factory-era administration and styles of learning are dysfunctional. But we have barely begun to create alternatives. I have argued that we can find the beginnings of appropriate postindustrial education in the features of the school restructuring movement that have gained force in the 1990s. The most promising restructuring efforts seek to invigorate the education system by adopting participative styles of management that support local creativity, autonomy, and problem solving. At the same time, we need to adopt active, constructivist learning for students as a central goal for schooling. Beyond that, we need imaginative, supportive federal and state policy making and financing. Such efforts are not unlike those that are helping to revitalize American industries and would tap the strength of the core values of the American democratic tradition.

If concern for democratic values emerges on top, I believe that there is room for hope— hope for creating a political economy and a form of education that could bring high technology and democratic values into creative collaboration. We would become a learning society at the workplace, in the schools, and in our communities. We could become a society in which the processes of technological change are disciplined by the political wisdom of democracy—a society in which we would adopt only those technologies and social systems that match our best sense of who we are and what we want this society to be. Capitalism with a human face?

References

Bailey T. (1991). *Jobs of the future and the skills they will require.* Berkeley: National Center for Research in Vocational Education, University of California.

Beyond rhetoric: A new agenda for children and families. (1991). Washington, DC: National Commission on Children.

Cole, K. C. (1990, January 7). Science under scrutiny. *Education Life Supplement, New York Times,* p. 18.

Cooper, K. (1989, May 20). Education secretary calls for restructuring of public schools. *Center Daily Times.*

Dewey, J. (1916). The need of an industrial educaton in an industrial democracy. *Manual Training and Vocational Education, 17,* 409-414.

Goodman, K. S., and others. (1988). *Report card on basal readers.* Katonah, NY: Richard C. Owen.

Harrison, B., & Bluestone, B. (1988). *The great U-turn.* New York: Basic Books.

Light, J. D. (1992). *A study of technology transfer through a United States action training program in the ministry of defense of an East African country.* Unpublished doctoral dissertation. Washington University.

Meier, D. (1991, Summer). Bush and the schools: A hard look. *Dissent.*

Piaget, J. (1973). *To understand is to invent: The future of education.* New York: Grossman.

Reich, R. (1991). *The work of nations: Preparing ourselves for 21st century capitalism.* New York: Knopf.

Sarason, S. B. (1990). *The predictable failure of school reform.* San Francisco: Jossey-Bass.

White, L. (1968). *Dynamo and virgin reconsidered.* Boston: MIT Press.

Zuboff, S. (1988). *In the age of the smart machine: The future of work and power.* New York: Basic Books.

2

Growth Patterns
in Workplace Training*

By Anthony P. Carnevale and Ellen S. Carnevale
Reprinted with permission from *Training and Development*, May 1994.

THE essential trends in training on the job are optimistic. Formal company training increased 45 percent from 1983 to 1991. The increases in training are broadly distributed among industries and occupations, although the general distribution of increase tends to favor more highly skilled workers. At the same time, we need to remember that overall training levels in the workplace are still low; optimistic increases are building on a paltry base.

The Surveys
Most of the data reported here were gathered by the Bureau of the Census's Current Population Surveys in 1983 and 1991 and analyzed by the U.S. Department of Labor's Bureau of Labor Statistics. In the 1991 Census Bureau survey, trained interviewers asked people from a random sample of 60,000 households about occupational mobility, job training, and length of employment at their current job.

The data do not report annual training levels; they show the amount of skill-im-

provement training received at any point in a worker's current job, as reported in the 1983 and 1991 surveys. The data define four sources of skill-improvement training:

• schools (including high school, post-secondary, junior college or technical institutes, and four-year or longer college programs),
• formal company training,
• informal on-the-job training,
• other types of training.

Several tables report only skill improvement training provided through formal company programs, because those are the numbers that reflect the amount of formal job-related training taking place in the workplace. The increasing levels and scope of training from 1983 to 1991 result from changes in the occupational structure of the labor force, with a shift toward more managers, professionals, and technical workers. These three occupational categories traditionally are at the head of the receiving line for training, and the 1991 data continue to reflect that preferred status.

Significantly, all four of the categories of skill-improvement training (school, formal company, informal on-the-job, and other) increased between 1983 and 1991. But formal company training showed the biggest gain. The rapid shift in formal company training demonstrates that more employers are committed to providing employer-based training for employees.

Also, employees who are educated beyond high school are still getting more training than those with only high-school educations. Education and training tend to go together. And technical workers, managers, and professionals usually have more education than other occupational groups and get the most training on the job. But overall increases in training across industries and occupations suggest that we are moving steadily toward the development of a culture of lifelong learning.

Studies show that employees wait until their mid- to late twenties to settle into their careers. Employers tend to provide training to employees after they make a serious job commitment. Formal company training is concentrated among workers between the ages of 25 and 44.

Females outpaced males in the amount of skill-improvement training received from 1983 to 1991. These data conform with findings of other studies that suggest that females tend to use learning as a lever for employment and earnings—and that they tend to pursue training more aggressively than males.

The manufacturing sector continues to be more training-intensive than the service sector, probably due to economic and technological change in this most globally competitive industry. The most technology-intensive environments are still shop floors, and the most radical competitive impacts of technology act like restless tectonic plates beneath them. The changes in manufacturing processes and competitive standards require new learning among employees.

With the acceleration of economic growth, these patterns in training probably will accelerate as well. Growth accelerates economic and technological change, and change encourages training.

More workers are getting training in their current jobs, so trainers will need to find ways to deliver training in more embedded contexts. As a growing share of workers needs training, it will become even more expensive to take people off the job to train them—lost wages and even short-term decreases in productivity will prove too costly. In other words, on-the-job training and alternatives to classroom-training methods will reap the biggest paybacks for employers and employees, both in terms of cost efficiencies and learning effectiveness.

Because of the high education and experience levels of trainees, trainers must not treat trainees as unskilled and unknowing workers. The trainer's role must change from expert teacher to expert facilitator. A trainer's power might just be in how "street smart" he or she is knowing an organization's structure and staff well enough to pinpoint the resident experts (very often the line employees) in technical knowledge and skills and to use these experts to design, deliver, and evaluate training.

Who Receives What

From 1983 to 1991, there was a 17 percent increase in the number of employees who reported getting skill-improvement training while in their current jobs (Table 1). In 1983, 35 percent of workers reported receiving skill-improvement training; in 1991, 41 percent of workers reported this kind of training.

Of the four sources of skill-improvement training (school, formal company, informal on-the-job, and other), the biggest gains occurred in formal company training. In 1983, 11 percent of employees who reported receiving skill-improvement training since beginning their current jobs received this training through formal company training. By 1991, the percentage had jumped to 16 percent, a 45 percent increase over 1983.

No other training source had that significant an increase. Informal on-the-job training ranked second, at 15 percent, in 1991, which represents a 7 percent increase from 1983. Schooling ranked third, at 13 percent, in 1991, an 8 percent increase since 1983.

TABLE 1
Skill-Improvement Training: All Employees

Employee Group	Percent with skill-improvement training, 1983	Percent with skill-improvement training, 1991	Percent change, 1983-1991	Percent formal company, 1983	Percent formal company, 1991	Percent change, 1983-1991
Total, all employees	35	41	17	11	16	45
Nontechnical professionals	66	72	9	9	13	44
Management support specialists	52	57	10	20	28	40
General managers	47	53	13	17	25	47
Clerical	32	40	25	10	16	60
Sales	32	35	9	13	16	23
Service	25	29	16	8	9	13
Transportation	18	25	39	6	10	67
Machine operators	22	25	14	4	8	100
Laborers	14	15	7	2	5	150
Technical professionals	62	70	13	23	31	35
Technicians	52	59	13	18	26	44
Craft	26	27	4	7	9	29
Precision production	36	38	6	13	17	31
Mechanics & repairers	44	48	9	22	24	9
Extractive	34	39	15	16	23	44

Sources: DOL bulletins 2226 and 2407.

The category of "other training" ranked fourth, at 7 percent.

Nine occupations registered larger-than-average percentages of workers who took formal company skill-improvement training while in their current jobs. Those occupations: general managers, technical professionals, technicians, precision production workers, management-support specialists, clerical workers, salespeople, mechanics and repairers, and extractive workers. Six occupations registered smaller-than-average percentages: nontechnical professionals, service workers, machine operators, laborers, craft workers, and transportation employees.

As in the 1993 survey, technical professionals continue to be the occupational group that gets the largest amount of employer-provided skill-improvement training (31 percent of all technical professionals received training). In descending order are management-support specialists, general managers, and technicians. But these occu-

TABLE 2
Skill-Improvement Training by Age of Trainee

Age	Number taking training (numbers in thousands) 1983	1991	Percent change from 1983 to 1991	Percent of total taking skill-improvement training, 1991
All workers, 16 and over	33,901	46,814	38	100
16-19	1,039	972	-6	2
20-24	3,703	3,707	0	8
25-34	10,879	13,438	24	29
35-44	8,573	14,660	71	31
45-54	5,713	9,015	58	19
55-64	3,471	4,239	22	9
65+	523	784	50	2

Souces: DOL bulletins 2226 and 2407.

TABLE 3
Skill-Improvement Training by Sex of Trainee

Sex	Number taking training (numbers in thousands) 1983	1991	Percent change from 1983 to 1991	Percent of total taking skill-improvement training, 1991	Percent of total in labor force, 1990
Male	19,238	25,120	31	54	54.7
Female	14,663	21,694	48	46	45.3

Sources: DOL 2226, 2402, and 2407.

pational groups did not differ significantly from the 45 percent average change in skill-improvement training among all employees.

Occupational groups that show significantly large increases in skill-improvement training for all employees include laborers (150 percent), machine operators (100 percent), and clerical personnel (60 percent).

Age, Gender, and Race

Table 2 looks at the percentage of employees in different age groups who have received training. With the exception of 16- to 19-year-olds and 20- to 24-year-olds, all age groups report increases in the percentage of people trained.

The data show that the workforce is growing older and that training is being concentrated among the older age groups. Workers between the ages of 35 and 44 experienced a 71 percent increase in the number of workers reporting skill-improvement training from 1983 to 1991. This age group also represents the biggest share of skill-improvement training, 31 percent.

In the general labor force (in 1990), work-

ers aged 35 to 54 make up 42 percent of all workers (52.5 million workers). But this age group represents 51 percent (23.6 million workers) of all skill-improvement training recipients.

Skill-improvement training is less prevalent among 16- to 24-year-olds. While representing 17 percent of the labor force (21 million workers), this age group garnered only 10 percent of skill-improvement training (4.7 million workers). The 16- to 19-year-olds group also represented the only decrease in skill-improvement training reported in the survey period from 1983 to 1991, with a drop of 6 percent.

In 1991, females represented the biggest change in the incidence of skill-improvement training received through any of the four sources. Forty-eight percent more women reported receiving training in the 1991 survey than in the 1983 survey compared with a 31 percent increase for males (Table 3).

Of all employees reporting skill-improvement training in the 1991 survey, males reported a 54 percent incidence, and females reported 46 percent. In the workforce in

TABLE 4
Skill-Improvement Training by Race and Ethnicity of Trainee

Race or ethnicity	Number taking training (numbers in thousands) 1983	1991	Percent change from 1983 to 1991	Percent of total taking skill-improvement training, 1991	Percent of total in labor force, 1990
White	30,581	41,461	36	84	85.9
Black	2,528	4,019	59	8	11.8
All other races	792	1,333	68	3	2.4
Hispanic	1,081	2,380	120	5	7.7

Sources: DOL 2226, 2402, and 2407.

TABLE 5
Skill-Improvement Training by Level of Education Completed

Level of education	Number taking training (numbers in thousands) 1983	1991	Percent change from 1983 to 1991	Percent of total taking skill-improvement training, 1991	Percent of total in labor force, 1990
High school or less	14,635	17,936	23	38	53
Some college	7,698	11,670	52	25	22
College graduate	11,568	17,208	49	38	25

Sources: DOL 2226, 2402, and 2407.

general, males represent 54.7 percent of all workers; females represent 45.3 percent. In other words, both males and females are receiving training roughly proportionate to their distribution in the workforce.

Of all employees reporting skill-improvement training in the 1983 and 1991 surveys, females' share of skill-improvement training increased 3 percentage points, or 6 percent. Males' share of skill-improvement training decreased 3 percentage points, or 4 percent.

Employees of Hispanic ethnicity saw a 120 percent increase in the amount of skill-improvement training received through any of the four sources (school, formal company, informal on-the-job, and other) from 1983 to 1991 (Table 4). Blacks saw a 59 percent increase in this training, and whites saw a 36 percent increase.

Whites make up 86 percent of the labor force and received 84 percent of skill-improvement training. Blacks make up 12 percent of the labor force but received only 8 percent of the training. People of Hispanic ethnicity, who make up 8 percent of the labor force, received 5 percent of the skill-improvement training.

Level of Education

People with the most and the least education get the most skill-improvement training on the job (Table 5). But those with the least education get a disproportionately smaller share of skill-improvement training relative to their numbers in the workforce, while those with education beyond high school get a greater share of skill-improvement training relative to their numbers in the workforce. Moreover, increases in training between 1983 and 1991 favor those with some college education or with a college degree.

In 1991, those with high-school educations or less got 38 percent of the skill-improvement training. Those with some college received 25 percent of the training, and college graduates received 38 percent.

Those with high-school educations or less got 38 percent of the training but represent 53 percent of the workforce. Those with some college got 25 percent of the training and represent 22 percent of the workforce. Those with college degrees received 38 percent of the training and represent 25 percent of the workforce.

TABLE 6
Type of Employer Involvement in Adult Education, 1991

			TYPE OF EMPLOYER INVOLVEMENT				
Participation in adult education	Percent of total in labor force	Any type	Given at place of work	Employer paid some portion	Employer provided course	Employer required course	Employer provided time off
47,143	41	74	37	60	44	35	56

Note: Adult education is defined as all non-full-time education activities such as part-time college attendance, classes, or seminars given by employers, and classes taken for adult-literacy purposes or for recreation and enjoyment.

TABLE 7
Estimated Hourly Cost of Training in Small and Large Firms

Training Category	FIRM SIZE			
	1- 24 employees	25-99 employees	100-499 employees	500+ employees
Hourly cost of formal training	$19	$17	$26	$22
Hourly cost of informal training	$12	$15	$16	$18

Source: SBA report, "Job Training Approaches and Costs in Small and Large Firms."

The fastest increases in training are occurring among those with the most education. Those with some college or with college degrees experienced increased skill-improvement training on the job between 1983 and 1991—by 52 percent for those who attended some college, and by 49 percent for those who earned degrees. Skill-improvement training among employees with high-school educations or less increased by only 23 percent over the same time period.

How Employers Are Involved

The employer's role in retraining American workers extends far beyond formal training on the job. The data shown in Table 6 describe the extent of employer involvement in adult-education activities for workers. In 74 percent of cases, employees who received adult education cited some type of involvement from their employers.

Clearly, employers are payers but not necessarily providers of adult education. Employers paid for part of this education in 60 percent of the cases—and 56 percent of adult-education participants received time off from work to attend the activities. But only 37 percent of the education occurred at the workplace.

Those data were collected by the National Center for Education Statistics. In its survey, *adult education* is defined as any type of education taken by adults. This includes work-related training, but it also includes education taken for recreation or personal enhancement. So the data do not describe job-specific skill-improvement training.

But according to the BLS data, 13 percent of workers who took job-specific skill-improvement training got that training through school. Employers paid in full for that schooling 29 percent of the time. An additional 13 percent of the trainees had their employers pay for some of the cost.

What Training Costs

In 1992, the Small Business Administration conducted a nationwide survey to determine the incidence of training for newly hired employees in small and large firms. The researchers collected data on two sources of training:

● formal training (includes on-site training and off-site training),

● informal training (includes training by

TABLE 8
Formal Training Programs in Small and Large Firms

Business Category	FIRM SIZE			
	1-24 employees	25-99 employees	100-499 employees	500+ employees
Percent of all firms with formal training programs	18.56	25.94	36.06	44.37
Percent of service firms with formal training	21.97	31.08	41. 18	50.72
Percent of nonservice firms with formal training	16.02	23.19	33.57	41.67

Source: SBS report, "Job Training Approaches and Costs in Small and large Firms."

TABLE 9
Skill Improvement Training: Type of Training by Occupational Group

Occupational group	Workers who took training (numbers in thousands)	TYPE OF TRAINING				
		Managerial or supervisory training	Reading math, or writing training	Computer-related training	Occupation-specific technical training	Other training
Total, all occupations	46,814	12, 484	6,587	15,021	29,949	7,811
Percent of occupational employment	41	11	6	13	26	7
Executive, administrative, and managerial	7,853	4,277	1,205	3, 175	4, 466	1, 100
Percent of occupational employment	53	29	8	22	30	7
Professional specialty	10,847	2,545	2,054	3, 424	7,298	2,338
Percent of occupational employment	67	16	13	21	45	14
Technicians and related support	2,365	326	315	946	1,722	237
Percent of occupational employment	59	8	8	24	43	6
Sales occupations	4,809	1,703	574	1,303	2,826	913
Percent of occupational employment	35	12	4	10	21	7
Administrative support	7,342	1, 459	1, 112	4,223	3, 420	877
Percent of occupational employment	40	8	6	23	19	5
Private household occupations	39	4	0	4	17	19
Percent of occupational employment	6	1	0	1	2	3
Service workers, except private household	4,339	689	413	390	3, 130	1,056
Percent of occupational employment	29	5	3	3	21	7
Farming, forestry, and fishing	602	153	27	68	420	126
Percent of occupational employment	21	5	1	2	14	4
Precision production, craft, and repair	4,949	1,000	555	867	3,992	480
Percent of occupational employment	38	8	4	7	30	4
Machine operators, assemblers, and inspectors	1,913	115	211	390	1, 473	261
Percent of occupational employment	25	1	3	5	19	3
Transportation and material moving	1, 112	132	64	117	750	267
Percent of occupational employment	25	3	1	3	17	6
Handlers, equipment cleaners, and laborers	643	84	56	113	434	139
Percent of occupational employment	15	2	1	3	10	3

Source: DOL bulletin 2407.

managers, training by co-workers, and training by watching others).

Table 7 looks at the estimated cost of training for newly hired employees. It appears that firms with 25 to 99 employees enjoy a cost advantage over even smaller firms, probably because the fixed costs of training are spread over more employees. The largest firms (more than 500 employees) enjoy a cost advantage over midsize firms (100 to 499 employees). This leaves a discrepancy between the large and the small firms.

Perhaps these cost figures show that there is a critical point at which firms must adopt the more expensive formal training practices that are common in large companies. It would appear that this point is between 100

TABLE 10
Formal Company Training by Industry

Industry	Workers who took formal company training (numbers in thousands)	Percent of total taking formal company training, 1991	Percent of total in labor force, 1990
Total	17,973	100	100
Agriculture, forestry, and fisheries	102	0.6	3.0
Mining	174	1.0	0.6
Construction	460	2.6	4.6
Manufacturing	3,629	20.2	17.2
Transportation, utilities, and communications	2,046	11. 4	5.2
Wholesale and retail trade	2,268	12.6	23.3
Finance, insurance, and real estate	2, 185	12.2	6.1
Business and repair services, personal services, and entertainment and recreational services	1,292	7.2	9.9
Professional and related services	3,733	20.8	13.6
Public administration	2,084	11.6	16.5

Sources: DOL bulletins 2226, 2402, and 2407

and 499 employees. These firms are too large to depend on the less expensive formal training methods used by smaller firms, but they are not quite large enough to spread the increased fixed costs over the additional employees, as the largest firms do to enjoy a lower average cost.

Size of Company and Type of Training

The 1992 Small Business Administration survey also shows a significant statistical difference in the existence of formal training programs for newly hired employees in small and large firms. Table 8 indicates that the likelihood of receiving training is a function of the size of an employee's firm. Large firms are more likely to implement and sustain formal training programs. In fact, the survey discovered that firms with more than 500 employees are more than twice as likely to provide formal training to new hires as are firms with fewer than 25 employees.

The data also indicate that the trend remains consistent among the service and nonservice industries. Within both sectors, the number of training programs increases with company size; firms with more than 500 employees are more than twice as likely to offer formal training as are firms with fewer than 25 employees.

Type of Training

Data in this category were not collected in 1983, so the discussion reflects 1991 responses only. Occupation-specific technical training was the most common type of training reported by all respondents in the survey. It was also the most common type of training reported by individual occupational groups, except for administrative-support and private household workers (Table 9). Among workers employed as administrative support staff, computer-related training was the most common type. Also, computer-related training was the second most common type of training received across all occupation groups.

The data do not specify the sources for the training. Providers could include a whole host of training suppliers, such as schools and independent consultants, as well as companies.

Formal Company Training by Industry

According to Table 10, the distribution across industries of formal company skill-improvement training shows that employees in the manufacturing industry (both durable and nondurable goods) receive 20.2 percent of the training. Employees in professional services receive 20.8 percent of the

Learning to Learn for Professional Growth

Knowing how to learn is the most basic of all skills because it is the key that unlocks future success. Learning to learn involves knowing the principles and methods that allow us to perform in three domains:

- the cognitive domain of skills we use to collect, know, and comprehend information,
- the psychomotor domain of skills we use to control our bodies in order to accomplish tasks, and
- the affective domain of skills we use to know, understand, and respond to feelings and behaviors.

Why Is Learning to Learn Important in the New Economy?

Equipped with this skill, a person can achieve competency in all other basic workplace skills. Learning skills are required in order to respond flexibly and quickly to technical and organizational change; make continuous improvements in quality, efficiency, and speed; and develop new applications for existing technologies, products, and services

What Is the Curriculum?

Learning-to-learn curricula include procedures for self-assessment, exposure to alternative learning styles, and training specific to the work context in which learning needs to occur. Specifically, these curricula should:

- identify personal learning styles, capabilities, and sensory preferences (seeing, hearing, or feeling), using testing instruments such as the Myers-Briggs Type Indicator; the Learning Styles Inventory; or Memorize, Understand, and Do.

- develop awareness of cognitive, psychomotor, and affective learning strategies and tools.
- match the employee's job contents and career trajectory to his or her learning needs, using such instruments as the Instructional Systems Design and Job Learning Analysis.

What Constitutes Competency?

Competency in learning includes demonstrated ability to assess what needs to be learned, apply learning techniques, and use new learning on the job.

Specifically, a person must be able to conduct a learning needs assessment and demonstrate personal learning skills such as understanding her or his own learning styles and capabilities.

A person must also be able to demonstrate skill in the cognitive domain by organizing, relating, recalling, and evaluating knowledge; moving from knowing to understanding and applying knowledge; understanding how to think logically, divergently, critically, and intuitively; understanding some alternative learning strategies and tools; and understanding how to mobilize and organize learning resources.

The learning process is ultimately cognitive and individual. But learning in applied settings often involves interacting with others. So an individual must have a complementary set of interpersonal learning skills, including giving and receiving feedback, learning collaboratively, and using others as learning resources.

—*Adapted from* America and the New Economy *by Anthony P. Carnevale, Employment and Training Administration, U.S. Department of Labor, Washington, DC: U.S. Government Printing Office, 1991.*

training. People in finance, insurance, and real estate garner 12.2 percent. In transportation, communications, and utilities, employees receive 11.4 percent of all skill-improvement training given formally by employers.

Formal company training for skill improvement is particularly intensive in several industries, which all receive more intensive training than their share of the overall labor market:

• The manufacturing sector, which represents 17.2 percent of the economy of the United States, receives 20.2 percent of the formal company training for skill improvement.

• Professional and related services (including health and education services) represent 13.6 percent of the economy but receives 20.8 percent of the formal company training.

• The finance industry represents 6.1 percent of all employees in the labor force but receives 12.2 percent of the formal company training.

• Transportation represents 5.2 percent of the labor force, but receives 11.4 percent of the formal company training.

Less intensive industries include the wholesale and retail trade industries. While representing 23.3 percent of the labor force, they receive only 12.6 percent of the formal company training for skill improvement. And the construction industry receives 2.6 percent of this training but represents 4.6 percent of the labor force.

Sources for Tables

Digest of Education Statistics, 1993, Washington, DC: U.S. Department of Education, National Center for Education Statistics.

Job training approaches and costs in small and large firms. Washington, DC: U.S. Small Business Administration, Office of Advocacy, February 1993. This report was prepared by Dan A. Black, Mark C. Berger, and John Barron.

How workers get their training: A 1991 update. Bulletin 2407, Washington, DC: U.S. Department of Labor, Bureau of Labor Statistics, August 1992. This bulletin was prepared by Thomas A. Amirault, under the supervision of Alan Eck.

Outlook: 1990-2005. Bulletin 2402, Washington, DC: U.S. Department of Labor, Bureau of Labor Statistics, May 1992.

How workers get their training. Bulletin 2226, Washington, DC: U.S. Department of Labor, Bureau of Labor Statistics, February 1985. This bulletin was prepared by Max Carey and Alan Eck, under the supervision of Neal H. Rosenthal.

3

Best Practices
in the Second-Chance System

By Kate Gerstle

THE *second-chance system* is a collection of programs, funded through both public and private sources, for people who did not acquire sufficient "education, discipline, or life skills" (Public Policy Institute of New York State, Inc., 1995, p. 10) through traditional education to find or keep decent jobs. People who fail to make a successful transition from school to work are the principal beneficiaries of opportunities offered through this system. The second-chance system is primarily administered through a complex web of federally subsidized training programs that fall under the auspices of the Job Training Partnership Act (JTPA) of 1983.

The federal government initiated workforce development programs during the Kennedy administration, with the Area Redevelopment Act of 1961. This was followed by a series of acts in the 1960s and early 1970s that formed the job-training infrastructure. In 1962, the Manpower Development and Training Act (MDTA) was passed to provide skill training for dislocated workers. By all accounts, MDTA had great success—at least three-quarters of the workers trained for new skills obtained employment and earned higher wages than those without retraining.

Federal policy moved to focus on minori-

ties and other disadvantaged populations in the mid-1960s, a shift symbolized by the enactment of the Economic Opportunity Act (EOA) of 1964. President Johnson staunchly advocated programs for poor youth, such as the Neighborhood Youth Corps and the Job Corps. MDTA and EOA were subsequently amended to sponsor initiatives aimed at older workers (Operation Mainstream), the economically disadvantaged (New Careers and the Work Incentive program), urban slums (Special Impact Program), and unemployment (Concentrated Employment Program). President Nixon continued the convention of sponsoring separately funded and administered programs. When a severe recession hit the nation in 1970, he authorized the Public Employment Program. However, by 1973 when expenditures for federal training and employment programs reached $5 billion, the President and Congress agreed that reform was needed. In 1973 the Comprehensive Employment and Training Act (CETA) was passed. CETA, according to Carnevale and Johnston (1989)

> provided for a comprehensive program of training and related services for the economically disadvantaged; a program of transitional public service employment for the most severely

disadvantaged and for eligible veterans in areas of very high unemployment; special federal training programs for . . . [Native Americans] and migrant and seasonal farm workers; a reauthorization of the Job Corps; and a National Commission for Manpower Policy to make recommendations about meeting the employment needs and goals of the nation. (p. 32)

CETA did not produce results as favorable as those expected. Supported by 26 separate appropriations in eight years, it lacked stable and secure funding. Workforce development programs run under CETA had limited accountability, which resulted in significant waste of federal funds. Shortly after the Act passed, a severe recession, induced partly by an OPEC oil embargo, struck the U.S. This forced CETA agencies to shift their emphasis from training to job-creation activities. The Congressional Office of Technology Assessment evaluated CETA's overall success as moderate, but most policy makers considered it a bottomless pit. During the 10 years of its existence, CETA programs consumed $53 billion in federal funds but placed only 15 percent of its participants (Lee, 1986).

Ronald Reagan assumed the presidency in 1981, with a clear intention of reducing government spending. Due to Congress's general disenchantment with CETA, it became an immediate target for elimination. Lawmakers struggled for nearly a year to develop a manageable and affordable plan for federal training of the economically disadvantaged. In 1982, with Americans confronting another recession, the dissolution of heavy industry, and millions of displaced workers, Congress passed the Job Training Partnership Act (JTPA). The legislation represented "a major shift in national employment and training policy and philosophy" (Cook, 1986, p. 74).

Unlike CETA, JTPA was devised to decentralize federal training and move power from the national to the state and local levels. State governments received authority to designate service delivery areas (SDA), approve program proposals, distribute funds, and assess performance. In addition, each SDA has a private industry council (PIC) that shares administrative authority with the state government. PICs comprised local government, education, and business leaders. By "bringing representatives from various segments of the private sector into the active management of job training programs" (Laabs, 1992, p. 36), PICs link private industry with intended clients of the JTPA: disadvantaged youths and adults, youths, and dislocated workers. The more than 600 private industry councils nationwide serve as the mechanisms that make the JTPA work, because they manage the daily activities associated with executing training programs. This partnership with local industry insures that workforce development programs funded by the federal government are responsive to the needs of local economies, which improves the likelihood of successful job placement. PICs, which often have state and county monies as well as federal JTPA funds at their disposal, are authorized to

● provide training or contract it out to external vendors;

● supplement the income of participants who are receiving on-the-job training; and

● offer career guidance, job search, and job placement services.

The JTPA's principal goal is to provide training for economically disadvantaged Americans, primarily young people, welfare recipients, and high school dropouts (Cook, 1986). This represents a shift in emphasis from CETA, which also engaged heavily in job development. The law specifically outlines the percentage of JTPA funds allowed for administration, stipends for participants, and support service costs, so that programs will remain strictly attuned to the job training required to create second chances. JTPA objectives are much more specific than those outlined by previous legislation; they "include better employment, higher earnings, increased skills and decreased welfare dependency—all designed to improve the quality of the workforce which, in turn, would enhance the nation's productivity" (Barnes, 1994, p. 12).

In addition to provisions of the JTPA, the second-chance system includes opportunities created through other federal legislation. In a 1988 reform, Congress mandated that welfare include human capital development programs and specifically that states create a Jobs Opportunities and Basic Skills Program (JOBS). This is somewhat integrated with the existing JTPA infrastructure as the intent was not to create another training delivery system. Furthermore, JTPA programs have been more efficient in their use of funds, spending more on education and training and less on participant support and administration than JOBS programs (JOBS and JTPA, 1994). Displaced workers are also supported through the Trade Adjustment Assistance (TAA) provisions of the Trade Act of 1974. "TAA benefits, including unemployment compensation, training, and related employment services, are due to workers adversely affected by increased imports of articles similar to those produced by the workers' firms" (Carnevale & Johnston, 1989, p. 38).

Furthermore, each state provides its own unique programs to encourage workforce development. This includes but is not limited to components of state systems of higher education (community colleges, four-year colleges, and universities); tuition assistance programs; programs sponsored by correctional services; training offered by mental and physical health agencies; and privately-supported activities. For example, the New York State 1993-94 Catalog of Workforce Preparation Programs, published by the New York State Job Training Partnership Council, listed 104 programs sponsored by 23 different agencies. The table shown below provides a synopsis of the breadth of second-chance system programs offered by just 1 of the 50 states.

The chart indicates that individual states may offer training programs not specifically covered here. However, the majority of services, as previously stated, are sponsored through the Job Training Partnership Act and, therefore, that is the focus of this chapter.

Second-Chance System Beneficiaries

Youths aged 14 to 21 who are at risk for dropping out of school or failing in the labor market after high school graduation are JTPA's first group of recipients. Many people

Program Activities

Activity	Definition	Programs
Assessment	Includes a general assessment of the client's employability.	44 programs; 11 agencies
Counseling	Includes any generally accepted form of peer or professional counseling, individual or group.	42 programs; 9 agencies
Classroom Training	Any training provided in a classroom setting.	37 programs; 12 agencies
Occupational Specific Skills	Vocational instruction.	35 programs; 12 agencies
Life Skills	Includes a broad range of pre-employment and work maturity skills.	40 programs; 9 agencies
Basic/Remedial Education	Includes where this is a specific strategy incorporated into the program design.	29 programs; 6 agencies
On-the-Job Training	Job specific training provided by a public or private employer in a work setting where the client is paid by the employer.	33 programs; 13 agencies
Work Experience	Includes try-out employment, job simulation and other simulation and other subsidized work.	32 programs; 9 agencies
English/Second Language	English language instruction.	23 programs; 5 agencies
Information/Data Collection	Informational services including labor market information, employment trends, etc.	24 programs; 8 agencies

Source: The Public Policy Institute of New York State, 1995.

realize that because of the difficult employment prospects for youth who do not earn a secondary school diploma, the number of dropouts must be reduced (*What's Working*, 1995). Under Title II-A of the JTPA, 40 percent of an SDA's spending on programs for disadvantaged youths and adults must go to services for those aged 16 to 21. These services include outreach to in-school youth, out-of-school youth, and young single mothers.

Disadvantaged young people who are enrolled in high school primarily can take advantage of part-time work opportunities and summer experiences offered by the second-chance system. Some of these programs have shown moderate success at reducing the dropout rate, but most have had ambiguous results. No existing evidence proves that programs like the Summer Training and Employment Program (STEP) or the Summer Youth Employment and Training Program (SYETP) positively influence graduation rates or long-term employment success. The Youth Incentive Entitlement Pilot Project (YIEPP), which was operative between 1978 and 1981 and provided summer employment and part-time jobs during the school year, improved youth employment rates but did not necessarily increase rates of school retention. This project demonstrated that the participants wanted to work if given the chance, but students failed to make a connection between completing high school and securing meaningful employment (*What's Working*, 1995).

In 1994, the School-to-Work Opportunities Act established a foundation for additional second-chance programs for disadvantaged in-school youth. The legislation advocates alliances between employers and schools to create workforce skill development opportunities so that non-college-bound students receive better preparation for work. Although the School-to-Work Act has insufficient funding, it has already been endorsed by business leaders nationwide. Ford Motor Company CEO Alex Trotman chairs the School-to-Work National Employer Leadership Council (NELC), a group of top executives who have committed to advancing the goals of the Act. Members of the NELC "have pledged to promote work-based learning for students in all sorts of educational institutions—high schools, community colleges, vo-techs, and proprietary schools" (Lee, 1995, p. 34).

The JTPA mandates that "school dropouts be served in proportion to their incidence in the local population" (Carnevale & Johnston, 1989, p. 33). Therefore, some SDAs must offer several concurrent training programs for out-of-school youth.

Experience with these programs has shown that relatively short-term (three to six months) interventions have little impact, but residential, high-intensity programs can result in improvements in future earning power.

> Consistent with findings for in-school youth, subsidized work experience for disadvantaged out-of-school youth has produced substantial gains during the period of subsidized employment. However, it has generally not had long-term positive effects on employment or earnings. . . . [Furthermore,] job search assistance may produce short-term benefits for disadvantaged youth, but the evidence is mixed—some models have worked and some have not. (*What's Working*, 1995, p. 8)

The second major category of Americans served by the second-chance system is disadvantaged adults. This group includes poor single parents, recipients of Aid to Families with Dependent Children (AFDC) benefits, migrant, or seasonal farm workers, and Native Americans. Outcomes for this group have shown greater promise than those for youth. Evidence suggests that, among programs designed for disadvantaged adults, the greatest accomplishments come through workforce development activities that combine on-the-job training with career guidance and job placement services. Short-term classroom training programs have been the least successful (*What's Working*, 1995). Some adult training programs have resulted in increased income and a decline in dependence on welfare, particularly among female participants. However, trainees' initial financial situations combined with low earnings available to less-skilled women causes participants to remain in poverty despite improvements attributed to training programs (*What's Working*, 1995). The Department of Labor reports that a majority of the adult female AFDC recipients who participated in JTPA programs in 1986 found job placements. Unfortunately, of those placed, only 16 percent and 22 percent were above the poverty line in their first and second post-training years, respectively (Romero, 1994).

Dislocated workers comprise the third group of second-chance system beneficiaries. According to Carnevale and Johnston (1989), displaced workers can take one or more of three possible courses of action: they can "wait and see;" they can "retrain for new jobs at similar or better wages;" or they can "accept new jobs that are relatively less skilled and pay lower wages" (p. 37). Most dislocated employees chose a combination of the first and third options, which is unfortunate because training activities can and do make a difference.

JTPA relief offered under the auspices of Economic Dislocation and Worker Adjustment Assistance is for workers who lose jobs due to plant closings or downsizing. In addition, the U.S. Secretary of Labor has a special discretionary fund for grants to "businesses working with organizations that provide training and employment services for laid-off workers . . ." (Barnes, 1993, p. 19). Job search assistance and early intervention have been found to shorten the time it takes displaced workers to find new positions with wages similar to those earned before a layoff. Analysis of JTPA programs for dislocated employees shows that long-term training is the most effective workforce development activity for this group of Americans, but only a very small number of displaced workers ever seeks long-term training (*What's Working*, 1995).

The second-chance system generally concentrates most heavily on providing services to other categories of disadvantaged youth and adults. Whenever the economy's industrial sector experiences significant problems with maintaining the workforce, however, the federal government and its training partners step in to help. Assisting displaced workers has been part of national employment policy since Johnson initiated the Manpower and Development Training Act in 1962, followed by Trade Adjustment Assistance, Title III of the Job Training Partnership Act, and most recently the Omnibus Trade and Competitiveness Act of 1988.

Models for the Nation

Second-chance system training consists of four primary types of employment services: job search assistance (JSA), short-term classroom training, long-term classroom training, and subsidized employment. The following anecdotes describe some of the most successful training programs in each of these four areas.

Job Search Assistance Programs

Job search assistance programs begin with career guidance and move participants through to job placement. Career guidance helps youths, disadvantaged adults, and dislocated workers assess their skills and identify positions, companies, and industries that suit their skills. In addition, job search assistance training instructs participants about how to complete job applications; how to respond to job announcements and postings; how to dress and speak in an interview; appropriate oral and written communication; and proper job search etiquette. PICs and agencies that provide these services also assist clients with finding a job once they have completed their self-assessment and job search preparation exercises. According to a 1995 Department of Labor report that evaluates JTPA successes and failures:

> Job search assistance has produced significant short-term positive impacts for every population group. The results for youth are somewhat mixed, though, as some JSA interventions have

succeeded and some have not. JSA appears to accelerate the process of finding a job, but not to have a lasting effect on the quality of job obtained.

JSA is generally one of the cheapest interventions. So JSA is usually a worthwhile investment, with benefits outweighing costs by a substantial amount. (p. 14)

Several job search assistance programs for dislocated workers or disadvantaged youths and adults have shown significant results. In Central Utah, the Mountain Lands JTPA career guidance program produced job placement percentages between 75 percent and 79 percent in the late 1980s (Armstrong, 1989). JSA was provided to Mountain Lands' clients by one contractor at one location, which made it convenient and simple to take advantage of the services. Once a counselor determined an individual's eligibility for JTPA benefits, the participant completed a self-assessment questionnaire. Those who had experience and a correlated job preference were channeled to basic assessment. Others progressed to extended assessment.

Basic assessment involved completion of a detailed personal data form followed by administration of "a modest battery of traditional vocational assessment instruments, including an interest inventory, a learning ability instrument, an academic achievement instrument, and, when indicated, a personality inventory" (Armstrong, 1989, p. 84). Counselors then met individually with each client to determine the appropriate course of action. This usually involved referral to a job-seeking skills class but varied somewhat based on the participant's level of preparation and readiness. Flexibility and intense individual client evaluation contributed greatly to the program's success in career guidance and job placement.

Extended assessment, for those who needed more assistance, involved completion of a wide range of work samples and inventories over at least two days. This was followed by an introduction to career exploration resources and an opportunity to work in groups with other job seekers to discover the value of these resources. As with basic assessment, when clients finished the comprehensive self-evaluation, they generally advanced to the job-seeking skills class.

Small cohorts of 10-15 participants met together with a counselor for 10 days for the job-seeking skills component of Central Utah's JSA program. The first 5 days involved instruction in attitude, appearance, resume writing, interviewing techniques, networking, and completing job applications. The second 5 days went to searching for jobs through the agency's job development division, as well as through external sources. It was "not uncommon for half or more of the clients to have secured employment by the end of the class in this client-centered placement program" (Armstrong, 1989, p. 86). Those still searching for employment after they had completed the training program were not abandoned. Counselors and job developers continued to work with these clients until they found work.

The overwhelmingly successful results of the Central Utah Mountain Lands' career guidance and job placement program came about through a holistic, interactive, individual, and dynamic approach to training. In addition, a teamwork approach to some of the activities helped clients develop a support system that helped them succeed. Finally, counselors, job developers, and participants maintained open lines of communication, and the system was consistently evaluated and updated in response to client reactions to the program (Armstrong, 1989).

By providing internships for a JTPA summer youth program, the Los Angeles County Health Department became acutely aware of the need for career and vocational guidance for disadvantaged teens in Southern California. Young people obviously benefited greatly from their involvement with Health Department's employees, so the youth program coordinators decided to take on a more ambitious agenda. They developed a very different job search assistance program from that sponsored by Central Utah, yet it proved very successful. One of the California project's unusual characteristics is that it was instituted and supported by private resources, not money obtained from JTPA or PIC funds.

The Health Department engineered a training program that was specifically tailored for the distinctive needs of economically and educationally disadvantaged teenagers. The program aimed to help young people "improve their work and communication skills, build their self-esteem, clarify their life goals, and have opportunities to practice employment skills that would help them get and retain good jobs" (Laabs, 1994, p. 35). One of the keys to the success of this program was that each participant was assigned a mentor who worked with that teen individually. Organizers recognized that many at-risk youths were starved for attention and had interacted with few positive role models before joining the Health Department's initiative.

In addition to meeting with their mentors, the teens gathered on a monthly basis for job-readiness preparation. Each session had a specific job search theme such as gathering and completing job applications, interviewing skills and rehearsals, creating resumes on the computer, and speaking in public. Further, the teens took field trips to broaden their perspectives and heighten their tolerance for diversity.

Ultimately, the participants emerged from this career guidance program with an awareness of what the world beyond their neighborhoods has to offer and an understanding that they could improve their lives significantly through education and hard work. The positive relationships they developed with peers and mentors showed that they could overcome obstacles to success and achieve goals. "Through this teen program, disadvantaged kids were inspired to reach into themselves and find the place where strength and courage lies, with the help of some people who cared about their development" (Laabs, 1994, p. 43).

In 1984, the San Diego private industry council learned that the last remaining local tuna cannery was going out of business and that hundreds of low-skilled workers, mostly older women, would lose their jobs. Because PIC members knew about the demise of the Van Camp Seafood Co. several months before it closed, they could intervene early and make a genuine difference for these employees. The Van Camp employees were offered counseling, skill and vocational interest assessment, job placement services, and English-as-a-second-language classes.

The San Diego PIC specialized JSA skills training for participants. It could provide tailored services because counselors met with Van Camp employees before their layoff, which gave time to develop appropriate training programs. Aggressive marketing and a diversified advertising campaign also proved advantageous. "More than 700 workers entered the PIC-sponsored training, and after . . . nine months . . . 445 landed jobs with private employers at an average wage of $5.11 per hour [in 1984 dollars]" (Lee, 1986, p. 58).

Among Job Training Partnership Act programs for in-school youth, the Quantum Opportunities Project (QUOP) has been one of the most distinguished. QUOP provided college guidance, career counseling, and mentoring to children in AFDC families. A program evaluation "found that QUOP participants were far more likely to graduate high school and go on to college. . . . Fully 42 percent of QUOP students went on to college, while only 16 percent of the control group did" (What's Working, 1995). These job search assistance programs experienced a positive cost-benefit ratio, but each did so for unique reasons. The above examples show that best practices in JSA include a holistic, well-integrated approach; peer and mentor interaction; early intervention; aggressive marketing; individualized training; open channels of communication; and regular program evaluation.

Short-Term Classroom Training

Short-term classroom training programs last from three to six months and generally help clients develop vocational or technical skills. Other short-term programs provide basic education such as preparation for the General Equivalency Diploma (GED) for those who have dropped out of secondary school or English-as-a-second-language instruction for immigrants. The Department of Labor's 1995 JTPA evaluation report concludes that:

> The impacts of relatively short-term classroom training have in most cases not been particularly positive, especially for youth. However . . . such training can have strong positive effects when it is closely tied to the labor market and very well implemented. In addition, classroom training has produced modest earnings gains for disadvantaged adults in the JTPA program. Results for programs which provide short-term training to displaced workers are not particularly encouraging so far. (*What's Working*, 1995, p. 14)

Despite this relatively negative appraisal of short-term training, the San Jose Center for Employment and Training (CET) demonstrates that the outcomes can be extraordinary. The San Jose CET is a clear example of a best practice in the second-chance system. Between 1985 and 1988, a JTPA initiative known as the JOBSTART Demonstration was instituted at 13 sites in nine states, including the San Jose CET. Developed and overseen by the Manpower Demonstration Research Corporation (MDRC), the project received funding through the Department of Labor (JTPA), the National Commission for Employment Policy, nine family and corporate foundations, and The Chase Manhattan Bank. "JOBSTART's major goal was to increase the employment and earnings and reduce the welfare receipt of young, low-skilled school dropouts" (Cove, Bos, Doolittle, and Toussaint, 1993, p. xx). Of the 13 sites, only the San Diego CET showed a significant earnings impact—average income increases of $6,700 over four years compared with a mean increase of $214 for all sites (Lee, 1995). The private, nonprofit CET was established in 1968 to teach occupational skills to unemployed migrant workers in East San Jose. Since then it has expanded to offer disadvantaged youth and adults 28 short-term training options, all developed in response to labor market demands. These vocational training options prepare participants for a wide range of employment possibilities, from heavy manufacturing trades to service positions to clerical and sales occupations. Staying attuned to the local labor market has contributed to the CET's 90 percent placement rate (Lee, 1995, p. 31).

Another factor in the CET's success is its truly integrated approach to providing remedial education along with vocational skills training. Referred to as *concurrent training* by the MDRC and *contextual learning* by Lee (1995), this method emphasizes technical instruction without ignoring the basic English or math skills deficiencies. Students enter job simulation activities directly, which teach academic concepts in the context of the job training, rather than through traditional classroom instruction. This approach lets participants focus on the positive rather than the negative, thereby improving their work attitudes and self-perception.

"Other unique features of CET/San Jose's JOBSTART program include a clear organizational focus on employment as the program goal, little upfront screening of applicants, . . . [and] relatively intensive services concentrated during a short period of time" (Cove, Bos, Doolittle, and Toussaint, 1993, p. xl). Participants are neither screened nor tested on entry and they have the option to continue training until they have mastered the necessary skills and/or found work. Like the concurrent teaching method, this open-entry and open-exit strategy creates a nonthreatening environment. Students attend training sessions for 35 to 40 hours each week for three to six months, so they are both constantly immersed in the program and continually interacting with instructors, counselors, and peers. The intensity of the schedule forces clients to remain focused on skill development and finding decent employment.

CET has expanded to 25 locations in California, Arizona, and Nevada, where it has served over 60,000 disadvantaged youths and adults. The remarkable accomplishments of the San Jose Center for Employment Training have been recognized by the Department of Labor in recent years. It serves as a model second-chance project, and attempts are now being made, under federal government sponsorship, to replicate its success through agencies in New York, Maryland, and Virginia.

On the island of Maui, the Hawaii State Employment Service created a demonstration program in 1991 to train disadvantaged adults to fill the local economy's need for child care services. The Family Child Care Training Project is a joint effort of state agencies, special interest groups, the Maui County PIC, Maui Community College, and University of Hawaii. Because there were only 22 licensed child care providers on the island, they seized an opportunity to prepare people for an occupation that clearly had labor market demand.

"This program recruits prospective home-based child care providers and offers them intensive [short-term] training and follow-up support services to ensure quality child care" (*Leaders of Change*, 1993, p. 7). As in the CET, instruction is conducted in a simulated work environment, in this case a model home. Children of the participants are cared for by a Family Child Care Training Project provider during the training sessions, giving students the chance to apply what they learned on site.

The agencies and institutions that support this project have taken extra steps to guarantee its success. For example, so the newly trained providers are not thwarted by the necessary capital investment in cribs, high chairs, toys, and other pertinent items, the project has established a free "library" that lends these materials. An advisory committee that evaluates activities and monitors progress oversees the Family Child Care Training Project. The ingredients appear to have been properly mixed because in the first two years of operation, 54 clients received training and 39 new child care providers earned a state license. The impact was significant in that more than 100 "additional

child care slots were created in the community, thereby allowing more people to enter and remain in the workforce" (*Leaders of Change*, 1993, p. 7).

What leads to a successful short-term classroom training program? The best practices showcased here indicate that using an integrated approach and operating in a simulated work environment are two key elements. Maintaining close contact with the local business community, and therefore remaining constantly aware of workforce needs, also emerged as a critical contributor to the success of short-term training projects.

Long-Term Classroom Training

Long-term classroom training—designed for those who need significant intervention for job placement—extends over more than six months. Assessment of compulsory schooling regulations indicates that remaining in secondary school has a meaningful impact on employment. Since these "laws tend to affect students who are the least advantaged and the least academically skilled, this suggests that basic education programs for the disadvantaged have a positive long-term effect" (*What's Working*, 1995, p. 12). Elementary and secondary education provided through traditional delivery systems, however, is beyond the scope of the second-chance system. Higher education offered by community colleges, four-year institutions, and universities is another common form of long-term training, but again is not relevant to a discussion of the second-chance system.

Note, however, that community colleges do play an essential role in providing services to disadvantaged youths and adults. Many JTPA contracts, for example, are awarded to two-year institutions that design and provide training programs on their campuses. These projects often lie outside the conventional community college curriculum. They are routinely offered in response to a service delivery area's demand for specific job search programs, occupational training, or long-term training.

Long-term training seldom exists outside

formal educational institutions, due to cost and desire to avoid unnecessary duplication of services. Since high schools and colleges provide appropriate training, other providers usually focus on job search assistance, short-term training, and subsidized employment. The Job Corps, however, is the exception to this rule and it has achieved a remarkable performance record. Established in 1964 under President Johnson's Economic Opportunity Act, the Job Corps is now supported through Title IV-B of the JTPA. The program's objective "is to provide an environment for severely disadvantaged youth in which they can learn the academic and vocational skills needed to enhance employability" (Johnson & Troppe, 1992, p. 339). A total of 111 residential centers in the United States and its territories serve over 65,000 of the nation's profoundly at-risk youth each year, at a cost of approximately one billion dollars. According to the proceedings of a recent Senate hearing on federal training programs, "The average Job Corps student is 18 years old, reads at a seventh grade level, has a disruptive home life, has never held a full-time job, and comes from a family with an income of under $7,000. More than 80 percent are high school dropouts" (*The Job Corps Program*, 1994, p. 6). Furthermore, Job Corps participants are usually racial minorities with 7th-grade math skills, and fewer than 10 years of formal education. Although participants can enroll in the Job Corps for up to two years, the mean duration of study is approximately 6.5 months (Johnson & Troppe, 1992).

The Job Corps system gives young people a comprehensive package of services, including but not limited to basic education, occupational training, health instruction, counseling, and job placement. Serving students with overwhelming fundamental academic deficiencies and many socio-economic problems is a challenge that the Job Corps has met head on. It does this by offering a flexible, individualized curriculum that is self-paced and directed by the mastery-learning method. This curriculum has

six component programs: reading, mathematics, high school equivalency (GED) exam preparation, world of work, health instruction, and social skills development. Since the Job Corps operates with an open-entry and open-exit philosophy, students enroll in and terminate from their training with varying levels of preparedness for employment. Some find the boarding-school environment and strict rules too restrictive, and consequently may leave before they take advantage of all that the Job Corps has to offer.

Workforce expectations and the population that the Job Corps serves have changed dramatically in the 30 years of its existence. The program has been dynamic, implementing change as necessary to meet evolving demands. After a 1986 pilot study, many centers began using computer-assisted instruction as a supplement to traditional paper-and-pencil pedagogy. A second initiative includes the introduction of a competency-based academic program in a number of test sites (Johnson & Troppe, 1992). This new project encompasses implementation of an automated educational tracking system aimed at creating capital efficiencies. Many Job Corps centers also work to build bridges to local high schools and state agencies as part of an effort to create more opportunities for Job Corps graduates.

The evidence of the Job Corps' success is staggering and therefore establishes the program as a model for the nation. Research clearly shows that enrollment in the Job Corps results in increased earnings, educational attainment, employment, and savings for society. It also leads to decreases in reliance on government subsidies and serious criminal offenses. Compared with nonenrolled disadvantaged youth, Job Corps enrollees on average earned $1,300 more annually, worked three more weeks per year, and were more likely to earn a high school diploma or GED (*What's Working*, 1995). Senator Simon of Illinois reported that

[a]ccording to a study by Mathematica Policy Research, for every dollar invested in Job Corps,

$1.46 is returned to the economy through reductions in income maintenance payments, the costs of crime and incarceration, and through increased taxes paid by Job Corps graduates. In addition to improving their future earnings, Job Corps participants are less dependent on welfare and unemployment insurance. (*The Job Corps Program*, 1994, p. 6)

The Job Corps represents a best practice in the second-chance system for reasons similar to those noted with Mountain Lands and the San Jose CET. It uses an integrated, full-service approach that is tailored to the individual participant's needs. The Job Corps has evolved throughout its history, maintaining a keen awareness of what it takes to help severely disadvantaged youths succeed.

In another second-chance program, the Siemens Corporation has recently begun to adopt the centuries-old apprenticeship system at plants in Florida, Kentucky, and North Carolina. An impromptu visit to East Wake High School near Raleigh, North Carolina, inspired Siemens to extend this program beyond the plant and into the classroom. Now East Wake and Siemens have cultivated a school-to-work partnership, which is consistent with the Clinton administration's vision of workforce development.

Company management and school officials worked together to design a plan of study that would meet secondary school educational requirements; provide participants with relevant occupational training; and prepare students for technical work at a Siemens energy and automation plant, so the corporation could get a return on its investment. To secure a commitment from all parties, resources were drawn from Siemens, the county, and the school.

Students enter the Siemens' long-term training program during their junior year in high school and remain in it until graduation. As with other successful second-chance projects, the East Wake students immerse themselves in a simulated work environment. They are pre-screened based on academic and citizenship credentials, complete job applications, attend employee orientation, and sit at work tables, not desks. Instructors present an integrated curriculum, focusing on electronic training and principles of technology. The classroom experience is tested over the summer when students work, for competitive pay, in entry-level assembly jobs at a Siemens facility.

"Since a college degree is seen as the ticket to the American dream, educators, parents and kids often dismiss the value of technical programs" (Lee, 1995, p. 36). But advocates disagree, arguing that youth apprenticeship programs give participants the qualifications they need for entry-level vocational jobs, but do not preclude their going to college. The practical experience these high school students gain prepares them for the transition to either work or higher education (Lee, 1995).

The Job Corps and the Siemens apprenticeship program clearly demonstrate that long-term classroom training can work for disadvantaged youth. Further, a recent study of dislocated workers found that long-term training resulted in a considerable increase in earnings (*What's Working*, 1995). Too few displaced workers took advantage of this option, however, to currently report it as a distinguished practice in the second-chance system. Note that postsecondary institutions provide substantial long-term training opportunities to disadvantaged populations, but the barriers to entry are somewhat higher than those associated with targeted training programs.

Subsidized Employment

Subsidized employment arrangements, in which both the employer and the government contribute to employee wages, can be either short term or long term. On-the-job (OJT) training, the most common form of subsidized employment, consumes about 22 percent of the JTPA's annual basic training block grant (Barnes, 1994). OJT places disadvantaged individuals with insufficient skills and experience in high demand fields. This enhances the participants' chances for long-term employment without forcing the employer to assume all the extraordinary costs associated with hiring at-risk youths and adults (Barnes, 1994).

According to the latest Department of Labor report on the economic impact of workforce development programs, subsidized employment has "proven quite successful for single mothers on welfare. The record in helping other adult populations is more sketchy, but generally positive" (*What's Working*, 1995, p. 15). Also, similar "programs for disadvantaged youth have boosted employment considerably during the program period . . . but have not been successful in producing lasting gains in employment or earnings. . . ." (*What's Working*, 1995, p. 15)

In Florida, the Palm Beach County PIC has had great success with on-the-job training programs. The PIC allocated $330,000 to subsidized employment agreements for both adults and young people in 1993-94. K-Rain, a local manufacturer of valves, controllers, and lawn sprinklers, worked with the Palm Beach PIC to hire 13 percent of its workforce through OJT programs (Barnes, 1994, p. 13). The program has achieved its objectives because the participants are well screened for minimum skill levels that closely match employer requirements for OJT candidates.

Ross Stores, Inc., a California-based chain of discount clothing stores, has also taken advantage of subsidized employment programs. A few months before a new outlet opens, Ross management contacts the local PIC to discuss ways that JTPA-eligible youths and adults can fill the company's employment gaps. The company had had great difficulty finding capable people for a large number of hourly retail positions, so the human resources department sought a new source. Working with PICs has enabled it to find a larger pool of qualified candidates.

PIC referrals usually need more comprehensive training because many have not been previously employed, but Ross is willing to provide the additional instruction because the government subsidizes a por-

tion of the costs. In addition, OJT programs have had a positive impact on turnover, which is generally very high in the retail industry. "People recruited through these alternative sources stay with [Ross] about 50 percent longer than those individuals recruited from the general market" (Laabs, 1992, p. 36). Top management has been committed to the Ross-PIC partnership from its inception, and the investment has paid off. Taking advantage of JTPA resources has been so advantageous that Ross's corporate human resources department has created a separate government programs office to work with the Department of Labor, state agencies, and private industry councils.

Disadvantaged adults have benefited from two model subsidized employment projects, the Supported Work demonstration and the Home Health Care Aide demonstration. Both programs resulted in average earnings gains of about $1,500 to $2,000 annually. These gains were sustained over a period of several post-training years (*What's Working*, 1995). By combining subsidized employment with job search assistance, these demonstrations helped participants to develop practical job skills in a realistic environment, and then to find unsubsidized work where they could apply their experience.

Does the Second-Chance System Work?

President Clinton's 1992 election platform included a commitment to federal government reinvestment in workforce development to better position the United States for competition in the global marketplace. Does the second-chance system make a meaningful contribution to this goal? In many respects, the evidence discussed here indicates that employment counseling and training for disadvantaged adults, at-risk youth, and displaced workers *do help* participants find and keep decent jobs. These model programs, however, represent only a small minority of all second-chance system activities. Research about the effectiveness of JTPA and other workforce development projects clearly indicates a substantial need for improvement, restructuring, and continuous change in the system. Also, more and better assessment of the return on investment is absolutely essential. Sufficient mechanisms to judge which programs work and which squander taxpayer dollars simply do not exist.

No system will likely make an impact on the neediest members of the groups that these programs serve (Lee, 1986). Despite this fact, the Mountain Lands' JSA project, the San Jose CET, the Job Corps, and the Ross Stores OJT initiative have succeeded in helping people become more productive members of the U.S. workforce. How can the models highlighted in this chapter inform the entire second-chance system? What lessons can be learned? Recurring characteristics of these distinguished programs include:

- use of an integrated approach;
- individualization based on the participants' needs;
- close connection to the local labor market;
- use of teamwork concepts and group dynamics;
- simulation of a realistic work environment;
- flexibility (often allowing open entry and open exit); and
- a dynamic quality, changing with demands of the clients and the market.

Other programs should duplicate these qualities when appropriate and avoid repeating serious errors when possible. Note, however, that just because something works well in Utah, does not mean that it will work equally well in Georgia.

Thousands of Americans have improved the quality of their lives through JTPA projects and other initiatives that have similar objectives. These programs have resulted in positive consequences for the welfare system, for employers, and for taxpayers. Clearly, the second-chance system is, and will continue to be, a critical component of workforce development in this country. After all, giving people a second chance is one of the guiding principles on which the political, social, and economic fabric of the United States was built.

References

Armstrong, R. N. (1989). Central Utah's JTPA career guidance and job placement program. *Career Development Quarterly*, 38 (1), 82-89.

Barnes, K. J. (1993). Economic dislocation and worker adjustment assistance. *HR Focus*, 70 (10), 19.

Barnes, K. J. (1994). Government program supports on-the-job training. *HR Focus*, 71 (6), 12-13.

Carnevale, A. P., & Johnston, J. W. (1989). *Training America: Strategies for the nation*. Alexandria, VA: American Society for Training and Development and Rochester, NY: National Center on Education and the Economy. (ERIC Document Reproduction Service No. ED 309 034)

Cook, R. F. (1986). Implementation of the Job Training Partnership Act: A field network process evaluation. *Evaluation and Program Planning*, 9 (1), 73-84.

Cove, G., Bos, H., Doolittle, F. & Toussaint, C. (1993). *JOBSTART: Final report on a program for school dropouts*. New York, NY: Manpower Demonstration Research Corp.

The Job Corps program. (1994). (Hearing of the Committee on Labor and Human Resources on examining proposals to reform and consolidate federal job training programs. United States Senate, One Hundred Third Congress, second session). Washington, DC: Senate Committee on Labor and Human Resources. (ERIC Document Reproduction Service No. ED 377 346)

JOBS and JTPA: Tracking spending, outcomes and program performance.(1994). (Report to the Chairman, Committee on Labor and Human Resources, U.S. Senate). Washington, DC: General Accounting Office, Health, Education, and Human Services Division. (ERIC Document Reproduction Service No. ED 372 269)

Johnson, T. R. & Troppe, M. (1992). Improving literacy and employability among disadvantaged youth: The Job Corps model. *Youth and Society*, 23, 335-355.

Laabs, J. J. (1992). How federally funded training helps business. *Personnel Journal*, 71 (3), 34-39.

Laabs, J. J. (1994). Disadvantaged teens work toward a better future. *Personnel Journal*, 73 (12), 34-43.

Leaders of change! Successful workforce development projects. (1993). Projects presented at the workforce development forums 1993. Washington, DC: U.S. Department of Labor, Employment and Training Administration.

Lee, C. (1986). What's the word on JTPA? *Training*, 22 (5), 54-55, 57-61.

Lee, C. (1995). Out of the maze: Can the federal job-training mess be fixed? *Training*, 32 (2), 29-34, 36-37.

Public Policy Institute of New York State, Inc. (1995, July). *Workforce get ready.* Albany, NY: Public Policy Institute of New York State, Inc.

Romero, C. J. (1994). *JTPA programs and adult women on welfare: Using training to raise AFDC recipients above poverty* (Research Report No. 93-01). Washington, DC: Department of Labor, National Commission for Employment Policy. (ERIC Document Reproduction Service No. ED 372 304)

What's working (and what's not): A summary of research on the economic impacts of employment and training programs. (1995). Washington, DC: U.S. Department of Labor. (ERIC Document Reproduction Service No. ED 379 445)

4

Human Capital and the New Economy

By Scott R. Sweetland

Introduction

MORE than 200 years ago, Adam Smith (1776, 1952) stated that "the wealth of nations included the acquired and useful abilities of all the inhabitants or members of the society" (p. 119). He further explained that acquired abilities, which were useful for production, constituted a form of capital that was fixed and realized in person. In 1960, Theodore Schultz (1961b) formally announced an economic research agenda that included the study of human capital. Similar to Smith's perspective, Schultz's analytic approach supported the theory that costs of education and training were actually "investments" that provided future flows of income. Since that time, *human capital* has meant *investments in people that provide economic benefits.*

While contemporary discussions of workforce preparation and human resource development occasionally use the term human capital, nearly all endeavors that improve work skills and worker productivity qualify theoretically as human capital investments (Becker, 1964, 1975, 1993; Mincer, 1974, 1989, 1994). Moreover, as the skill requirements of the modern day workforce shift toward knowledge-application (Drucker, 1993), the prime human capital investments—education and training—become ever more important to productivity at individual, corporate, and national levels.

This chapter will explore workforce preparation from a human capital theory orientation. It begins with a brief historical overview of human capital theory and then considers recent observations made by Deming, Drucker, Reich, and Thurow. The viewpoints of these prominent authors are further considered to show the relevance of the human capital theory orientation to learning, working, and earning.

Human Capital Theory

During the late 1950s, economists pursued human capital theory for two distinct but related reasons: First, conventional means of economic measurement did not account for a significant portion of U.S. economic growth. Second, increased levels of education accounted for a significant portion of personal income growth.

From the macroeconomic standpoint, economists long believed that changes in the factors of production—land, labor, and capital—could explain economic growth (Samuelson, 1980). However, studies by Abramovitz (1956), Solow (1957), Kendrick (1958, 1961), and others indicated that these economic inputs did not explain a significant portion of economic growth. Kendrick's preliminary calculations strongly supported Fabricant's (1959) illustration that the proportion of unexplained economic growth had grown at an increasing rate throughout the 1889-1957 period. Fabricant asserted that this growth was unexplained because conventional definitions of labor did not adequately reflect improvements in the economic quality of human resources. To support this position and provide a basis for expanded dialogue, Fabricant defined intangible capital as "all the improvements in basic science, technology, business administration, and education and training that aid in production" (p. 22).

Schultz (1961b) synthesized his analyses (1959, 1960, 1961a) with others to assert that the concept of intangible or human capital presented one plausible explanation for the otherwise unexplained portion of economic growth:

> Although it is obvious that people acquire useful skills and knowledge, it is not obvious that these skills and knowledge are a form of capital, that this capital is in substantial part a product of deliberate investment, that it has grown in Western societies at a much faster rate than conventional (nonhuman) capital, and that its growth may well be the most distinctive feature of the economic system. (1961b, p. 1)

As part of his 1960 presidential address to the American Economic Association, Schultz revealed that the stock of inputs which contributed to economic growth had changed dramatically from 1900 to 1956. He suggested that while the stock of nonhuman capital had increased 4.5 times, the stock of education in the workforce had increased 8.5 times. In relative terms, this nearly twofold increase provided strong evidence that "investment in education . . . by itself may well account for a substantial part of the otherwise unexplained rise in [national] earnings" (1961b, p. 10).

We refer to the macroeconomic perspectives of Schultz and Fabricant as *residual analysis*. In this context, the residual repre-

sents that portion of economic growth unaccounted for by conventional means of economic measurement. The human capital theory perspective suggested that this residual would be explained if new empirical approaches that accounted for investments in people were adopted.

Denison (1962) developed a special case of residual explanation that supported human capital theory. Based on the Cobb-Douglas (1928) aggregate production function, Solow (1957) had developed a mathematical model of the U.S. economy and suggested that the residual was attributable in part to education. Denison's creation was an alternative production function model that specifically included education and advances in knowledge as economic inputs. The first stage of his analysis estimated that the average annual rate of growth in U.S. national income was 2.93 percent from 1929 to 1957. The second stage attempted to explain the sources of this growth and to arrive at a residual of zero. To accomplish this, Denison attributed 43 percent of national income growth to human capital investment through education and knowledge inputs.

Friedman and Kuznets conducted a pioneering analysis of personal incomes in 1945. Their study demonstrated that personal incomes within the medical profession were largely explained by investments in formal education and training. Mincer (1958) found that personal incomes across the U.S. were largely explained by investments in two types of training: formal education and work experience. The results of both studies suggested that high incomes justifiably reflected human capital investments in training. Through his cross-sectional analysis, Mincer also found that the incomes of workers rose at a greater rate in occupations that required higher levels of training and skill. He believed that this occurred because human capital investment increased as people developed higher-order skills and improved them through work experience.

Becker (1960) explored differences in personal incomes between high school and college graduates in the U.S. He related income differentials between the two groups to the cost of acquiring a college education through a methodology that derived an internal *rate of return* on investment. On average, Becker estimated that graduation from college provided a 10 percent rate of return on private human capital investments. Perhaps more important than his original estimates, however, was the way Becker arrived at an internal rate of return. The derived statistic was important because it summarized the cost-benefit relationship of college education and allowed comparisons among alternative investment opportunities. For example, if an individual had the opportunity to earn 15 percent on a business investment, then a 10 percent return on college education would not be very attractive. However, if the individual's only investment alternative was to earn 5 percent interest on a bank account, then a 10 percent return on college education would seem profitable.

Becker's approach was also relevant to national assessments of human capital investment. In fact, his original research hypothesis dealt with "American policies and procedures relating to economic growth and military technology" (Becker, 1960, p. 346). Becker hypothesized that cumulated private investments in education and training, as well as public subsidies that supported and promoted education and training, were a form of national investment. The internal-rate-of-return statistic provided a means to gauge national investments in education and training relative to other national investments in such diverse areas as military technology, interstate transportation, and mass communication.

While the pursuit of human capital theory in the 1960s did not capture the value of education and training in absolute terms, scholarship in the field created an analytical framework for assessing the economic consequences of learning. At both the individual and national levels of analysis, human capital theory studies repeatedly demonstrated that "learning was earning." Perhaps this is why the field flourished for more

than a decade and led to the publication of more than 2,000 research studies, journal articles, and books on the economics of education (Blaug, 1978).

Since that time, the larger economics of the education field and the study of human capital theory have continued to grow. Although theoretical and practical criticisms have been ignored throughout this historical overview, the selected studies provide a strong foundation and opportunity for comprehensive understanding of the human capital theory orientation.

The New Economy

Human capital theory studies consistently provided economic observations that correlated earning with various forms of learning. For those who became convinced that the economic relationship was causal, studies of national and individual economic progress produced evidence of the significance of learning at the corporate level of analysis.

Within this conceptual framework, the learning-to-earning transformation depended on the qualities of both the corporate organization and the national economy: The economic progress of individuals relied on corporations and other institutions to provide employment in an environment that demanded and compensated learned skills and abilities. In turn, corporations and institutions relied on a vibrant national economy that supplied the components of production and demanded finished goods and services. In this closed economy (that is, one that existed primarily inside national boundaries) the relationship of education and training to productivity and earning seemed obvious. Throughout the last decade, however, many scholars have observed fundamental changes in the structure and organization of the national economy as well as the operations of its corporate component.

Before he became President Bill Clinton's Secretary of Labor, Robert Reich (1991) predicted that national products, corporations, and industries would become vestiges of the past. He pointed to an emergent, highly competitive global economy in which "high-value businesses" (p. 84) summoned the forces of supply and demand across the globe to meet the needs of narrow customer segments with specialized, even customized, solutions. Reich further described the emerging "global webs" (p. 113) through which corporate ownership and financing, production materials and laborers, marketing and sales distribution, and research and development were accomplished—all in diffused geographic locations that seemed to transcend national boundaries. Because of these and other global conditions, Reich asserted that the economic significance of nationality would become stratified among people who were able, or unable, to participate in the global arena.

Although Reich's analysis largely confronted issues of national sovereignty and multinational corporate organization, nearly all of his illustrations pointed to the value of human capital skills, education, training, and experience. Similar to his conceptualization of high-value businesses, Reich described symbolic analysts (p. 178) as members of the workforce who identified, solved, and brokered problems for individuals, organizations, industries, governments, nations, and so forth. He asserted that symbolic analysts commanded the highest levels of compensation in the global economy because their efforts to conceptualize problems, devise solutions, and plan implementation strategies contributed the most value to products and services. His global perspective suggested that individuals would aspire to become symbolic analysts and that national labor policies should seek to maximize the number of symbolic analysts in the workforce.

Lester Thurow (1992) also discussed dramatic global changes. However, his interpretations suggested that the economic continuity of nations would be maintained. The major shift that Thurow conceived was a United States that no longer dominated the world economic order, but rather stood with Japan and the European Economic Commu-

nity (EEC) as a relatively equal economic contender. Thurow predicted that intensified competition among the three predominant economic powers would necessarily lead to nationally planned economic goals and strategies. He contended that this new economic necessity would prove especially problematic for the U.S. because "America's most comfortable hypothesis is to tell itself that it does not need an economic game plan. The old ways are the best ways" (p. 259). According to Thurow, this myopic characteristic of Americans and American systems of organization would inevitably undermine the economic competitiveness of the U.S.

Beyond the context of national economic goals and strategies, Thurow discussed the necessity of *teamwork* for economic survival, observing that Americans, on the whole, did not traditionally nurture and support teamwork. American heroes were historically individuals, not teams, and American business and government negotiated as adversaries rather than as allies. To illustrate this characteristic as a weakness in the new competitive game, Thurow contrasted it with the strategic strengths of America's competitors. These included the Japanese government's interactions with Japan's industries and the cooperation required among European nations to enter the EEC.

Thurow contended that individual and corporate rationale in the American economic system naturally led to a collective irrationality. This could only be overcome, he believed, by cooperative investments in key industries that would support high wages, and hence, improve the standard of living. Among other recommendations, Thurow forcefully asserted that cooperative public and private investments in formal education and work-skills training would be required to prepare a world class workforce that could compete with Japan and the EEC.

Peter Drucker (1993) pointed to the history and evolution of economies to assert that society around the world was in a state of profound transformation. While he did not contest the continued existence of nations or nationality, Drucker stated that the nation, as an entity, was losing its sovereign power. His observations included the shared military operations witnessed in the Persian Gulf as well as the shared identity of the nations in the EEC. Within nations, Drucker observed that sovereign powers had become weakened by political interactions with powerful lobbyists and the delegation, or relegation, of social responsibilities to diverse institutions and other organizations. His conclusion on this point was that the nation-state would not disappear, but it would no longer be indispensable.

Drucker felt that throughout the history of complex interactions between political entities and economies, the free market was "the one proven mechanism of economic integration" (p. 7). However, his analysis clearly differentiated the free market from classical capitalism which, along with Marxism and communism, had all but disappeared. Drucker's rendition of transformational society was neither socialist nor capitalist; it was postcapitalist. Drucker maintained that many of the institutions and mechanisms of the old world would survive, although each was to play a new role in modern society. Even the traditional factors of production—land, labor, and capital (Samuelson, 1980)—would be affected.

Where for centuries economic development had depended on the factors of production, comparatively and competitively, Drucker asserted that they had become secondary to the primary resource of productivity—knowledge. He argued that the traditional factors were already traded, bought, and sold at will, but that the primary resource of knowledge was required to procure and use them productively. In the current and future economic environment, asserted Drucker, the means to economic growth will be essentially the application of knowledge to knowledge.

In his last book, W. Edwards Deming (1994) further dispelled the common misconception that he was preoccupied with total quality management (TQM). In fact, his first chapter related the epitome of quality control—"zero defects" (p. 16)—to a larger system that only existed as long as it produced a product or service that the market demanded. Deming stated that innovation, communication, cooperation, and learning were required in all systems, including industry, government, and education, to achieve a system of "profound knowledge" (p. 92)—learning and knowledge of a system that developed outside the system. Deming asserted that through the existence and recognition of this outer dimension of knowledge, nations, corporations, institutions, and other organizations could initiate and endure major transformations that would benefit economic growth and the quality of living.

Deming's analysis defined all systems to include "interdependent components that work together to try to accomplish the aim of the system" (p. 50). He sharply criticized Western theory and practice for its propensity to arrange interdependent components competitively. Cooperation was required both across and within systems, Deming maintained, because interdependent components—individuals, departments, corporations, institutions, governments, and so forth—could not be separated. He also asserted that the rank and file organization of people and their current skills and knowledge further promoted the harmful effects of competition and that the source of this harmful trend was social, beginning in schools which assigned grades and taught win-lose games.

While each of the prominent authors discussed here may have disagreed on some of the specific implications posed by the new economy, they concurred in their observations in several areas. We can summarize these into three key points.

First and foremost, the new economy is globally organized in terms of economic inputs, the distribution of outputs, and the processes used to acquire inputs and create outputs. Second, competition with producers, intermediaries, and consumers—from across the street and across the globe—affect all levels of economic activity. Third, economic systems must respond to global organization and competition proactively to bridle internal competition and release the spirit of cooperation. The human capital theory orientation places further emphasis on these economic points by considering the human condition as it relates to education, training, and employment.

Human Capital Development

The human capital theory's analytical framework usually considers the most quantifiable aspects of human capital, such as those that relate to the correlation between income and educational attainment. Its broadest interpretation, however, encompasses all elements that affect the human condition, including good nutrition, appropriate medical attention, and all other healthful activities (Schultz, 1961b). A more narrow definition of activities that support the development of human capital include formal education, work-skills training, and work experience. We will now discuss these activities in relation to the key economic points that were emphasized above.

Faced with a new, globally organized economy, any nation must answer this fundamental question: What do we have to offer the worldwide market? In the U.S., we must ask: Do we want to provide the best labor at the lowest price? Probably not. In fact, our massive public and private expenditures on K-postsecondary and work-skills training education most likely preclude us from offering cheap labor to the rest of the world. We have made our choice to support human capital investment; furthermore, the systems that support human capital investment in the U.S. have long since been established, expanded, and entrenched economically, politically, and socially.

When economic competition in the U.S. was contained largely within the nation's boundaries, there was sufficient reason to believe that human capital investments were providing adequate returns. The addition of increased competition from across the globe will likely affect the U.S. economy in such a way that we will require greater returns on those investments.

Without considering the effectiveness and efficiency of the current level of human capital investment, we could argue that the new economy requires increased levels of spending for formal education and work-skills training. While educators and human resource development officers would probably applaud this action, it would most certainly diminish the capacity of the U.S. to compete in the global market because it would increase the price of goods and services. Overinvestment in human capital would simply drive the price of American goods and services out of the competitive market.

We can no longer measure the effectiveness and efficiency of human capital investment in the U.S. against what we believe to be the status quo. The effectiveness and efficiency of other nations' human capital investment programs will determine the new benchmarks of performance. To remain competitive, formal education and work-skills training in the U.S. must be at least as effective as those of the competition. Otherwise, the market price of goods and services will reflect investment inefficiencies, which, as discussed earlier, will hurt American competitiveness.

The bottom line is that failure to provide formal education and work-skills training effectively will prevent the U.S. from offering a labor resource that the world market demands. Consequently, people will lose jobs. Failure to efficiently provide effective preparation will prevent the U.S. from offering products and services at world-market prices and, consequently, people will lose jobs. When American jobs are lost, most people are sensitive to the immediate losses incurred by individuals, their families, and their communities. Corporations and institutions become aware of their own losses in terms of profits and funding. The nation is then compelled to recognize its economic and political losses.

The compound function of these losses extends further when we consider a third aspect of human capital development: work experience. Without work experience, initial investments in human capital become nonperforming assets, and they eventually obsolesce (Schultz, 1963). In addition, the effects of human capital development on work are never realized. To capitalize on human capital investment, people must engage in meaningful work, which occurs in an environment where continual learning takes place. Whether by design or chance, people who are working preserve and maintain initial human capital investments and, through work experience, increase the value of those investments.

By now, it should be clear that any nation's workforce requires preparation through education and training, as well as employment opportunities that allow workers to practice their skills and build on initial human capital investments. In the U.S., we accomplish the first stage of preparation by a system of mass education which is, at some point, supplemented by work-skills training. For the most part, people gain work experience from another system—the workforce. Of course, there are more than two systems involved in the creation of human capital in the U.S., but the relationship between them is similar to those between myriad public and private systems. Each depends on the other because each loses some of its value or potential without the efficient performance of the other.

Formal education, work-skills training, and relevant work experience cannot be accomplished by one autonomous system. Human capital is created through many stages of development which depend on a multitude of systems. The common denominator throughout this complex process of development is the individual. The success or failure of systems is ultimately experienced by individuals, who naively progress through the education system and are helped or discarded by another system that reacts hastily to the economic environment. Each system along the way may view itself as autonomous, even competitive, in relation to the others, but the most devastating

and immediate losses are borne by individuals and their families.

Considered in the aggregate, we in the U.S. depend on two internal systems, which are ultimately accountable to the worldwide economic system. If we refuse to recognize global economic pressures and fail to transform the disjointed activities of our systems into a coordinated program of human capital development, the rest of the economic world will leave us behind. U.S. history has taught that an unbridled market economy elicits many misgivings. We can be certain that the unrestrained global market will show no mercy, economically or otherwise.

References

Abramovitz, M. (1956). *Resource and output trends in the United States since 1870.* New York: National Bureau of Economic Research.

Becker, G. S. (1960). Underinvestment in college education? *The American Economic Review, 50,* 346-354.

Becker, G. S. (1964). *Human capital: A theoretical and empirical analysis, with special reference to education.* New York: National Bureau of Economic Research.

Becker, G. S. (1975). *Human capital: A theoretical and empirical analysis, with special reference to education* (2nd ed.). New York: National Bureau of Economic Research.

Becker, G. S. (1993). *Human capital: A theoretical and empirical analysis, with special reference to education* (3rd ed.). Chicago: University of Chicago Press.

Blaug, M. (1978). *Economics of education: A selected annotated bibliography* (3rd ed.). New York: Pergamon Press.

Cobb, C. W., & Douglas, P. H. (1928). A theory of production. *The American Economic Review, 18* (Supplement), 139-165.

Deming, W. E. (1994). *The new economics: For industry, government, education* (2nd ed.). Cambridge, MA: Massachusetts Institute of Technology, Center for Advanced Engineering Study.

Denison, E. F. (1962). *The sources of economic growth in the United States and the alternatives before us.* New York: Committee for Economic Development.

Drucker, P. F. (1993). *Post-capitalist society.* New York: Harper.

Fabricant, S. (1959). *Basic facts on productivity change.* New York: National Bureau of Economic Research.

Friedman, M., & Kuznets, S. (1945). *Income from independent professional practice.* New York: National Bureau of Economic Research.

Kendrick, J. W. (1958). *Productivity trends in the United States.* Unpublished manuscript.

Kendrick, J. W. (1961). *Productivity trends in the United*

States. New York: National Bureau of Economic Research.

Mincer, J. (1958). Investment in human capital and personal income distribution. *The Journal of Political Economy, 66*, 281-302.

Mincer, J. (1974). *Schooling, experience, and earnings.* New York: Columbia University Press.

Mincer, J. (1989). *Human capital responses to technological change in the labor market.* Cambridge, MA: National Bureau of Economic Research.

Mincer, J. (1994). *Investment in U.S. education and training.* Cambridge, MA: National Bureau of Economic Research.

Reich, R. B. (1991). *The work of nations.* New York: Vintage Books.

Samuelson, P. A. (1980). Economics (11th ed.). New York: McGraw-Hill.

Schultz, T. W. (1959). Investment in man: An economist's view. *The Social Service Review, 33,* 109-117.

Schultz, T. W. (1960). Capital formation by education.

The Journal of Political Economy, 68, 571-584.

Schultz, T. W. (1961a). Education and economic growth. In N. B. Henry (Ed.), *Social forces influencing American education* (pp. 46-88). Chicago: University of Chicago Press.

Schultz, T. W. (1961b). Investment in human capital. *The American Economic Review, 51,* 1-17.

Schultz, T. W. (1963). *The economic value of education.* New York: Columbia University Press.

Smith, A. (1776/1952). An inquiry into the nature and causes of the wealth of nations. In R. M. Hutchins & M. J. Adler (Eds.), *Great books of the western world: Vol. 39 Adam Smith.* Chicago: Encyclopaedia Britannica.

Solow, R. M. (1957). Technical change and the aggregate production function. *The Review of Economics and Statistics, 39,* 312-320.

Thurow, L. (1992). *Head to head: The coming economic battle among Japan, Europe, and America.* New York: William Morrow.

5

An Emerging Perspective on Policies for American Work and Education for the Year 2000: Choices We Face

By Arthur G. Wirth

Reprinted with permission from the *Journal of Industrial Teacher Education*, Vol. 31, No. 4, Summer 1994.

THE generalization that provides the background for the remarks to follow is that we are living in the beginning stages of one of the great social transformations in human history—a computer-driven, postindustrial revolution that is replacing the factory industrialism that we opened the century with.

A hundred years ago, the decade of the 1890s was another great watershed decade. Frederick Jackson Turner called it the decade of the closing of the frontier. We were leaving the stage of pioneering exploration and agricultural expansion to enter a new urban industrial America. The assembly line was the new dominant tool of production; it replaced farm- and craft-centered hand skills, and its influence permeated the society, including the schools.

We excelled in it and by mid-century dominated the world's economy, but by the 1990s it appears to have run its course. Its features, once so powerful, can become dysfunctional for meeting the new realities.

The new realities of postindustrialism are (a) the electronics-communications revolution, (b) the emergence of a competitive global market, (c) serious ecological damage, (d) ethnic, racial, and sexual diversity, and, above all, (e) turbulent change—rapid and unpredictable.

We are struggling to adapt. Some are making it and some are not. In the past 15 years, we have been confronting a disturbing new phenomenon—an overall decline in the American standard of living.

In the 1980s, American productivity rose by one percent, Japanese productivity by three percent. As we saw the hollowing out of well-paying manufacturing jobs, 70 percent of new jobs were lower-skill/lower-pay jobs. We have moved toward a more polarized society. The well-educated top 25 percent prospered, but the median wage fell by 5 percent. Real wages in 1992 for male high school graduates with up to five years of work experience were 27 percent below 1979 levels (Faux, 1993, p. 467). In 1991, 21.8 percent of American children (one-third of families with children) were living in poverty (Bernstein, 1993, p. 279). In the 1980s, 50 percent of additional income went to the top 1 percent; the middle class shrank by 4.5 percent (Harrison & Bluestone, 1988, p. 164). Another fact of major importance is that in the early 1990s, the labor pool in third-world countries increased by 554 million versus 35 million in mature industrial countries.

We face a third world awash with hundreds of millions ready to work for much lower wages than American workers and new high-tech competitors from Europe and the Asian rim.

Before considering proposals for meeting the challenge, a few words about the social transformation that is needed.

With the advent of assembly-line production at the opening of the century, the basic problem was how to harness an ill-educated immigrant labor force with power-driven factory machinery. Frederick W. Taylor's scientific management offered the solution: break production into easily learned, repetitive tasks; design work as a dual system with thinking, supervision, and control limited to qualified technicians and managers at the top; expect compliant, unthinking execution by workers on the line. It was the system we entered the 1980s with—at a time when the suspicion was growing that it lacked the flexibility and intelligence to cope with turbulent change.

In 1980, William Duffy, vice-president of General Motors in charge of new plant construction, told us at a Washington University luncheon, "General Motors used to boast that its production line had been broken into job segments so simple that any task on the line could be learned in 15 minutes or less—any idiot could do it. If workmanship and morale were poor, the answer was to step up supervision and control. But by 1980, GM was beginning to fear that a production process based on increased control by supervisors of a reluctant, unmotivated, antagonistic workforce that produced shabby products was not viable for survival."

By 1980, GM and other companies were looking for an alternative to Taylorism. In the late 1970s, they were turning to an alternative theory of work, developed in Scandinavia, called *democratic socio-technical work theory*. Scandinavians saw Taylorism as fundamentally flawed. Human work, in postindustrialism, they said, is socio-technical. The technical side of the hyphen refers to the power of electronic technology. But the *socio* refers to the important human qualities needed to troubleshoot, communicate, innovate, and collaborate to meet change (Wirth, 1983, p. 26).

Taylorism, they said, is guilty of the "technical fix fallacy"—the assumption that all problems will yield to expert-designed technical solutions; it ignores the "socio" (human) dimension, critical for high-tech work. We may note that while workplace democracy contributes to human dignity at work, the Scandinavians made it clear that ensuring the *democratic* dimension of *socio-technical* requires strong involvement by democratic unions. Echoing this sentiment, Owen Bieber, president of the United Auto Workers (UAW), called in 1990 for an end to management's "charmed circle of privilege," saying that industry's survival depends on workers' involvement in deciding investments, products, prices, working conditions, and decisions to send work overseas (Wirth, 1983, p. 39). In emerging high-tech work, any organization that fails to tap the brains and commitment of people at work will fail.

By the beginning of the 1990s, American theorists were making their own analyses of what was happening and their recommendations for change. I'll refer to four of them that I will call our Informing Gurus. They all see classical Taylorism as dysfunctional and are proposing alternatives.

Informing Gurus

The first guru is Robert Reich (1991, pp. 200-208), author of *The Work of Nations: Preparing Ourselves for 21st Century Capitalism* and [recently] President Clinton's secretary of labor. His central argument is that the standardized mass production of the Taylorized assembly line era is obsolete. Our former near monopoly of the American market is gone, as that market is now just another part of the one competitive global market, with everyone in it.

In the 1970s, while American producers were venturing forth with the bright idea of planned obsolescence, new international rivals were doing end runs around them with ideas like "the perfect car," and consumers loved it. The consumers are global; they have diverse, changing needs; and they have plenty of producers beckoning for their attention.

The result, says Reich, is that American corporations that can no longer generate large earnings from the high-volume production of standard commodities are gradually turning toward serving the diverse special needs of customers dispersed around the globe. They are surviving by shifting from high-volume to high-quality production. National corporations are being transformed into international corporations with offices and personnel located all over the world.

Global communication networks of computers, fax machines, satellites, and modems link engineers, designers, contractors, and dealers worldwide. This global system, which is in a constant state of change and refinement, is made possible not only by evolving technology but also by four key human skills that drive high-value enterprises. Reich (1991) says that these are the skills of symbolic analysis:

• *Abstraction*–the capacity to order and make meaning of the massive flow of information, to shape raw data into workable patterns.

• *System thinking*–the capacity to see the parts in relation to the whole, to see why problems arise.

• *Experimental inquiry*–the capacity to set up procedures to test and evaluate alternative ideas.

• *Collaboration*–the capacity to engage in active dialogue to get a variety of perspectives and to create consensus when that is necessary.

The result, says Reich, is a growing trend: those with the symbolic analytic skills (the top 25 percent) prosper, those with routine skills are slipping, and those with low skills and dropouts are obsolete, with poverty as their life prospect.

A second guru is Harvard's Shoshanna Zuboff, author of *In the Age of the Smart Machine: The Future of Work and Power,* who studied companies on the frontier of high technology (Zuboff, 1988). She found managers in these places facing an interesting choice. The first, which she termed the *automating* choice, assumes that you can succeed competitively primarily with new technology, retain top-down controls, and deskill labor. You can go overseas with this model or cheapen labor at home. It is a powerful temptation. The flaw, Zuboff says, is that over the long haul, it tends to lack the flexibility required to remain competitive under turbulent change.

The second possibility Zuboff calls the *informating* option. It grows out of the recognition that the centrally controlled automated choice is not flexible enough to cope with the new order of change and complexity. In the informating choice, computer technology becomes a source for designing innovative methods of sharing information with the workforce–informating them. New types of skills and knowledge that depend on the understanding and manipulation of information are needed to tap the potential of an intelligent technology. As the workforce is given access to data from an information-rich environment, hierarchical distinctions begin to blur. Managers and workers fashion new roles that permit them to invent creative ways to add value to products and services.

Zuboff gives detailed examples of how work in the age of the smart machine gets transformed by the emergence of an "electronic text." The change is from the manual skills of physical production to work marked by abstract intellective skills. This requires a kind of learning that demands the constructing of meaning from a symbolic medium.

Learning becomes a top priority. Managers begin to see that all workers in the system need access to data so that they can understand the system in order to trouble-shoot and innovate. Beyond the need for access to data, the organizational climate must support the essential conditions of a learning environment—freedom to play with ideas, to experiment, and to enter into dialogue. Such a democratic environment enhances competitive effectiveness, but at a cost that can be threatening to management. Thus the dilemma of management: choose the automating option, which preserves control from the top level at the cost of the flexibility required to be globally competitive, or choose to informate, which shifts power to people in more democratic work settings. A competitive edge is gained, but at the cost of losing the traditional command prerogatives of management.

A third guru is W. Edwards Deming (Gabor, 1990), with his concept of total quality management (TQM). He argues that the only way to survive in a world awash with cheap labor and high-tech competitors is to be superior in quality and innovation—to keep a step ahead of the pack. The key ingredient is a highly educated, competent workforce with an individual and group commitment to a *relentless pursuit of quality.*

The key to quality, he says, is trust between management and the workforce. Trust is undermined by the mainline management by objectives tradition, which uses the motivation of fear to pit people against each other. The fixation on merit ratings, Deming says, diverts leadership from its central task which is to create trust, competence, commitment to quality, and even joy in work. Deming does advocate teaching workers competence with quantitative methods only so that workers themselves can get feedback on their performance and do their own quality control, for which they take responsibility. At Xerox and Ford, performance appraisal ratings are based primarily on the performance of the team and include contributions to cooperative efforts.

Another point often overlooked is Deming's contention that a spiritual issue is involved. We ought to be informed, he says, by the passage in Ecclesiastes that says that we were created "a little higher than the animals" and "a little lower than the angels."

Organizations that treat us as mere organisms miss our distinctive human strengths—our capacities for analyzing, problem solving, innovating. But we also are "lower than the angels." So harm can occur with the wrong kind of freedom; freedom needs to be balanced by self-discipline and responsibility for high-quality work. There is a never-ending search in good human organizations to find the right balance.

The fourth guru is the National Center on Education and the Economy, together with people loosely associated with the Clinton administration. The Southern Regional Education Board is one of the educational groups putting the ideas into practice. From the National Center came the volume *America's Choice: High Skills or Low Wages* (National Center on Education and the Economy, 1990). The thesis is that our basic choice is either to drift toward a polarized, low-skill/low-wage society or to follow Germany and Japan in creating a high-skill/high-wage society based on two key features: (a) have all front-line American workers educated at middle-level academic, communications, technical, and managerial skills so that they can handle emerging technology, implement quality controls, be involved in self-management groups, and be prepared for continuing learning at new levels and (b) have industrial leaders committed to a collaborative, participatory management style that taps the strengths of such a workforce.

Such a workforce will have to come from the non-college-bound sector of American students, the group that schools are doing their least effective job with.

Proposals for a major overhaul are based on several assumptions: (a) that a high school diploma will be less and less viable for entry into the work world of the year 2000; (b) that President Bush's Project 2000 pointed correctly to one key problem—the need to raise academic achievement—but failed to recognize that different pedagogical strategies are required to motivate unengaged students; and (c) that a whole new attitude needs to be taken toward non-college-bound students. So, instead of "dumbing down" instruction for students in the general track, follow the lead of Henry Levin in his Accelerated Schools Program for at-risk students—give them the kind of enriched programs that are provided for the gifted, including experiential, hands-on, active learning (Wirth, 1992, pp. 111-116).

With these assumptions in mind, the National Center is proposing three bold steps: (a) restructure the three-track school system that reflected Taylorist-era realities, (b) employ new pedagogical theory and strategies, and (c) create new forms of assessment.

The ideas for restructuring the system and employing different pedagogical strategies are interrelated. The argument is that cognitive psychology tells us that learning tends to be most effective when tied to real-world experience—when more of our human capacities are engaged like our manipulative capacities, opportunities for social interaction, the chance to puzzle things out, to generate hypotheses and act on them.

Where structure is concerned, the proposal is to eliminate the ill-functioning three-track system created in the era of Taylorism and replace it with a tech-prep program. All academic courses will be given at the college-prep level. Non-college-bound students (some say all students) will have academics complemented by various forms of applied/experiential learning. The tech-prep program, eventually replacing the high school diploma, would involve new linkages between secondary schools and junior colleges, so that the goal would be to have all students completing something like the first year of junior college before entering work.

Changes in pedagogical theory and practice are just as important as curriculum re-structuring. Factory-era schools were based on a knowledge accumulation concept of learning rooted in the Thorndikean behaviorist tradition. The strategy of mastery of basal texts plus testing fails to produce the quality of learning needed for postindustrial reality. That style has been a demonstrable failure with too many students. The need is for more experimentation with active styles of learning based on cognitive psychology—for example, constructivist learning that has students construct understanding in group problem-solving projects.

No single formula is proposed, but a variety of ideas are in the hopper. Robert Reich is pushing hard with the School-to-Work Opportunity bill for the expansion of apprenticeship programs and employer internships, where academic study is integrated with work world experiences. Others like Thomas Bailey and Sue Berryman are recommending cognitive apprenticeships, where apprentice-type methods are applied to academic learning (Berryman & Bailey, 1992). I gave other examples in *Education and Work for the Year 2000*, such as the Apple Classrooms of Tomorrow (ACOT) program where students and teachers invent ways of using computer technology to advance their learning (Wirth, 1992).

A third proposal is to replace standardized testing assessment with a system of performance standards that students could explicitly prepare for. (Final assessments would be based on portfolios, performance tests, exhibitions, etc.) The goal is to create certification programs beginning in tech-prep and continuing throughout work careers that would improve lifetime employment opportunities for all, thereby, avoiding a society of "education haves" versus "have nots." To give dropouts a second chance, states could establish local youth centers through employment training boards with a family-like atmosphere, counseling, basic education, and a strong mentoring program.

Finally, incentives would be offered to employers to invest 1 percent of payroll in programs of further education and training as a permanent part of the American work world. The aim is to build a new philosophy, where skill upgrading for a majority of workers throughout their work lives becomes a central aim of policy.

Technical Education as General Education for All Students?

A possibility that jumps out of all of this is that by 2000 we may be moving toward the idea of making some form of technical education a part of general education for all American students.

I am not sure of just what issues that possibility would pose for vocational/technical educators. I do, however, want to call attention to one critical issue that may get overlooked. The pressures will be strong to focus sharply on how to upgrade skills for a high-skill workforce—a worthy and necessary goal. The question is whether such a sharp focus on utilitarian goals could lead us to miss a deeper educational opportunity—one more important for our postindustrial needs perhaps than skill upgrading itself.

We may see the underlying issue by noting John Dewey's way of grappling with the same question as we entered this century. A major urban industrial revolution was replacing our rural past. As apprenticeship weakened, there were strong pressures to add a vocational training component to the schools—and also a groping for what kind of learning was needed to help the young make their way into a transformed America.

In the 1890s, Dewey was simultaneously pioneering his instrumentalist philosophy, and creating his University of Chicago Laboratory School. A noteworthy feature of his school was his decision to make the study of the occupations the integrating center of the curriculum. His argument was that imaginative study of human occupations contained an extraordinary potential for giving America's children the kind of an illuminating or liberalizing education that they needed to cope with the problems of an era of revolutionary change.

His argument makes sense only by seeing how it was embedded in that instrumental philosophy he was creating—a philosophy informed by the evolutionary perspective. Dewey, born in 1859, the year of Darwin's *On the Origin of Species*, was part of a generation whose major intellectual challenge was to come to terms with the disturbing evolutionary perspective.

Dewey came to hold that an image of humans as *homo faber* (humans as tool users) could reveal the unique human strengths that made it possible for us to experience life in an extraordinarily unique way—to experience life with awareness and growing understanding that could increase through time. He saw our human capacity to use objects as tools and our "tool of tools"—language—emerging out of the active occupations of daily life—out of our being occupied with meeting the needs of survival like food, clothing, and shelter and with our need to increase our knowledge of what was happening in order to act more effectively—and beyond that simply to meet our deep need to understand. How could this be? We may conjecture about prehistoric beginnings. Someone first saw the possibility of using a rock as a tool to kill a ground squirrel or as a tool to grind with. Names had to be given to these objects transformed into tools, and language was needed to communicate with companions about what had been learned. Language itself was expanded to the powerful tool of reflective inquiry as we learned to combine the processes of acting with reflecting on the meaning of our actions. The humanly ennobling process was under way to create understanding and meaning of our condition.

In evolutionary perspective, the introduction of each new tool transformed human life. Thus, with the power of domesticated animals harnessed to the wheel, we entered an age of agriculture. With the harnessing of the energy of coal and steam power, we moved into the stage of industrialism, and now the power of computer technology hurls us into a new postindustrialism. Each transformation has been marked by wrenching changes in institutions: economic life, government, family, education, religion, and the arts. With each new challenge our tool of tools, language—as the active process of reflective inquiry—itself expanded and grew in power. Dewey held that language in its most advanced form, had emerged as the tool of scientific inquiry, the most powerful instrument of human learning to date. It opened new realms of meaning about the world and ourselves and new means to cope with the turbulent change that scientific inquiry itself produced. Dewey's technical definition of education reflected this perspective of transformative learning. Education, he said, is that active "reconstruction or reorganization of experience which *adds to the meaning* [italics added] of experience, and which *increases the ability to direct* [italics added] subsequent experience" (Dewey, 1916, pp. 89-90).

Dewey explored the meaning of this perspective for the schools of the 1890s. As he saw it, by the twentieth century the long struggle of inquiry had produced the impressive bodies of organized knowledge stored in books and libraries—the glorious understandings that had emerged from the inquiries. From these sources, extrapolations had been made into the basal texts of our children.

By 1900, rows of classrooms were being built into massive school buildings where children sat quietly to have the accumulated knowledge transmitted to them. This was a well-intentioned and notable accomplishment, but by Dewey's instrumentalist concept of learning, it contained a fundamental flaw. Knowledge, the end product of the long struggle of inquiry, was being transmitted, but the transmission was divorced from the active process of reflective inquiry that had produced it.

For Dewey, this was untenable because the inquiry process itself was the most important tool of learning twentieth-century children needed. In effect, he probed his instrumentalist philosophy to see if there could be an alternative to school seat work. His instrumentalist analysis had led him to

see that reflective inquiry itself had come out of the daily active occupations of people grappling with the demands of life with the tools at hand. Not so surprising, then, was his hypothesis that to get students engaged in the occupations and all the questions and inquiries they opened up would be a better alternative to seat work.

Thus we find the famous occupation of weaving in the Dewey School—not, he hastened to add, to meet the new demands for vocational training, but because he and his teachers could get students involved in the active, problem-solving, reflective inquiry that the occupations opened up and because they could help students get insight into the revolutionary stage they were living in and understand something of the human history that had got them there.

Thus, he got children actively struggling with the processes of shearing wool, carding it, and spinning it to get it ready for a loom to produce a scarf. Forcing them to face the nitty-gritty of production required them to employ a wide range of learning to complete a difficult task—manipulating tools, reading and researching, interacting socially, communicating, analyzing sources of hang-ups, conjecturing ideas, and actions to resolve them—in short, to be involved in the active process of inquiry. As Jim Garrison (1990, p. 405) once put it, they learned that "meaning is made originally, by doing, by being occupied with, and operating upon something or other."

But beyond the production process itself, students were led to work out historically how the human need to turn raw wool into clothing had been transformed by the introduction of new tools and processes. They could see the changes in human experience that came with changes in technology from primitive hand looms to power-driven or eventually electronically-driven looms of the twentieth century. And they could be led to evaluate the consequences for human life, good or bad. All of this could be accompanied by exploring connections with organized knowledge in academic subject matter.

Thus, Dewey argued that one can "concentrate the history of all mankind into the evolution of flax, cotton, and wool fibers into clothing" (1916). The other technologies of daily life can attain the same potential of liberating learning with one important proviso. They must be approached with an imaginative commitment to plan learning experiences so that they disclose ever-widening contexts of meaning. Technology, so to speak, can be educative if you dialogue with it. It is more monologic if you only train for it.

In the 1990s, there are once again strong pressures to upgrade occupational skills for an increasingly high-tech workforce. What I have been trying to suggest, however, is that technical educators informed by John Dewey's instrumentalist philosophy will know that to settle for this focus in a narrow sense will be to miss what Dewey saw as a larger, exciting opportunity: that technical educators, in collaboration with academic colleagues, could take students through in-depth studies of human occupations and their technologies in ways that would provide deeply illuminating, liberalizing educational experiences—that is, the kind of education needed to help students confront the radically new, uncharted challenges of the twenty-first century.

This may seem far-fetched. It just might gain support, however, as we get serious about the mind-boggling postindustrial realities we are moving into and the understandings we need to cope, among them the following:

• The need to understand that economic survival requires a global perspective—and a multicultural perspective.

• The need to understand that postindustrial complexity requires letting go of the demeaning Taylorist dualisms that arrogated to technical elites the authority to think and to manipulate and control people, as well as the need to replace such dysfunctional work styles with alternatives that tap capacities for innovating, reflective learning, and collaborative troubleshooting by all members of the workforce—a style that combines democratic values with the power of high technology

• The need to understand that a relentless concern for quality of product must be extended to a relentless concern for the quality of the *oikos* (our house)—the global ecology

• The need to understand that a high-tech learning society is ill served by a dualist separation of vocational training from liberal studies, that the times require liberalizing integrations of technical and general studies—to provide both the conceptual skills for new work and the skills for making quality-of-life value judgments

• The need to understand that with all of the power of technology we can still be torn apart as a society if we fail to address the injustice, despair, and rage spawned by an economically polarized society

In short, we may be moving into a time when it becomes practical to be moral. I hope so. If we are, we'll have to think to the core what the meaning of that is for the education of our children—and for the workers and managers of our workplaces.

References

Bernstein, J. (1993). Rethinking welfare reform. *Dissent, 40* (3), 277-282.

Berryman, S., & Bailey, T. (1992). *The double helix of education and the economy.* New York: Institute on Education and the Economy, Teachers College, Columbia University.

Bottoms, G., Presson, A., & Johnson, M. (1992). *Making high schools work through integration of academic and vocational education.* Atlanta: Southern Regional Education Board.

Dewey, J. (1916). *Democracy and education.* New York: Macmillan.

Faux, J. (1993). Industrial policy. *Dissent, 40* (4), 467-474.

Gabor, A. (1990). *The man who discovered quality.* New York: Times Books.

Garrison, J. (1990). Philosophy as (vocational) education. *Educational Theory, 40* (3), 391-406.

Harrison, B., & Bluestone, B. (1988). *The great U-turn.* New York: Basic Books.

National Center on Education and the Economy. (1990). *America's choice: High skills or low wages.* Report of the Commission on the Skills of the American Workplace. Rochester, NY: Author.

Reich, R. B. (1991). *The work of nations: Preparing ourselves for 21st century capitalism.* New York: Knopf.

Wirth, A. G. (1983). *Productive work in industry and schools: Becoming persons again.* Lanham, MD: University Press of America.

Wirth, A. G. (1992). *Education and work for the year 2000.* San Francisco: Jossey-Bass.

Zuboff, S. (1988). *In the age of the smart machine: The future of work and power.* New York: Basic Books.

Part II

Corporate Practices

6

Corporate Training in America: A Primer for Today

By Deborah M. Buffamanti

CORPORATE America wants to train you. In fact, it has a vested interest in seeing you grow intellectually. Every company, regardless of industry, size, degree of globalization, or core business enterprise would like to make you a more productive, more efficient member of the team. One of the best ways to ensure continued skill growth is through the use of *corporate training*.

Formal corporate training is frequently called America's "shadow educational system" (Special Section, 1993, pp. 29-34). And for good reason. In 1990, *Training Magazine* estimated that approximately $45.5 billion went to formal corporate training programs. By 1994, *Training Magazine*'s yearly industry report of corporate training in America indicated that this figure had risen to $50.6 billion. In 1995, the figure once again increased by an additional 3 percent to approximately $52.2 billion. At this point, it shows no sign of slowing. Remember, too, that this figure only represents the structured training that companies provide—it does not include the informal, ad-hoc sort of training that frequently takes place on the job site.

Why Train?

Most training today is geared toward a particular skill objective. Generally, the type of training provided is "learning focused on the employee's present job" (London, 1989, p. 1). Along with providing direct skills education, corporate training programs address a variety of other internal needs. For example, training programs help to socialize new employees. They can strengthen corporate culture, increase competitiveness, reinvigorate the workforce, help a company meet equal opportunity and affirmative action guidelines, and act as the "glue" for hiring and retaining valuable staff members. Corporate training can prevent "occupation obsolescence" (Casner-Lotto, 1988, p. 2) by assisting in redefining, enlarging, and identifying emerging jobs. Along with advancing the skill level of the individual and the enterprise, training eases the transition between the more traditional bureaucratic, hierarchical style of management and the new flatter management styles now emerging in many organizations.

Training clearly benefits both the employee and the employer. According to Goldstein & Associates (1989, p. 351), a 1987 Work in America Institute report indicated that:

- a stable, motivated, well-trained workforce plays a critical role in the long-term prosperity of an enterprise.

- long-term prosperity enables the enterprise to fulfill its commitment to employment security.

• employment security motivates employees to identify with the goals of the enterprise and to learn continuously.

• continuous learning appeals to one of the most powerful drives among employees: the desire for self-development, growth, and career advancement.

• continuous learning makes sense because employees have unexplored capacities for education, and educated employees can adapt, to a surprising degree, to the changing needs of the enterprise.

In terms of advantages for individuals, the more skills people can bring to employers, the more likely it is that they will be hired and ultimately, trained, retrained, or more fully trained in a larger-size company. For today's workforce, work-based learning can be the deciding factor between welfare and a living wage.

Other pressures, both internal and external, have forced companies into the education realm. The need for constant innovation, reductions in cycle times and defect rates, and the demand for massive gains in efficiency across all corporate systems have produced intense strains on personnel. Further, efficiency gains have not come at the expense of decreasing customer service levels. Instead, companies institute them along with progress toward better customer relations; enhanced environmental programs; increasing levels of customization; and overall superior levels of employee, supplier, and customer rapport. In the constant search for better ways of doing things, corporate training can provide the mechanism that transforms an idea on paper—or one that lurks in the back of someone's mind—into a new way of working.

The persistent problem of an under-educated workforce presents one of the most pressing reasons for the existence of formal training programs. Job growth between 1992 and 2005 appears divided between two polarities: jobs that tend to be low-paying, require low skills, and contain relatively few rewards in terms of personal growth and satisfaction, and, alternatively, jobs that require high skills and are high-paying and generally seen as rewarding career choices (Bureau of Labor Statistics, 1993).

Where jobs require advanced skill levels, such as those of systems analysts (the second-fastest-growing occupation between 1992 and 2005, according to the Bureau of Labor Statistics study cited above), today's system of academic learning clearly falls short. Academics alone have failed to give these types of professionals the hands-on experience they need to grapple with complex, interrelated technological problems. To complicate matters further, most programs of applied learning, like those for home health aids (the fastest-growing occupation between 1992 and 2005) tend *not* to meet the highest academic standards. This substantial discrepancy between the level and type of learning required and that delivered by the school systems creates a "skills gap" within the labor pool. This gap must be addressed. To remain competitive in the new world economy, companies must ensure that they have the most skilled workforce available today—and tomorrow. Anticipating that need, they've begun taking on the task of educating workers themselves.

In the last 20 years, a complete reengineering of many major systems of business has occurred. Manufacturing concerns have been technologically reworked or moved offshore to less expensive environments. Inventory and accounting systems have moved to just-in-time processes, controlled by supplier and vendor databases that reorder, purchase, and make payments automatically. Even management itself is evolving into something flatter, more responsive, and increasingly more widespread and innovative within the enterprise. The next logical progression of this movement toward rationalization and utility calls for a shift from viewing personnel as a cost, to viewing it as a benefit; from viewing labor as a drain on resources, to viewing it as a constantly renewable resource. Ultimately, the labor pool will take its rightful place as the most valuable business asset—*human capital*—which requires development and management like any other asset or advantage.

Types of Training

Most major corporate training efforts cover a variety of broad content areas. If a company needs a specific skill set, it's highly likely that it's offering a course in that particular area. Of course, the type and duration of each training program differs according to the company's needs, size, budget, and time constraints. In general, though, most companies offer at least a short training program under the heading of "new employee training."

According to a survey by the U.S. Department of Labor (1994) conducted between February and July 1994, 71 percent of large companies provided at least some formal training to their employees at some point during 1993. Company size played a major role in determining whether or not training was provided. Of companies that responded to the survey, 99 percent of those with 250 or more employees offered some type of formal training. (The USDL survey findings are based on 12,000 surveys sent to nonagricultural business between February and July 1994. The survey had a usable response rate of 71.3 percent.)

Broadly speaking, the larger the company, the larger the corporate training investment, the greater the number of trainers available to train, and the greater the number of student days during which training occurs. Some companies have very extensive training programs, while others concentrate on skills that will most enhance the core business enterprise. Texas Instruments, a company with more than $10.3 billion in revenues during 1994, has more than 500 different course offerings spread throughout its seven divisions. (These divisions include Semiconductors, Defense Electronics Systems, Software Productivity Tools, Consumer Electronics, Custom Engineering and Manufacturing, Electric Controls and Metallurgical Materials.) While not all corporations require employees to attend training, they do strongly encourage it. In some cases, failing to attend leads to termination of employment.

Training frequently covers remedial or basic skills, which include mathematics, literacy, English as a second language, reading comprehension, and writing. Customer relations training includes telemarketing, interpersonal skills, time management, and problem solving. Sales and marketing training covers selling techniques, forecasting, pricing, territory management, and business-writing skills. Management and supervisory skills training will normally include programs on topics such as personnel, human resources development, performance evaluations, finance and productivity enhancement, and working with unions. Executive education programs include topics like diversity, leadership development, strategic planning, sexual harassment, and stress management. Other types of training can include professional, scientific, engineering, and technical skills training designed to improve specific competencies in a wide range of fields. For example, these programs hone skills in banking, physics, accounting, mechanics, and information systems. (For an in-depth introduction to training programs available in the private sector, see Bard and Elliott's *The National Directory of Corporate Training Programs*).

While only certain groups within an organization receive some types of training, other types are sufficiently important to be offered at all levels of the organization, and on a fairly continuous basis. These may include training in time management, problem-solving skills, business writing, sexual harassment prevention, and stress management. Transferable skills like these are necessary for all employees and constitute some of training's basic education within the workforce.

One type of training that continually emerges as essential is computer training. According to *Training Magazine's* 1995 Industry Report (p. 61), "the single type of formal training most likely to be provided by employers, large and small, is a course that teaches some kind of computer skill. In 1990, three quarters of U.S. organizations with 100 or more employees provided computer-skills training. [In 1994], that figure rose to 88 percent. Today, 93 percent of employers offer computer-skills training." The other two types of training most frequently taught through formal programs were sales and customer relations, and management skills (U. S. Department of Labor, 1994).

Many companies also engage in training mandated by local, state, or federal agencies. Training in environmental health and safety procedures and equal opportunity employment provide examples. Health and safety training may include courses offered through the Department of Labor's Occupational Safety and Health Administration (OSHA). These courses run the gamut from basic accident prevention through construction standards, fire protection, and hazardous materials handling. OSHA courses have also begun to include topics such as industrial noise control and ergonomics. Equal opportunity employment training now includes materials on the 1990 Americans with Disabilities Act. The act extended the prohibition against discrimination on the basis of race, sex, religion, and national origin to persons with disabilities. Hence, recruitment training programs must now include materials on preemployment screening, hiring, promotions, layoffs, and terminations, with respect to individuals with disabilities.

While much training takes place in the classroom, on-the-job training is also a significant component of workplace learning. It may involve mentoring and coaching by supervisory staff in a one-on-one style. It can also include rotational assignments throughout the plant, factory, store, or enterprise. While training directors like in-house classes, it's no longer unusual for corporations to outsource some training to a local college.

Training in each of these areas fosters the core workplace competencies necessary for economic survival. In the new world economy, the most successful labor pool will contain participants who have strong learning skills—in other words, solid skills in reading, writing, comprehension, computation, and reasoning. These workers will also have well-developed interpersonal skills. They will have the ability to resolve problems in a timely fashion and exhibit leadership and visioning regarding their job-related duties. Further, most in this well-educated group will want to manage their own educational and career development.

The scope of corporate training efforts within a company can range from small, ad-hoc, and inexpensive, to large, complex, and expensive. Training can sometimes be a significant budget item as seen in Table 1 below. The table, taken from a recent *Fortune* article by Ron Henkoff, shows just how extensive—and expensive—major training efforts can be.

Course Materials

Training programs normally begin with a needs *assessment* developed by a company's training department to determine exactly what skills trainees will need. Course curriculum can come from a variety of sources. Trainers can purchase off-the-shelf materials from established vendors, consultants, colleges and/or universities. This approach is fast, easy, and, while not always inexpensive, trainers can normally reuse much material. Trainers or training managers can also build their own course materials by assembling exercises, labs, and other items. This allows for designing the course in a way that addresses targeted needs at an appropriate depth for the intended audience. Trainers can also use a combination of the two approaches by purchasing generic course material, then customizing it. In many cases, trainers can also outsource the training itself. This proves especially useful if they know an instructor or other expert authority in the particular field in which they want to offer training. In this instance, the company trainer contracts

TABLE 1
Training at Selected Companies

Company employees worldwide	Percent of payroll spent in 1992 on training	Average hours per employee per year	Comments
Motorola 107,000	3.6%	36	The gold standard of corporate training. The company says every $1 spent on education returns $30 in productivity gains.
Target 100,000	N.A.	N.A.	Rapidly expanding retail chain has used Disney-type training to empower front-line employees and improve customer service.
Federal Express 93,000	4.5%	27	Workers take computer-based job competency tests every 6 to 12 months. Low scores lead to remedial action.
General Electric Aircraft Engines 33,000	N.A.	N.A.	Training budget has shrunk, but new focus on teamwork has helped the division boost productivity in a slumping industry.
Andersen Consulting 26,700	6.8%	109	Replaced 40-hour business practices class with interactive video, saving $4 million per year, mostly on travel and lodging.
Corning 14,000 Domestic	3.0%	92	Ordinary employees, not professional educators, do most training. Pay of factory workers rises as they learn new skills.
Solectron 3,500	3.0%	95	Training helped this fast-growing Silicon Valley company win a Baldrige Award in 1991. The 1993 goal: 110 hours per worker.
Dudek Manufacturing 35	5.0%	25	Had to teach basic literacy and math before introducing quality management. Hefty investment has paid off in profits.

Source: *Fortune*, March 1993.

with an instructor who provides his or her own materials and then designs, delivers, manages, and evaluates the course on behalf of the firm's training department.

Delivering Training

While the standard classroom-based lecture is one of the most common training methods available, trainers rarely use it as the sole delivery method, and the use of videotapes has recently surpassed it in popularity. Video has a number of advantages that most corporations can appreciate—it is readily available, virtually indestructible, cost effective, portable, reusable, and requires very little maintenance and overhead.

Most training has at least a partial lecture component, although normally training is not delivered exclusively through this format. Frequently, training managers strive to provide their audience with the delivery method most appropriate to the topic and audience. Usually, this results in a wide mix of delivery methods presented during every training session. The mix of methodologies changes according to audience age, audience size, room and time constraints, and the trainers' experience with the particular method of delivery. While videotapes and lecture are the two prime methods for delivering instruction, the one-on-one approach runs a close third. Other methods include (but are not limited to) role playing, simulations and games; discussion groups; one-on-one training; demonstrations; case studies; slides; overheads; films; audiotapes; computer-based training; video teleconferencing; multimedia; and CD-ROM-based learning. Due to some recent technological breakthroughs, a small amount of training now sees delivery through virtual reality, distance-learning programs, and audio teleconferencing.

Who Gets Trained?

According to *Training Magazine*'s October 1995 (p. 46) issue, more than 49.6 million people received some sort of formal training from their employer during that year. This is up strongly from 39.5 million in 1990. In terms of a general breakdown by occupational type, by 1995 more than half (54 percent) of all training dollars went to training managers and professional staff. Another 14 percent went to training salespeople (Special Section, 1995, p. 46). The remainder was spent on administrative positions.

Regarding the duration of training by job category, salespeople received an average of 38 hours of training, followed by professionals, who received 35 hours. Those classed as middle managers received 32 hours of training, first-line supervisors received 31, senior managers received 30 and were tied in terms of training hours with customer service representatives and production workers. These groups were followed by executives, who received approximately 29 hours of training annually, and finally, administrative employees, who generally received 19 hours of training.

The amount of training employees may receive partially depends on the industry in which they work—not just their occupation. Leaders in the amount of training provided (based on expenditures) tend to be within the financial sector—brokerage houses, financial institutions, insurance companies, and banks. Closely following those are manufacturing concerns of all types, educational institutions, and employees within public administration. Companies in the transportation sector, communications, or utilities offer somewhat less training.

Evaluating the Training

Roughly speaking, there are four measurable ways to determine the effectiveness of training. According to *Training's* Industry Report, in 1995 approximately 84 percent of all industries surveyed evaluated 85 percent of their courses for the trainees' reactions to the course. Companies normally do this through a survey given to trainees after the course, and this method appears to be the most popular way of assessing training. Further, 69 percent of all industries within the survey evaluated 50 percent of their courses by testing the trainees to determine what they learned. Again, companies normally do this immediately after completion of the course. Another 60 percent of survey firms evaluated 50 percent of their courses to determine how their trainees' behavior had changed when they returned to the job, and finally, almost 43 percent of surveyed firms, evaluating almost half (46 percent) of their courses, addressed the change in business results attributable to the training taken.

Creating a Learning Organization

Today's workforce clearly needs to learn *how to do the work*, as well as *how to work more effectively*, all the while *learning to learn within the workplace*. Corporate training programs can facilitate this. Without these most basic of learning competencies, any individual stands at significant risk of economic displacement. Simultaneously, the corporation must replicate this process on the individual level, the team or group level, the division or department level, and finally, across all corporate divisions on all continents. It's an overwhelming, daunting task. Ultimately, the company must reflect on the *learning-to-learn process itself* and become what is currently called a *learning organization*. (For further information on the learning organization, see Peter M. Senges' *The Fifth Discipline: The Art and Practice of the Learning Organization*. Senge is credited with coining the phrase *learning organization*.)

To assist with the evolution toward learning organizations, corporate training mechanisms must deal with a wide variety of issues. Internal trends affecting corporate training include issues of need, resource allocation, motivation, learning styles, corporate culture, and assumptions about learning in general. External trends, like those within the workplace and society, all impact the design, delivery, and evaluation methods that corporate trainers employ. Trends toward building diversity, dealing with sexual harassment, team building, AIDS, drug testing, smoking, and the move toward responsible corporate citizenship all impact the training agenda and, ultimately, the strategic planning functions of the organization.

The benefits of becoming a learning organization are many. According to D. R. Tobin (1993) in *Re-Educating the Corporation: Foundations for the Learning Organization*, a learning organization has an increased level of corporate creativity. It promotes responsive personnel and systems. Learning organizations nurture flexible employees who know how to resolve uncertainties and to create new ventures. Finally, learning organizations act in a timely fashion. Taken together, these traits nourish individual growth while enhancing the corporate capability to manage and benefit from change. Everyone is a learner in this type of organization. All learn from each other, constantly and continuously, and all can function as change agents.

Building Corporate Universities

Developing this culture of continuous learning implies that companies must take a proactive role in educating their workforce. As late as the mid-1970s, business concerns had more interest in instructing their own employees than anyone else, and they couldn't quantify the value in training someone not directly on their payroll. After all, why train your suppliers? Why train future employees? Companies at that time were much more concerned with how their training courses supported and reinforced other course offerings, or how training could be made to address real organizational requirements, rather than addressing a completely different audience. Today, the training paradigm has shifted from the approach of only training employees, to something more like "supply-chain management." In this new approach, training—as well as every other business operation—focuses increasingly on

identifying, cultivating, and managing all the aspects of developing relationships that continually enhance the firm's competitive advantage.

According to an article in the August 1995 issue of *Chief Information Officer Magazine* (Baatz, 1995), the business supply chain begins with procurement of the raw supplies an enterprise needs to produce its final products or services. It ends with the eventual disposal of a good or satisfactory completion of a service. The supply chain includes all the activities that a business concern tracks between these starting and finishing points. Fundamentally, this chain includes sourcing, managing, and integrating suppliers; purchasing or developing raw materials and products; manufacturing the goods or services; warehousing and distribution of the items; managing the sales and advertising functions; developing personnel and accounting functions to support each of these activities; and implementing disposal or recycling programs, when necessary.

Management of the enterprise supply chain is a complex matter. It doesn't fall under the control of any particular department or employee. However, developing and managing the supply chain is becoming central to a firm's ability to increase its market share and profitability. Supply chain management allows the business to get the finest product possible to the customer's choice of locations, in the most timely fashion—all without a hitch.

In many cases, especially for firms with more than 500 employees, this need to begin managing the supply chain has resulted in a new corporate entity: the corporate university. So popular are these operations that "at least 400 businesses presently include a building or campus labeled 'college, institute, or education center'" (Meister, 1994, p. 19). Currently, Motorola, Xerox, Intel, General Electric, American Express, Arthur Anderson, and Sprint have some of the most notable of these universities. Much like its public, private, or research counterparts, the corporate university is a place of learning—although it is not necessarily bounded by four walls. Corporate universities provide the learning labs of the company; they build training curricula for each job; they give all employees a shared corporate vision; and they extend training to employees and, when necessary, beyond.

According to J. C. Meister (1994) in *Corporate Quality Universities: Lessons in Building a World-Class Work Force*, the success of corporate universities depends directly on four criteria. First, these universities must give special emphasis to evangelizing, espousing, developing, and understanding their unique corporate culture. In effect, to developing strong corporate citizenship among members of their workforce. Second, the universities must tie essential business needs to corporate training agendas. They must develop training plans that provide a progressive path for employees to develop within their job rank and beyond. Through them, employees can master skills for effectively navigating a career path, while meeting the organization's need for succession planning. The third criterion for success requires the supervision of the training transformation from a single event to an unflagging stream. This most fully integrates training in the mainstream of business functions, and it makes training as responsive as possible to shifting strategic needs. Finally, corporate universities must extend training beyond the corporation to include all constituencies—from future employees to current and possible suppliers.

Training: A Systems Approach

Many large organizations—such as Motorola, IBM, General Electric, and Xerox—train not only their employees, but their customers, vendors, suppliers, and future employees. They also train other groups—such as educators—who may ultimately impact the profitability of the company.

Companies looking to enhance their future competitive advantage willingly provide training to constituencies on whom they depend. By developing close relationships, companies can get a large lead on their competition. One example of training's evolution into a system comes when firms begin to train their most valued suppliers. Anderson Screw Products, a manufacturer of custom precision-turned parts based in Jamestown, New York, works closely with the Remington Arms Co. In 1991, due to their close working arrangements, Remington declared Anderson Screw Products a preferred supplier, with a defect rate of a mere .04 percent. The symbiosis between the companies came about through joint training programs, which ensured that both parties understood what they had to do. In this example, Anderson maintains a profitable long-term relationship that provides Remington with a quality, nearly defect-free product.

While training suppliers represent one type of "partnering"—in which a company links closely with a supplier, customer, or interested other party to mutual benefit—other examples abound. Motorola, a respected name in corporate training circles, has sponsored a group of students at the British Columbia Institute of Technology to help develop prototype software necessary for networkable wireless data communications. Students who began the assignment in January 1995 made major contributions to a real-life project that was global in scope. The software prototype was ready for release in May 1995. In this sort of partnership, students get valuable employment experience and possible internships, while Motorola and its customers get a real product.

The shift toward training outreach is increasingly common, and it is expected to be more so in the future. While the outreach effort now goes primarily toward suppliers, vendors, and customers, it is also moving rapidly down the supply chain into the educational arena to include potential employees, suppliers, and others. To illustrate, IBM has eight partnerships with the higher-education community that revolve around the application of total quality management (TQM) practices in higher education. IBM, through the American Association for Higher Education, made available eight cash and equipment awards in May 1992. The IBM-TQM Partnership began in October 1991. IBM announced that it would make a significant commitment to work with higher education to accelerate the teaching, research, and use of quality management practices in college and university operatons. Its commitment was a series of eight cash and equipment awards—$1 million in cash or $3 million in equipment, or a combination, to each institution over five years. Awarded institutions were also offered partnerships with IBM facilities that included loaned executives, speakers, and faculty, and student internships with IBM.

After receiving more than 200 proposals from a variety of institutions, IBM ultimately granted eight universities an IBM-TQM partnership. The winning institutions were Clark Atlanta University/Southern College of Technology, Georgia Institute of Technology, Oregon State University, Pennsyslvania State University, Rochester Institute of Technology, University of Houston-Clear Lake, University of Maryland-College Park, and University of Wisconsin-Madison. The proposals indicated the following four prime motivators for the institution's involvement in the partnership program: (1) improving national competitiveness, (2) conforming to customer requirements, (3) renewing the academy, and (4) improving operational performance.

Other outreach efforts go even farther back along the educational continuum to the public or secondary school levels. Mobil Oil entered into a partnership with the Beaumont, Texas, school district in 1993. Mobil's Operation Breakthrough was designed to give students stronger technical skills through enhanced math, science, and language arts courses. Specific goals were set, with evaluations to occur over the course of three years. More than 200 teachers participated in "shadowing" experiences for one work day at one of 18 participating companies. Moreover, five teachers worked at paid internships within Mobil, and they incorporated their experiences into a revised course curriculum. As a result of their cur-

riculum changes, enrollment in algebra increased by 62 percent over the last two years, and math and reading scores have also improved significantly. Even more important, the school district was one of the very few districts chosen to participate in the National Science Foundation Center for Science Education Reform. The benefits to Mobil include a more educated workforce from which to draw future employees, suppliers, and customers. The school district benefits from increased student strength in critical areas identified in Goals 2000.

The Future of Corporate Training

Like most other business systems, corporate training will continue to evolve. It will increasingly contribute to the bottom line of firms by enhancing the sorts of skills that the organization most requires to stay competitive. Like other business processes, training will become more modular and more prepackaged. More courses will appear on videotape or audiotape or in computer simulations. They will be made to be used and reused and will be increasingly interactive in nature. Training in the future will also be more flexible and more customized. While formal training will still be a somewhat structured activity, it will become more adaptable to input from developers, trainers, and audience alike. Moreover, a given course curriculum will be delivered in a variety of methods to accommodate different learning styles. In terms of the customization of training, course design will continue to contain items like exercises and videos, each of which can be replaced with different activities developed to emphasize a distinct training need.

Training in the future will reach more areas of the enterprise, touch more individuals, and become increasingly more measurable and quantifiable. It will become more important relative to corporate activities like accounting, sales, and supply chain management, since it can positively affect all of these. The link between strategic planning and training will become tighter, and ultimately, the two areas will impact each other on a continual basis. Strategic planning will indicate what skills are needed now and in the future, and training will deliver those skills. After a certain skill level has been reached, planning will raise the standard to further increase skill capabilities.

Other evolutions in the future of corporate training will likely include training that occurs at a faster pace and more often. This fits with the idea of establishing or developing a learning organization. Moreover, business should expect an increase in the total number of course offerings available. As business becomes increasingly complex, training needs should continue to escalate and become more differentiated. The duration of training per course offering will shorten, as time constraints increase for employees and others. Training budgets should continue to outpace inflation, and the demand for training professionals should also increase. Major social trends will continue to affect training. Some of these trends—like the movement toward self-managing teams, reengineering, and the use of contingent workers—will impact training in a significant way. Other trends, like total quality management, visioning, and outsourcing will also impact training in the workplace, though less dramatically.

Since the 1700s, when the industrial revolution began, training has played an expanding role in American business. During the last 50 years, it has evolved from the 1940s wartime effort of teaching basic job skills to the 1950s emphasis on psychology and human relations training. By 1960, training began to examine group behavior—especially motivation and attitude change—while at the same time, professionals in the field refined their notions of evaluating training to include its effect on business results. The training focus continued to evolve so that by the 1970s, it began to include wider social concerns like discrimination and pollution. Parallel to this, "management by objectives" and the nature of leadership both became hot topics of public discussion and debate. By the 1980s, both the rise of the service sector and considerable downsizing

among some icons of corporate America had begun. This led to more changes within the training agenda, which began to include topics like teamwork, adventure training, and quality circles.

Finally, in the 1990s, training has continued to develop in a way that embraces the concepts of the learning organization, reengineering, and outsourcing. In this era of high performance economies, global systems, and constant change, training will need every technological and human advantage it can muster to continue its role as a major tool of competitive advantage for business.

References

Baatz, E. B. (1995, August). The chain gang: Best supply chain/logistics practices. *Chief Information Officer Magazine, 8*(19), 46-52.

Bard, R., & Elliott, S. K. *The national directory of corporate training programs,* 2nd ed. (1988). New York: Stonesong Press.

Bureau of Labor Statistics, Office of Employment Projections. (1993, November). *Occupations with the largest job growth. 1992-2005.* Washington, DC: Moderate Alternative.

Casner-Lotto, J., & others. (1988). *Successful training strategies: 26 innovative corporate models.* San Francisco: Jossey-Bass Publishers.

Goldstein, I. L., & Associates. (1989). *Training and development in organizations.* San Francisco: Jossey-Bass Publishers, p. 351.

Kimmerling, G. (1993, September). ASTD benchmarking forum. *Training and Development Magazine, 47*(9), 29-36.

London, M. (1989). *Managing the training enterprise: High quality, cost-effective employee training in organizations.* San Francisco: Jossey-Bass Management Series.

Meister, J .C. (1994). *Corporate quality universities: Lessons in building a world class workforce.* New York: American Society for Training and Development & Irwin Professional Publishing.

Senge, P. M. *The fifth discipline: The art and practice of the learning organization.* (1990). New York: Doubleday.

Special section: Industry report. (1993, October). *Training Magazine, 30*(10), 29-34.

Special section: Industry Report. (1995, October). *Training Magazine, 32*(10).

U.S. Department of Labor. USDL #94-432. (Sponsored by the Employment and Training Administration of the U.S. Department of Labor.) Washington, DC: Author.

7

Diversity Training Makes JCPenney a Special Place to Work

By Gale Duff-Bloom

JCPENNEY was established as a small-town dry goods store in 1902 by James Cash Penney. The store was called The Golden Rule. In the 93 years since our inception, JCPenney has experienced phenomenal growth. Today, the company operates department stores in all 50 states, as well as Puerto Rico, Chile, and Mexico. We also own and operate the JCPenney Catalog, JCPenney Insurance, Thrift Drug, and the JCPenney National Bank.

The dominant part of our business, however, focuses on retailing apparel, shoes, jewelry, accessories, and home furnishings through our 1,200 department stores. JCPenney has recently put together three back-to-back great years. Retail sales for 1993—our 91st year in the business—were $19.6 billion. Net income was $940 million. In 1994, we topped that, with retail sales of $21.1 billion and a net income of $1.1 billion.

Developing Initiatives for the Advancement of Women and Minorities

It's a fact that in sheer numbers women dominate the retail industry—except when it comes to the management and senior executive ranks. At that level, they have represented a clear minority. Our women and minorities were mainly in the entry and middle-management levels, with few minorities at any level.

In 1987, our then chairman/CEO, William R. Howell, believed it was time to change the face of our workforce. He took advantage of two key historical events that really became the catalyst for our diversity initiatives.

First, in 1988 the company's home office relocated from New York to Dallas. A number of our managers from all levels elected not to make the move—which gave us the opportunity to better balance our workforce.

Around the same time, JCPenney essentially completed a 10-year, $10 billion repositioning from being a mass merchandiser to being a national department store in the fashion business. With this transition —and the change in customer demographics— came the absolute need for our company to better understand the needs of both women and minorities. We believed it was important for us to reflect on diversity issues, and then spell out our concerns in a "diversity positioning statement." This would allow us to tell ourselves, and then tell our communities, exactly where we stood on the issue.

First we looked at diversity as individuals. We saw that as our society, our company, and our customers become more diverse, it became more important for us to respect and appreciate the uniqueness of each human being. Because each person is an "original," a one-of-a-kind combination of skills and characteristics—physical, personality, cultural, ethnic, racial, religious—each is special and different.

For the company, valuing diversity means including our associates' and customers' differences as part of our overall business strategy. We think that we can best respond to a diverse customer base if people within the company represent the diversity that exists outside it. Our diversity initiative isn't just the nice thing to do. It's a vital and obvious bottom-line strategy that we believe will impact our financial future as much as anything else we do at JCPenney.

Diversity Training within JCPenney

A major component of our diversity initiative involves *training*. Management development has always been a strong part of our heritage. Developing our associates is part of a process that is planned, executed, and monitored as carefully as any other business activity we undertake.

To develop and strengthen the managerial skills needed to lead a diverse workforce, the company initiated a series of workshops. All management employees must attend the one and one-half day Valuing Cultural Differences program. The workshop aims to create an awareness of all cultures represented within JCPenney, to develop an awareness of each associate's impact on the workplace environment, and to increase communication among our increasingly diverse workforce. Approximately 18,000 management people have been through the program, which is now also being offered to administrative associates.

The workshop objectives are met through the use of experiential exercises, videos, case studies, and much open discussion by the participants. Attendees are encouraged to share who they are personally, and then challenged to explore their own inner baggage of stereotypes and prejudices. Two key

videos are used to show the destructive power of prejudice both morally and economically. A broad definition of "culture" is used in the workshop, including issues of race, ethnicity, gender, age, physical ability, and sexual orientation, along with the often-forgotten concerns of white males. The content of the entire workshop might be briefly summarized as: Treat people as they want to be treated, and communicate with people as individuals, not as members of a cultural group.

To build on the success of Valuing Cultural Differences, we implemented a second program titled Leadership in the 90's. This new two-day course aims to take the awareness generated in Valuing Cultural Differences and use it to marry the diversity process with the JCPenney management process. This helps people develop the actionable, practical skills needed for leadership in a multicultural environment.

Leadership in the 1990s is built around a caring leadership style advocated by James Autry in his book *Love and Profit,* which emphasizes fair treatment, as well as special treatment when the situation warrants. In this context, *special treatment* means being flexible enough to meet the problems facing individual associates, and handling them one on one, in a caring manner, while not creating new policies across the board. Some of the other workshop components are cross-cultural communication; overcoming filters caused by differences; coaching for associate growth; networking as a positive tool for the mutual benefit of all parties; motivation in today's environment; and building strong team members on both functional and cross-functional teams. This workshop also uses a combination of activities, videos, case studies, and participant discussion to accomplish course objectives.

In addition to the in-house training, 125 key senior managers attended the special, week-long Multicultural Workshop. This workshop is an immersion in diversity issues and experiences. Its primary objective is to transfer awareness to commitment for change through relationship and team building. We also conducted the Corporate and Individual Realities for Women Workshop to assist women in their professional development and help them manage gender-related issues.

Aside from these diversity workshops, JCPenney has developed a number of individual training programs that deal with special topics. Beyond Compliance: Serving Customers with Disabilities, was developed in 1994 and distributed to more than 1,200 stores. The program explains how to break away from old attitudes of biases and stereotypes and learn to treat the physically impaired customer as simply a customer.

Another topic was sexual harassment. We developed a communication program to help make all associates aware of situations, language, and actions that could be construed as sexual harassment. The program, distributed to all JCPenney units, was modified to accommodate differences in state laws, where applicable.

In 1991, we established a mentor program specifically to help new management associates, either new hires, or associates recently transferred to our home office. Each new associate is paired with an experienced management associate. The mentors guide and coach their protégés during the transition.

Mentors and protégés are assigned in round-robin order within the same functional work-activity family, such as Finance, Systems, Merchandising, and Catalog. In making the assignment, factors considered are the mentor's level, which must be the same or higher than that of the protégé, and the mentor's present job responsibilities.

The mentor and protégé meet once or twice a month, usually over lunch, and they also exchange telephone calls. This gives associates an opportunity to branch out and form relationships that can help them understand the work environment as they experience the transition into a new company or work assignment. We support this program with half-day training sessions for the mentor, and a separate session for the protégé, to help each prepare for his or her role.

The mentor program proved so successful that in 1994 it was expanded to include the Tier II level Management Career Planning Program. This program aims to provide protégés with a mentor who will help them develop more confidence about their careers. It also gives protégés more awareness and knowledge to enable them to make better career choices. Protégés in Tier II interact with mentors who have at least five years experience with the company.

In keeping with our management development philosophy, we also have a General Management Performance and Career Management Program that identifies for our associates opportunities that exist in other parts of the company. We provide a description of the management jobs available up to the senior management level, and the requirements for those jobs. This is accompanied by a cross-department career grid that shows specific positions in each department. These tools facilitate manager/associate career discussions on possible career paths outside of their departments.

Training Technology

As we move into the 21st century, JCPenney is keeping pace with technology in many of our training efforts. For several years we have used our own internal television network to broadcast (via satellite) to all of our stores and district offices. This network, originally established for the merchandise-buying function, was also used to broadcast training sessions to our stores via a one-way video transmission. Participating stores could call in questions.

Today, we use distance learning. Communication is still one-way video, transmitted via satellite, but students in remote locations use a touch keypad, with a built-in microphone which allows personal interactivity. Via the keypad, students respond to questions from the instructor, thereby giving the instructor immediate feedback on student comprehension of material. When necessary, students can also press a call button to signal when they have questions. A simple touch of the facilitator's computer screen will activate the student's microphone. Distance learning benefits the student by increasing participation and by providing a quick way to signal the instructor when necessary.

Distance learning gives JCPenney (1) an ability to train more associates at a less overall cost; (2) "just in time" learning opportunities to meet immediate business needs; and (3) an opportunity to use a medium proven to increase learning and retention. We plan to have distance learning capability present in all of our stores and business units by 1997. In addition to our "functional" training, units will also be offered developmental learning topics to build their personal skills.

Another aspect of "just-in-time training" is our desire to provide technical training in a way that is performance based and mirrors the actual system. JCPenney recognizes that learning transference is best when there is (1) a direct correlation between learning and the job and (2) the learners are in control of their own learning. So, if systems training is needed, JCPenney wants to provide that training using the same system—even if we must duplicate the system to provide specific practice or common scenarios.

Multimedia and computer-based training (CBT) is a future direction that can't be ignored in a learning organization. The real beauty of multimedia or CBT is that they provide for self-paced and self-guided instruction. The pace of the learning is in the control of the learner. It also affords associates in training the ability to assess their knowledge in a "learning environment" and to control their learning by reviewing those concepts that may be more difficult.

Our technological advances also now include college recruiting efforts on the Internet. Via the Internet, potential JCPenney employment candidates can now get a sampling of the training programs we offer for entry-level positions.

Currently we average between 180 and 200 daily inquiries over the Internet. Thirty-three percent of those inquiries come from educational sites. The page most accessed (following our home page) is the Information Systems department, at 27 percent of total inquiries.

We also accept resumes over the Internet. We have received resumes from countries other than the U.S., including Russia.

Internal Advisory Teams

The heart of the diversity initiatives are our advisory teams, such as the Women's Advisory Team and the Minority Advisory Team. The teams work with people in human resources and senior management to identify issues and barriers to the development of women and minorities. Results and recommendations are reported to the Diversity Steering Committee, which consists of top senior managers. Each year, this committee reviews the management status of women and minorities in each department and makes recommendations concerning their future development.

The advisory teams made several recommendations, most of which we implemented. We initiated basic workday improvements, such as flexible staffing, a career pathing system, and a true state-of-the-art home office child care facility.

We now have networking programs where women and minorities identified as upper-management candidates have a chance to interact with senior executives at regularly scheduled luncheons. We began roundtable discussions where all associates have the opportunity to talk to senior management.

At one point early in our initiative, we also identified a shortage of both female and minority role models and a way to solve the problem until the company could grow more of its own. The answer was and is our continuing leadership forums, where noteworthy outside women and minorities of singular accomplishment come in and speak to our associates.

Our first forum drew an audience of about 300 women and men. For the second event, held two months later, over 700 showed up and TV monitors had to be set up in the hallway to accommodate the overflow.

Along with those, we have regular brown-bag lunch seminars to communicate different aspects and programs of the ongoing diversity initiatives. We sponsor external programs so that our efforts do not remain isolated within the company, but rather become part of the community's fabric.

Every year across the nation, JCPenney sponsors 25 women's conferences and 16 multicultural conferences. These are trade fair events attended by well over a million people that include seminars and exhibits on a variety of subjects vital to women and minorities. We have assumed a leadership role in achieving gender equity in women's sports. We have backed Indianapolis 500 race car driver Lyn St. James, as well as the National Girls and Women in Sports Day. Every year, we sponsor both the Memorial Day Weekend LPGA Skins Game on ABC and the network's mixed-team event, the JCPenney Golf Classic, in the fall.

In 1994, JCPenney began sponsoring the Susan G. Komen Foundation's Race for the Cure in the fight against breast cancer. These hugely popular race and walk events across the country have raised tens of millions of dollars for cancer research, education, and treatment.

A true highlight every year is our Juanita Kreps Award, which celebrates the Spirit of the American Woman. Named after the first woman on the company's board of directors, this annual award is presented to a woman who has professionally distinguished herself on a national basis.

Receiving the Catalyst Award

In 1995, JCPenney was given the prestigious Catalyst Award which annually honors business organizations for outstanding initiatives to advance women. We are the first retailer to receive this award. In addition to receiving national and local attention, our Catalyst Award-winning programs will be used to educate the business community about cutting-edge initiatives, and will serve as examples of best practices that can be replicated by other organizations. Winning this award gives our company national dis-tinction, and reinforces our commitment to continue to develop vital roles for women and minorities.

The most important element in the success of our women's and minority initiatives—ranking just ahead of the Advisory Teams—is, of course, a *total commitment from the top*. Senior management's support, combined with patiently educating people, is the key to our success. We didn't achieve what we have today overnight—it's taken six years of steady, persistent application. This is a journey, and it will continue to be a journey.

Since the inception of our diversity efforts, W. R. Howell, as well as others in the senior management ranks, have been steadfastly behind all diversity initiatives. In six short years, we have made extraordinary progress:

- We have the first female senior executive vice-president in the company's history.

- For the first time, we have a female president in one of our four merchandising divisions (the $4 billion dollar Home Division). Also for the first time, we have an African-American president in one of our four regions.

- As of 1995, women represented 60 percent of our entry-level managers and minorities represented 16 percent. Thirty-one percent of our mid-managers are women, while minorities represent 11 percent. Also, women fill 15 percent of our senior manager positions, with minorities at 5 percent.

Our goal is to have women eventually represent 46 percent of every management level, with minorities representing 16 percent. Our approach to diversity fits within our corporate culture. When founded in 1902, JCPenney called his store The Golden Rule. This concept has permeated the company's culture ever since. It is natural in such an environment that our diversity efforts would have a chance to succeed. In 1913, the company adopted "The Penney Idea," a series of seven principles which serves as the basic policy for conducting our business. One of these principles is "To improve constantly the human factor in our business." Although we have numbers that measure how many women and minorities work at JCPenney, how can we actually measure the improvement in the "human factor"? It is not measured in numbers only, but also in terms of the moral and ethical principles by which we conduct our daily lives. Here again, the company's value system is naturally in synch with the spirit of diversity.

Our company harnessed its natural culture to energize our multifaceted initiative, and nurtured it every step of the way. Our chairman, W. R. Howell, has provided staunch support that has indeed set a strong example for all management in accomplishing diversity goals. JCPenney's senior management has recognized how all this is in consonance with a strong diversity initiative. These initiatives permeate our company culture today, and they will continue over the long term.

8

Learning at Hewlett-Packard

By Jim Fuller

Background on Hewlett-Packard

Bill Hewlett and Dave Packard started the Hewlett-Packard Company (HP) in a small garage in 1937. They aimed to create technology products that were of the highest quality, while at the same time offering customers significant value. The two men led their company through significant growth and change. At the close of 1995, HP employed 102,000 employees located across 113 countries. The company sells more than 25,000 products in diverse technology markets such as home and business computer products, electronic test instrumentation, medical measurement products, electronic components, and high-precision analytical test products.

Worldwide sales in 1995 amounted to $31.5 billion, making that year the fourth straight with revenue growth above 20 percent. Profits for the year were up by 52 percent, and investment in product research and development reached more than $3 billion. What allows a company such as HP to continue to be so successful in rapidly changing markets amidst fierce competition? It's the people.

When HP CEO Lew Platt accepted *Fortune* magazine's Most Admired Corporation award, he commented that the company's 100,000 employees around the world deserved this recognition. "HP people are intelligent, hard-working, and passionate in their pursuit of excellence. In an era of dizzying change, they illustrate the timelessness of HP's values: teamwork, flexibility, contribution, respect for people, and integrity. I'm grateful to HP's people for how well they've put those values into play in a turbulent industry environment. And I'm delighted to have their accomplishments recognized."

HP has always held its employees in high regard. This belief and practice comes directly from the company founders. Bill and Dave have always believed that people want to do a good job, and given the opportunity, will do so. This has significant impact on how the company views its employees, and the investment it makes in their professional development.

Dave Packard expressed it best in an objective that he created for the company. "The most capable people available must be selected for each assignment within the organization. Especially in a technical business where the rate of progress is rapid, a continuing program of education must be undertaken and maintained. Techniques that are good today will be outdated in the future and every person in the organization from top to bottom must continually be looking for new and better ways to do his work." Those words were written in 1961. They have shaped our focus on people development, and are just as meaningful today as they were in 1961.

Lessons for Change

HP's entry into digital video products provides a vivid example of keeping up with rapidly shifting business needs. The Microwave Instrument Division (MID) was one of HP's oldest product divisions, creating precision measurement equipment for engineers working in microwave-range electronics. The market for MID's instrumentation had begun to slow. There was ongoing demand for the products, and the division could continue for many years producing its current products. It would be safe, comfortable, and profitable, but it would not provide opportunity for growth.

In a bold move, the division recreated itself in a surprisingly short period of time. The division manager transferred all the existing MID products to HP's other instrument division, leaving the organization with no products or source of revenue. Unless MID could create and successfully market an entirely new line of products, the division would have to close and its employees would have to find new positions within HP.

The general manager gathered all the MID employees in the division cafeteria and outlined the changes that were occurring. From that day forward, the division would be called VID, and it would focus exclusively on digital video products. In a period of only 12 months, VID introduced 12 new digital video products that took the market by storm.

Nice story, you might think, but what does this have to do with learning? Moving from microwave instrumentation to digital video products required the R&D organization to make significant shifts. The MID designers created products for microwave engineers, who they understood quite well. They wore crewcuts and plastic pocket protectors. Now they would have to design for video engineers. These people wore pony-

tails and earrings—and they were the guys! The new technologies and new customers represented a dramatic transformation. While none of the design team attended a single training class, all had to engage in significant learning.

Library and bookstore shelves were emptied of books on digital video technology. Every video trade show was attended by at least one engineer or marketing person. VID design team members spent time at major video production studios to understand their new customers, what they did, how they did it, and what products they needed. Our people needed meaningful technology information and customer insights to transform themselves. Training courses could never have created the rapid, pragmatic learning needed for success.

Hewlett-Packard takes a rather unusual approach to employee development. There are several issues that drive the current philosophy. Each needs to be explored a bit to understand the practices that are now in use.

Formal Training May Not Be the Best Solution

"Walking school" and "talking school"—we don't send our children to either of these, but they seem to learn the skills involved to the level of performance. I ride a bicycle perfectly well, but have never been to a single related class. As human beings, we have the innate capability to learn. We do it from the moment that we enter this world. What is our obsession with attempting to institutionalize and regulate learning?

Very few people would say: "I have a pesticide problem." The real problem is insects in the house. Pesticide is a potential solution, as is installing screens to keep the bugs out. "I have a water problem" is rarely heard. "Fire" is more common, and the real problem. Water is a solution to the problem. Both of these statements are rather silly, and they represent backwards thinking. "I have a training problem" is a similar example. Performance is the true problem. Training is a potential solution, but not always the correct or sufficient one. An attendee at a training course summarized the issue in written evaluation comments: "This was 30 minutes of valuable information packed into a three-day course."

The Software Reuse Project

Hewlett-Packard was not immune to the pervasive "training problem" approach. We created training courses for important skill areas. People took them. Lots of them. In the midst of this burgeoning training activity, something caught our attention: an undeniable failure.

HP was creating many software products. To increase the productivity of software developers, we introduced a program called *software reuse*. The basic idea behind software reuse is that many software programs share common functions, and therefore can share code. Rather than write each line of code, a developer can create software product by assembling already written blocks of code. Software reuse can reduce development time by 80 percent. We created a wonderful training course on software reuse. We had the class develop blocks of code, then put them together to create a simple product. The class went well using these new skills. Back on the job was a different matter.

Graduates from the software reuse class went to work on a major project. Reuse was immediately abandoned. Why? None of the developers had access to the server where the code blocks were stored. Without access to the building block, progress was halted. We solved the problem and software reuse went into full swing for about a week before it again stopped abruptly. We discovered that the building blocks had bugs. Developers spent more time fixing the block than they would writing the code from scratch. After fixing the problem, Software reuse saw extensive use until it was abandoned a third time. The developers discovered that the management team had not changed the criteria for evaluating performance. Evaluations and pay increases would be driven from the amount of new code

written. The managers were using a powerful reinforcer (pay) to reward the old behaviors and punish the new. When confronted with this dilemma, they immediately changed the criteria to reward reuse. The project concluded well ahead of schedule and exceeded sales projections.

The software reuse experience caused significant concern. Skills and knowledge, while important, proved insufficient for achieving performance. At that point, we needed a bigger picture of how to improve the performance of HP's employees.

The Human Performance System

The software reuse experience demonstrated that improving the knowledge, skills, and attitudes (KSAs) of employees was not enough to improve on-the-job performance. Performance represents a much more complex issue. As we looked at the barriers to performance, it became clear that people work within a performance system and that many external factors affect performance. To optimize performance, all components of the system must operate correctly.

Figure 1 illustrates the performance system that is used at Hewlett-Packard. It shows a system where inputs and processes create outputs that are fed back through the system to the people and organization. All the components of the system exist within a work environment that also affects performance.

The human performance system begins with organizational inputs. Every organization provides inputs to its people. The inputs can be fixed or variable, formal or informal, documented or not. Inputs from a variety of sources exist within HP. The organization has goals, values, and a climate that affects the way people operate within the organization. Hewlett-Packard has organizational values and norms that people in the company refer to as "the HP Way". The philosophies that comprise the HP Way were created by the company founders. Every employee clearly understands them. The HP Way creates expectations for behavior (how things get done) within the company.

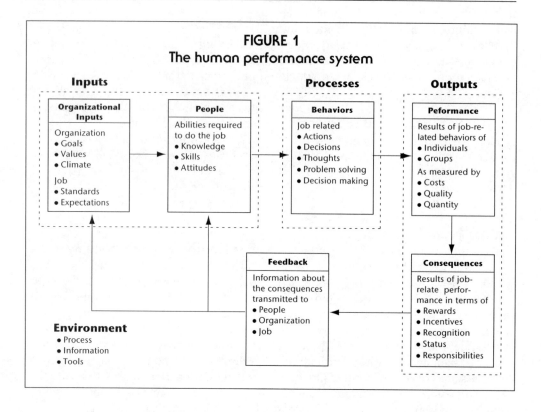

FIGURE 1
The human performance system

(For detailed information on this topic, refer to David Packard's book *The HP Way*).

In addition, all employees have a written position plan that indicates their role in the organization and the results they are expected to achieve in their job. This creates a clear picture of what is to be done. If the position plans are poorly written or out of date, the employee could easily be striving for the wrong performance. We have seen instances of training programs where the most valuable outcome involved providing clarity on job expectations. Employees knew how to do the tasks, but they didn't know the specific desired tasks or the additional tasks needed to successfully perform in their position.

Within HP's human performance system, people take the available inputs and use their existing knowledge, skills, and attitudes (KSAs) to produce behaviors. If the KSAs are inadequate, the tasks may be performed incorrectly, inadequately, or not at all. Like each component in the performance system, the KSAs are a necessary but insuf-

ficient element for achieving optimum performance. One major error typically made by training organizations (the same error we encountered with the software reuse project) is to focus exclusively on KSAs and ignore other components. This produces highly capable people who strive to achieve in a suboptimal environment.

Behaviors that are created result in performance—the output component of the human performance system. Output within this system consists of the desired accomplishments for which the job exists. This performance can take place on an individual or group level. Typically, performance is measured in terms of desired outcomes that are valued by the organization. These include reduced product costs, increased quality, and increased productivity. It is important to distinguish between the behaviors and the performance of the employee or individual. Behaviors are measured by specific actions or activities. Performance is measured by outcomes. It is quite possible to have employees working within a system, demonstrating the desired behaviors, while failing to achieve any desired outcomes. HP uses a management philosophy commonly referred to as management by objectives (MBO). This method of managing sets clear performance goals (desired outcomes) and allows the employee to select the best method (within the guidelines of the HP Way) to achieve the performance. The focus is not on behaviors, but on the performance.

The resulting performance has specific consequences associated with it. If the consequences reinforce the desired performance, then the desired performance will likely continue. If the consequences punish the performance, then the performance will likely diminish over time. B. F. Skinner demonstrated this simple stimulus-response relationship in his classic experiments. When looking at causes of performance problems of groups and individuals, "incorrect consequences" shows up as a surprisingly frequent performance barrier. We have looked into organizations and found multiple examples of:

- correct performance that was ignored (so why bother?),
- correct performance that was punished (which discourages its continuance),
- incorrect performance that was ignored (so why improve or change?), and
- incorrect performance that was rewarded (which encourages its continuance).

Once the consequences of poor performance are established, they need to be fed back to the people and the organization. A system that does not provide feedback is an open loop, and the results will likely be unpredictable. When provided with regular feedback on their performance and the consequences, people will modify their own behavior to optimize their performance and the associated consequences. Without frequent, accurate feedback, people are less likely to improve their performance over time.

The last component of the human performance system is the environment. Aspects such as work processes, information, and tools can have a significant impact on performance. If people receive bad information and/or inadequate tools, they will not achieve optimal performance. This will occur even if the organizational inputs, people abilities, performance consequences, and feedback are of the highest quality. All the human performance components must be optimized to produce top-level performance.

Causes of Top Performance

The concept of the human performance system was reinforced by a study that was done to determine *why* top performers excelled. The study identified top performers and median performers who worked in the same jobs. After careful observation of their work, the causes for the performance differentiation were identified. The results indicated several reasons for superior performance. In general, top performers consistently

- do away with unnecessary steps,
- perform an extra step that is needed but not documented,
- use available information or documentation that others do not use,
- possess a self-created job aid unavailable to others,
- have information or data that others do not have,
- possess better tools than those that others have,
- have a different motive for performing,
- work in a different environment,
- receive different guidance and feedback during their working life, or
- receive different incentives.

Receiving more, different, or better training was not found to be a major contributor to top performance. The ability to optimize the other components of the human performance system appeared to be the key. With this information in hand, Hewlett-Packard began to question the value of its investment in classroom-oriented training. The human performance system model indicated that training alone did not produce improved performance. Other questions began to arise as well.

Questionable Assumptions Regarding Classroom Training

Within industry, most training activity occurs within the classroom environment. This appears to be an artifact from how we learned during our school days—it is not necessarily a consciously selected strategy. There are many assumptions implicit in the classroom environment. If asked, most educators would say they consider these assumptions false. However, business continues to build courses that reinforce certain false assumptions. Some of these false assumptions include:

● *Everyone starts with the same knowledge.* We know that if you gather 20 adults, you will find a distribution of knowledge on almost any topic. Different people will come to a classroom experience with different levels of experience. However, when in the classroom, everybody is assumed to be at the same level. Almost without exception, courses start every learner at the same place regardless of actual knowledge or capability.

● *Everyone learns at the same pace.* Again, we know that this is false. Different learners learn at different rates on different subjects. In the classroom, all learners are paced by the instructor and the slowest learners.

● *Everyone learns best from listening.* There are actually several learning modalities. Unfortunately for nonauditory learners, listening to the instructor talk is the primary means of instruction used in the classroom.

● *Everyone should learn individually rather than collaboratively.* When we were in school, collaborative learning was called "cheating." Most courses are still designed around the individual learner. Employees are taught individually, then sent back to the work environment where they are expected to operate in teams and work collaboratively.

Declarative Versus Procedural Knowledge

In addition to the concerns caused by classroom assumptions, questions began to arise at HP regarding the appropriateness of the classroom for delivering the type of learning that our business needed. To greatly simplify types of knowledge, we can divide them into two categories: declarative and procedural. Declarative knowledge is easily communicated and typically can be evaluated through written or verbal testing. Facts regarding American history or world geography exemplify declarative knowledge.

Procedural knowledge is more complex and defies verbal information. As an example, try to use words to explain how to drive a car. Decisions based on dynamically changing information make the task nearly impossible. While learning about history may work in the classroom environment, learning to drive a car will not.

As we looked at the types of knowledge necessary for HP employees, we found that the vast majority were procedural in nature. We wanted employees to determine how to troubleshoot complex systems, work collaboratively to address customer opportunities, and design products not previously in existence. Classroom learning was clearly not making the most of our efforts to develop leading-edge employees. We needed a different approach to human development.

HP's New Learning Strategy

Historically, HP had taken a classroom-oriented curriculum approach to employee development. The professional success of education managers was partly measured by the depth and breadth of course curriculum available to the employee, typically measured by the overall weight of the course catalog. With the assistance of their manager, employees would scan through the catalog and select courses that would help them achieve their yearly development plans. This might have worked in the past, but the demands of the 1990s required a learning strategy consistent with the prevailing business demands. Rather than strategizing to create ever-expanding curriculums, we shifted to a strategy that described what learning should look like within HP. We decided that learning at HP would have the following characteristics:

• *Right Time*—Training should occur when a solution is needed.

• *Right Place*—Training should occur where a solution is needed.

• *Right Solution*—Training should effectively and efficiently meet the learning/performance improvement need. At this point, HP should attempt to find or create training that resolves the performance barrier.

While this view appears very simple, it radically transformed the company's view of developing learning. Traditional training approaches did not meet the requirement of HP's "right time" learning. To respond to customer/market demands, employees need to develop new knowledge rapidly—when they need it—not when the next course is available. When employees solve a problem, they need "right place" solutions—not ones that require them to travel. In the past, attending a three-day training course was an acceptable use of time. No longer. Also, more and more, employees are demanding "right solution" learning resources. They will no longer tolerate attending a three-day course to extract the 30 minutes of learning that they need. They want solutions that are efficient (require as little time as possible) and effective (provide all the learning necessary to improve performance).

The HP Corporate University

Many large companies have centralized universities. Some are even renowned for their corporate university resources and size. Many people are quite surprised to discover that Hewlett-Packard has no centralized corporate university. HP has chosen not to build a campus for many reasons. For HP, a centralized university sends the wrong message to our employees. It says that learning occurs at a specific time in a specific place, and we want every employee to be learning all the time, in every place possible, as they are engaged in their daily work.

A centralized corporate university can also have an adverse effect on the education professionals within the company. The large campus and expansive curriculum allows training and development educators to

fall into the trap of believing that they are in the business of *training* rather than increasing corporate ability to achieve business needs through improving employee performance. Companies with corporate universities also tend to have poor measures of success for their training organizations when measured using such key indicators as training expenditure per employee; number of classroom days per employee; number of available courses; and course evaluation through student reactions.

These measures lead organizations into the training business, rather than the business of improving employee performance and company competitiveness. Establishing a traditional corporate university was clearly the wrong solution for Hewlett-Packard. However, HP's employees needed access to learning solutions consistent with the Right Time, Right Place, Right Solution strategy. HP needed to create a different kind of university.

Establishing the HP Virtual University

The nature of work is changing at Hewlett-Packard. The classic 9 A.M. to 5 P.M. Monday through Friday office work week is disappearing. HP now has a very geographically dispersed workforce. A manager at HP can have employees in Atlanta, San Jose, Barcelona, and Hong Kong, all at the same time. Segments of this workforce are mobile—working on the road, or even permanently at a customer's site. Others telecommute, working at home some or all of their work week, connected to HP through phone, fax, and remotely networked computers. HP is in a 24-hours-per day, seven-days-per-week global business that requires alternative and flexible work schedules. Manufacturing and customer support centers operate around the clock, placing employees on highly unusual work hours. Learning solutions at HP need to be adaptable so that all employees around the world can take part in professional development.

As a result of these workforce changes, Hewlett-Packard decided to develop a *vir-*

tual university. This learning resource would be available to employees regardless of time, space, and location constraints. Development solutions would be available to meet their performance needs whenever required. HP's virtual university would use a wide variety of methods to achieve this unusual goal.

● *On-line resources* – The Hewlett-Packard Company is in an enviable technological position. As a leading manufacturer of computer and network solutions, we can create an unparalleled network learning system. HP is the world's largest client/server solution provider, with more than 75,000 desktops networked together without a single mainframe computer. Since the system comprises all HP equipment, a desktop in Hong Kong is compatible with a desktop in Boise. This allows HP and its partners to design and develop learning solutions that can work on every employee's desktop computer. Once a computer-based training (CBT) or electronic performance support system (EPSS) is installed on the system, any employee on the network can run any learning solution at his or her desk at any time. Hence: Right Time, Right Place, Right Solution.

● *Desktop video* – A number of video-based learning solutions exist. Many can be quite useful, but they present at least two problems inconsistent with HP's learning strategy. First, employees must leave their work areas to view them (not right place) and they must frequently watch or interact for the entire duration of the presentation to find the information they need (not right solution). Both of these approaches are inconsistent with HP's learning approach. Hewlett-Packard manufactures a product called a *video server.* These systems are designed to store video programs digitally, and deliver them on demand to desktop computers using advanced compression techniques. Placing video learning solutions on video servers allows employees to view videos at their desktop on demand – resolving both the right place and the right time issues. Further, because each video is stored digitally, an index can be created for it to

permit the employee to select specific information rather than view the entire video. This addresses the right solution.

● *AI work analysis* – If you have ever attended a computer software training course, you are probably aware of some of the limitations that it presents. With only one instructor and 20 students, each participant receives limited coaching time. Having a personal coach who watches you and makes recommendations to improve your performance is optimal, but unrealistic. Unless of course, your coach is also your computer. Using an artificial intelligence (AI) program running in the background, HP's virtual university network can monitor how you use software and make recommendations for productivity improvements. You can call up a performance coach wherever and whenever desired.

● *Learning centers* – Some Hewlett-Packard employees work in positions that do not offer them immediate access to a desktop computer. For these employees, HP has created learning centers where they can gain access to the HP Virtual University. Open everyday, 24 hours per day, these centers are heavily used by employees seeking to advance their careers and remain current on technology. In some cases, HP has also worked with local community colleges to allow HP employees to earn college credit for education acquired in HP's learning centers.

● *Satellite courses* – Some HP employees prefer to receive learning from leading academic institutions. Unfortunately, few employees would have the opportunity to pursue a degree from MIT or the Stanford Business School. Unless, of course, the school came to the employee. Through strategic partnerships with leading schools, university courses are broadcast to HP sites through HP's own satellite network. Employees can view these courses in a common room with other HP students, take them in taped form for viewing at home, or access them directly through their desktop computer system via HP's learning network.

● *World Wide Web conferences* – Almost every HP employee has access to the World

Wide Web (WWW). Through the development of tools and technologies to complement WWW capabilities, HP has been able to simulate conference attendance. Rather than spending days and dollars traveling, the conference attendee simply connects to the conference electronically. All readings are available for review and are linked to additional learning resources. The sound files from the presentations are downloaded to the employees desktop computer and played while the presentation visuals are displayed on the screen. As the attendees pose questions to the presenter electronically, their responses are available to all participants. The nature of the technology allows attendees to connect at any time, and the materials and discussions are available for their constant review. This allows attendees to participate anywhere in the world, regardless of time zone.

Avoiding the Problem of "Technolust"

Hewlett-Packard's use of technology to improve learning is exciting—and highly seductive. Therein lies a potential difficulty. If you want to start a stampede, introduce a new technology into the education profession. There is little doubt that thousands will flock to the new technology and hail it as the solution that will revolutionize education. We all witnessed this reaction first with television, and subsequently with the video recorder, satellite broadcasting, computer-based training, interactive video, and now with multimedia. Rather than the foretold revolution, what typically occurs is a rapid adoption of the technology, with little thought to design of the learning that the media is supposed to deliver. This is what we refer to as *technolust*—the application of education technology for the sake of technology itself. This can be a very bad habit.

In the book *Self-Directed Learning*, author George Piscurich makes a rather bold statement: "Video set distance learning back 30 years. It made it possible to take the same boring lecture technique that has been putting students to sleep for generations and

distribute it for use at any time, to hundreds of sites simultaneously. No design methodology, just convenient access to bad training." This is a clear example of technolust, and its resulting product, "shovelware."

The rapid adoption of technology creates a large and impatient market for learning solutions that use the technology. Vendors and developers find that they must create or provide solutions rapidly. "Shovelware occurs when a training vendor takes a learning solution in its current format (such as videotape) and simply shovels the same content to a new technology (such as multimedia). The effectiveness of the resulting products is highly questionable, and the quality rarely tolerable."

Recently, a major university came to HP for technical assistance in implementing a multimillion-dollar, high-technology distance-learning system. As we applied the design/delivery process to the project, we quickly discovered a case of technolust. The desire to create an international satellite broadcast system overshadowed the real learning needs that could be easily and inexpensively best achieved by using a printed-publication strategy instead.

To avoid the natural tendency toward technolust, Hewlett-Packard has adopted a design/delivery process. This structured approach to learning begins with the desired learner performance and clearly identifies what the learner should be able to do (perform) as a result of the learning solution. Then, the best learning method is selected to achieve the desired learner performance. The learning method and a number of practical constraints then dictate the most appropriate delivery methods. Frequently, the most effective and efficient delivery method can be the least technical. This has prevented HP from investing in learning solutions that either do not work or cost significantly more than necessary.

Career Self-Reliance and the New Employment Contract

As you read through this chapter, you have probably sensed a significant change in Hewlett-Packard's employee development strategy. Most employees in private industry have found that the employment contract has changed significantly. At one time you could work for the same company, sometimes in the same job, for your entire life. Today, very little loyalty exists between employee and employer. Mass layoffs are frequently used to eliminate employees with old skills and bring in employees with new capabilities. In its 57-year history, HP has never had a major layoff. The company does not pursue a hire-fire strategy to ensure that employee capabilities meet the current business need. Hewlett-Packard uses a very different employment and development philosophy.

HP embraces the philosophy of career self-reliance. Within HP, every employee is personally responsible for managing personal career and professional development. Fundamentally, there are two complementary aspects necessary for career self-reliance to operate effectively. First, the company or employer has responsibility for offering employment opportunities and development resources. The employee has responsibility for taking the initiative to understand HP's future business needs and ensure that his or her selected career path will be needed by HP in the future. Using the development resources provided by the company, the employee ensures that his or her personal development keeps pace with the demands of the job. When the company offers employment and the employee offers employability, the needs of both are met.

The employees of HP's VID division used the power of career self-reliance when they moved from their old comfortable products to designing new products for a new market in record time. Every employee took responsibility for personal professional development, and each discovered that the theme for the division transformation is true: "The future is ours to create."

References

Gilbert, Thomas F. (1978). *Human competence: Engineering worthy performance.* New York: McGraw-Hill.

Ormond, Jeanne E. (1990). *Human learning: Theories, principles, and educational applications.* New York: Merrill.

Piskuritch, George M. (1993). *Self-directed learning: A practical guide to design, development, and implementation.* San Francisco, CA: Jossey-Bass.

Romiszowski, A. J. (1988). *The selection and use of instructional media.* New York: Nichols.

Stolovitch, Harold D., & Keeps, Erica J. (Eds.). (1992). *Handbook of human performance technology.* San Francisco: Jossey-Bass.

9

Creating a Culture of Learning at Rich Products Corporation

By Mary Beth Debus

MANY organizations offer various degrees of education and training opportunities to their people. A primary challenge for companies is to develop these opportunities in such a way that they communicate a consistent message to both a company's internal people and the external world in which it operates. The creation of structures to support this commitment to learning becomes crucial if both the individual and the organization are going to benefit from this approach. This chapter explores how one company, Rich Products Corporation (RPC), has designed—and continues to design—its structures and messages such that all associated with the company will benefit from its commitment to learning.

Rich Products Corporation is one of the world's largest family-owned manufacturers of frozen food. Headquartered on the Niagara River in Buffalo, New York, with sales of more than $1 billion a year, Rich Products has a national and international work force of more than 6,000 associates (Rich Product's term for employees) and more than 30 manufacturing facilities and field offices throughout North America, Mexico, Asia, and Europe. Rich's manufacturing facilities, warehouses, and subsidiaries produce a wide spectrum of premium-quality products including nondairy creamers, toppings and icings; frozen doughs, baked goods, and sweet goods; bakery finishers; specialty meats; barbeque; pastas; and frozen seafoods, to name a few.

Rich Products was founded by Robert E. Rich, Sr., now the chairman. RPC's president is his son, Robert E. Rich, Jr., and Melinda Rich, Bob Rich, Jr.'s wife, is president of Rich Entertainment Group. The Entertainment Group operates eleven restaurants, a golf course, and three baseball teams, including the Triple-A Buffalo Bisons franchise.

Rich Products' world headquarters houses a state-of-the-art research center, a truly unique conference center, Rich's Mother and Child Center (Rich's in-house day care facility for the children of associates), and a wellness/fitness center.

Linking Training with Company Strategies

To benefit from its commitment to a learning environment, an organization must provide a focus for learning and training opportunities. The organization must provide training consistent with the company's mission and business strategies as well as focus on associates' individual development needs. The organization must also make itself aware of the greatest needs in both business and indivdual-development areas.

Mission: World Class (M:WC)

Rich Products began its Mission: World Class journey in 1991 with the realization that 46 years of financial and business success were not necessarily enough to keep the company competitive in the future. This realization emerged from a study the organization undertook to answer a question that chairman Bob Rich, Sr., raised as to whether Rich Products should pursue the Malcolm Baldridge Quality Award. While the organization saw the award as a fine recognition, those involved felt that an ongoing internal focus, rather than a goal with an end result, would better serve the company. The leaders agreed that Rich Products needed a more clearly articulated mission that all associates would embrace. Simply put, what was needed was a shared focus for all members of the company.

In 1992, Rich Products appointed a director of Mission: World Class. Mission: World Class is RPC's statement of mission and strategies. (See Appendix A.) The creation of this unique position within the organization helped associates understand how strong the leadership's commitment was and is to the Mission: World Class philosophy. The director took responsibility for designing communication strategies for effecting a cultural change in a company that already enjoyed great success. As another indication of its commitment, senior management formed an executive steering team.

The first communication efforts of Mission: World Class included the publication of *Rich's Magazine*. The first issue, introducing M:WC, was sent to each associate's home. Throughout the organization, M:WC steering teams were formed and trained, and individuals were chosen and trained to be M:WC facilitators. What followed was the roll-out of Block I training for all associates in the company. Vendors and brokers also received M:WC training. The main theme of Block I was "Why change?". It further explained each of the M:WC strategies and

provided hands-on approaches to integrating these strategies into everyday work life.

During this time, the concept of the *learning organization* was introduced. The organization heard many times: "The only competitive advantage we have is to learn faster and react more quickly than the competition." This was important to Bob Rich, Jr.'s vision for the company. Today, this message has matured into the Rich Products Corporation Learning and Development Philosophy. (See Appendix B.)

RPC continues its focus on the M:WC philosophy and strategies. Each year a new training series has been introduced to associates. The company has also been reinforcing the relationship between its business strategies and the M:WC philosophy. For each associate, the expectations of how to behave, and what to work toward grow clearer each year as the ongoing commitment to learning and development continues.

Associate Development

While the mission and business strategies are crucial to the company's success and to each associate's ability to contribute, RPC soon realized that addressing individual needs could not be overlooked. Neither the M:WC Department nor other areas in the company were set up to address these needs. As a result, the Associate Development Department within human resources was formed in 1995. The department's focus is unique in that it emphasizes development as well as strategic compensation practices. (Further descriptions of the department's activities will follow later in this chapter.)

The Associate Development Department was established to develop "talents, agility, and leadership qualities in associates such that all could accomplish business plans and effectively utilize resources." Immediately, the Associate Development Department and the Mission: World Class Department began to discover a synergy in their work and focus. For example, while team building had been a focus in M:WC, it eventually became an area that associate development undertook.

Needs Assessment

Regardless of its source, all training should relate to business goals and the M:WC philosophy and strategies. In that spirit, associate development and M:WC join in partnership to address and assess the overall needs of the organization. Both formal and informal needs assessments contribute to the departments' ability to best meet the needs of the company and the individual associates.

Formal needs assessments include in-depth meetings with each steering team and other representatives from throughout the company. Steering team members are questioned about the current and future needs of associates in their department, whether related to business skills, technical skills, team skills, or individual development. The meetings are analyzed by counting the number of responses in various categories and comparing those responses against both the short-term and long-term business objectives. Priority goes to skill areas that will best meet company objectives and those that are most often requested by the organizational members.

Other informal conversations also result in the identification of needs for individuals, teams, or departments. Members of the Associate Development Department and M:WC have become very adept at listening to what associates say, and they can translate what they hear into identified needs of the company.

Building Partnerships for Development

Once the training and development needs of the organization are identified and matched against the company's mission and business needs, the organization seeks to build a partnership with each individual. Individuals take ultimate responsibility for their own development and learning, but the organization must actively support individual efforts and provide resources. RPC offers many resources to its associates.

Tuition Assistance

Many companies recognize that the continuing education of their people greatly benefits the organization. Individuals engaged in continuous learning are better prepared to handle the ever-changing business environment and are more prepared for new positions within the company (either promotions or lateral moves). Rich Products, like many progressive companies, has adopted a tuition assistance program. The expense of college courses chosen to help enhance a present or future career are paid for 100 percent by the company (75 percent on passing a course and the balance a year later).

Rich Products has created a partnership between the associate and his or her manager in an attempt to involve both in the development of the individual's career. The college degree sought should either be part of a planned career transition or related to future or present job duties in the current position. This helps to ensure that education dollars are spent wisely and are part of a larger plan benefiting both the company and the individual.

In-House Training

While training has been conducted at RPC all along, the company recognized that it could not fully realize its commitment to learning without forming a staff dedicated to that purpose. Associate development has begun offering and sponsoring courses to RPC associates through a catalog of training seminars. The first catalog covered one quarter of the business year and offered six different "open" courses. Associates from a wide cross-section of departments registered for these courses. The open enrollment allows for targeting associates' individual needs in areas identified as those most needed by the company. One such course, Time Management, is certainly not a necessary course for every individual, but it should be available to those who need to enhance their organization and time-management skills. Other courses offered in the first catalog were Building a Team, Giving and Receiving Feedback, Communication and Listening, Interviewing Skills, and Work/Life Balance.

Associates and their managers ideally work together to target individual needs. Individuals who attend classes have a responsibility for creating opportunities to apply their newly learned skills, and the manager's support is crucial in this process. Both also need to be concerned about developing the skills that the company most needs and that will support the company's objectives. Any courses offered by associate development need to be related in some way to RPC's objectives, and most will have an obvious connection.

While individuals have unique training needs, specific departments or teams may also want or need to train together. This would be most likely when the theme of the training is more general and applicable to the stage the team or department is in. For example, as new teams are formed, or new transitions are made in a department, many request team-building activities. It is not unusual for associate development to develop and provide activities designed to address issues such as communication, trust, and leadership for an entire team or department.

Teams may also need such skills as feedback or consensus decision-making to enhance their interaction with each other or with their customers. Associate development is committed to enhancing the performance of a department or team so that it can better meet its business objectives and operate more efficiently and effectively.

External Training

Internal resources cannot meet every training need. Some needs are too specific, technical, or even too advanced to be provided internally. Sometimes the timing of the need and the training that can be provided internally simply don't match. From time to time, associate development receives requests for information on specific skills classes such as basic math. Although this course is not currently offered by the company, associate development finds resources to address the individual need.

RPC is committed to providing opportunities for associates to attend outside seminars or classes. Many associates attend either local or national seminars for their own development, paid for completely by RPC. Associate development serves as a "clearinghouse" of catalogs and course descriptions for individuals searching for an external learning opportunity.

The Corporate Library

Rich Products has developed a corporate library which houses training videos, business books, resources on local educational opportunities, and information specific to various departments. This library provides a good example of the individual being responsible for his or her own learning, while the company provides the resources.

Developing Support Structures

Simply providing opportunities for learning is not enough to support the individual's and organization's goals. Organizations need to develop *support structures* tied to the development of their people. Rich Products has restructured its Human Resources Department into *centers of excellence* and is updating its compensation, recognition and reward, performance management, and succession-planning systems to reflect the new needs of the company.

Centers of Excellence

The centers of excellence were created as a result of analysis of the key business strategies of RPC and their implications for human resources. The department analyzed the responses to the question "What are the implications for human resources if we are to support the vision?" The result was a focus on five strategies:

- associate development,
- organization planning,
- cultural change,

• reward and recognition to support M:WC, and

• effective human resource information systems.

Corporate human resources was then restructured into centers of excellence to reflect these strategies and to provide the fuel for their implementation. The centers of excellence, responsible for companywide strategy development and implementation, are Associate Benefits, Human Resources Services, Associate Relations, and Associate Development (including Training and Compensation).

• **Associate Benefits** is the center of excellence that has responsibility for the development and administration of all benefits throughout the company. This includes such areas as health insurance, life insurance, wellness programs, disability, retirement benefits, and savings plans.

• **Human Resources Services** was designed as a separate center of excellence to develop effective human resources information systems, improve administrative procedure, and provide effective data on RPC human resources. Its goal is to remove the administrative burden from other human resources areas so that they can focus on strategic planning and initiatives rather than day-to-day transactional processes. HR services has responsibility for all automated human resources activities, including payroll.

• **Associate Relations** serves as the center of excellence responsible for the overall human resources policies and legal/contractual affairs. This center also deals with diversity issues and work/life concerns.

• **Associate Development** is uniquely designed as a center of excellence. In most companies, compensation is linked with benefits. At Rich Products, Associate Development includes the function of compensation and training. An argument can be made—and at Rich Products it is—that it is crucial to link the education, development, and performance of associates to how we choose to recognize and reward them. One supports the other. Associate Development,

then, is responsible for training, organizational development activities, and designing strategic compensation policies. The efforts to develop reward and recognition processes to support M:WC results in an initiative named Performance, Accountability, and Recognition (PAR).

Performance, Accountability, and Recognition

PAR's goal is to establish a direct link between associates' rewards and recognition and the achievement of RPC's business goals. The process of accomplishing this includes linking performance and reward, providing appropriate recognition for accomplishments, driving productivity and goal attainment, and supporting M:WC behavior. A team of cross-functional associates examined the current systems and have made recommendations for new systems that will support the company's new culture. A part of this is a performance management system that includes individual development plans and that more directly recognizes behavior that accomplishes RPC's business objectives.

Associate Development Planning

Associate Development Planning is the name given to RPC's succession planning process. It aims to provide a basis for developing high-potential associates (with special attention on women and minorities), assimilating knowledge of the company's collective strengths and weaknesses, and identifying talent gaps. The expected results of this program are the effective staffing of RPC, developing a talent pool of associates, identifying key positions within the company, and establishing a base for determining the competencies valued at RPC.

Extending the Boundaries of the Learning Environment

While an organization needs to expend time and energy, and demonstrate commitment to its internal people, the most successful organizations will extend that learning culture beyond its boundaries. Rich

Products has a number of avenues for creating a culture of learning with customer groups and the community at large.

Tech Schools

Rich Products has two tech schools for our customers, which operate 46 weeks of the year. World Headquarters in Buffalo, New York, houses one school, while the other resides in Fresno, California. The schools take up approximately 2,500 square feet and are fully equipped for hands-on work. Their primary purpose is to provide Rich Product's customers a better appreciation of the company's products, both in terms of quality and application. The schools also develop and enhance basic food-handling skills, menu presentation techniques and merchandising, and in-house food safety.

Classes are offered at no charge to customers. Rich Products pays for their accommodations and provides meal stipends. Some customers can earn travel vouchers to offset outside travel expenses. This is an investment on the part of Rich Products in the skills and abilities of the company's customers. The classes certainly highlight RPC's products, but, more important, they enhance our customers' ability to function in their own businesses. RPC's commitment to each operator's success helps build loyalty to RPC's products, promotes product sales, and ensures the products' best performance.

Technical Consultants

Not all customers will be able to attend our tech school classes. To further educate the users of RPC's products, the company deploys technical consultants into its territories to work with customers on site.

The technical consultants' main focus is the versatility and quality of RPC products. Through them, our customers learn more about food preparation and can better present their products professionally. The technical consultant will work with operators on menu analysis and food costing as well as such skills as proofing and baking,

decorating, product presentation, and merchandising. Many RPC technical consultants have operator experience, which helps to establish their credibility and further enables them to help customers learn.

Training Videos

RPC has produced training videos for many of its product lines and it continues to develop more. The main purpose of each video is to show the benefits and advantages of the product, to promote appropriate product handling, and to demonstrate multiple variations of the product for the menu. Each video contains a suggested hands-on approach supported by the following material: an instructor's guide, a materials checklist, attendance sheet, menu tips, recipe slicks (notes on preparing a variation to the product), and an evaluation summary.

Each of these handouts fits neatly in the video case, and is printed such that enlarging them 200 percent on a photocopy machine will produce an 8-1/2" x 11" handout. The videos can be shown either by a technical consultant or by an operator who has been through a demonstration, or who has attended our tech school.

Rich Products/Canisius College Institute

Canisius College is a Buffalo-based college that has developed a new curriculum of restaurant and hotel management in cooperation with the Statler Foundation. The college has included in its curriculum a strong focus on marketing and it requires students to spend a year abroad studying to build international management techniques.

In an effort to introduce and promote the new school, Canisius College has joined in partnership with Rich Products to create the Rich/Canisius Institute. The institute will provide two- to three-day seminars to those involved in the operations for food service, hospitality, or related businesses. The seminars are designed to target middle management up through directors and multi-unit supervisors.

The institute will provide a further opportunity for Rich Products to associate its name with learning opportunities. The institute will be an additional forum for educating and supporting customers of Rich Products while enhancing the overall food service field. The institute will also provide an additional avenue for RPC to train its own associates.

Community

Rich Products has obvious business reasons for extending its learning philosophy to its customers. RPC, however, extends this commitment beyond its traditional business boundaries. The company is involved in a not-for-profit educational agency, a school partnership program, an internship program, and a day care center/preschool. It also provides opportunities for its associates to speak at outside functions.

Western New York United Against Drug and Alcohol Abuse is a community-based prevention agency dedicated to reducing the personal tragedy and social cost of alcohol and other drug abuse by increasing awareness, educating, and mobilizing area residents to participate actively in proven strategies to prevent substance abuse. Bob Rich, Jr., and Mindy Rich co-chair this agency. Their commitment of time is complemented by the provision of other Rich Products resources. RPC provides meeting rooms for board meetings, associates volunteer at events, and even the outside of RPC's world headquarters building in Buffalo is "dressed" in an enormous red ribbon for Red Ribbon Week—a national campaign against drug and alcohol abuse. Perhaps most significantly to the agency, Rich Products has provided office space to Western New York United virtually rent free, and has provided use of company resources for such services as legal help and insurance advice.

Certainly, Western New York United has other business supporters, but none as active and visible as Rich Products. It is interesting to note that while RPC supports many organizations, its primary efforts go to an organization focusing on learning and awareness. This highlights, again, RPC's commitment to a learning environment—even beyond the business.

Rich Products also participates in a school partnership program with Community School 77, which is located in the neighborhood of Rich Products' world headquarters. RPC's school partnership, themed "Together Today for Tomorrow," began in 1993. Both the school and RPC look for opportunities to enhance students' learning experience in order to create lifelong learners. In one case, RPC supplied a variety of rewards that provided the impetus for the school staff to develop a recognition program for exemplary behavior.

In another special sponsorship, Rich Products arranged for Thurman Thomas Day. Because Thurman Thomas is the star running back of the four-time AFC champion Buffalo Bills, children were thrilled to hear his motivational message of setting goals and staying in school. In the spirit of partnership, the children also performed for Thurman Thomas, building their sense of self-esteem and worth.

These events, as well as a quasi mentorship program, are only a few of the many large and small ways that Rich Products has been and will continue to be supportive of the learning environment of the neighborhood children.

RPC sponsors a summer internship program to extend a learning opportunity to college students. Each student is placed in a department and works on a specific project. The student has an opportunity to learn about the work environment in a field in which they have an interest. It is not unusual for a very positive relationship to be built between the intern and the department. Many interns return for a second learning experience.

Rich's Mother and Child Center is an on-site day care and preschool for the children of Rich's Associates. One of only 13 accredited centers in western New York, the center focuses on learning and development of enrolled children. This philosophy demonstrates again RPC's commitment to learning, this time extended to the youngest in the community.

RPC associates have participated in formal and informal speakers' bureaus. RPC encourages and supports extending the learning philosophy beyond the confines of the office. Educational institutions, professional organizations, and community organizations have sponsored events featuring RPC associates as guest speakers. Topics range from technical expertise areas such as international human resources, logistics, and food service marketing, to more general topics, such as leadership, delegation, or team building. RPC associates have also led strategic-planning sessions for other organizations in need of such process facilitation.

Moving into the Future

Rich Products has learned much in its efforts to support the learning philosophy. As improvement opportunities are identified, Rich Products is chartering cross-functional teams to identify new processes. In some cases, the teams themselves take over a process that once flowed from department to department. When opening a new facility, the company sees the benefit of investing heavily in new state-of-the-art technology that allows for improved communications and understanding of the business processes. Clearly, all levels of the company, from the leadership to the individual associate, have been impacted by the organizational commitment to learning. Decisions connect more closely to business needs and individuals are better prepared than ever to do their jobs. The company continually creates new structures to support the changes. There is no end in sight. Everyone at Rich Products is well aware that continued learning is crucial to the company's future growth and prosperity.

Appendix A
Mission: World Class—Our Philosophy Statement

Our Mission
Rich Products Corporation is a dynamic growth-oriented company on a World Class Mission to set new standards of excellence in customer satisfaction and achieve new levels of competitive success in every category of business in which we operate.

Our Strategy
We will achieve our World Class Mission by working together as a team in a total quality effort to:

Impress Our Customers
Provide exceptional service to our external and internal customers the first time and every time.

Improve, Improve, Improve!
Continuously improve the quality and value of the goods we produce and the services we provide.

Empower People
Unleash the talents of all our Associates by creating an environment that is safe, that recognizes and rewards their achievements, and encourages their participation and growth.

Work Smarter
Drive out all waste of time, effort, and material—all the barriers and extra steps that keep us from doing our jobs right.

Do the Right Thing
Maintain the highest standards of integrity and ethical conduct and behave as good citizens in our communities.

Appendix B
Rich Products Corporation Learning and Development Philosophy

Mission

Rich Products Corporation develops the knowledge, skills, and leadership capabilities of its Associates through a dynamic learning environment which drives the continued achievement of unparalleled customer satisfaction and the organization's global business strategies.

Strategy

We will accomplish this mission by:

● Providing learning opportunities and resources for personal and team growth and development.

● Recognizing the shared responsibility between the individual and Rich's. Individual associates are ultimately responsible for initiating and managing their own development. Rich's will be a partner in this journey.

● Emphasizing that change is inevitable. Associates must be willing and able to accept change. Associates who do not embrace learning opportunities will be unable to meet the organization's performance expectations.

● Developing technical skills training to support and increase our competitive edge.

● Developing and aligning Associates' skills and knowledge with business needs.

● Providing mentoring and career development programs which add value to the Associate's and the organization's growth.

● Assessing the talents and development needs of Associates and the Company to fulfill the future leadership positions within Rich Products Corporation.

10

The Bank of Montreal Institute For Learning

By Diane Blair

The Bank of Montreal

The Bank of Montreal, founded in 1817, is Canada's oldest bank and one of the largest in North America. Since 1990, The Bank of Montreal has experienced record earnings, an annualized return on investment of 14.3 percent, and substantial worldwide growth. During this time, the bank also acquired two premier investment firms—Nesbitt Thomson and Burns Fry—and created what is currently Canada's largest investment house, Nesbitt Burns. In 1994, the bank became the first Canadian bank to be listed on the New York Stock Exchange. On May 20 of that year the Bank's $40 million state-of-the-art Institute for Learning (Canada's first dedicated conference center) was opened by Prime Minister Jean Chretien. For the fiscal year ending October 31, 1995, net income for the bank was $986 million, up 20 percent from the same period in 1994.

Chairman and Chief Executive Officer Matthew W. Barrett oversees more than U.S. $152 billion in assets and about 33,000 employees. As with many companies moving toward globalization, approximately 50 percent of the bank's income comes from sources outside of Canada.

Why an Institute For Learning?

The Institute For Learning (IFL) opened for business in January 1994. Its purpose: to change the culture of Canada's oldest bank.

Founded in 1817, the Bank of Montreal (or BMO, pronounced "Bee-mo") is one of the five behemoth financial institutions that have made up Canadian banking for well over a century. Banking in Canada has traditionally been synonymous with one thing: lending. BMO's reputation: big and stable, but slow moving and impersonal. In 1987, BMO's current chairman, Matthew Barrett, became the youngest president in the bank's 170-year history. He inherited an organization that was, like its cohorts, a sleeping giant awakening in a new era.

Waves of Change

It could be argued that BMO had been in a quiet decline since the 1930s. With the explosion of the computer age the bank was at risk of developing into something of a dinosaur. During the late 1970s and early 1980s the organization underwent a much needed but radical reengineering. By 1987, the bank's internal processes and structures had undergone a successful "modernization." The change was impressive and effective, but did not come without cost. The approach used to bring about such radical change was a traditional, heavy-handed one.

The bank's culture was in a fragile state—characterized by resistance and low morale. Furthermore, some of the new ways of doing business, particularly those imposed on the personal and small business banking divisions, were severely straining relations with the bank's core customers.

In 1989, the waves of change facing BMO became a tidal force as the Canadian banking industry was transformed overnight. Specifically, the Canadian Bank Act, which limited banks to "banking", was deregulated. This allowed any financial institution to engage in any facet of the financial services industry—from serving as a trust company, to managing mutual funds, to stock brokering, to insurance. This shift has had a profound effect on the Bank of Montreal in terms of what institutions comprise the bank's major competitors and of the expectations of "bank" customers.

In addition, as the world economy becomes more globalized and trade barriers continue to crumble, large foreign investors in Europe, Asia, and the U.S. are turning their sights on the Canadian market. Ten years ago, Canada's big five banks were among the 50 largest in the world. Today, not one Canadian bank has this status; not because the banks have shrunk, but rather because the virtual explosion of international mergers has created a new breed of "superbank". These new banks benefit from obvious economies of scale when doing business. In addition, due to their strength and magnitude, they are redefining the banking industry. These superbanks have the capacity to create increasingly sophisticated financial products—in house, at greater speed and lower cost than ever before.

For Matt Barrett, this is the new playing field for which BMO's current business strategy has been crafted and on which BMO must continually learn how to compete to sustain a competitive advantage.

BMO's Vision

From the start, Barrett's approach to revitalizing the Bank of Montreal was differ-ent. He toured the organization from one end to the other, asking employees at all levels about their thoughts on banking, the future of banking, and their roles within this new future. In April 1990, the bank unveiled its new strategy, Vision 2002. This vision is about becoming a "full service North American bank"—a bank that can compete in the global marketplace by achieving and sustaining a distinctive competitive advantage with its customers. At the core of this vision is one prime objective: to serve the four groups of people who are the bank's stakeholders: (1) shareholders, (2) employees, (3) customers, and (4) people who live and work in the communities the bank serves.

The fundamental belief underlying this vision is the strategy that the only sustainable competitive advantage is our *human capital*. "Without our employees," says Matt Barrett, ". . . there would be no customers." Furthermore, as the rate of change accelerates, we can no longer consider new technology and other real assets a distinctive competitive advantage as these things can now be copied, replaced, or acquired with ease.

For BMO, the value of human capital involves more than the quality of training or the ability of a workforce to perform skills for today's needs. It is also the capacity of the organization to cultivate human potential and leverage it. That is, to continually learn and constantly transform the organization to best leverage new opportunities and create new futures. Leveraging the bank's human capital involves establishing an organizational culture that engages employees' energy, ideas, and experience, and that invites creativity and innovation.

Over the last five years, the Bank of Montreal has been a real success story. It has achieved record annual profits each year and has outperformed Canadian competitors in terms of return on equity. Furthermore, there's a new verve about it. At one time, it was not uncommon for BMO employees to be a little evasive when asked where they worked. Now, it's a badge of distinction! Employees feel proud about what the bank represents and about the new energy, enthusiasm, and commitment they are contributing to achieving the bank's vision.

TAKING RISKS

. . . the riskiest thing is risk aversion. You've got to do something unless you want to end up characterized as a competent steward who just kept order in the organization. But keeping order is easy—you don't become CEO unless you know how to run the place—what you really get paid for is the transformation of the organization, the repositioning of it, the catching of the big trends. Because the global environment isn't stable, nothing is stable, and there have been a lot of very large companies that were household names that got into serious trouble because they missed the waves.—Matt Barrett, CEO, Bank of Montreal

Today's BMO consists of four lines of business: (1) Canada's largest investment house, (2) Canada's second-largest personal and commercial bank, (3) a global corporate financial institution, and (4) Harris Bank (including recently acquired Suburban Bank) in the United States. Change has been dramatic in the last decade, as BMO had grown from 22,000 to approximately 34,000 employees and now spans three continents and some 2,500 work locations. Growth and change for the bank have become part of everyday business.

The Institute for Learning

The Institute For Learning is a critical part of the bank's strategy for future success. It is a $40 million (Canadian funds) investment in ongoing organizational renewal. It reflects the commitment of Matt Barrett and the Bank "to create an organization that can achieve and sustain competitive advantage in a world that is rapidly, radically, and continuously changing . . . an or-

ganization capable of constantly learning and transforming itself . . . a learning organization."

IFL's Offer to the Bank of Montreal

The Institute for Learning is a natural extension of what Canada's *Maclean's Magazine* dubbed, "The Bank's New Weapon—Being Nice!" (July, 1990) The new approach is really nothing more than the old adage "The customer is always right." As Matt Barrett recounts: "I was struck all my life by how pompous bankers are. They seem to love being seen as imperial and aloof. . . . [T]hat's dangerous for banking and not good for business." The bank surveyed customers about all the things people were saying about banks—in summary, that they were "remote, insensitive, mean-spirited, and black-hearted." Then BMO built a strategy based on the assumption these customers were *right* and the bank needed to change its image. IFL is a part of the resulting strategy for change.

Becoming a Learning Organization

The bank's new business strategy is based on two major premises:

1. Organizations that learn faster and better will meet the needs of customers faster and better.

2. The goal is not only to compete now, but to prevail in the future.

IFL's mission is to help the bank cultivate an organization of excellent learners by instilling a spirit of lifelong learning and organizational renewal.

INSTITUTE FOR LEARNING: CORE PURPOSE

To serve as partners in achieving and sustaining exceptional performance by inspiring and leading the creation of a learning culture where all employees achieve personal and professional excellence and we are recognized by our customers as truly distinctive.

The IFL's offer to BMO is best articulated in the Institute for Learning's Charter:

> IFL is the nexus for inspiring lifelong learning and exceptional performance within the Bank of Montreal. The goal of IFL is to assist the bank and its business units to achieve their strategic goals and cultural aims:
>
> 1. By developing requisite individual and organizational competencies.
>
> 2. By promoting and facilitating organizational renewal.
>
> We choose to be judged on our contribution to PERFORMANCE. The bank's customers will recognize and value the difference they see in the bank's staff.
>
> To deliver we will become pre-eminent in the field of adult learning through the development, design, and delivery of superior learning experiences.

How does the IFL go about changing the culture of Bank of Montreal? How does it create a Learning Organization? IFL plays two key roles to help the Bank achieve its vision by functioning as (1) a world-class learning institution and (2) a nexus for learning.

World Class Learning Institution

The main campus for the Bank of Montreal's Institute For Learning is a spectacular residential facility north of Toronto, Ontario. Details about the building and its design are provided in the sidebar titled "IFL: An Award-Winning Design."

While the building itself symbolizes the value the organization places on continuous learning and growth, becoming a "world class learning institution" means more than bricks and mortar. It means becoming a "professional service firm;" that is, multi-faceted and dedicated to helping clients achieve exceptional performance. To accomplish this goal, IFL's strategy is to offer not only traditional training courses on core banking skills, but comprehensive, well-integrated performance solutions.

In terms of targets, IFL has already achieved its 1997 goal of providing five training days per employee per year. That's twice the national average in Canada and more than double BMO's pre-institute targets. Currently, however only 28 percent of training actually occurs at the Institute For Learning in Scarborough. The other 72 percent of training takes place at or near the workplace. This is part of IFL's commitment to providing just-in-time training (i.e., delivering the right skills and knowledge, at the right time and in the right place). Some of this training occurs at field campuses in Calgary, Montreal, and Chicago, but more and more frequently, this type of learning

IFL: An Award-Winning Design

Everyone learns in different ways. The Institute for Learning offers a wide variety of learning opportunities and room for experimentation and growth. In addition to 12 large classrooms with the best of learning technology, the center offers a high-tech business information center, 20 break-out rooms and 8 role-play rooms outfitted with audiovisual equipment ready for use. Wide open spaces, natural light, and a wellness center help to inspire energy, enthusiasm, and imagination for the possibilities we can accomplish.

Learning takes place not only between teacher and student, but between colleagues: student to student, and student to teacher. IFL was designed to allow employees from all regions and levels within the bank to get together, exchange ideas and experiences, and learn from each other informally. As a 150-room residential center, cloistered hallways punctuated with windowed alcoves, and college-style dining room, IFL provides every opportunity for the kind of spontaneous, informal conversations that can lead to meaningful learning and new ideas.

is being done closer to work. That is, via self-study or small-group learning at the workplace or, where possible, embedded directly in the tools and practices of daily work

At first glance, a contradiction appears to exist here. Why create a sophisticated learning center and then develop a strategy to shift learning to the workplace?

If we believe that the bank's success lies in the ability of its people to learn, IFL's responsibility is to recognize that learning occurs everywhere and to create comprehensive performance solutions that best leverage each learning opportunity. IFL's strategy can be summarized as follows:

Exceptional Performance =
Skills & Knowledge +
Environment & Tools + Management

Exceptional performance results best from aligning resources with opportunities. IFL is a bankwide resource center where performance solutions that best lead to exceptional performance can be created, designed, developed, and, when appropriate, delivered.

The Organization

The key to IFL's success as a professional service firm, is a learning-centered approach, not a training-centered approach.

IFL is organized around two considerations:

● Who are the learners?

● What centers of competence are needed to create performance solutions?

IFL currently has seven major client groups: each of the bank's four lines of business; two internal service groups—operations and corporate services; and the bank as a whole, through its corporate management committee. IFL services these clients through ad hoc professional service teams comprised of three centers of competence:

● **Client relationship management**—Relationship managers work directly with each major client group; they understand

their client needs and opportunities, and align them with IFL resources.

● **Subject matter expertise**—Faculty address what learning will occur; they understand the specific skill and knowledge requirements of each line of business.

● **Domains of learning**—Learning managers and technicians address *how* learning will occur; they understand how to best leverage the methods and technologies of learning and the environment in which learning will take place.

The ways in which these professional service teams work together is dynamic: as the needs of our clients evolve, so does IFL's role in servicing these needs.

IFL's Evolving Role

Before IFL, BMO used to have a traditional training department. Its role was that of "order taker." That is, clients put in orders for training and the training department found or created the courses to fill these orders. There was little interaction regarding needs and desired outcomes, and little consideration of whether the training intervention fit both needs and possible opportunities. Now, through its centers of competence, IFL can work with its clients as partners, designing *what* and *how* learning is best achieved.

Through its relationship managers, IFL can help clients articulate their training needs and seize opportunities. Relationship managers are seasoned professionals with considerable experience in the line of business they support through BMO. With a clear understanding of where the client is going, and the ability to recognize opportunities and align them with the most appropriate resources and services, relationship managers can impact learning and performance at a more powerful, strategic level. Also, by working in close association with each other, the relationship management team can now capture strategic learning opportunities between the bank's differing lines of business.

Subject matter expertise is centered around three faculties. Each faculty broadly represents one of the key success factors for the bank: (1) leadership and change, (2) technology and change, and (3) core banking skills (relationship selling and lending/finance). Courses can be designed and delivered at the institute from a single faculty member working with a specific client to fill a specific performance gap. Increasingly, though, faculty are building a more strategic model, where courses are linked and offer learners a continuum of learning. Further, faculties now work together to design courses that recognize the diversity of learning experiences involved in enhancing performance.

Also, IFL has developed three centers of competence representing each of the environments, or *domains*, in which learning takes place: (1) campus learning, (2) distance learning, and (3) embedded learning (or performance support). Each center brings a specific technical expertise to the design of a learning intervention. This support allows the IFL to ensure that each learning opportunity is best leveraged. However, and most important, these domains of learning also serve as centers for the research, experimentation, and new development that allow IFL to continually evolve with our clients and generate new learning environments and tools that are state of the art.

In summary, being a professional service firm at the Institute for Learning means providing well-integrated, whole system, performance solutions. We have come to recognize several important factors in achieving this:

● establishing a well-informed relationship with all clients,

● engaging IFL early in a business planning process,

● developing a thorough understanding of each client's specific performance goals and gaps,

● engaging appropriate expertise,

● recognizing and realizing opportunities to leverage learning, and

● creating comprehensive learning solutions that take best advantage of all available learning environments (dedicated, at-work, in-work) methods and technologies (e.g., classroom, textbook, computer-based, multimedia, interactive small groups, mentoring, coaching, performance assessments and compensation plans.)

Delivery of Learning

IFL's role in the delivery of learning support takes many forms: direct program delivery, brokering for appropriate external vendors, or supporting clients to allow them to deliver their own learning solutions. Client needs, time constraints, and the nature of the learning required are key factors in the selection of a method of delivery.

● **Direct program delivery**–IFL produces an annual catalog of courseware targeted both to individual learners (as a personal development resource) and managers (as a tool for staff development). Classroom learning is delivered both at the Institute for Learning and in the field. The selection of courses to be held at IFL is based predominantly on the extent to which the program allows participants to take advantage of the institute's rich learning environment beyond the classroom. Courses are usually delivered by IFL faculty or, in some circumstances, by an external vendor. (For more details, see the section titled IFL: A Nexus for Learning.)

● Brokering vendors–IFL has developed a wide network of external vendors representing a broad range of professions and fields of expertise. External vendors are used in both a consulting capacity and for course delivery where appropriate. IFL may broker an external vendor to serve two important functions:

(1) *Decrease fixed cost if the need is generic.* When the training is not specific to BMO, or if the demand is either very low or highly variable, or the technology involved has a "short shelf life" and requires frequent upgrading to facilitate, these programs can be purchased from a vendor. (Basic computer skills training is an example.)

(2) *Obtain access to a highly current or specialized field of expertise.* When the level of expertise required cannot be sustained

in house by the institute, or would involve a prohibitively large amount of time and/or cost to produce, a field expert may be retained to design a custom program. (Examples include developing competence in new or emerging technologies, such as derivatives.)

• **Client delivery**—Most of the more than 50,000 days of training delivered by the Institute for Learning in 1995 were delivered at a distance or through performance support tools. Most of the learning in these domains is specifically designed to be self-directed. Some of this learning is also designed for small group experiences or one-on-one learning with a coach. In any case, all of this learning is delivered in the absence of IFL staff. In this situation, IFL's role is to work with the client in creating a learner-centered strategy that considers not only the learning tools themselves, but also things such how to best introduce these tools, how to develop coaches, how to manage performance, and how to align personnel policies with the learning. (See the sections titled Critical Success Factors and Learning for Success.)

The key to designing, developing, and delivering a learning-centered approach is the capacity of IFL's relationship managers, faculty, and learning managers to work together as a professional service team.

IFL: A Nexus for Learning

The charter for IFL states, "We choose to be judged by our contribution to performance." So far, we have discussed the institute in terms of its ability to recognize performance gaps and create performance solutions. For Matt Barrett, this is only part of the picture. He envisioned a second role for IFL that would make it:

A nexus for learning—a place not only for training skills and knowledge but exchanging ideas and creating futures. At any given time, a cross section of the bank would be there and able to communicate freely, discuss common concerns without fear, and make change happen!

Preparing for the Future

IFL's contribution to performance is determined not only by its ability to provide learning support for the future that we can predict, but also, the future *beyond* that, the "unknowable" future! To elaborate, most corporate training is designed to help people acquire the skills and knowledge they need to do their current job, or, possibly, a job we expect them to do soon. However, the shelf life of these jobs is getting shorter and shorter.

Looking further down the road, we see a point at which we can no longer predict our needs, where the future becomes "unknowable". While this has always been the case if one looked far enough, as the rate of change accelerates, the "unknowable horizon" gets nearer and nearer. As a result, the opportunities to simply forecast needs and plan training are reduced.

Thus, IFL's second and greater challenge involves determining how to prepare our people to succeed in the future even when we don't know where its going! Creating a nexus for learning at IFL's main campus is one way IFL can address this challenge.

By *nexus* we mean a central hub for learning—not just formal learning, but informal and serendipitous learning. If the Institute for Learning is to help prepare for the "unknowable" future, it must do more than create *opportunities for learning;* it must also develop the *capacity for learning* individually, in groups, and as a whole organization.

Recognizing that what we believe, value, and know determines the way we conduct our lives and our work, we must consider how we know what we know. According to Jim Rush, senior vice president and director of IFL, a fundamental premise of a nexus for learning is that "[m]uch of what we do as adult learners is not the result of learning that happened in a classroom, rather, we know what we know because we chose to learn it at a point in time when it was important to us and in a way that was most meaningful to us." Thus, the learning experiences that take place at the IFL are designed both for *learning* and *learning how people learn.*

One of the ways the IFL accomplishes this is by broadening the way we think about the IFL and IFL learning experiences. As the BMO's nexus for learning, IFL has been defined in terms of four "places" or metaphors for learning:

- the "marketplace," where the whole community can gather and share resources,
- the "practice field," where new ideas can be tested in a safe environment,
- the "workstation," where bank-wide problems can be addressed through active learning, and ultimately
- the "water cooler," where employees from all areas and levels of the bank can get together and share ideas and experiences that will create the future of the bank.

The impact of thinking about the IFL in this way is evident both in the design of some IFL courseware and in the creation of other unique learning experiences at the institute.

Critical Success Factors

A model learning organization. Broadly speaking, one of the most critical factors to success for IFL is its ability to become a "model learning organization," one that IFL employees live every day and that IFL's clients and guests experience first hand when they take a course or work with our staff. Some of the qualities IFL seeks in becoming a model learning organization include:

(A) *Recognizing that learning occurs everywhere and with all employees.* The Institute for Learning is involved not only in providing training but building comprehensive, integrated performance solutions, involving on-campus, at-work, and in-work learning support. Further, IFL is for *all* BMO employees, not just management.

(B) *Identifying opportunities across functions and between pillars and engaging appropriate expertise.* The relationship managers for each of IFL's client groups also work together as a team to identify learning opportunities between their clients. Relationship managers can develop learning interventions to best meet these opportunities by engaging a professional service team with the centers of competence (subject matter and learning approach), and/or external vendors appropriate for the situation.

(C) *Maintaining a state of constant transition.* The nature of the projects IFL undertakes, and the resulting roles, responsibilities, and approaches used, constantly change and evolve to best meet customer needs and new opportunities.

(D) *Establishing a high capacity for learning, creativity, and innovation.* At any one time, the community of learners visiting the Institute for Learning represents a microcosm of the bank itself. Through a rich environment for learning informally and serendipitously, IFL provides an excellent opportunity to leverage this microcosm. Furthermore, IFL is becoming recognized as the BMO's center of research and experimentation around learning—a place to work on problems and create innovative solutions.

(E) *Recognizing learning culture as part of a performance culture.* For IFL, our success in supporting learning is not only about "days of training" it's about impacting learning capacity and work practices. Likewise, the effectiveness of an IFL learning intervention is not only a measure of skills and knowledge acquired, it is a measure of individual capacity for learning and the design of tools and work practices that promote continuous learning and improved performance. IFL is committed to researching and developing new ways to assess learning in terms of changes in thinking, behavior, and practice in the workplace.

Three other factors are also critical to IFL's success: balancing short- and long-term thinking, building informed relationships, and effective program design and delivery.

Short- and long-term thinking. Success for IFL is serving the needs of our clients not only for the present and knowable future but, also, for the unknowable future. If we focus only on delivering excellent training programs to fill perceived gaps, we may succeed in developing a workforce that can perform for every *foreseeable* situation, but not for the *unforeseeable.* Conversely, by focusing solely on creating better lifelong learners, we may let our clients down in terms of preparing employees to compete successfully for the present.

Fiscal responsibility is a very powerful driving force in banking. It plays a paramount role in the strategic planning of IFL's clients and a critical one in serving the needs of the bank's shareholders. We do not have the luxury of pursuing long-term sustainability at the expense of short-term performance. At the same time, as competitive forces accelerate the rate of change, we cannot afford to be short sighted! IFL's success depends on our ability to consider goals in both what we do and how we do it.

Relationship building. The key to creating the right mix of what and how learning takes place lies in the relationships IFL builds with its clients. The foundation for this relationship is dialogue. Through dialogue, rather than monologue, both the client and IFL are better informed, better able to recognize opportunities, and better able to make effective decisions about how to best leverage each learning opportunity.

Program design and delivery. For the IFL, the design and delivery of a successful program means meeting the essential business needs of our clients and adding real value. As previously discussed, the factor that is most critical to meeting needs is relationship building. The two factors most critical in adding real value are found in the roles first envisioned for IFL by Matt Barrett. First, by becoming a world-class learning institution—where a learning culture is developed by cultivating the individual learner's capacity to learn how to learn while learning. Second, by taking advantage of IFL as a nexus for learning where serendipity can strike, problems are shared and resolved, and new futures are created.

Some examples of value-added programs at the Institute for Learning include the following:

Integrated performance solutions through courseware. IFL's "classroom" courseware has evolved in many ways. Rather than being discrete, single-subject-area designs, they tend to integrate a number of learning support vehicles to best support the client's desired performance outcomes. One way this has occurred is by integrating different faculty disciplines. One example is sales and leadership, using a variety of learning approaches that are both practical and theoretical.

A number of other IFL courses are evolving by integrating different levels of learning. That is, as clients begin to value developing not only immediate skills but a capacity for life-long learning, courses have begun to integrate a broad range of more experiential approaches to learning that help learners recognize *what they learned while they were learning.* At the IFL, this is referred to as *meta learning.* One of the ways IFL achieves meta learning is through adventure-based learning. The IFL now has an on-site, outdoor "challenge course" where facilitators can work with groups to develop their ability to learn from their own experience, in the moment.

Mentorships. Mentoring is a natural extension of IFL's commitment to creating courseware that is part of an integrated performance solution, aligned with the client's specific needs. IFL mentors work directly with learners when they leave the institute to help them integrate classroom learning into everyday work practices.

Open forums. IFL recently brought together 150 employees from all levels and areas of BMO for an open forum about productivity. Productivity Forum '95 was created specifically to establish the nexus for learning at IFL. That is, the forum was designed to offer the kind of rich learning environment where informal learning is the norm—and serendipity may strike at any time! To achieve this, the open forum was completely void of what normally constitutes formal learning. There were no lectures, no speeches, no presentations, no predetermined agenda and no imposed processes or action plans. The open forum served as the ultimate "watercooler." Furthermore, unlike other meetings, participants were not selected or assigned. The invitation to attend was open to those who chose to come because they have an interest or concern about the topic (productivity at BMO) and a desire to do something about it. During the forum, participants identified important issues, created their own agenda, convened their own sessions, generated their own book of proceedings, and, in the process, developed a new level of understanding about common issues and a new way of thinking about resolving problems through collective learning.

Learning for Success. As a comprehensive, self-directed learning system, Learning for Success (LFS) takes the notion of providing an integrated performance solution to new heights. LFS was designed to help branch banking achieve a critical strategic objective: to transform its workforce from a transactional culture into a more dynamic, relationship/sales culture. The first LFS program targets first-line employees; the second, first-line managers. LFS is a series of learning modules that incorporate product and systems knowledge, technical competence, and sales skills with personal effectiveness, team building, leadership development, and learning how to learn. While LFS is predominantly a distance-learning program, it also takes advantage of a broad spectrum of at-work, in-work and on-campus learning approaches, including:

- a set of pocket-book-size self-study modules that learners can use at work or take home,
- an on-line help program that can be accessed when the time is right—either when help is needed in the middle of a task, or when things are quiet and there's an opportunity to take some time to explore and discover,
- a set of small-group learning modules that work in the staff room or local learning center, usually with a peer or manager as coach, and
- some dedicated classroom-learning time at the IFL, focusing on developing new leadership skills and learning and sharing ideas with colleagues from all across the bank.

As an integrated performance solution, Learning for Success also incorporates other important learning support opportunities. These include workplace policies and practices, human resource management practices, performance reviews, and compensation plans.

The Institute for Learning is also developing a new Learning for Success CD-ROM that integrates personal effectiveness and the fundamentals of relationship selling. The compact disc can be used for self-study or as part of a small-group learning experience at one of the bank's community learning centers.

Electronic classroom and C-100. Commercial Lending 100 is the first in a series of intense accreditation courses to become a commercial lender. Generally viewed as a highly technical skills-based course, C-100 has traditionally been a two-week, residential, lecture and assignment, "killer" course. Targeting account managers and aspiring account managers all across the bank, the course is considered effective at ensuring that learners gain a uniform set of skills and knowledge. While it is a successful, well-established and necessary course, C-100 has sometimes been criticized because of the high cost involved in terms of travel, accommodations, and lost person-power for the two weeks during which an employee takes the course.

To address some of these challenges, the IFL piloted its first electronic C-100 course. Twenty-five account managers, in 14 bank locations in Canada, the United States, and Japan, could attend class without leaving their office or home. Unlike a self-study course, learners could communicate on-line with their facilitator at the IFL and with their classmates. Assignments were also delivered and returned on-line. Another feature of this integrated learning system is the class project, based on "real work" in the learner's own locale. By grounding the learning in "real work," the learner not only develops practical skills and knowledge but a unique network of learning and working colleagues in the field. Also, local area managers have the opportunity to become personal coaches, providing another rich dimension of practical learning through their years of experience.

Institute for Small Business. The Institute for Small Business is an institute within the Institute for Learning. It is a center for research supporting the emerging needs of small businesses in Canada, which is an important priority for the Bank of Montreal. A variety of research projects in partnership with Canadian university management programs, the private sector, and government are all designed to yield new understandings about nonfinancial factors that can contribute in significant ways to success in small business.

While each of the critical success factors described in this chapter are of great importance to IFL's success, it is of greater importance to recognize that in the dynamic of a learning organization, these factors represent only the current chapter in an ongoing story!

Looking Toward the Future

As a "nexus for learning", the IFL itself has clearly laid claim to a belief that, ultimately, successfully preparing for the future is not only about predicting that future, it's about managing the "unknowable" by developing the capacity to continually learn and transform.

At the horizon where the unknowable begins to take shape, there are a few important assumptions about the future of learning for IFL in planning to meet the needs of its clients. Future learning can take a variety of forms:

Systematic. Learning interventions will no longer be considered as discrete events, but rather, as part of a continuous stream or system of learning.

Strategic. The development of a business strategy and a learning strategy will occur as one seamless strategic approach—such that learning interventions are directly linked to essential business needs.

Timely and customized. Training de-

MANAGING THE TRADE-OFF:

Eliminating the cost of a dedicated, residential learning course benefits the customer if that dedicated learning experience is not providing value. However, this is not always the case. In a dedicated learning environment, people can observe, interpret, and learn. Learning comes not only from one's own successes and failures, but from the experiences of others. A dedicated learning environment is an opportunity for focused learning, without the distraction of other work pressures. This is a safe environment to try new things without fear of failure. In fact, it is in testing one's self beyond what can be accomplished at work—even to the point of failure—that real learning occurs. This kind of learning opportunity multiplies in the company of others.

Sometimes, a combination of distance, dedicated, and classroom learning best accomplishes the right learning, at the right time, and in the right place. While this notion is not novel, it has not traditionally been an interactive process. In other words, more typically instructors may give self-study assignments purely as pre-classroom preparation, or for post-course practice. By considering the electronic classroom as an extension of the on-campus classroom, IFL offers its clients the best of both worlds. On the one hand, learners achieve not only a common standard of practice and base of field experience. They also begin to interact with colleagues before coming to the IFL. On the other hand, their time at the institute can then be much richer, as well as briefer. In addition, when these learners return to the workplace, their capacity for learning at a distance has been enhanced, increasing the likelihood of on-going learning.

partments have traditionally developed competencies to deliver mass training. The training provided is usually fairly standardized, has a fairly lengthy course development and refinement period, requires extensive training for course leaders and a delivery horizon of at least one to five years. In a rapidly changing competitive environment, our clients increasingly need solutions that target small groups of people in a more immediate, more focused way. Frequently this involves a delivery horizon of weeks or months, rather than years. Action learning, and our ability to continually create new ways and means to leverage it, will be critical to meeting this challenge.

Experimental. In keeping with our commitment to achieving sustainable competitive advantages over the long term, the Institute for Learning approach to meeting the changing needs of our clients will be one that constantly seeks new opportunities. Experimentation and new research will be a part of every initiative. IFL is now beginning to experiment with new program *theme weeks* designed to enhance the residential experience and to best leverage opportunities for learning beyond the course curriculum.

Partnership oriented. As the electronic information highway expands rapidly, it is increasingly evident that opportunities for meaningful links between business and education, between the public sector and the private sector, are growing and will play a key role in learning in the future. Partnerships provide unique opportunities for experimenting and working together to push the envelope of new learning. IFL is currently involved in a number of partnerships with academia, businesses, and the community. These partnerships focus on both current reality, through practical problem solving, and on creating futures through new research. Developing more and more diverse partnerships will be critical to IFL as we continue to evolve our understanding of learning and ways in which we can positively impact our client's learning and performance.

If we stop for a moment and consider this list in the context of the traditional corporate training paradigm, it speaks volumes about how far the paradigm has shifted. As we prepare our clients for the unknowable future, IFL has redefined its value in terms of performance, and we "choose to be judged by our contribution to that performance." It is the qualities of learning that will be foremost in defining our evolution as true corporate partners in "achieving and sustaining exceptional performance."

11

Evaluation of Corporate Training Programs

By Michael P. Lillis and Jerry M. Newman

BY all accounts, American businesses spend over $50 billion per year on training programs (*Training*, 1995). That is approximately $500 per year for every employee in the country. Is this investment in human resources worthwhile? Unfortunately, we don't know! Evaluation of training program effectiveness is one of the least-well-developed areas of human resources management. Why is this so? Perhaps because we simply do not view training as an investment. Consequently, we do not insist that training ideas compete for investment dollars alongside other investment options (Belcourt & Wright, 1995). If the return on investment (ROI) for training is less than that for other investment options, we would, under a standard financial-planning scenario, choose to finance the more profitable ventures.

The reality of training evaluation is considerably less sophisticated. Frequently, training programs are not evaluated at all. If evaluation does occur, it is often confined to merely asking employees if they liked the training and considered it useful. Is it any wonder, then, that training budgets are among the first cut during economic downturns (Milkovich & Boudreau, 1994)? In the most recent economic downturn (1991) training budgets declined by 5 percent (Training Budgets, 1992). Business leaders simply have too few hard facts to evaluate the effectiveness of training programs. When cutbacks occur, it is hard for money spent on training to stand the test of economic value.

If we are to reverse this process, to begin viewing training dollars as a legitimate investment option with a credible ROI track record, we need to identify ways to evaluate training programs effectively. This chapter looks at the practice of training evaluation today and recommends steps for continued evolution. We cover three main concerns: conceptual issues in evaluating the training process, conceptual issues in evaluating training outcomes, and a review of recent empirical studies evaluating different types of training.

What to Evaluate in Training

One way to determine a program's effectiveness involves determining whether the process under which it was designed was logically carried out according to standard business practices. Were the procedures followed reasonable and defensible? As an alternative, we could focus on the outcomes of the training program. Is there an outcome that can be directly attributed to the program that has value for the organization?

Did employees view the training positively? Did they learn new skills? Did their behavior change for the better in the post-training work setting? Did the training lead to better business results? As Table 1 shows, companies spend time assessing these outcomes.

If training cannot demonstrate value-added qualities, conventional wisdom suggests that it does not matter how well conceived the training-design process was. In addition, we think companies should assess the effectiveness of processes used to design and administer programs. Armed with this information, they can more easily identify processes important to successful outcomes. It is just a short step, then, to provide prescriptive details on how to design training programs that maximize the chances of positive training outcomes. The next two sections cover process and outcome evaluations.

Evaluating the training process is, at best, subjective. But any effective program should consider the elements that follow.

Identifying Training Content

External forces. Forces outside the organization sometimes determine selection of training programs. The dramatic increase in use of computers influences the way people perform jobs. Remaining competitive requires increased training in computer skills. One survey lists training in basic computer skills as the most common type of training program, with 93 percent of all companies reporting programs in this area (*Training*, 1995).

Demographics of the workforce may also shape some of our training needs. The aging of the workforce, the rapid rise in numbers of minority and women workers, and the continuing influx of immigrants makes training programs on cultural diversity and understanding differing viewpoints/behaviors high priorities for training.

Organizational analysis. Robert Eaton, president of Chrysler Corporation, likes to talk about the way strategic objectives should cascade down an organization, act-

TABLE 1
Training Evaluation
(survey of 82 organizations)

Measured trainee reactions to program 85%
Measured amount of learning that occurred 50%
Measured whether trainee behavior changed 50%
Measured whether business results
   improved because of training 46%

Source: Training, October 1995 (p.64). Numbers represent average percentage of all courses in an organization's curriculum that are evaluated this way.

ing as a beacon that guides both employee behavior and programs designed to improve employee behavior. This includes the design of training programs (Harp, 1995). Table 2 shows how this process should work. If, for example, we decide that our competitive advantage rests in innovation, we need to find ways to identify and market new products more quickly than our competitors. As different units of the organization define what this means for them in terms of strategic goals, we begin to see the types of behavior that are needed to help achieve innovation goals. Every one of our human resource programs, including training, should focus on promoting innovation. This may well dictate emphasizing a different set of training initiatives than another strategic alternative might warrant.

The organizational analysis should also include evaluation of the corporate culture. Are key people prepared to support the training initiative? Employees may like a training program, learn from it, and develop new behaviors. But if they go back to a culture that is unreceptive or, worse, hostile, new behavior will die for lack of reinforcement. Diversity training programs, for example, have long suffered from this problem. Trainees come back from diversity programs energized to find ways to make diversity work for the company. Sometimes, though, these trainees are "strangers in a strange land." Others in the work unit have not received the same training. No effort is made to develop communications programs that explain the role of training in building a workplace where the value of diversity is recognized. The end result: trainees drift back to the old way of doing things.

Identifying training needs. Does the organization use an effective process to identify training needs? Sometimes, for example, training content is the outcome of a popularity contest. What's hot today determines what's included in training tomorrow. More appropriately, training content should come from one or more of the following sources:

- Interviews or surveys of employees and their managers. Such audits might be combined with the annual budgeting process to both identify training needs and earmark sufficient funds to ensure program completion.

- Review of performance trends as uncovered by the performance appraisal process. If raters report similar kinds of developmental needs across categories of employees, this is one of the most credible sources of data supporting training.

- Post-training test data that show patterns of continuing deficiencies.

- A training committee comprised of representatives from the training department, from other functional areas, and from top management can combine to translate strategic plans into meaningful training agendas.

Prioritizing training needs. Inevitably, the training wish list exceeds the training budget. Part of training evaluation includes setting and following priorities. Typical questions include: (1) Is the program necessary to comply with legal mandates? (2) What is the cost? (3) Are the behaviors targeted for training essential to achieving strategic objectives? Table 3 shows the most common types of current training programs.

Legal landmines. Numerous laws mandate training. For example, the Occupational Safety and Health Act requires training related to workplace hazards. Similarly, federal contractors and subcontractors must, under the Drug Free Workplace Act, provide employees with drug awareness training. Other laws encourage training as an "affirmative defense" should a law suit be filed. For example, companies that do not have training related to sexual harassment prevention will be more vulnerable if a harassment charge is filed. Although training alone isn't a sufficient defense, it is part of the package of evidence employers use to show awareness and attempts to comply with legal mandates.

Course development. Part of the evaluation process also should include a look at course development procedures. Have we established objectives?

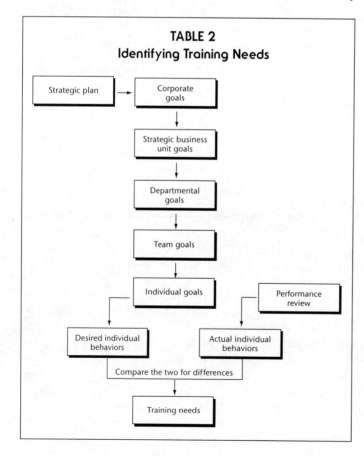

TABLE 2
Identifying Training Needs

Strategic plan → Corporate goals → Strategic business unit goals → Departmental goals → Team goals → Individual goals → Desired individual behaviors

Performance review → Actual individual behaviors

Compare the two for differences → Training needs

TABLE 3
Types of Training Programs

Types of Training	Percentage of Companies Providing
Basic computer skills	93%
Management skills/development	86%
Technical skills	85%
Supervisory skills	85%
Communications skills	85%
Customer relations/services	82%
New methods/procedures	80%
Executive development	75%
Personal growth	71%

Source: *Training*, October, 1995, p.60.

Absent clearly defined objectives, it is hard to determine if training succeeds. For example, a computer training program must specify what types of behavior or knowledge employees should demonstrate after training.

The content of the course also should "map" into both task analyses and performance analyses. If we identify skill/knowledge deficiencies either through analysis of what employees do (task analysis) or how well they do it (performance analysis), there should be clear evidence that this information spurs the direction of course development.

Course scheduling. Something like scheduling may seem a small factor in training success. Any trainer knows, though, that absenteeism problems are a major explanation of program failure. "We're too busy to be trained" is a commonly heard lament. Unless the program has management support and a time schedule that minimizes work disruptions, empty seats may result.

Evaluating the Outcomes of Training

Training evaluation asks the deceptively simple question: "Was there improvement after the training program occurred?" This question begs two further questions: (1) "What is the definition of improvement?" and (2) "Was the improvement caused by the training program and not some other concurrent change in the organization?"

Defining Improvement: The Criterion Question

Most people involved in training agree that four things can be measured to determine whether a training program resulted in improvement. First, we could ask for trainee reactions to the program. If employees like the program, as indicated by postprogram surveys of attitudes, the program is judged a success. The inference here is either that positive attitudes are a desirable goal in and of themselves or, more likely, that positive attitudes will lead to positive bottom-line impacts. Second, employees could be asked to show learning or knowledge gain from the program. Both before and after the program, employees would take a written exam or formally demonstrate on the job some type of knowledge. Again, the inference here is either that knowledge as an end result is good or that knowledge gains will translate into positive bottom-line impacts. Third, a successful training program might be judged by the amount of desired behavior change that occurs. Fourth, it is easy to make the inferential leap that more frequent exhibition of desired behaviors will be reflected in the bottom line. In fact, notice that each successive criterion moves closer to the type of outcome that carries weight with top management. Indeed, Table 1 shows that the least common way to evaluate a training program is to ask directly if improvement occurred in an operating measure (e.g., on-time deliveries, number of accidents) or financial measure (e.g., operating income, return on assets) deemed vital to organization success. Clearly, evidence of financial improvement traced directly to a training program would indeed justify continued training expenditures.

As Table 1 illustrated, fewer than half of all training programs evaluate bottom-line impacts of training. Rather, the most common way to evaluate training involves asking employees about their subjective reactions—a method that is highly difficult to link with the bottom line. This differential popularity can be explained by looking at the second question linked to training evaluation: Was the improvement caused by the training program and not some other concurrent change in the organization?

Identifying the Cause

Organizations today change constantly. New strategic plans, new operating procedures, new capital investments, new employees, new policies and procedures—any new thing makes it difficult to trace the cause of bottom-line changes. Did the new training program lead to fewer customer complaints, or did that occur because we switched to a different overnight carrier with a better on-time delivery record? Did the new safety training program cause the drop in number of our OSHA incident reports, or can we trace improvements to the new VP of operations who constantly reminds all supervisors that *safety comes first!* Sometimes organizations get ambitious and set up control groups that don't receive training, then compare those groups with others that do receive training. If nothing else differs between the controls and the trained groups, we may be able to say that differences are caused by training. But most of the time, other differences exist between the groups as well. This weakens our ability to claim training as the clear cause of success.

This type of confounding is most likely to occur when we want to trace the impact of a training program on some bottom-line measure. As we move down the list of criteria for evaluating training—toward bottom-line measures—progressively more things other than the training can affect results. Each of the first three measures—affective reaction to training, knowledge increments, or behavior change—are individually based (i.e., change occurs in the individual trainee). Hence, if the cause of change is not the training program, other "likely suspects" would be fairly easy to isolate. When we get to bottom-line measures, it is more difficult to trace the causes of change. Literally hundreds of people, processes, and policies could have direct or interactive effects on important corporate goals. Intro-

duction of a training program might be just one of the possible explanations. In part because of these barriers, most training programs focus on trainee reactions, knowledge/skill gains, or behavior-change measures for training effectiveness.

Evaluating Effectiveness

Human resource departments are under increasing pressure to show how investments in training can lead directly to business objectives such as increased revenue and higher productivity. While some training programs might pursue measurement of the company's return on training investment, the effectiveness of training can also be evaluated in terms of reaction, learning, and/or behavioral criteria (Kirkpatrick, 1967). This is especially true for programs targeting "soft-skills" such as problem solving, team building, communication, listening, and stress management (Pine & Tingley, 1993). The lack of consensus about how to measure program effectiveness makes difficult the task of creating programs that would be generalizable across the organzation.

Any review of the training literature must consider training evaluation methodology. In light of the very real constraint on organizations regarding the feasibility of formal experimental designs, many studies cannot provide a rigorously controlled basis of evaluation. This threat to validity further limits our ability to draw inferences from existing research. In a recent review, Goldstein (1991) pointed to the anecdotal nature of the literature, calling into question the usefulness of many evaluation efforts. Certainly, to minimize concerns about the utility of research and to facilitate efforts at comparison across studies, high-quality evaluation research is needed.

Much research in corporate training focuses on the effectiveness of a particular instructional method. In other words, is the effectiveness of training partially a function of the way training is delivered, independent of training content? In a comprehensive review of the organizational training literature, Tannenbaum and Yukl (1992) suggest that all well-known training methods have been shown to be effective for at least some learning objective. The question, then, is not whether a particular method "works," but for what specific results criteria it proves effective.

Organizational trainers have a wide variety of instructional methods from which to choose. Table 4 reveals the most common types used for employee training and their frequency of use. A formal training program will often use a combination of these methods, switching from one to another as course content and objectives change. The following sections review research on the three most frequently evaluated training methods: games/simulations, role plays, and computer-based training.

Games and Simulations

Games and simulation are widely used by trainers. They have experienced a significant resurgence of interest in the past few years. Wexley and Latham (1991) trace the popularity of games and simulations to three factors: (1) increased expertise and sophistication in computer simulations; (2) increased interest in understanding organizations from a systems-level perspective; and (3) increased awareness of the importance

TABLE 4
Common Instructional Methods

Method	Percentage of Organizations
Videotapes	92
Lectures	90
One-on-one instruction	82
Games/simulations	63
Case studies	57
Audiotapes	50
Slides	49
Role-plays	49
Self-assessment/self-testing	49
Computer-based training	48
Self-study programs	33
Multimedia	27
Videoconferencing	18
Teleconferencing (audio only)	16
Distance learning	9
Virtual reality	3

Source: *Training,* October 1995, p.62. Numbers represent percent of all organizations using these methods for employee training. Based on 982 responses.

of the managerial decision-making process— a focal area for many games and simulations. The latest stimulant of the business gaming movement has been the availability of powerful inexpensive personal computers, which make computer-driven games and simulations available to a wider range of people (Keiser & Seeler, 1987).

Games and simulations vary widely in terms of the types of activities to which they relate. This section focuses on instructional methods that combine the interactive processes of a game with the real-world characteristics of a simulation, or what is formally called *gaming simulations.* In a recent review, Thornton and Cleveland (1990) characterized gaming simulation activities along a continuum of complexity, ranging from simple individual-level skill practice games (one-on-one interview simulations, in-basket exercises) or group interaction games (leaderless group discussions) to more complex-level system games representing large-scale multidimensional simulations. Despite the various levels of complexity, effective training can be accomplished with any simulation that represents relevant processes of management, organizational behavior, and organizational systems (Sackett, 1987).

Research on other types of games and gaming simulations have been reviewed by Hsu (1989), Keys and Wolfe (1990), Wolfe (1990), and Lane (1995). Building on these reviews, we discuss some of the evidence that relates to the teaching power of business games. In particular, we focus on two instructional approaches frequently used in human resource training and assessment applications: the in-basket technique and large-scale behavioral simulations.

The *in-basket exercise* was originally developed as a simulation game to study administrative skills among military officers (Frederiksen, 1962). The technique requires a participant to play the role of a supervisor with a fictitious company, who must make decisions about a set of hypothetical letters and memos that have accumulated in the supervisor's in-basket. As a training technique, the in-basket method is frequently used to elicit behaviors considered useful in evaluating many dimensions of managerial competency, such as planning, organizing, decision-making, and administrative control (Thornton & Byham, 1982).

Virtually all assessment centers for managerial development use an in-basket. Although evidence shows that assessment centers are useful predictors of subsequent managerial success (e.g., Gaugler, Rosenthal, Thornton, & Bentson, 1987; Thornton & Byham, 1982), it is often hard to determine the in-basket's contribution to the prediction of performance apart from other assessment tools. Schippmann, Prien, and Katz (1990) conducted a recent review and evaluation of the psychometric properties of in-basket measurements. Their findings provided sufficient evidence to support the development and use of the in-basket procedure, although evidence for the validity of the in-basket is somewhat marginal. A lack of discriminant validity among dimension ratings has led others to question the validity of the in-basket method (e.g., Sackett & Dreher, 1982; Brannick, Michaels, & Baker, 1989).

A *large-scale behavioral simulation* is a noncomputerized management game that attempts to reproduce individual and collective behaviors normally exhibited in managerial work environments (Wolfe, 1993). Keys and Wolfe (1990) identify this type of simulation as one that focuses on interpersonal skill assessment and behavioral learning rather than the strategic management focus of computerized business games. *The Looking Glass* (Lombardo, McCall, & DeVries, 1983), *The Business Policy Game* (Cotter & Fritzsche, 1986), *Kombinant* (Gernert, 1986), *Mansym IV* (Schellenberger & Masters, 1986), and *The Organization Game* (Miles & Randolph, 1979) are all popular examples of this type of large-scale simulation. More recently, a number of industry-specific simulations have been developed. Stumpf and Dunbar (1990) describe a number of complex simulations for a wide variety of industries, in-

cluding life insurance companies, not-for-profit organizations, food-manufacturing companies, and financial service organizations.

Behavioral simulations attempt to create real-world experiential environments that contain enough reality to induce real-world-like responses from those engaged in them (Wolfe, 1993). A simulation is "valid" if a manager in the simulation behaves as he or she would under similar circumstances in the organization (McCall & Lombardo, 1979). However, there is little evidence that large-scale behavioral simulation training results in improvements in managerial effectiveness. Further, much of the work on the evaluation of these games has been anecdotal, descriptive, or judgmental in nature.

The Looking Glass, Inc., simulation (Lombardo, McCall & DeVries, 1979) is one of the best-known examples of a large-scale behavioral simulation. It was designed to simulate the demands of a typical managerial job by requiring participants to recognize and solve complex problems regularly encountered in the daily running of a business. Research evidence provided by Kaplan, Lobardo, and Mazique (1985) supports the use of *The Looking Glass, Inc.,* for building team trust and managerial effectiveness. More recently, VanValsor, Ruderman, and Phillips (1989) have shown that this technique is capable of eliciting behaviors on the part of manager participants quite similar to that of managers in real organizations.

Most empirical studies on the educational value of management games have been conducted for large-scale computer-based simulations. In a study by Byrne (1979), participants in *The Executive Game* (Henshaw & Jackson, 1984) were able to perform 8 of the 10 real-world managerial roles and skills identified by Mintzberg (1973). Another study by Hemmasi and Graf (1992) employed the *Micromatic* business simulation (Scott & Strickland, 1985) and determined that practitioners, as compared with students, attribute significantly greater overall educational utility to business simulation gaming as a teaching pedagogy. A study by Wolfe and Roberts (1986) found some degree of external validity for the business game used in their study, *The Business Management Laboratory* (Jensen & Cherrington, 1984). More specifically, they found that students' game performance predicted their career success as a manager five years after graduation. More recently, a study by Wolfe and Chanin (1993) found that a participant's strategic skills significantly affected the economic results they could obtain in *The Business Management Laboratory*. Further, individuals who initially possessed low skills could improve them to a significant degree over the simulation run. Results from these and other studies seem to indicate that management games have some educational benefit. However, as suggested by Keys and Wolfe (1990), failure to provide a realistic organizational context significantly limits the generalizability of these games.

Behavioral Role Modeling

Behavioral role modeling (Goldstein & Sorcher, 1974) has a formidable history as a tool used to facilitate organizational training. In recent years, it has emerged as a popular approach for teaching interpersonal and supervisory skills (Decker & Nathan, 1985). This technique draws its origins from Bandura's (1977) social learning theory, which stresses the use of observation, modeling, feedback, and reinforcement as steps for modifying human behavior. Behavioral role modeling usually begins with a live or videotaped demonstration of required or appropriate behaviors. Trainees then imitate these behaviors in practice or work situations. Finally, trainers provide constructive feedback and reinforcement to further enhance or develop the trainees' behavioral repertoire.

Published research has largely supported behavioral role modeling's effectiveness in organizational training (e.g., Burke & Day, 1986; Latham & Saari, 1979; Mayer & Russell, 1987; Russell, Wexley, & Hunter, 1984; Robertson, 1990; Manz & Sims,

1981). Applications of this research have shown positive and significant findings for a variety of learning objectives. Behavior modeling is particularly effective for training in such diverse areas as interviewing skills (Ivancevich & Smith, 1981), supervisory skills in coaching and handling complaints (Decker, 1982), computer software skills (Gist, Schwoerer, & Rosen, 1989), cross-cultural management skills (Harrison, 1992), and conflict resolution skills (Nunns & Bluen, 1992).

Although much of the existing research supports the utility of this training method, several writers have expressed concerns about conclusions drawn from research. One concern relates to the transfer of learned skills back to the job. For example, in a review and meta-analysis, Russell and Mayer (1985) found that although studies showed an increase in paper-and-pencil learning criteria, they did not assess trainees' abilities to generalize modeled skills to settings outside the training context. In a subsequent article (Mayer & Russell, 1987), they note that most studies on behavior modeling examine only immediate learning, while neglecting other important outcomes such as trainee generalization and transfer.

Recently, Greenberg and Eskew (1993) identified three key dimensions that influence the generalizability of findings from role-playing research: the subject's level of involvement (paper-and-pencil response vs. overt behaviors), the role being played (themselves vs. another), and the degree of response specificity (restrictive vs. nonrestrictive). They concluded that to enhance generalizability outside the laboratory, studies should (1) encourage research subjects to be more actively involved in the roles they play; (2) ask participants to play themselves, rather than take on the role of a specific or generalized other; (3) match the background of the participant and the role-playing context; and (4) allow subjects to be free to improvise their reactions to the role playing by allowing them to respond in a free and spontaneous manner (as opposed to a highly restricted specified manner). Following these four prescriptions increases the likelihood that trainees will carry their training over into the work setting. For example, in a recent study by Yuille, Davies, Gibling, Marxsen, and Porter (1994), eyewitness memory of police trainees during realistic role plays was more intact after a 12-week interim for participants (high-involvement subjects) than for observers (low-involvement subjects).

A second concern relates to the types of training for which this instructional method is most appropriate. Behavior modeling appears useful for teaching concrete behaviors that are clearly optimal for a particular type of task, such as operating equipment or assembling a machine (Tannenbaum & Yukl, 1992). However, writers (Decker & Nathan, 1985; Gist, 1989; Robertson, 1990) have questioned the effectiveness of this technique for teaching the kinds of flexible adaptive behaviors needed in the workplace. It appears easier to train and retain simple, redundant, and, therefore, unrealistic behavioral repertoires (Parry & Reich, 1984). Baldwin (1992) noted that a lack of variability in role models' behavior may limit usefulness for such complex subjects as interpersonal skills training. Baldwin's research showed that exposing trainees to greater variability in the modeling design had a significant positive effect on a trainee's ability to generalize learning to contexts outside of training.

Gist (1989) identified an alternative strategy for increasing the adaptability of the behavior modeling technique. More specifically, Gist found that a variation called *cognitive modeling* can be useful for training in the areas of innovation and creativity. This form of modeling is based on a process of attending to one's thoughts as one performs an activity and using self-instructional thoughts to guide performance. By focusing on thoughts and cognitions as opposed to observable behaviors, Gist argues that modeling techniques can be used to train employees on tasks that are performed primarily through cognitive processes (e.g., problem solving, idea generation, or any

tasks drawing heavily on memory or judgment). This form of modeling has received limited empirical support in a training context (Meichenbaum, 1975).

Computer-Based Training

The computer-based training (CBT) method uses a computer as a main medium for delivering training. Hart (1987) identified two key advantages of CBT tutorials over other instructional methods: reduced cost and increased training effectiveness. CBT can reduce costs in several ways, including

• reducing employee travel (especially in larger companies with dispersed workforces),

• shortening the length of training (by keeping trainees from being held back to the pace of the slowest person in a training session),

• improving the timeliness of training (helping new employees become productive faster), and

• lowering staffing requirements.

In addition to increasing efficiency, CBT can make training more effective by standardizing delivery/feedback, individualizing employee programs (allowing for the tailoring of a program to suit an employee's capabilities), and providing sufficient opportunity to practice a skill until proficiency is attained. One major disadvantage is cost, if you can't buy CBT off the shelf. It is expensive to develop. However, computer software now exists that simplifies and speeds the design process and facilitates programming (Tannenbaum & Yukl, 1992).

A large body of literature supports the benefits of computer-based training in education research. Most studies have reported that CBT proves more effective than conventional methods. For example, in investigating the impact of CBT on accounting courses, several authors found computer-assisted instruction superior to conventional group instruction (e.g., Friedman, 1981; Groomer, 1981; McKeown, 1976, Oglesbee, Bitner, & Wright, 1988). Others have reported similar findings in elementary school settings (e.g., Edwards, Norton, Taylor, Weiss, & Dusseldorp, 1975; Vinsonhaler & Bass, 1972). Kulik, Kulik, and Cohen (1980) conducted a comprehensive review and meta-analysis of 59 studies evaluating computer-assisted instruction in education. In 37 of the 59 studies, computer groups outperformed control groups in a variety of subject areas, indicating a clear dominance of computer-assisted instruction (King, Premkumar, & Ramamurthy, 1990). However, Clark (1983) noted that much existing research failed to control for differences in content, novelty, and/or teaching methods, thereby allowing considerable potential for confounding the results. More recently, researchers have investigated how specific features of a CBT program should be changed to improve the effectiveness of the computer-based instructional method (e.g., Gal & Steinbart, 1992; Pei & Reneau, 1990). Reviews of the training literature continue to call for more rigorous empirical work. Although each training method has demonstrated some utility, more research is needed to determine the types of content for which a method is appropriate and to discover how different aspects of the method affect training outcomes (Tannenbaum & Yukl, 1992).

References

Baldwin, T. T. (1992). The relative power of training evaluation designs under different cost configurations. *Journal of Applied Psychology, 77,* 155-160.

Bandura, A. (1977). *Social learning theory.* Englewood Cliffs, NJ: Prentice-Hall.

Belcourt, M. (1995). Costing training activity: a decision maker's dilemma. *Management Decision, 33* (2), 5-15.

Brannick, M. T., Michaels, C. E., & Baker, D. P. (1989). Construct validity of in-basket scores. *Journal of Applied Psychology, 74,* 957-963.

Bryne, E. T. (1979). Who benefits most from participation in business policy simulations: An empirical study of skill development by functional area. In S. C. Certo, & D. C. Brenensthl (Eds.), *Proceedings of the Sixth Annual National ABSEL Conference* (pp. 257-260).

Burke, M. J., & Day, R. R. (1986). A cumulative study of the effectiveness of managerial training. *Journal of Applied Psychology, 71,* 232-246.

Clark, R. E. (1983). Reconsidering research on learning from media. *Review of Educational Research, 53* (4), 445-460.

Decker, R. J. (1982). The enhancement of behavior modeling training of supervisory skills by the inclusion of re-

tention processes. *Personnel Psychology, 32,* 323-332.

Decker, R. J., & Nathan, B. R. (1985). *Behavior modeling training.* New York: Praeger Publishers.

Edwards, J., Norton, W., Taylor, S., Weiss, M., & Dusseldorp, R. (1975). How effective is CAI? A review of research. *Educational Leadership, 33,* 147-153.

Frederiksen, N. (1962). Factors in in-basket performance. *Psychological Monographs, 76* (22, Whole No. 541).

Friedman, M. E. (1981). The effect on achievement of using the computer as a problem-solving tool in the intermediate accounting course. *The Accounting Review, 56,* 137-143.

Gal, G., & Steinbart, P. J. (1992). Interface style and training task difficulty as determinants of effective computer-assisted knowledge transfer. *Decision Sciences, 23,* 128-143.

Gaugler, B. B., Rosenthal, D. B., Thornton, G. C., III, & Bentson, C. (1987). Meta-analysis of assessment center validity. *Journal of Applied Psychology, 72,* 493-511.

Gernert, G. R. (1986). Kombinant: The multilevel management simulation game. *Simulation & Games, 17,* 320-326.

Gist, M. E. (1989). The influence of training method on self efficacy and idea generation among managers. *Personnel Psychology, 42,* 787-805.

Gist, M. E., Schwoerer, C., & Rosen, B. (1989). Effects of alternative training methods on self-efficacy and performance in computer software training. *Journal of Applied Psychology, 74,* 884-891.

Goldstein, A. P., & Sorcher, M. (1974). *Changing supervisor behavior.* New York: Pergamon.

Goldstein, I. L. (1991). Training in work organizations. In M. D. Dunnet & L. M. Hough (Eds.), *Handbook of Industrial/Organizational Psychology, 2,* 507-619.

Greenberg, J., & Eskew, D. E. (1993). The role of role playing in organizational research. *Journal of Management, 19,* 221-241.

Groomer, S. M. (1981). An experiment in computer-assisted instruction for introductory accounting. *The Accounting Review, 56,* 934-941.

Harp, C. (1995, August). Link training to corporate mission. *HR Magazine,* 65-68.

Harrison, J. K. (1992). Individual and combined effects of behavior modeling and the cultural assimilator in cross-cultural management training. *Journal of Applied Psychology, 77,* 952-962.

Hart, F. A. (1987). Computer-based training. In R. L. Craig (Ed.), *Training and development handbook* (pp. 470-487). New York: McGraw-Hill.

Hemmasi, M., & Graf, L. A. (1992). Managerial skills acquisition: A case for using business policy simulations. *Simulation & Gaming, 23,* 298-310.

Hsu, E. (1989). Role-event gaming and simulation in management education: a conceptual framework. *Simulation & Gaming, 20,* 409-438.

Ivancevich, J. M., & Smith, S. V. (1981). Goal setting interview skills training: Simulated and on-the-job analyses. *Journal of Applied Psychology, 66,* 697-705.

Jensen, R. L., & Cherrington, D. J. (1973). *The business management laboratory.* Dallas: Business Publications.

Kaplan, R. E., Lombardo, M. M., & Mazique, M. S. (1985). A mirror for managers: Using simulations to develop management teams. *Journal of Applied Behavioral Sciences, 21,* 241-253.

Keiser, T. C., & Seeler, J. H. (1987). Games and simulations. In R. L. Craig (Ed.), *Training and development hand-book* (pp. 456-469). New York: McGraw-Hill.

Keys, B., & Wolfe, J. (1990). The role of management games and simulation in education and research. *Journal of Management, 16,* 307-336.

King, W. R., Premkumar, G., & Ramamurthy, K. (1990). An evaluation of the role and performance of a decision support system in business education. *Decision Sciences, 21,* 642-659.

Kirkpatrick, D. L. (1967). Evaluation of training. In R. L. Craig (Ed.), *Training and development handbook* (pp. 18-1-18-27). New York: McGraw-Hill.

Kulik, J. A., Kulik, C. C., & Cohen, P. A. (1980). Effectiveness of computer-based college teaching: A meta-analysis of findings. *Review of Educational Research, 50,* 525-544.

Lane, D. C. (1995). On a resurgence of management simulations and games. *Journal of Operational Research Society, 46,* 604-625.

Latham, G. P., & Saari, L. M. (1979). Application of social-learning theory to training supervisors through behavior modeling. *Journal of Applied Psychology, 64,* 239-246.

Lombardo, M. M., McCall, M. W., & DeVries, D. L. (1983). *Looking glass.* Glenview, IL: Scott, Foresman.

Manz, C. C., & Sims, H. P. (1986). Beyond imitation: Complex behavioral and affective linkages resulting from exposure to leadership training models. *Journal of Applied Psychology, 71,* 571-578.

Mayer, S. J., & Russell, J. S. (1987). Behavior modeling training in organizations: Concerns and conclusions. *Journal of Management, 13,* 21-40.

McCall, M. W., Jr., & Lombardo, M. M. (1979). *Looking Glass Inc.: The first three years* (Vol. 8). Greensboro, NC: Center for Creative Leadership.

McKeown, J. C. (1976). Computer-assisted instruction for elementary accounting. *The Accounting Review, 51,* 123-130.

Miles, R. H., & Randolph, W. A.(1979), *The Organization Game.* Santa Monica, CA: Goodyear.

Milkovich, G. T., & Boudreau, J. W. (1994). *Human Resource Management.* Burridge, IL: Irwin

Mintzberg, H. (1973). *The nature of managerial work.* New York: Harper & Row.

Nunns, G. G., & Bluen, S. D. (1992). The impact of behavior modeling training on self-reports of white supervisors in two South African mines. *The Journal of Applied Behavioral Science, 28,* 433-444.

Oglesbee, T. W., Bitner, L. N., & Wright, G. B. (1988). Measurement of incremental benefits in computer enhanced instruction. *Issues in Accounting Education, 3,* 365-377.

Parry, S. B., & Reich, L. R. (1984). An uneasy look at behavior modeling. *Training and Development Journal, 30* (3), 57-62.

Pei, B. K. W., & Reneau, J. H. (1990). The effects of memory structure on using rule-based expert systems for training: A framework and an empirical test. *Decision Sciences, 21,* 263-286.

Pine, J., & Tingley, J. C. (1993). ROI of soft-skills training. *Training, 30,* 55-60.

Robertson, I. T.. (1990). Behavior modeling: Its record and potential in training and development. *British Journal of Management, 1,* 117-125.

Russell, J. S., & Mayer, S. (1985). *Behavior modeling: A re-view and future directions.* Unpublished manuscript, University of Oregon.

Russell, J. S., Wexley, K. N., & Hunter, J. E. (1984). Questioning the effectiveness of behavior modeling training in an industrial setting. *Personnel Psychology, 37,* 465-481.

Sackett, P. R. (1987). Assessment centers and content validity: Some neglected issues. *Personnel Psychology, 40,* 13-25.

Sackett, P. R., & Dreher, G. F. (1982). Constructs and assessment center dimensions: Some troubling empirical findings. *Journal of Applied Psychology, 76,* 401-410.

Schellenberger, R. E., & Masters, L. A. (1986). *Mansym IV: A dynamic management simulator with decision support system.* New York: Wiley.

Schippmann, J. S., Prien, E. P., & Katz, J. A. (1990). Reliability and validity of in-basket performance measures. *Personnel Psychology, 43,* 837-860.

Scott, C. R., Jr., & Strickland, A. J., III. (1985). *Micromatic: A management simulation.* Boston: Houghton Mifflin.

Stumpf, S. A., & Dunbar, R. L. M. (1989-1990). Using behavioral simulations in teaching strategic management processes. *Organizational Behavior Teaching Review, 14,* 43-62.

Thornton, G. C., III, & Byham, W. C. (1982). *Assessment centers and managerial performance.* New York: Academic Press.

Thornton, G. C., III, & Cleveland, J. N. (1990). Developing managerial talent through simulation. *American Psychologist, 45,* 190-199.

Training budgets declined in 1991. (1992). *HR Focus, 69,* 14.

Training budgets: 1995 industry report. (1995, October). *Training,* 41-66.

Van Velsor, E., Ruderman, M., & Phillips, A. D., (1989). The lessons of the looking glass. *Leadership and Organizational Development Journal, 10,* 27-31.

Vinsonhaler, J. F., & Bass, R. K. (1972). A summary of ten major studies on CAI drill and practice. *Educational Technology, 12,* 29-32.

Wexley, K. N., & Latham, G. (1991). *Developing and training human resources in organizations* (2d ed.). Glenview, IL: Scott-Foresman.

Wolfe, J. (1990). The evaluation of computer-based business games: Methodology, findings and future needs. In J. W. Gentry (Ed.) ABSEL *Guide to Experiential Learning and Simulation Gaming,* New York: Nichols Publishing.

Wolfe, J. (1993). A history of business teaching games in English-speaking and post-socialist countries: The origination and diffusion of a management education and development technology. *Simulation & Gaming, 24,* 446-463.

Wolfe, J., & Chanin, M. (1993). The integration of functional and strategic management skills in a business game learning environment. *Simulation & Gaming, 24,* 34-46.

Wolfe, J., & Roberts, C. R. (1986). The external validity of a business management game: A five-year longitudinal study. *Simulation & Gaming, 17,* 45-59.

Yuille, J. C., Davies, G., Gibling, F., Marxsen, D., & Porter, S. (1994). Eyewitness memory of police trainees for realistic role plays. *Journal of Applied Psychology, 79,* 931-936.

12

Quality Learning: A Cooperative Venture in Control and Responsibility

By Paul J. Poledink

Introduction

A friend of mine, a former college-level teacher of teachers, now a designer of training programs and a trainer for business and industry, made a rather blunt statement some time ago. We met at a conference, exchanged pleasantries with some of our old colleagues and talked about families, work activities, projects, successes, and getting older. Regarding his switch from academia to the industrial training sector, my friend fired off this comment about his new profession. "You know," he said to his former education department colleagues, "when learning doesn't take place in your line of work, students fail; they get bad grades. When learning doesn't take place in mine, the instructor or the course designer gets fired."

My friend was, of course, pointing to one aspect of the well-documented differences between the fields of education and training. We went on to discuss other things at lunch later that day, but my friend's observation about the education and training professions familiar to both of us kept nagging me for some time after that. I kept coming back to his hard-nosed differentiation between the two areas. My friend's statement placed the responsibility for education's success on the student, and the responsibility for training's success on the instructor or course designer.

What I have come to believe more and more though, after spending time with representatives of both points of view, is that while the discussion of the differences between education and training is still interesting, the argument itself is outdated and wastes our mental energy and valuable time. Given what we presently know and what we continuously discover about learning, especially the learning needs of adults, I think it more appropriate to spend our time discussing and promoting effective, high-quality learning rather than interacting with those who continuously resurrect the education-vs.-training argument.

What we do know for sure about adult learning, however, takes on added importance when we consider the increasing necessity of learning in the workplace and the emerging prospect of the *learning organization*. This organizational phenomenon can be defined as one in which all levels of management, production, marketing, research, design, accounting, human resources, and maintenance—in other words, people from all areas of the organization—consciously and actively involve themselves in learning in order to improve the organization's viability and enhance individual job security.

Also labeled at times *high-performance organizations*, these new entities thrive not on a static, defined pattern of operation, but on a dynamic, strategic, and at times unpredictable modus operandi. The success of the organization and the individuals in it depends on the knowledge base. Wisdom is the chief form of capital.

While there are many elements that contribute to traditional organizations becoming high-performance learning organizations, the heart of the change process—and the organization's successful continuing operations—is learning. In a learning organization, the acquisition of knowledge becomes a shared responsibility of both the organization and the employee. Training and education programs offered by the organization support this learning, but they make up only a part of the organizational and employee development process. I suggest that quality adult workplace learning must become a cooperative venture between the organization and its employees, one in which certain elements play critical roles. The responsibility for learning becomes a shared function, with all involved understanding and fulfilling their roles and responsibilities. For the learning process to succeed, all elements that support it must be identified and integrated into a systematic approach. The outcome of this approach can only be suggested rather than explicitly defined, and it may not be immediately apparent. The total organizational output usually becomes greater than the sum of the inputs—a long-term commitment is made to a strategic vision rather than to an immediate objective.

Rather than arguing for or against the value of education versus training, theory versus practice, the concrete versus the abstract, the academic versus the applied, the immediate versus the long range, we should accept the values and strengths of all components of learning. More important, though, we ought to ask—and answer—the following questions:

- What is quality learning?
- What are the critical elements neces-

sary to ensure quality learning by motivated individuals who must function in high-performance organizations?

Traditional Practices and Quality Learning

To begin answering these two questions, we must realize that many traditional education and training beliefs and practices will not work well in the new paradigm. Situations in which the learning provider strongly controls and directs content development and the instructional delivery process—or in which the learner is considered a simple recipient of instruction—will negatively affect the outcome of any high-performance learning process. Learners cannot be viewed by the learning provider—or by themselves—as empty vessels waiting to be filled with information, skills, and knowledge. Nor should they be considered passive receivers of instruction who quietly await infusion of new capabilities.

The organization cannot assume a one-sided role in designing learning activities independent from the learners themselves. Learning cannot, moreover, be considered a simple sequential or hierarchical building-block process for learners. One style, one sequence, and one delivery system cannot fit all learners and all outcomes. Members of the organization, whatever their level of responsibility, cannot separate their learning from their work responsibilities. They also cannot view learning activities as mere add-ons, perks, rewards, or, in a negative sense, retribution for poor performance.

Quality learning, then, is the formation of insight, perspective, competency, and judgment that occurs through the organization's provision and support of learning opportunities and the employee's active participation in acquiring knowledge, skills, and attitudes. It occurs when the following basic assumptions are understood, accepted, and practiced by all members of the organization:

- There are broad, comprehensive learning goals that everyone involved in the learning process understands and accepts.

• Learning goals are recognized as beneficial to the organization and the individual, with the goals being related and integrated whenever possible.

• Learning outcomes may be broad or focused, depending on their identified and agreed-upon purpose.

• Learning content is always contextualized to allow easy application to ongoing and future operational needs.

• Learning activities are both formal and informal, with both modalities receiving the input of the involved parties.

• Learning is clearly considered a metacognitive activity, with learners assuming responsibility for creating beneficial outcomes and applications for the organization and for themselves.

• The learning process recognizes the effectiveness and appropriate use of instructional technology and information accessibility.

• The learning context is comprehensively analyzed to provide quality-control measures and ensure system accountability and effectiveness.

Three primary elements support these basic assumptions and form the basis for their application and effectiveness within the organization:

• the identification and integration of quality learning goals.

• the identification and integration of quality learning content.

• the implementation of a quality learning context.

All three elements play important roles in assuring quality learning.

Quality Learning Goals

Learning goals broadly identify and define the general purpose of any adult learning activity. The use of learning goals recognizes that adults lead multiple lives with varying demands and expectations, and that they spend their learning currency and time in pursuit of academic goals, life goals, and work goals.

Learning undertaken primarily to meet *academic* goals traditionally takes place early in one's adult life and is designed to meet the standards of academic institutions. The outcomes of these learning activities—in addition to the acquisition of knowledge and skill—include diplomas, credits, grades, degrees, certificates, and licenses. Each of these credentials verifies that the learner has met an established and recognized set of standards. When individuals choose to pursue academic goals, their learning is substantially defined and controlled by the institution granting the credential. The learner assumes responsibility for meeting standards, with the promise of receiving the credential upon their successful completion.

Individuals pursue learning aimed primarily at attaining *life* goals to enhance some aspect of their personal lives. Outcomes of this learning are varied, but they generally include leisure learning activities, learning-for-learning's sake, enhanced personal or financial well-being, avocational/hobby pursuits, social interaction, intellectual stimulation, or preparation for the next stage in life, such as retirement. When learning is undertaken to achieve life goals, control of the process rests primarily with the individual learners. They choose a convenient time and place, they choose the content, and they choose the learning mode—books, tapes, lectures, or workshops, for example. After completing this learning activity, participants achieve a sense of satisfaction and well-being or a more fulfilling individual or social lifestyle. Providers of this type of learning maintain responsibility for identifying the interests of the general population and providing the appropriate form of learning activity.

Work-related learning goals have usually focused on the increased effectiveness of the organization through the enhancement of employees' job performance. Work-related learning may include the skills and knowledge necessary to maintain or upgrade current job skills, to move to another level or type of work assignment, or to acquire a new or different job or career. Commonly known as training, career development, or vocational preparation, this form of learning is usually looked on as a singular event or terminal activity rather than a lifelong endeavor. Work-related learning usually provides the organization with a more productive and capable employee and enhances the employee's job security and economic well-being. The organization traditionally controls the content and delivery of this learning, sometimes with minimal employee validation of the usefulness of the training outcomes. Employees have responsibility for actively participating in the training and for using their newly acquired skills to the best of their ability in the performance of their jobs.

In the new high-performance learning organization, the three learning goals of academic achievement, life-skill development, and work-related skill acquisition become much less differentiated. The blurring of differences and overlapping of boundaries between the three goals magnifies and intensifies the outcomes. The return on the investment of time, effort, and money by the individual or the organization increases. The outcomes transfer to another application with little or no additional cost or effort.

For example, the design and development of training that not only meets a work-related need but also qualifies for academic credit at a college or university serves work and academic goals at the same time. The development of interpersonal communication skills can serve a life-skill goal as well as increase an employee's workplace performance capabilities. Achieving a higher level of competency in reading or writing skills may serve all three goals. It may earn employees a certificate or academic credit. It may increase their social skills. In addition, it may enable them to better participate in a work-related training activity.

Working directly to integrate and interrelate academic, life, and work goals whenever possible motivates adults to learn. Clear evidence of a multiple payback and a higher rate of return on investment of time and energy leads to greater individual effort. Organizational return also increases in magnitude when learning goals are combined rather than allowed to remain discrete. This synergistic effect supports and reflects a major aspect of a high-performance learning organization and its high-performing employees—knowledge increases exponentially by combining separate knowledge bases and expanding traditional patterns of learning. Once the organization realizes that learning can achieve several goals at the same time, and individuals understand the benefits learning can produce in several areas of their lives, acquiring knowledge and skill becomes a more positive, lifelong activity.

Quality Learning Content

The second element supporting quality learning is *content:* the learning outcomes that are suggested, mandated, or individually selected for acquisition by the organization or the learner. The wide-ranging types of organizations and the imaginative possibilities of individuals make it quite impossible to provide a comprehensive listing of this content. What can be learned and then synthesized into new forms and applications has no limit. There are, however, several groupings of knowledge, skills, and attitudes in the prospective high-performance learning organization. These groupings include foundation competencies, general work-related competencies, and specific work-related competencies. Successful learning practices include all of these competencies in their repertoire and interrelate them whenever possible. Foundation competencies deserve the most attention, however, because of their general nature and transferability to many types of work organizations.

Foundation Competencies

Foundation learning has commonly been referred to in a simplistic manner as mastering the "basic skills." Foundation skills have been considered the means for allowing the acquisition, analysis, interpretation, and presentation of the skills and knowledge necessary to attain academic, daily living, and work-related goals. Reading, writing, oral communication, and mathematical competencies traditionally comprise the list of basic foundation skills. With our primary focus on the learner in a high-performance organization, however, the emphasis must go to the acquisition of foundation skills for doing or performing, not just for acquiring other skills or knowledge. School-based or academic programs usually emphasize the use of these skills for acquiring further academic knowledge. Their new use is measured by performance or "getting things done." People read, compute, and converse to solve problems, make decisions, or formulate new approaches. This application must also be specifically taught and learned. High performance learning and performance activities take the traditional basic skills categories and add outcomes and nuances not traditionally offered by academic disciplines. Reading, for example, falls under four major categories or types: reference, prose comprehension, document comprehension, and application skills.

Reference skills help us find the information we need or want. We scan titles, skim tables of contents, quickly flip through screens on a computer to search out the source of needed information. In the workplace, we use reference skills to look for a particular manual, job aid, file, or database, and to determine the relevance of information for a particular job or problem.

Prose comprehension skills allow us to read written material for general ideas and specific details. We interpret information gained and start thinking beyond the words themselves. We may ask such questions as, "Is this information complete? Is it based on opinion or fact? Where can I get more information?" Or, we may simply say to ourselves, "I don't agree with this." The large amount of written material encountered in all aspects of life demands quick and accurate comprehension for successful high performance.

Traditional academic reading-skill development focuses on material presented in sentences and paragraphs. Much of the material in the workplace, however, requires different reading strategies. Document comprehension skills are necessary to interpret charts, graphs, forms, diagrams, schematics, illustrations, and maps. Documents demand visual scanning perceptions that differ from the usual left-to-right and top-to-bottom techniques used in prose comprehension.

Finally, high performers read as much to do as to know. We use written information to complete a task or solve a problem. We compare information from different sources. We verify that our work matches written specifications. We make decisions based on the information we have read. We use a set of critical reading application skills to do this.

Writing as a foundation skill usually comprises three categories: mechanics, transfer and creation. Mechanics provide the accepted standards for spelling, grammar, punctuation, and format, and they make writing easy to read and understand. We use these mechanics to record or transfer information from one document or conversation to another as part of daily work life. Many times, we take mechanical accuracy for granted. However, we cannot overlook the importance of mechanics. Composing and creating documents on paper or on a computer are an essential facet of high performance. As individuals in an organization gain knowledge, the clear and concise transfer of that knowledge to other members of the organization for their understanding and possible use is of great importance.

Traditional writing skills, however, are being augmented by a new set of competencies in the high-performance workplace as conditions change. The new writing skills include the production of crisp, bulleted memos transferred quickly through an electronic-mail medium; the formation of flow charts and time lines annotated with words, phrases, and acronyms; and the generation of reports and memos that reflect the beliefs, values, and culture of the organization. Other high-performance writing skills include taking notes at meetings, recording ideas on a chart pad, translating numerical data into words, and designing materials on slides or transparencies for use in presentations. When combined with traditional writing standards, the new skills allow the organization to benefit from a full sharing of the accumulated thoughts of individual employees.

Oral communication has also gained importance. The traditional academic educational system has not emphasized oral communication, and people often lack skills in this area. Oral communication takes place more rapidly than written communication. It involves listening skills, interpersonal communication, group participation skills, and presentation skills.

At times, we can view oral communication as one-way communication, such as when we listen to a formal presentation or lecture. Here, the speaker speaks and the listener listens. Most oral communication in a high-performance organization, however, is an interactive process. Much of the best communication takes place when skilled communicators—interactive speakers and listeners—engage in informal dialogue. As listeners, we involve ourselves actively. We ask questions, seek clarification and elaboration, interrupt at appropriate times, and provide feedback. Similarly, as speakers we must have awareness of our listeners. We can't do all the talking. We ask questions to be sure our message has been understood. We solicit opinions, advice, or suggestions, and respond to listeners' feedback.

These interpersonal communication skills take on added importance when we participate in organized group discussions or team meetings. A high-performance work group succeeds when active speaking and active listening take place. This leads to an open exchange of ideas that allows all participants to express and support their points of view. Group conversations flow smoothly and productively when everyone has good communication skills and the self-confidence to express opinions and ideas.

At times, people may need to make a formal presentation to a large group. A report of findings, the results of a project, or a proposal for a change in operations may be best delivered orally. While making effective public presentations does not come naturally to many of us, practice brings improvement.

Math competencies, the final of the four foundation skills, grow increasingly important in a high-performance organization. Typical indicators of quality are most frequently represented by numbers. "You can't manage or control what you can't measure," according to a commonly heard quality slogan. All members of a high-performance organization must know how to quantify—and thus control—their areas of responsibility to the extent they are empowered to assist in managing them. To do this, people must know how to use basic math principles, apply specific mathematical functions when necessary, and interpret numbers both graphically and verbally. One specific area of math that has gained importance in recent times is statistics and probability. We can attribute much improvement in the quality of goods and services to the control of variability in process and product, an achievement predicated on the ability of individual employees to measure processes, statistically analyze data, and predict outcomes and events using probability theory.

Although people must acquire an appropriate level of competence in each of these four foundation areas, doing so is still not enough for success in the new high-performance workplace. Additional sets of foundation skills are emerging and becoming necessary for high-performance individuals.

Knowing how to learn is becoming an expected personal ability. Individuals must have awareness of their own learning style and adapt it to various situations. They must become professional learners. They must realize what they know and what they don't know. They must know where to go for information—what databases to access, people to ask, references to seek. They must become appropriately curious and imaginative and possess the desire and skill to satisfy their curiosity. The organization, in turn, must recognize this search for knowledge and provide the appropriate learning support systems to meet the need.

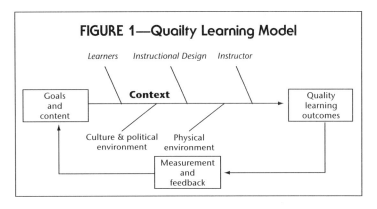

FIGURE 1—Quailty Learning Model

Knowledge and appreciation of systems theory is also becoming necessary. In its broadest definition, this understanding of what systems are and how they operate serves as a fundamental tenet of the learning organization. For example, having a basic understanding of economic theory—how local, national, and, in many cases international, financial systems operate—can lead to an appreciation of the economic factors that influence workplace decisions. Human behavior systems, while subject to unpredictable imagination and free will, do operate according to recognizable principles. The introduction of new processes demands an understanding of the properties of physical systems, primarily technology and electronics. The internal political and cultural systems of an organization certainly influence, if not control, much of the behavior of the individual employees. An awareness of computer systems is mandatory. Compliance with an organization's health and safety systems is quite possibly a matter of life or death.

How to "work within the system" reactively, and how to "work the system" proactively to support one's own growth and development as well as the organization's viability, is an emerging requisite skill in the high-performance learning organization.

Quality Learning Context

With the identification of learning goals and content, a final question remains: How can we ensure achievement of goals and mastery of content? The answer lies in controlling the context of the learning process. *Context* is defined as the identification of the variables that affect a learning activity, those elements that impact the process of providing and acquiring skills and knowledge. Examples of context variables can be graphically shown and related through the use of the *fish-bone process model*, a pictorial representation of the variables and their location in the learning process. (See Figure 1.) This model also describes a measurement and accountability system that is important to all who have responsibility for the success of the learning activity. In its generic form, this model lists inputs, variable activities, expected outcomes, and a measurement feedback loop for designed-in continuous improvement. Our high-quality learning context identifies areas of potential variability, assigns responsibility for control of these variables, and systematically enhances the probability of successful learning outcomes through a process of measurement, feedback, and change.

The variables involved in the quality learning context include:

● the learners, who bring their existing skills and knowledge, their motivation to learn, their personal, academic, and work-related backgrounds, and their own career goals,

● the cultural and political environment,

● the instructional design,

● the physical environment, and

● the instructors.

Learner Variables

The responsibility for controlling individual learner variables and ensuring their positive impact lies, to some extent, with those who select or assign employees to educational and training programs. If there is an organizational need for increased workforce knowledge or skill, the organization must assume responsibility for assuring that the right people receive the right training at the right time. The "right people" are those who understand the need for the training and possess the prerequisite skills and knowledge necessary to successfully participate in learning activities. The "right time" involves offering training as close as possible to the period when the knowledge or skills must be used. The "right training" is learning content that addresses the immediate need or long-term goal. When the organization initiates the learning, those who administer the training process must address these variables.

Participants in the training, however, also bear responsibility for the behavioral variables under their control. They must actively involve themselves in the learning process, recognize their work-related learning responsibilities, and have awareness of their skill development and educational needs. In addition to reacting to training situations, individuals must initiate learning activities in accordance with their individual perceptions and needs whenever appropriate.

Environmental Variables: Cultural and Political

Cultural and political variables include the norms, organizational attitudes, and unwritten rules that describe the way things are done in an organization and determine the way people should behave. How people are valued, how initiative is rewarded, how imagination is fueled, how status is defined, which relationships are formed—all are part of the political and cultural underpinnings of every organization. All members of an organization have some responsibility for maintaining these contextual variables in a constructive and positive manner, but it is primarily the function of leadership. Both formal and informal leaders, those with official and unofficial influence or authority, affect these variables. If learning is recognized as important and encouraged, it will

most likely take place. If competency and knowledge are looked on with envy, guarded as the province of the elite, or allocated only on a need-to-know basis, they will not flourish, but will wither and fade. Overt support is important, but often the quiet, intangible recognition of the quality learning process through informal words and supportive actions most enables it to occur.

Instructional Design Variables

Education and training administrators have responsibility for the design and delivery of the learning process. They have control over the choice of the overall instructional design and the production of learning materials for computer-assisted instruction, video-based training, and distance-learning systems. The addition of media technologists compounds the variables. Whatever the delivery medium, the training administrator must take into account the principles of adult and competency-based learning theory. These design variables include the belief that

● adults bring a wide range of experience and knowledge to the learning situation and are a reservoir of existing wisdom,

● a wide variety of learning styles exists in any adult population,

● adults seek concrete solutions and applications of skills and knowledge for immediate effect and turn to principles and concepts when dealing with long-term, strategic goals,

● feedback on learning progress and achievement is important,

● adults acquire learning outcomes through building patterns and relationships.

An appreciation of these and other adult learning principles results in the design of learning activities suitable for adult learners. Multiple approaches to the delivery system through a variety of sensory applications, varying thought patterns, and effective instructional materials achieves this goal.

Physical Environmental Variables

The quality of the physical surroundings affects the teaching-learning process. Training administrators cannot ignore the comfort of the learners and instructors. Suitable temperature levels, acceptable ambient noise levels, ease of access, and sufficient space all seem obvious. Yet, some traditional non-learning organizations that consider education and training an adjunct to the organization's operations do not provide acceptable physical surroundings for learning activities. While they may not totally prevent learning from taking place, less-than-favorable physical surroundings interfere with learning. These conditions imply that the learning process is not worth significant investment of effort or financial resources. The physical environmental variables in a high-quality learning organization reflect the importance of the learning process and visibly support both group and individual learning.

Instructor Variables

Given the wide array of our individual beliefs, temperaments, philosophies, styles, experiences, and other personal qualities, instructor variables may be the most difficult to control. Who we are as people becomes who we are as instructors. In spite of personal differences, though, instructor performance must meet a generally recognized set of standards. At a minimum, instructors must know and be interested in their subject matter, have skills and knowledge in adult learning theory and practice, have the physical and psychological stamina to interact with learners, and appreciate the culture of the organization and its learners. Training administrators bear the responsibility for assuring that the variables initially are at acceptable levels of quality. They must periodically monitor instructor performance to maintain these levels.

Monitoring and controlling contextual process variables associated with the learner, the cultural and political environment, the instructional design, the physical environment, and the instructor will help ensure acquisition of needed skills, knowledge, and attitudes.

Conclusions

In the final analysis, achieving a high-performance learning system is a shared responsibility that rests on independent initiative. Individuals and organizations must identify and integrate their shared goals, define general and specific content outcomes, and gain control of the variables that impact the enterprise's success.

When these actions become part of the deep core of the culture and begin to drive individual and organizational actions and decisions, high performance ceases to be a singular act and becomes an ingrained habit.

References

Baugh, R. (1994). *Changing work: A union guide to workplace change.* Washington, DC: AFL-CIO Human Resources Development Institute.

Carnevale, A., Gainer, L. J., & Meltzer, A. S. (1988). *Workplace basics: The skills employers want.* Report prepared by the American Society for Training and Development under contract by the Department of Labor. Alexandria, VA.

Cohen, A. R., & Bradford, D. L. (1990). *Influence without authority.* New York: John Wiley & Sons.

Drucker, P. F. (1989). *The new realities.* New York: Harper and Row.

Eurich, N. P. (1990). *The learning industry: Education for adult workers.* Princeton, NJ: Carnegie Foundation for the Advancement of Teaching.

Marshall, R., & Tucker, M. (1992). *Thinking for a living: Education and the wealth of nations.* New York: Basic Books.

National Alliance of Business. (1988, July). *Building a quality workforce.* Washington, DC: U.S. Department of Labor, U.S. Department of Education, U.S. Department of Commerce.

Senge, P. M. (1990). *The fifth discipline: The art and practice of the learning organization.* New York: Doubleday/Currency.

Schein, E. H. (1985). *Organizational culture and leadership.* San Francisco: Jossey-Bass.

Smith, R. M., & others. (1990). *Learning to learn across the life span.* San Francisco: Jossey-Bass.

U.S. Department of Labor. (1993). *Road to high performance workplaces.* Washington, DC: Author.

Wlodkowski, R. J. (1993). *Enhancing adult motivation to learn.* San Francisco: Jossey-Bass.

Part III

School Practices

13

How We Will Learn in the Year 2000: Reengineering Schools for the High-Performance Economy

Deborah Buffamanti and Albert J. Pautler
Reprinted with permission from *Journal of Industrial Teacher Education,*
Vol. 31, No. 4, Summer 1994.

A recent issue of *Fortune* magazine (May 1993) posits a radical new world of work. Something revolutionary, not evolutionary, awaits us in the not-too-distant future. The cover story, "How We Will Work in the Year 2000," paints a portrait of organizations that have metamorphosed from the hierarchical into the web-like and other, newly unfamiliar forms; from the tidy, cubicled arrangement of bureaucrats to the scurrying, pager-carrying technocrat. With computational infrastructure currently meshing into a global network of resources, the world of work is about to be thrown into a convulsion of change.

The author of the article, Walter Kiechel, claims there are at least six trends beginning to influence America that will have an intense and lasting impact on the nature of the workplace. Three of these trends directly target the nature of the organization itself; the other three, the nature of work. Altogether, this brave new world will be unlike anything the American labor market has experienced.

Changes in the Nature of Organization

The first of Kiechel's organizational trends revolves around the size of the company of the future. Generally, the trend toward corporate downsizing or rightsizing will become much more commonplace and acceptable.

This trim organization model will help usher in the birth of other new, unconventional, organizational types. Kiechel's second organizational trend is the proliferation of diversity in organizational structure. According to Kiechel, the Taylorist, factory-like workplace may well compete for business with companies that resemble a spider's web. Other competitive firms will be radically flat in structure and could contain many sites linked to a central hub.

These smaller, unorthodox corporate entities will help foster Kiechel's third organizational trend: the shift from a vertical division of labor to a horizontal one. This shift is the impetus behind the disintegration of the corporate ladder. This will be replaced by a classification of individuals based on their knowledge, skills, or specialties. The issue of transferable skills, and their current market value, will become the deciding factor in employment options, salary, and position within the organization. By the year 2000, skill—not longevity—will be the only item rewarded.

Taken together, these three trends profoundly impact the nature of today's organization and, ultimately, of tomorrow's as well. The change toward a more complex but smaller organization, the shift from the common hierarchy to a variety of organizational structures, and the movement from a horizontal to a vertical division of labor will all produce tremendous change in the nature of the American company.

Changes in the Nature of Work

Kiechel goes on to illustrate three more trends, each impacting the essential nature of work as it is currently known. The first of Kiechel's trends altering the nature of work is the rise of the technician as the elite of the American worker. Many new technician and specialist jobs are dependent upon knowledge and use computer technology as integral to the task. With this type of specialized knowledge, technicians don't fit well within any sort of hierarchical organization. They tend to operate as individual contractors and work extremely well within the new, compact organization.

Kiechel's second movement redefining the nature of work is that business will increasingly become the act of providing a service rather than merely producing tangible goods. Business will no longer be making things. It will instead be adding value, providing services, delivering experiences, and coordinating dependencies.

The rise of the technical elite and the idea of business as service will combine with the organizational trends to produce a new form of work, one drastically different from today. Kiechel's final, and most important, trend postulates that the very nature of work will be redefined by the year 2000. Kiechel

reasons that work will be more refined, more specific, more intense, more wide ranging, more involving, and more demanding. It will involve much more learning, both on the job and in academic arenas.

These three final trends—the rise of the technician, the emergence of the service economy, and the changing nature of work—all impact the future of America and the place of work within it. In combination with the organizational trends, they will surely alter the American worker, and the global economy, in some fundamental fashion.

How We Will Learn in the Year 2000

"How We Will Work in the Year 2000" begs a response from educators. How will the national public school system deal with the requirements of Kiechel's high-performance workplace? And what sorts of trends are currently underway within education to facilitate the move to this type of world? Educators, already on the defensive for the past decade, will inevitably be required to address the needs of this emergent economy. A companion piece to the Kiechel article might well be called "How We Will Learn in the Year 2000." This piece is already hovering, in bits and pieces, in the periphery of our collective unconscious, and we would like to suggest some of its key ideas here.

"How We Will Learn in the Year 2000" might well begin with an examination of the structure of future schools. Historically, the controversy regarding restructuring schools reappears with cyclic frequency and has done so almost since the inception of the national public school system. Recently, a number of respected publications have done a fine job of outlining the current reasons for structural change: *Influences in Curriculum Change* (Unruh & Leeper, 1968); *What Work Requires of Schools* (U. S. Department of Labor, 1991); *Learning a Living: A Blueprint for High Performance* (U. S. Department of Labor, 1992); and *Education That Works: Creating Career Pathways for New York State Youth* (New York State Job Partnership

Council, 1992). This call for change is not unusual given that the Taylorist, hierarchical structure of our schools was molded some hundred years ago. What is unusual, though, is that the historic call for restructuring has been replaced with a clamor for more than restructuring—for *reengineering,* a total rethinking of the educational realm. From the focus of education, to the place of students within the system, to the role of personnel, to content materials, and all the way through delivery and evaluation methods, nothing will be left untouched. Reengineering promises to turn education upside down.

"How We Will Learn in the Year 2000" will begin with the claim that the most important trend impacting education will be the need for reengineering learning. The act of reengineering an organization is radical. It is not incremental or ad hoc but a deliberate, calculating appraisal of the current conditions of the organization.

Shift toward Critical Thinking Skills

Reengineering schools for the high-performance economy will require a number of substantive changes. One of the first changes schools will experience by the year 2000 will be a shift in focus toward critical thinking skills. While the foundation subjects will still exist, the focus of learning will be much more on the development of reason, problem solving, logical analysis, and decision making within the context of real problems. These skills are particularly necessary in a working world where the responsibility for the achievement of goals is coupled with those performing the tasks.

Democratization of Learning

The second change that reengineering will produce will be a new impetus toward the democratization of learning. One of the components of the trend toward the democratization of learning concerns the transformation of school culture from a teacher-centered learning system to a learner-centered one. Old-style schools contained

teachers who knew the answers, planned the activities, provided the evaluations, and prevented social transgressions. This Taylorist factory model of learning assumed that students were empty vessels, waiting to be filled and processed from the fount of the teacher's knowledge—products, if you will. The school of the future will require that students take responsibility for many of these functions and assist others in doing the same. In the school of the future, all those involved in the learning process will routinely consult with teachers, peers, community members, and outside experts in the pursuit of information. Students, in addition to teachers and other professionals, will be forced to seek information more frequently from outside the school.

As one can see, the role of school personnel will not go unaffected during this reengineering process. Teachers, principals, and central office staff will have to change. As students become more active in the learning adventure, the role of teaching breaks out of the Taylorist mold. Teachers will facilitate learning. They will become guides, pointing out possible routes of exploration that may not be immediately apparent to the student. Principals will become facilitators for teacher learning, and central office staff roles will certainly be transformed to assist with this new learner-centered instructional style.

The process of democratization within education will clearly produce a better labor pool. The skills involved with self-management, self-discipline, and self-motivation will be crucial to the labor force by the year 2000. Jobs at that time will require individuals with the skills and personal qualities to see processes through to completion. Encouragement of this type of behavior will help learners transition into successful workers. They will have experience with planning, self-directed learning, and self-evaluation methods; teamwork; breaking out of boundaries to discover key information; well-developed problem-solving and reasoning skills; and the significant ability to manage themselves. This process of the democratization of learning is a fundamental precursor to a new world of work.

Reengineering schools will also lead to the democratization of fiscal control. This particular change is already visible in the emergence of site-based management and shared decision making. These particular changes have sought to move authority for fiscal management directly to the school itself. This flattening of the school hierarchy has led to a more complex, integrated scheme of school organization—relying more and more on teams of specialists drawn from affected audiences for the resolution of problems.

By encouraging this type of networking team structure within schools, educators can help students see the process of team formation, project analysis and completion, and then team dissolution around them. All experience the process and all can carry this skill into the twenty-first century world of work.

While reengineering the schools will promote a renewed strength in logic and reasoning abilities, as well as a shift toward democratization and the changing roles of personnel, this process also has some important implications for educational content.

Multidisciplinary Subject Matter

A third trend in "How We Will Learn in the Year 2000" will be increased content variety and an interest in the multidisciplinary nature of subject matter. With the new focus on critical thinking skills, reason and logic, and the shift to teaching these skills in a problem-solving context, course curriculum will become increasingly dense, sophisticated, and technological in nature. Learning will also become more applied.

This is particularly important given the complexity of the new world order. The global economy that Kiechel describes is an elaborate web of people, languages, technologies, processes, and time zones. It demands that workers be sufficiently skilled to understand not only the systems they are

familiar with but the underlying principles that make the process possible. When understanding eludes them, they must be able to formulate questions and probe for responses that can assist them in the completion of their duties.

Diversity of School Structures

The process of reengineering schools will lead, as in the workplace, to a fourth trend: the diversity of school structures. Some of the structured changes currently seen within schools are the emergence of magnet schools, schools-within-schools, and schools devoted to specific ends housed within a school of a broader intellectual context. America is experiencing a fragmentation of the schooling market into an increasing number of disciplines. In addition to this, proprietary schools, vocational schools, training schools, parochial schools, military, public, private, and performing schools are all contributing to this trend and encouraging a new political momentum toward school choice. This particular structural change has impacted students most but also impacts teachers, parents, and government. It remains to be seen whether or not the strength of these new substructures has any impact within the private sector and, ultimately, within Kiechel's high-performance global economy.

Move toward Lifelong Learning

Reengineering schools comprises more than changes in structure and shifts toward the democratization of learning. The new economy will require workers capable of lifelong learning; and the schools of the future, like the workplace, will encourage that.

Hence, contained within the reengineering of schools will be the rise of lifelong learning. As students become more active participants in the learning process, they will increasingly be able to plan and negotiate activities, assess themselves (as well as others) and outsource for information when the need arises; eventually, they will mature into capable, self-managing individuals who recognize that lifelong learning will be their mainstay to employability.

Schools of the future will encourage life-long learning in a variety of ways. First, they will focus efforts on the individual learner and customize curriculum opportunities to the individual's needs and abilities. This is especially valuable to workers and those most at risk in the new economic era. Second, schools of the future will encourage independent study—but probably in a variety of group formats. For example, learners could participate in large groups for introductory sessions to certain material, discussion groups for material not easily understood, and very small groups for projects requiring problem-solving tasks. Again, this would be a boon to those requiring retraining or those stumbling academically. Lifelong learning could also be facilitated through flexibility in terms of intellectual development. Learners could easily rotate into or out of modules of learning that suited their needs and developmental level at that particular time. All of these programs designed to promote lifelong learning have at their root the objective of creating intellectual excitement within the learner. When this is accomplished, learning continues.

In this new learning environment, the boundary between *learning to know* and *learning to do* becomes blurred. The notion of vocational or general or career or academic tracks is no longer viable when schools are committed to producing only the finest skilled graduates. And if those graduates are encouraged to pursue learning ad infinitum, then Kiechel's world of work will not be too far off.

These emerging educational trends are only the most visible part of the sweeping modifications housed under the umbrella of reengineering schools. Reengineering will impact not only the organizational structure of schools, the division of labor in schools, and the role of school personnel, including students, but also the nature of learning and, ultimately, the nation at large, by creating a workforce capable of sustaining Kiechel's high-performance, high-wage economy.

These trends will result in sweeping changes for the goals of education. Primarily, they will require the establishment of new, world-class standards of education for all, with no exceptions. Then, they will require the establishment of a new curriculum, focusing not on the development of basic academic skills but on the development of individual thinking and reasoning skills within the context of problem-solving. In conjunction with these, one should expect the incorporation of new teaching methodologies into education: for example, learning and testing in context and the rise of independent study and self-assessment. This will require the commonplace use of high technology to assist learners. Finally, new materials for learning, based in part on the emergent fields of interdisciplinary science and applied knowledge, will be developed.

Reengineering schools represents a sea change within education. With the advent of a more democratized learning system and the rise of lifelong learning, along with structured changes in schools, education will be poised to remake itself into the committed, vibrant institution it can be. It can ensure that all students learn to think and will later become productive citizens, able to make their way in Kiechel's world.

"How We Will Learn in the Year 2000" will suggest that the most important, all-encompassing shift beginning to convulse America's public schools will be the movement toward a complete reengineering of the system. This particular transformation includes a new focus toward critical thinking skills, the democratization of learning, an increase in the complexity of subject matter, and a movement toward structural diversity and lifelong learning. This groundbreaking process is fundamentally more influential, pervasive, and far-ranging than those trends impacting Kiechel's working world. The reengineering of the public school system contains the rebirth of America's economic future and a new world of learning more conducive to a successful working life than ever before.

References

Kiechel, W. (1993, May). How we will work in the year 2000. *Fortune, 127* (9), 38-41.

New York State Job Partnership Council. (1992). *Education that works: Creating career pathways for New York State youth.* New York: Task Force on Creating Career Pathways for New York State Youth.

United States Department of Labor. (1991). *What work requires of schools: A SCANS report for America 2000.* Washington, DC: Secretary's Commission on Achieving Necessary Skills.

U.S. Department of Labor. (1992). *Learning a living: A blueprint for high performance: A SCANS report for America 2000.* Washington, DC: Secretary's Commission on Achieving Necessary Skills.

Unruh, G. G., & Leeper, R. R. (Eds.) (1968). *Influences in curriculum change: Papers from a conference sponsored by the ASCD Commission on Current Curriculum Developments.* New York: National Education Association, Association for Supervision and Curriculum Development.

14

Improving the School-to-Work Transition of American Adolescents

By Robert W. Glover and Ray Marshall

Reprinted by permission of the publisher from Ruby Takanashi, *Adolescence in the 1990s: Risk and Opportunity.*
(New York: Teachers College Press, © 1993 by Teachers College, Columbia University. All rights reserved.)

AMERICA has the worst approach to school-to-work transition of any industrialized nation (William T. Grant Foundation, 1988, pp. 26-28; Berlin & Sum, 1988, pp. 22-23; U.S. General Accounting Office, 1990, pp. 33-41; Commission on Skills, 1990, 46-47; Osterman, 1980; Osterman, 1988, pp. 111-114). Put simply, we have no systematic processes to assist high school graduates to move smoothly from school into employment. Our secondary schools and counseling efforts are focused primarily on encouraging youths to continue their education in college and obtain a degree. Yet almost half of each graduating class—roughly 1.4 million young people each year—directly enters the labor market without enrolling in college, and only one-quarter of each graduating class ultimately obtains a baccalaureate degree. Most high school graduates not going to college are left to sink or swim—without advice or career counseling and without any job-placement assistance. A 1981 survey by the Educational Testing Service (ETS) revealed that almost half of all high school students never talked to a counselor about occupations and only 6 percent of high school counselors reported spending more than 30 percent of their time helping students find jobs (Chapman & Katz, 1981). Budget cuts during the 1980s eliminated federally funded job-counseling services through the public Job Service, which at its peak (in 1964) had served 600,000 youths annually in half of the nation's high schools (Barton, 1991).

The Commission on Skills of the American Workforce summarized the problems for youths going to work immediately after high school: "There is no curriculum to meet the needs of non-college bound youth, no real employment service for those who go right to work, few guidance services for them, no certification of their accomplishments and . . . no rewards in the workplace for hard work at school."(Commission on Skills, 1990, p. 47)

The Context

While school-to-work transition is among the weakest links in the American learning system, it is important for Americans to consider why we must be concerned about improving all of our learning systems. By our definition, the term *learning systems* includes families, community institutions, workplaces, media, and political processes—in addition to formal schools. Among the key questions we must address are: Why have learning systems become so much more important? How do American systems compare with those of other countries? What are the implications of, and policy actions required by, technological change and a more competitive global economy?

Economic Change

The need for increased learning and thinking skills is driven by some very fundamental economic developments. The main problem for the United States has been a shift from an economy based mainly on natural resources and economies of scale—made possible by mass production for a large, relatively insulated American market—to a more competitive global-information economy where economic success depends mainly on the quality of human resources. The United States had enormous advantages in the traditional mass-production economy, and although we retain advantages based on our past successes, we have serious disadvantages in the increasingly competitive global economy. These disadvantages relate to the obsolescence of our traditional learning systems, which were closely related to the skill requirements of a mass-production system.

A basic feature of the traditional American economy was the fact that it afforded very rapid increases in productivity and standards of living. This has been mainly due to an abundant supply of cheap natural resources, economies of scale, and reinforcing processes whereby market forces shifted resources to higher productivity uses (e.g., from agriculture to manufacturing) and caused improvements in one industry to lead to improvements in others (e.g., as when reduced steel costs improved auto and other industries, leading to higher sales and greater scale economies).

This mass-production system had its problems, but it ushered in the longest period of sustained, equitably shared prosperity in the history of the United States—perhaps even in world history.

The main forces eroding the mass-production system's basic institutions were the closely interactive effects of technology and international competition. Technology reduced the importance of physical resources and changed the nature of mass-production processes. Information technology and flexible manufacturing systems make it possible to achieve many of the advantages of economies of scale without large producing units. *Technology*—best defined as how things are done—is basically ideas, skills, and knowledge embodied in machinery and structures. Technological progress therefore represents the substitution of ideas, skills, and knowledge for physical resources. Schultz demonstrated this process in agriculture, where there have been great increases in output since the 1920s despite the use of less land, physical capital, and labor (Schultz, 1981). Moreover, other economists have demonstrated that almost all of the improvements in productivity since the 1920s have been due to factors associated with human capital and technology—natural resources account for none of the increase and physical capital for only 20 percent or less.

Learning Systems for a Mass-Production Economy

The skill requirements of the mass-production system resulted mainly from the hierarchical, fragmented nature of the work (or Taylorism) combined with the assembly line. This system required a few educated managerial, technical, or professional employees; most of the work was routine and could be performed by workers who needed only basic literacy and numeracy. Indeed, much work could be done by illiterates. Because the system was so productive, workers with limited education could earn enough money to support their families at levels that were relatively high by historical standards. This was especially true after the New Deal policies of the 1930s provided safety nets for those who were unable to work, collective bargaining to make it possible for workers to improve their share of the system's gains, and monetary and fiscal policies to keep the system running at relatively low levels of unemployment.

Learning systems reflected the mass-production skill requirements. Managerial, professional, and technical families prepared their children for occupations through family information networks and elite learning processes in public or private schools. With some notable exceptions, public schools were organized primarily to provide basic literacy and numeracy skills to lower-income native and immigrant students expected to work in mass-production factories or on farms. Although the system provided more upward occupational mobility than those in most other countries, especially after the reforms of the 1930s and 1940s, both family and school learning systems basically perpetuated the mass-production, resource-oriented occupational structure. This included education and training for the skilled trades through postsecondary school apprenticeship programs. The school-to-work transition processes were informal and largely family related but were perpetuated through formal learning systems.

Competing in the New Economy

Information technology has combined with international competition to alter conditions for economic viability and success. In a more competitive, consumer-driven system, quality—best defined as meeting consumers' needs—becomes much more important; mass-production systems were producer driven and emphasized quantity, not quality. Moreover, in competitive markets, economic success depends heavily on productivity in the use of all resources, not just economies of scale. Competitive systems thus must be more flexible in adjusting to changing market and technological conditions.

In a more competitive environment, com-

panies or individuals can compete in two ways: They can reduce their wages or improve productivity and quality. The easiest approach, the one we have followed in the United States, is the low-wage strategy. Most other industrialized nations have rejected this strategy because it implies lower and more unequal wages, with serious political, social, and economic implications (Commission on Skills, 1990, pp. 40-41).

Japan and Western European countries take several actions to encourage companies to pursue high-wage strategies. First, they build national consensus for such a strategy. The essential instruments to encourage companies to pursue high-wage strategies include wage regulation, full-employment policies, trade and industrial policies, and adjustment policies to shift resources from low- to high-productivity activities.

Japan and Western European countries promote various forms of worker participation to encourage companies to organize for high performance (i.e., for quality, productivity, and flexibility). It has been well documented that these organizations have lean management systems that decentralize decisions to front-line workers as much as possible. To encourage worker participation and decentralized decision making, other countries encourage collective bargaining and require or promote worker participation in management decisions at various levels, including boards of directors, but almost always in workplace decisions.

High-performance organizations likewise develop and use leading-edge technology. The mass-production systems depended on standardized technologies and relatively unskilled labor. As it has become clear that this combination is not competitive in high-wage countries, some American companies have attempted to automate—combining advanced technology with unskilled labor, an approach that rarely succeeded. High-performance organizations require well-educated workers who can adapt and constantly improve leading-edge technology in a process the Japanese call "giving wisdom to the machines."

Because high-performance organizations give workers much discretion, positive incentive systems are basic requirements for success. The incentives for front-line workers in mass-production organizations are often negative (e.g., punishment for failure) or perverse—penalizing workers for superior performance, as when workers lose their jobs when they improve productivity. Positive incentives include group bonuses for superior performance, participation in decisions, internal unity, and employment security.

Above all, high-performance organizations require workers who can analyze data, communicate with precision, deal with ambiguity, learn rapidly, participate in what were considered management decisions in hierarchical management systems, and work well in teams. These have come to be called "higher-order thinking skills," formerly possessed only by the managerial, professional, and technical elites.

Most industrialized countries have developed policies to ensure that a majority of their workers have higher-order thinking skills. These include high performance standards all young people are required to meet before they can leave secondary schools. It is each school's responsibility to see that these standards are met. Standards are important because they provide incentives for students, teachers, and other school personnel; information to employers and to postsecondary institutions; and a means for policy makers and the public to evaluate schools.

Standards are likewise important factors in strengthening school-to-work transition systems, because students who meet high standards are prepared for work, technical training, or other forms of postsecondary education. Since the United States has no national standards for secondary school leavers, our students in nonacademic tracks too often find their options to pursue higher levels of postsecondary education and training severely constrained.

Other countries do several other things that strengthen their learning systems. First, most have family policies to support children. The United States alone among industrialized countries has no child-support, universal-preschool, or parental-leave programs. The absence of such policies makes many of our families—especially our low-income families—very poor learning systems. Many of our children therefore start school far behind their more advantaged counterparts, and subsequently receive inadequate learning opportunities at home as well as in school. Families are not only basic learning systems but also provide information and services linking young people to labor markets. Families in most industrialized countries have experienced considerable structural change and stress since the 1960s that have reduced their effectiveness as learning systems. However, most other industrialized countries have done much more than the United States to provide public and community processes to help families compensate for these changes (Marshall, 1991). Second, most other countries also have well-developed labor market institutions and information systems to help match workers and jobs. Third, most other countries provide systematic postsecondary education and training opportunities for school leavers. Finally, they offer incentives for companies to provide on-the-job training for front-line workers. American systems in all of these areas are not very well organized or systematic. Few American companies provide formal education and learning systems for their employees and, as would be expected in Tayloristic work organizations, most of the systems they do have are devoted mainly to training managers—not front-line workers (Commission on Skills, 1990, p. 4).

Implications of Inadequate School-to-Work Transition

The lack of a systematic bridge between school and work most adversely affects poor and minority students. They have access to few resources or information networks to obtain mainstream jobs that lead to meaningful careers. In labor markets, word-of-mouth contacts among people who know and trust each other match learners with learning opportunities and jobs with job seekers. Many middle-class parents have the contacts and resources to be good job developers for their children. However, low-income parents are not so well positioned, especially if they are black or Hispanic. The problems are often compounded by powerful negative stereotypes youths and employers may have about one another. Employers often are influenced by what they see in the media about inner-city youths. Likewise, many minority youths have negative ideas about industry hiring practices. In addition, the location of available jobs may pose significant problems for inner-city and minority youths in isolated rural areas where they lack transportation to the available employment or training opportunities.

U.S. Bureau of Labor Statistics data on the employment status of recent high school graduates confirm these Hispanic and black labor market disadvantages. Unemployment rates for whites, Hispanics, and blacks were 14.9 percent, 29.1 percent, and 50.3 percent respectively. In addition, more black youths were out of the labor force and thus not counted as unemployed. Indeed, only 28.5 percent of blacks but 53.5 percent of white male high school graduates had jobs in October after graduation (U.S. Bureau of Labor Statistics, 1989). These data refer to whether youths have jobs at all without any reference to the quality of those jobs. The realization that relatively few minority youths obtain any job—let alone a good job—even if they study hard and obtain a diploma provides little incentive to excel in school.

Problems in making the transition from school to work are not confined to minorities or the poor. Negotiating the labor market is a difficult task for many American youths who have decided not to pursue a baccalaureate degree. In other countries, youths are provided occupational counseling, employment information, and job placement through local schools or labor-market institutions, and employers take an active role in youth development activities. The United States, by contrast, has no system for getting youth from school into work, and the employer community takes little responsibility for youth.

School dropouts and high school graduates are most at risk of unemployment, low incomes, and unsatisfying work. However, even college-bound youths often do not receive adequate career counseling. The result is high proportions of college students who are "undeclared" as to their major. College students are often ignorant of the options available. Many college graduates appear at a loss in making occupational choices; some even enter law or graduate school not so much out of choice but from lack of knowledge of other options.

America is thus not serving many of her youth well and is particularly neglectful of the needs of the three-quarters of her future workforce who do not obtain baccalaureate degrees. At the same time, it is becoming clear that the new, high-performance work organizations require that *all* workers be more highly skilled. Stated another way, in the modern global-information economy, few people will obtain a good job that pays well without significant learning beyond high school. The triple demands of efficiency, quality, and flexibility require line workers who have high levels of basic skills and who learn quickly. In short, the quality of America's front-line workers is the bottom line in our nation's economic future. In this light, a closer comparison of American school-to-work transition practices with those of Japan and Germany is especially instructive.

Japan

The largest and best Japanese firms, such as Toyota, Mitsubishi, and Sony, actively recruit not only the best university graduates but also the best high school graduates. They aggressively seek out the best high schools and request school staff to recommend students to them (Rosenbaum & Kariya, 1989). This gives high school students incentives to work hard and perform well in school and it puts power into the hands of teachers, whose recommendations carry significant weight (Rosenbaum, 1990, p.12). After hiring them, Japanese firms typically put these 18-year-old high school graduates into well-developed learning systems both on the job and off. Japanese foremen and other supervisors are evaluated in part by how well they instruct the workers they supervise; teaching is simply an integral part of their job. In addition, most firms expect their employees to continue learning on their own in self-development programs, conducted through correspondence and other professional development processes. Many employers circulate lists of recommended course opportunities and reimburse half of the tuition to any employee who passes such a course.

Germany

The involvement of German firms in the development of the teenage workforce is even clearer and more explicit than in Japan. Under the German apprenticeship system, youths beginning at age 16 spend four days per week in an industry-devised, nationally approved program of occupational instruction with an employer and one day in school. Because apprenticeships involve two learning tracks—on the job and in school—the German system is commonly known as the "dual system." The program of structured training normally lasts for three years. Germany's biggest and best companies participate and actively recruit the best-achieving youths. Americans on study tours of the German apprenticeship system are likely to find themselves at factories operated by firms such as Siemens or Daimbler Benz, or even subsidiaries of American firms, including Ford Motor Company or Corning.

The German dual system is supported by an impressive counseling and guidance system operated largely by the public employment service, so that German youths are acquainted with available options and are able to make decisions about careers as adolescents. Youths also have available to them a variety of exploratory activities, ranging from plant tours and job-shadowing experiences to "sniffing apprenticeships," in which youths spend two weeks in a selected apprenticeship on a tryout basis.

The German apprenticeship system is a socialization process as much as it is a training program. Through apprenticeships, the majority of German adolescents at ages 16, 17, and 18 spend most of their day in an adult environment—learning such work-readiness behaviors as coming to work on time and valuing quality in their workmanship. As in Japan, German youths are able to participate effectively in these on-the-job learning systems because they are required to meet high academic standards for graduation from secondary schools.

In both Germany and Japan, when young workers complete their formal training, they enter well-developed workplace learning systems. Teaching is an explicit, high-priority component of the training for foremen and other supervisors, and work is consciously organized as a learning system.

American Employers Avoid Responsibility for Youth Formation

The contrast with U.S. practices could not be sharper. Whereas Germany and Japan have systematic incentives and high expectations for performance of their adolescents and their expectations are generally fulfilled, Americans expect little of adolescents and our expectations are equally fulfilled.

America's preferred employers—those who offer good wages, attractive benefits, and career potential—ordinarily do not hire high school graduates immediately after graduation, even if they have good academic records. America's biggest and best corporations avoid hiring youths at all. Only a handful of the Fortune 500 firms hire fresh high school graduates for entry jobs offering career opportunities. Even member firms of the Business Roundtable, who so actively advocate school reform and form partnerships with schools, do not hire teenagers. Although almost all of these firms eventually employ high school graduates, they normally wait until the job applicants are "mature and settled down" in their mid-twenties and have accumulated some work experience. Other employers emulate the practices of our largest firms. Thus, American apprenticeship sponsors act like any other American employer in a position to be selective about applicants; they choose *against* youth. The average starting apprentice in the United States is in his or her late twenties. This delay in hiring for career-track jobs results in many youths spending five or six years floundering in jobs that offer opportunities neither for learning nor for advancement (Osterman, 1980; William T. Grant Foundation, 1988, pp. 26-28). More important, these conventional American hiring practices have at least four critical consequences for school-to-work transition:

1. The delay in hiring American youths provides German and Japanese youths a 5- to 10-year head start in gaining access to significant occupational skill training.

2. These practices remove some of our best learning systems—our finest corporations—from the processes that develop our youth. By shunning any responsibility for hiring teenagers, the best American employers have effectively disengaged from the process of instructing and socializing their future workers.

3. The delay in hiring high school graduates eliminates a natural communication loop for employers to feed clear information back to schools about what skills are needed in the workplace.

4. Most important, effort and achievement in school are disconnected from rewards in the workplace, thus undermining student incentives to work hard and achieve in school. Improving the school-to-work transition is thus an essential school reform issue.

Recent research by John Bishop and James Rosenbaum has demonstrated that effort and achievement in high school are not effectively rewarded for students who do not plan to go to college (Bishop, 1989, pp. 6-10, 42; Rosenbaum, 1989, pp. 193-197 & 1990, pp. 10-15 40, 42, 43). Few employ-ers ask for high school transcripts, and most of those that do find that they cannot obtain them on a sufficiently timely basis to make hiring decisions. The high school diploma appears to be valued by employers mainly as an indicator of persistence rather than as a measure of achievement. Although a high school diploma makes a big difference in earnings over the long run, it appears to make little difference in the type of employment and wages offered in initial jobs after high school graduation. Because many youths have a short time horizon, near-term employment prospects offer much more powerful incentives than do abstract arguments about lifetime earnings.

American employers currently are not communicating what they need very clearly either to schools or to students. Employers must therefore do a better job of identifying the skills they require of job applicants and reach agreement with schools about how to assess and certify those skills. Equally important, employers must act to hire youths with such skills, once certified. Surveying employers to find out what skills they say they need is not enough; the effort must be tied to action. A promising vehicle for achieving employer commitment to action is a formal agreement, an idea that started with the Boston Compact in 1982. Legislation introduced in October 1991 by Senators Edward Kennedy (D-Massachusetts) and Mark Hatfield (R-Oregon) and Congressmen Richard Gephardt (D-Missouri) and Ralph Regula (R-Ohio) contains provisions establishing community youth employment compacts in Title III B. Entitled the High Skills, Competitive Workforce Act of 1991, this legislation was drafted to implement the recommendations of the Commission on Skills of the American Workforce.

Important Design Features of a Communitywide School-to-Work Initiative

It is clear that we cannot simply transport the German or Japanese approach to American shores, nor should we want to. Each is embedded in its culture and has its own laws and deficiencies. Rather, we should learn from the approaches used in other countries and adapt the best aspects into our own homegrown solutions.

The design for the systematic yet flexible model envisioned here is based on several principles. *The first of these is to connect achievement in school with rewards in the labor market.* Incentives are important for everyone. Students must know that achievement in school pays off unmistakably in terms of economic opportunity.

Second, no single program or training approach can meet the needs of all youths or of all employers. Thus, it is important to make available a variety of training and learning services and opportunities, including work-based learning options.

Third, a system is needed that is available to all youths, rather than a series of short-term demonstrations for special populations. The initiative must be institutionalized with regular financing and thus not dependent on ad hoc grants for continued support. It requires a sustained commitment from the business community, which must see that it is in its own interest. To avoid stigmatizing the participating youths, the initiative must not be reserved exclusively for disadvantaged populations. Of course, helping minority youths and the disadvantaged is a key concern, but there are better ways to help assure their participation than by making poverty an eligibility criterion. Targeting can be achieved by selecting school districts with heavy poor and minority enrollments and by building in strong recruiting and outreach components to assure that poor and disadvantaged youths are well served by the system. Also, *an integral part of any school-to-work system is to serve those who have dropped out of school and who have enrolled in second-chance learning programs, connecting achievement and performance in these programs with rewards in the labor market.*

Fourth, in several respects, information is a key element of the proposed system. To manage the system properly, accurate feedback is needed about youths after they leave school. In order to provide the community with information about its young adults, an information system should be developed to follow young people who have left high school, graduated, and entered the labor market or postsecondary education or training programs. Such data are not commonly available now, and they are essential for accountability and for monitoring progress against goals. Information also is needed on the performance of various public and private training providers, including proprietary schools, community colleges, and other postsecondary training options. In order to make informed decisions about which path to take, youths need to know about the efficacy of various training options after high school. Such data should be collected regularly and made accessible to students and their parents, as well as policy makers and the general public. Finally, graduating youths need a better way to document their competence than conventional school transcripts. Skill certification procedures that are both user friendly and meaningful to employers need to be developed.

Fifth, if adolescents are expected to be in a position to make decisions about careers, providing better and earlier occupational information and guidance is essential. To be successful in the job market, moreover, students need better information on how to get and keep a job. Students must be able to present themselves on paper and in person; they must have opportunities to practice their interviewing skills.

Sixth, vocational options need to have a strong academic content. Critics of vocational-technical education often draw a false distinction between "vocational" and "academic" education. Properly taught, technical education always has required considerable academic content—and technical education will contain even more academic content in the future, as higher theoretical and conceptual skills are required. Most abstract and academic subjects can be taught more effectively through hands-on experience than through classroom lectures. In fact, learning probably is always more effective with the unity of thought and action. The importance of learning by doing has been rediscovered by much recent research (Resnick, 1988, pp. 13-20; American Association for the Advancement of Science, 1988, p. 146; Hutchings & Wutzdorff, 1988). Academic content is necessary also in providing a foundation for adaptability and learning how to learn. Narrow job training or task learning soon becomes obsolete in the changing world of work. It is essential that youths learn how to learn in order to constantly upgrade and improve their skills to match the needs of the workplace.

Finally, the system should not foreclose the option for higher education. Although students may identify themselves as "non-college-bound" in high school, many subsequently may decide to pursue further schooling. Attending college is not a one-time-only decision. In view of the need to promote continued learning as a valued skill essential in almost all jobs that pay well, it is best not to close the options unnecessarily for any youngster. Participation in the program should not preclude college attendance. On the contrary, a major objective of the initiative should be to foster lifelong learning of all types.

The Compact: A Foundation for an American School-to-Work System

The problem of bridging the transition between school and work requires a systematic regional and community response. One promising approach is to organize job collaboratives or compacts between businesses, schools, and community leaders along the lines of the Boston Compact (Spring, 1989 & 1987). Compacts have been established in several cities, but many are simply unfocused collections of business-education partnership activities. What we have in mind here is a version far more specific—geared to results in integrating school and employment and in creating incentives for learning.

The essential mission of the job collaborative is to stimulate academic achievement and career readiness among students. All of the parties in the compact agree to commit themselves to a set of measurable goals or outcomes and to a system for evaluating each through time. A primary aim is to provide students with incentives to stay in school and perform well in order to be eligible for jobs and financial assistance for higher education. Participating students agree to maintain certain standards of performance. For example, in Boston they must obtain certification that they are working hard from two teachers, must stay out of trouble with the law, and must maintain at least an 85 percent school attendance level. In return, businesses agree to preferential hiring of students who meet the specified standards. For their part, school authorities agree to make specific improvements in the participating schools.

To build a bridge between school and the business community, Boston copied the model of the British Careers Service, an arm of the local educational agency with responsibility for counseling and job placement, now a part of the Youth Training Scheme. Young counselors were placed in schools to help train youths in presenting themselves effectively to employers and to help connect participating students with jobs.

Begun in 1982 and renegotiated in 1988, the Boston Compact brought together the resources of the public schools, businesses, universities, labor unions, and the mayor's office to improve student academic achievement and work preparation in exchange for increased opportunities for both employment and higher education. This compact has been most successful in gaining jobs for high school graduates. In 1989, through the compact 1,107 graduates (in a class of just under 3,000) found full-time jobs averaging $6.75 per hour in over 900 businesses (Commission on Skills, 1990, p. 107). Over 85 percent of the youths placed are reported to have been satisfactory employees. Perhaps most impressive of all, among high school graduates, employment of blacks reached parity with that of whites at a level substantially above the national average. Youth unemployment rates in Boston were significantly lower than in other places, and the difference between the proportions of black and white unemployed youths was almost negligible—an achievement virtually unparalleled in any other major city (National Alliance of Business, 1989, p. 3).

Even though Boston's booming economy during the 1980s was a helpful factor, the compact's accomplishment in raising employment for black high school graduates to the level of employment of whites was due as much to the efficacy of the concept as to economic conditions. The Boston project focused on a fundamental difference between middle-class white youths and those from poor black families: namely, that white middle-class youths have better information and networks to obtain jobs than do poor black youths. Young people from poor homes lack the network of employed fathers and mothers, aunts, and uncles that smoothes the transition for the better connected. The recession of the early 1990s has diminished the program's number of placements, but the compact is still performing and evolving, with discussions underway in 1992 to form a vocational-technical school connected directly to a variety of apprenticeship paths into the workplace, with related training provided by area community colleges.

The Boston experience has revealed important lessons that should be incorporated into any program to help young people move successfully from school to work. Youth—especially those from disadvantaged families—must have access to information and job networks in order to find employment. Such networks can be established on an institutionalized basis within the high schools through establishing career services or similar functions. Assistance from an intermediary—including training in effective job-search techniques—is an important component. Job-related standards should not be ignored in student recruitment and selection, and special efforts are needed to articulate relevant standards on a clear, objective basis and to communicate those standards to schools, young people, and their families. Incentives are important for everyone. For students, it must be unmistakably clear that school pays off in terms of economic opportunity and personal satisfaction.

Establishing commitments to performance goals with measurable objectives, regularly measuring performance against those goals, and publishing the results are all critically important. Students need to be contacted after graduation to find out how well the compact is working and to provide feedback to improve future operations.

Of course, no uniform prescription is appropriate for all localities. Each process must be adapted to the needs, resources, and circumstances of both the employers and the youths in the community served. Successful compacts are not just single programs—rather, they become frameworks to organize a wide variety of initiatives or partnerships. Such efforts can refine job-entry requirements, foster the availability of effective mentor arrangements between youths and adults, create meaningful training and career paths for youths, improve occupational counseling, and offer training and education on a joint basis between schools and work sites, thereby putting learning into a practical context more likely to motivate students. In short, the process of bridging the school-employment gap must be systematic, focused, comprehensive, and flexible.

Building Effective Learning Paths from High School to Career-Track Jobs

A compact with measurable outcomes and a good information base offers the foundation for a community school-to-work initiative. Under its umbrella, a variety of effective training paths can be developed from high school leading directly to jobs and careers. No single training approach will suit the needs of every youth, every employer, or every occupation. The best arrangement may be to establish a portfolio of promising options including apprenticeships, cooperative education, vocational academies, tech prep programs, and national youth service, along with other learning systems that have not yet been envisioned.

Apprenticeships

Conceptually, the apprenticeship model offers many advantages in remedying the employment problems of young people. First, unlike most other forms of training, apprenticeship provides a built-in opportunity for youth to earn while they learn. Second, its mode of training—practical learning by doing—has natural appeal to many young people who are weary of conventional classroom instruction. Third, learning occurs in a real job setting, in direct contact with employers and older workers who can help socialize youths to the workplace. Apprenticeships thus offer built-in incentives and opportunities for mentor relationships.

The effectiveness of apprenticeship is well documented by research. Studies have demonstrated that craft workers trained through apprenticeship learn new skills faster, are promoted faster and more often, suffer less unemployment, and earn more than their counterparts trained in other ways (Marshall, Franklin, & Glover, 1975; Hills, 1982; Leigh, 1989; Cook & others, 1989). Likewise, follow-up surveys of former apprentices have indicated that as many as 15 percent have become business owners themselves (Maier & Loeb, 1975).

Since apprenticeship regulations specify a minimum age of only 16 years, it is technically possible for apprenticeship to serve teenagers in the United States. However, there are some impediments to using the American apprenticeship model for youth younger than 18. The child-labor provisions of the Fair Labor Standards Act and insurance regulations, for example, prohibit youth below that age from working in some hazardous apprenticeable job classifications in construction and other industries.

Another impediment is employer reluctance to hire youth as apprentices, especially disadvantaged youths. Sponsors feel that they are making a major investment in apprentices who may leave them before their investments are recouped. Like other investors, apprenticeship sponsors avoid risk. One public policy solution to this problem is to make disadvantaged youths less risky investments for employers, as has been done with a variety of preapprenticeship initiatives such as those provided in the Job Corps, programs registered by the state apprenticeship agencies in North Carolina and Florida, and a wide range of apprenticeship outreach and skill-development programs (Tolo, Glover, & Gronouski, 1980). However, the approach of expanding preapprenticeship programs is limited by what might be called a "funnel problem." Few apprenticeship positions are available and competition for many of these is intense. A means of expanding the number of apprenticeships, along with getting more youths into them, is therefore needed. One approach—school-to-apprenticeship linkage—has demonstrated that it can accomplish both. The concept of school-to-apprenticeship linkage is simple. High school seniors are employed on a part-time basis as registered apprentices with transition to full-time apprenticeships after graduation, when they become regular apprentices working full time while they complete their related training, ordinarily taken through special classes at local community colleges or vocational schools.

Experience to date reveals some weakness with school-to-apprenticeship programs, especially arranging post-high-school-related training opportunities for apprentices with small employers who sponsor only one or two apprenticeships, making it difficult to meet the minimum class size requirements in community colleges and vocational schools. An ideal solution to this problem is to get employers to join together in associations to sponsor apprenticeships. However, since many school-to-apprenticeship sponsors are new and inexperienced, this is easier said than done. Considerable work is involved in establishing effective programs of related study at the high school level and beyond.

Thanks in part to the work of a number

of individuals and organizations, interest in apprenticeship recently has increased dramatically (Hamilton, 1990 & 1987; William T. Grant Foundation, 1991; Lerman & Pouncy, 1990; Nothdurft & Jobs for the Future, 1991). In l991, the states of Arkansas (Jobs for the Future, April 1991), Wisconsin, and Oregon established a series of state-funded apprenticeship projects. Several bills have been introduced in the U.S. Congress to establish a major national demonstration of youth apprenticeship. Forces driving this movement include a new interest in the German apprenticeship system, the rediscovery by cognitive psychologists of the effectiveness of learning by doing, work by anthropologists in Third World countries confirming the success of informal apprenticeships, and the reaffirmation of the apprenticeship concept by the U.S. Department of Labor's Apprenticeship 2000 initiative during 1988-1989 (U.S. Department of Labor, 1989). In order to distinguish them from traditional apprenticeships, advocates usually call their new programs "youth apprenticeship" or "work-based learning."

Cooperative Education

Although apprenticeship is not well established in American high schools, another work-study training scheme, cooperative education, has a better foothold. Approximately 600,000 high school students, nearly one-tenth of all students who are enrolled in vocational education programs, participate in cooperative education.

Cooperative education differs from apprenticeship in that cooperative education is more school-based than industry-based, its training typically ends with high school, its work stations are designed to be training stations rather than permanent jobs, and it is best established in a different set of occupations than apprenticeship—primarily in retailing and clerical work. Cooperative education at the postsecondary level has grown significantly over the past two decades, especially among community colleges. Thus, there would appear to be great potential to link the two to offer more advanced training—especially in conjunction with the establishment of tech prep programs (see below). However, at the present time, collaboration between cooperative education at the secondary level and at the postsecondary level is remarkably uncommon.

Existing evaluations of cooperative education programs have yielded mixed results and incomparable findings, but these evaluations have been methodologically flawed (Stern & others, 1990). A key problem with cooperative education is the great variation in quality from program to program. One solution is to tie the programs to a certification scheme such as that used in German apprenticeships, in which the skills and knowledge of the program's graduates are tested in performance, written, and oral tests appropriate to the occupation (U.S. General Accounting Office, 1991, p. 13).

Vocational Academies

Restructuring high school vocational-technical education is a critical component of any system to improve the linkages between school and work. One promising approach is the career academy, originated in Philadelphia and replicated extensively in California.

Under the basic academy model, at the end of the ninth grade, students at risk of failure are identified and invited to volunteer for a program based on a school-within-a-school format, with a separate team of teachers for a portion of their courses. The resulting cadre of students and teachers remains together for three years. Students spend the tenth grade catching up on academics and integrating computers and field trips into the curriculum. In grade 11, every student has a mentor from industry who introduces the student to his or her workplace and joins the student for recreational activities at least once a month. By the end of the eleventh grade, the student obtains a summer job with one of the business partners. Students who stay with the program are promised a job on graduation from high school.

The academies have worked well because the students have a context for their learning and they have "found a home" in the small academies (about 100 students or less). Evaluations to date indicate that academies have an effect on reducing dropout rates (Stern & others, 1988 & 1989). Plans for a careful evaluation of the longitudinal effects of career academies using a random assignment design are being formulated by the Manpower Demonstration Research Corporation.

Partnership academies were subsequently funded in 12 school districts across California with matching grants of $67,500 from the state. By 1991, several additional California sites were being developed around occupational clusters in hospitality, media, health, or finance, depending on the local economy. Efforts were being made to expand even further.

Industry variations of the academy idea also have emerged. The American Express Corporation, for example, developed the Finance Academy in Phoenix, Arizona, to prepare youth for careers in banking and finance. The program has been replicated in other cities in collaboration with other financial service firms. American Express also began its Academy in Tourism and has established a foundation to promote the academy model generally. However, some of these examples simply involve adding a few vocational courses independent of academic courses without attempting academic-vocational integration or establishing multiyear school-within-a-school arrangements.

The partnership or career academy model offers several advantages over the traditional ways of organizing high school vocational education. First, clustering vocational education by industry rather than by occupation facilitates industry involvement while leaving open a wide array of occupations to which students can aspire. Second, partnership academies are less likely to become stigmatized than are vocational education programs organized along occupational lines. An academy in the health occupations, for example, includes students who aspire to

be physicians as well as those who wish to become nurses' aides. Third, partnership academies reach at-risk youths earlier and more effectively than other approaches alone. Identifying and beginning to work with students as early as the ninth grade may prevent some at-risk youths from dropping out. Using the small group school-within-a-school format provides a more personal setting for learning. All of these features make the partnership academy an attractive component of a school-to-work initiative.

Tech Prep Programs

Promoted by Dale Parnell and by the Center for Occupational Research and Development (CORD), "tech prep" provides an alternative to the "college prep" curriculum. The aim is to prepare youths for technical careers by aligning high school and community college curricula into a coherent, unduplicated set of courses (Parnell, 1985; Parnell & Hull, 1991). These were formerly called "2 + 2 programs" because they combine the last two years of high school with two years of community college. Tech prep requires the development of formal agreements between the secondary and postsecondary partners for integrating or articulating high school and postsecondary curricula. Unlike the predecessor 2 + 2 program, which could shorten the length of time required to complete work for a certificate or an associate degree because they were designed as a more efficient learning process, tech prep programs intend to provide students with more advanced skills within the traditional time period than do separate high school and community college programs. Students successfully completing the tech prep sequence obtain a high school diploma and a two-year associate degree or a certificate. Tech prep programs are flexible; they can include components for work-site training and work experience, and can even be combined with two-year apprenticeships.

The Carl D. Perkins Vocational and Applied Technology Education Act of 1990 authorized $125 million annually for planning and demonstration grants to consortia of local education agencies and postsecondary institutions to formulate a three-year plan for the development and implementation of tech prep programs. With such federal encouragement and funding, tech prep will become more pervasive.

While tech prep will certainly foster better school-to-school linkages between secondary and postsecondary institutions, its effectiveness in improving school-to-work transitions is yet to be proven. The effectiveness of tech prep in improving school-to-work connections is likely to rest on the degree to which the programs involve meaningful participation by industry, develop work-based learning that effectively integrates school and employment, and integrate academic and applied learning in new ways that engage students and bring life to the instructional process. It is hoped that the federally supported evaluations now under way will provide evidence of the effectiveness of tech prep approaches.

National Youth Service

The implementation of an effective program of National Youth Service could help improve the transitions from high school to work and to college or postsecondary training. National Youth Service obviates the need to find employers for all youths in need of work and opens up many more options. Such a program could offer special advantages if through participation in national service, youths could gain financial assistance for college or postsecondary training along the lines of the GI Bill. In addition, National Youth Service volunteers could be used to strengthen schools and second-chance learning systems. Service to others builds unity among youths from diverse backgrounds while offering valuable learning experiences for the volunteers.

Conclusion

We need to build on such successful experiences as school-to-apprenticeship linkage, cooperative education, the Boston Compact, the partnership academies, and tech prep. A primary objective should be to establish a scaled-up school-to-work initiative that makes a difference for substantial numbers of youths, including minorities and youths from poor families. In short, we propose a system that encompasses a variety of training/learning options. It would begin by providing earlier and better occupational knowledge and guidance for students (and their teachers)—starting at least in middle-school years. Secondary-level vocational education would be restructured along the partnership academy model. High school students would have the opportunity to participate in a compact in which employers promise preferential access to career jobs in return for meeting achievement standards in school. Students not intending to pursue a baccalaureate degree would have a variety of attractive training opportunities, including academies, youth apprenticeships, tech prep, and cooperative education. Adoption of the Commission on Skills of the American Workforce's recommendations to establish high national standards that all high school students would be expected to meet would help keep the options open for all students and therefore greatly facilitate the transitions to work, technical education, or four-year colleges.

Occupational guidance should be systematically improved, beginning as early as elementary school. By tenth grade, youths would be sufficiently prepared to choose a career academy that would provide a context for learning in their subsequent high school years. Career awareness and goal setting should be followed by career exploration, development of preemployment skills, and mentor relationships. Beginning in the eleventh grade, at least some of the academic training would be conducted in a functional context, using problems and real-life situations encountered on the job. Each participating school would have the equivalent of a careers service staff member on site to help conduct the preemployment training, counseling, and matching of mentors and summer jobs.

At the end of the eleventh grade, the program would branch into a variety of flexible options, including apprenticeships, cooperative education work stations, and tech prep programs. In choosing the tech prep option, students would be required to complete two years of community college. Likewise, apprenticeships would require student participation in related training beyond high school. In most cases such training would be conducted in community colleges.

These options would be presented to students, parents, and employers as high-quality opportunities that do not preclude possibilities of attending college later, especially for students who met world-class academic standards for high school graduation. Students would have to earn admission by achieving certain standards in basic skills and other competencies needed for employment. The training would be competency based, offering a variety of instructional strategies including an individualized, self-paced mode using instructional materials in a variety of media formats (including print materials, audiovisuals, and computer-assisted instruction). Group work would also be undertaken. The curriculum would need to be substantial and challenging, with a high academic content. For example, knowledge of mathematics (at least through algebra) is required for several apprenticed trades. Competency certification throughout and upon the completion of training would be an integral feature.

Fearing for their own survival in an increasingly competitive world, many American businesses are desperately seeking ways to improve public schools. Numerous partnerships and "adopt-a-school" arrangements have been initiated, and education issues are receiving greater attention from business lobbies. A key political theme from business is to make teachers and administrators accountable for student outcomes, but mandating that educators be "accountable" ignores the fact that learning is a joint enterprise involving both teachers and students. While good teaching can facilitate learning, it is ultimately the responsibility of the student to learn. Learning cannot occur without students taking action. Motivation is a key to effective learning.

Unfortunately, businesses often overlook a major lever in their own hands for motivating students: They control the most important incentive for workbound youngsters—access to jobs—yet most do not use it. In addition, businesses have not articulated clearly to schools their needs in terms of learner outcomes or skills required, nor have American businesses organized to develop a consensus on such standards—even for vocational education students. Within limits, many businesses have simply adjusted requirements to the job applicants available. Further complicating this picture is firms' disparate expectations from schools. Business is highly heterogeneous in terms of management practices and other important dimensions. Moreover, skill requirements change through time, and the demands of the global-information economy are raising standards significantly for line workers (Commission on Skills, 1990, pp. 37-42).

The issue of standards raises difficult questions. Which firms should set the standards? Ideally, should standards be set by the most progressive or leading-edge firms? If so, which firms are leading-edge and how is such an identification made? How often should the standards be updated and what are the processes for doing so? What are the roles of governments, schools, and other "outsiders" in establishing standards? These questions have no simple answers.

Given these complexities, a good place to start is with a compact that promises students who achieve at a specified level preferential consideration for jobs in the summer, after school, and, most importantly, at graduation.

In most communities, employers begin this process by focusing on students' grades and attendance. However, after accumulating experience with the first few graduating classes, recognition generally sets in that grades and attendance are not enough. Simple grade-point averages, for example, do not take into account that some courses are more rigorous than others. Even more fundamental, it is not clear that grades are useful indicators of the skills employers seek. Businesses must specify what skill assessments and certifications of performance they trust. Both the standards and the measures used to assess them must be reasonable, clear, and objective.

A primary requirement for success in any school-to-work initiative is getting employers committed to the effort. Business needs to recognize that inadequacies in the preparation of American youth are not just problems for schools. The development of a quality workforce requires active participation of many outside the schools, including parents, public officials, communities, and employers. Ultimately, American employers must shoulder part of the responsibility for the development of youths—their future workers. It is, however, the responsibility of government at every level to provide the incentive context within which employers operate. The federal government should build consensus for a high-skills development strategy, but business and labor representatives should be active participants in that consensus-building process. An effective process to facilitate the transition from school to work for the great majority of our young people who do not pursue baccalaureate degrees must be an integral component of any high-skills development strategy.

Authors' note: We are grateful to the Charles Stewart Mott Foundation and Jobs for the Future for generous financial support for Robert Glover during the preparation of this manuscript. For helpful comments on previous drafts of this paper, we want to thank Paul Barton, Jana Carlisle, Kenneth Edwards, Barbara Green, Samuel Halperin, Suzanne Hershey, Christopher King, Cheryl McVay, Edward Pauly, Ellen Sehgal, John Stevens, Ruby Takanishi, Ken Tolo, Joan Wills, and two anonymous reviewers.

References

American Association for the Advancement of Science. (1988). *Project 2061 Report*. Washington, DC: Author.

Barton, P. E. (1991, Spring). The school to work transition. *Issues in Science and Technology, 7*, 50.

Berlin, G., & Sum, A. (1988). *Toward a more perfect union: Basic skills, poor families, and our economic future*. New York: Ford Foundation.

Bishop, J. H. (1989, January-February). Why the apathy in American high schools? *Educational Researcher 18*.

Chapman, W., & Katz, M. (1981). *Survey of career information systems in secondary schools*. New York: Oxford University Press.

Commission on Skills of the American Workforce. (1990). *America's choice: High skills or low wages!* Rochester, NY: National Center on Education and the Economy.

Cook, R. F., & others. (1989, March). Analysis of apprenticeship training from the National Longitudinal Study of the High School Class of 1972 (Report prepared for the Bureau of Apprenticeship and Training, U.S. Department of Labor, & the National Training Program of the International Union of Operating Engineers). Rockville, MD: Westat, Inc.

Hamilton, S. F. (1990). *Apprenticeship for adulthood: Preparing youth for the future*. New York: The Free Press.

Hills, S. N. (1982). How craftsmen learn their skills: A longitudinal analysis. In R. E. Taylor, H. Rosen, & R. C. Pratzner (Eds.), *Job training for youth* (pp. 203-240). Columbus: National Center for Research in Vocational Education, Ohio State University.

Jobs for the Future. (1991, April). *A feasibility study of youth apprenticeship in Arkansas*. Somerville, MA: Author.

Leigh, D. E. (1989, October). What kinds of training 'work' for noncollege bound youth? (Report prepared for the U.S. General Accounting Office).

Lerman, R. I., & Pouncy, H. (1990, Fall). The compelling case for youth apprenticeships. *The Public Interest, 101*, 62-77.

Marshall, R. (1991). *Losing direction: Families, human resource development, and economic performance. The state of families*. Milwaukee, WI: Family Service America.

Marshall, R., Franklin, W. S., & Glover, R. W. (1975). *Training and entry into union construction* (Manpower R & D Monograph No. 39, U.S. Department of Labor, Manpower Administration). Washington, DC: Government Printing Office.

Maier, D., & Loeb, H. (1975). *Training and work experiences of former apprentices in New York state*. New York: Division of Research and Statistics, New York State Department of Labor.

National Alliance of Business. (1989). *The Compact Project: School-business partnerships for improving education*. Washington, DC: Author.

Nothdurft, W. E., & Jobs for the Future. (1991). *Youth apprenticeship, American Style: A strategy for expanding school and career opportunities*. Somerville, MA: Jobs for the Future, 1991.

Osterman, P. (1980). *Getting started: The youth labor market*. Cambridge, MA: MIT Press.

Osterman, P. (1988). *Employment futures: Reorganization, dislocation, and public policy*. New York: Oxford University Press.

Parnell, D. (1985). *The neglected majority*. Washington, DC: Community College Press.

Parnell, D., & Hull, D. (Eds.) (1991). *The tech prep associate degree: A win-win strategy*. Waco, TX: Center for Occupational Research and Development.

Resnick, L. (1987). Learning in school and out. *Educational Researcher, 16*, 13-20.

Rosenbaum, J. E. (1989). Empowering schools and teachers: A new link to jobs for the non-college bound. *Investing in people*. (Report of the National Commission on Workforce Quality and Labor Market Efficiency, U.S. Department of Labor). Washington, DC: Government Printing Office.

Rosenbaum, J. E. (1990, Winter). What if good jobs depended on good grades? *American Educator, 13*, 12.

Rosenbaum, J. E., & Kariya, T. (1989, May). From high school to work: Market and institutional mechanisms in Japan. *American Journal of Sociology 94*, 1334-1365.

Schultz, T. W. (1981). *Investing in people: The economics of population quality*. Berkeley: University of California Press.

Spring, W. J. (1989). From 'solution' to catalyst: A new role for federal education and training dollars. (Working paper prepared for the National Center on Education and the Economy).

Spring, W. J. (1987, March/April). Youth unemployment and the transition from youth to work. *New England Economic Review*, 3-16.

Stern, D., & others. (1988, Summer). Combining academic and vocational courses in an integrated program to reduce high school dropout rates: Second-year results from replications of the California Peninsula Academies. *Educational Evaluation and Policy Analysis, 10*, 161-170.

Stern, D., & others. (1989, Winter). Benefits and costs of dropout prevention in a high school program combining academic and vocational education: Third-year results from replications of the California Peninsula Academies. *Educational Evaluation and Policy Analysis, 11*, 405-416.

Stern, D., & others. (1990, March). Work experience for students in high school and college. *Youth and Society, 21*, 355-389.

Tolo, K., Glover, R. W., & Gronouski, J. (1980). *Preparation for apprenticeship through CETA*. Austin: Lyndon B. Johnson School of Public Affairs, University of Texas at Austin.

U.S. Bureau of Labor Statistics. (1989, June). Nearly three-fifths of high school graduates of 1988 enrolled in college. (U.S. Department of Labor News Release 89-308). Washington: Author.

U.S. Department of Labor. (1989). *Work-based learning: Training America's workers*. Washington, DC: Government Printing Office.

U.S. General Accounting Office. (1990). *Training strategies: Preparing noncollege youth for employment in the U.S. and foreign countries*. Washington, DC: Government Printing Office.

U.S. General Accounting Office. (1991). *Transition from school to work: Linking education and work site training* (GAO/HRD 91-105). Washington, DC: Government Printing Office.

William T. Grant Foundation Commission on Work, Family and Citizenship Youth and America's Future. (1988). *The forgotten half: Pathways to success for America's youth and young families*. Washington, DC: Author.

William T. Grant Foundation Commission on Work, Family and Citizenship, Youth and America's Future, & others. *States and communities on the move: Policy initiatives to create a world-class workforce*. Washington, DC: Author.

15

Developing Best Practices in Middle Level and High School Vocational/ Career/Occupational Programs

By Conrad F. Toepfer, Jr.

Introduction:
Into the Future . . . *Now*

Now more than ever, young people must develop the attitudes and skills they will need to achieve personal and economic self-sufficiency in their adult futures. Building on their childhood experiences, most people largely fashion their attitudes about learning, work, and their enduring adult values during early adolescence. Relatively few individuals substantially change attributes in those areas after their middle level school years. The high school years clearly are too late to begin efforts to help youth develop the skills they will need for stable and better employment in our changing society. Middle level school programs must include the here-and-now realities of life in local communities and in our broader society so that young people understand what they need to succeed in their adult lives (Toepfer, 1994).

Today, young adolescents face life in a society in which continued learning will determine their ability to qualify for upwardly mobile employment opportunities. Wirth (1992) considered that schools remain society's best instrument for educational and social transformation, maintaining that youth need to become aware of and understand the skills they will need in the twenty-first century.

Middle level school programs need to help students understand that they will encounter continually changing circumstances in their adult futures. As new occupations replace old ones, to remain employable, workers will need to learn skills required for new jobs and positions. This is a new, major challenge to middle level education. The Carnegie Commission Report (Hornbeck, 1989, p. 8) concluded that middle level schools are *potentially society's most powerful force to recapture millions of youth adrift*. Middle level and high school programs must help young adolescents see the need to become personally and economically self-sufficient. Young people need to develop skills in such areas as:

- defining and solving problems,
- accessing and processing information, and
- collaborating and networking (which involves the learning of risk taking and sharing with others).

People will need such attributes in professional and other workplace environments. Students must develop capabilities to maintain and improve their employability potential. In like manner, middle level educators must understand the importance of this need. Their success in developing experiences that help students to understand the societal shift and develop such attributes will have far-reaching consequences.

A Brief Historical Perspective

More than a decade ago, the report *A Nation at Risk* (Gardner, 1983) initiated a national campaign to improve American secondary education. While that report focused on high school education in grades 9 through 12, pressure soon mounted to move a number of high school learning experiences down to the middle level to "get students ready for high school." To counteract that, Johnston and others (1985) identified an agenda for improving middle level education which framed legitimate, middle level educational excellence issues. As schools continue to be a convenient and powerless scapegoat for various national woes, this chapter will consider the current attempt to revise vocational/occupational/career education as a cure for the American economy. I believe that will raise a number of critical concerns for middle level education. A brief review of events in recent decades could help us see what may lie ahead.

The wave of national reports initiated by *A Nation At Risk* noted the critical importance of schools preparing a greater number of young people with high technology skills. However, Duckworth (1984) saw things differently, and time has proven her correct.

The Bureau of Labor Standards presents quite a different picture of the demands for highly educated young people in the next 10 years. By the year 1990, the four fastest-growing high technology jobs together will create a total of 382,000 new jobs. The number of fast-food workers alone will increase by 400,000, and seven other kinds of work are above them on the list. (Secretaries top the list with 700,000, nurses' aides/orderlies are next at 508,000, followed by janitors, sales clerks, and cashiers.) The current crisis could be seen quite differently from the way these [national educational] reports suggest. One could instead propose that it is the economy which is in crisis, and that young people know that perfectly well. When the prospect for work is a fast-food job, if you're lucky, what economic incentive is there to invest in education? (p. 16)

I was working in a junior high school when the Soviet Union put Sputnik into orbit in 1958. Science and mathematics programs in American schools were blamed as the reason the United States failed to put a satellite into orbit first. It is interesting that American schools received no accolades when, less than a decade later, the United States put the first person on the moon. In like manner, could the rise in sales of Japanese and other foreign automobiles beyond those of American-made cars have been a major reason for *A Nation at Risk*'s indictment of our schools?

The issue of employment and jobs has risen to center stage during the past decade. Some predictions of the National Alliance of Business (1987) have proven painfully accurate. That organization noted that 75 percent of the people to be employed in the year 2000 were already in the workforce. It also predicted that

• youth unemployment would be three times higher than the overall unemployment rate,

• young workers would drop from 30 percent to 16 percent of the workforce between 1985 and 2000, and

• by the year 2000, an estimated 5 to 15 million service jobs would be obsolete.

Those predictions have been realized before the dawn of the next millennium. Some of Hodgkinson's (1989) data pointed to another unemployment problem that has been confirmed. Increasing numbers of college graduates and advanced degree holders now take jobs that do not require a college degree, and many of them work in fields other than the ones in which they have earned degrees. It seems clear that unless more than minimum wage jobs are generated, improving the educational achievement and skills of students will not "jumpstart" our economy.

A Misdirected Agenda

I strongly disagreed with the efficacy of the "goals" in *America 2000* (1991) and with those slightly expanded statements in the Clinton administration's *Goals 2000* (1993) initiative. Goals should set directions toward which progress can be planned and charted. What America 2000 listed as goals were actually time-lined mandates with neither programmatic nor financial means to achieve them. Besides being unachievable by the year 2000, the greater question is whether those targets are indeed the central purposes toward which our schools should be working. The Clinton administration's view has not changed from the educational rhetoric of *America 2000*.

The goals in the *Goals 2000* and *America 2000* initiatives were taken from *National Goals of Education* (1990) produced by the Governors' Committee, which was chaired by Bill Clinton, governor of Arkansas at the time. Although given no financial means for achieving them, schools that embraced the goals of all three statements stand accountable for not achieving them by 2000. We must ask ourselves whether the American scientific community would have accepted President Kennedy's challenge to put a person on the moon in less than a decade without significant financial and other support.

To succeed, the rethinking of vocational/occupational/career education must be integrated with efforts to provide jobs in specific areas. The effort to rethink those fields is best seen through the Secretary of Labor's SCANS report (Secretary's Commission on Achieving Necessary Skills, 1990), which does not build such an interfaced effort. However, isolated, single-thrust attempts appear to have little chance of reaching the SCANS targets for the year 2000 and may again render education liable to severe criticism.

SCANS states that by 2000, high school graduates must possess the following competencies for entry-level jobs in business and industry:

Resources: Identifies, organizes, plans, and allocates resources.

A) Time: Selects goal-relevant activities, ranks them, allocates time, and prepares and follows schedules.

B) Money: Uses or prepares budgets, makes forecasts, keeps records, and makes adjustments to meet objectives.

C) Material and facilities: Acquires, stores, allocates, and uses materials or space efficiently.

Interpersonal: Works with others.

A) Participates as member of a team: Contributes to group effort.

B) Teaches others new skills.

C) Serves clients/customers: Communicates ideas to justify position, persuades and convinces others, responsibly challenges existing procedures and policies.

D) Negotiates: Works toward agreements involving exchange of resources, resolves divergent interests.

Systems: Understands complex interrelationships.

A) Understands systems: Knows how social, organizational, and technological systems work and operates effectively within them.

B) Monitors and corrects performance: Distinguishes trends, predicts impacts on system operations, diagnoses deviations in systems' performance, and corrects malfunctions.

C) Improves or designs systems: Suggests modifications to existing systems and develops new or alternative systems to improve performance.

Technology: Works with a variety of technologies.

A) Selects technology: Chooses procedures, tools or equipment, including computers and related technologies.

B) Applies technology to task: Understands overall intent and proper procedures for setup and operation of equipment.

C) Maintains and troubleshoots equipment: Prevents, identifies, or solves problems with equipment, including computers or other technologies.

Chances are poor that most graduating high school seniors can develop such competencies through existing high school programs alone. First, new programs must be developed by educators in consultation with Department of Labor and business/industry and community leaders. Only then can a realistic timetable for preparing high school students for job entry be developed. The year 2000 deadline aside, high schools alone cannot achieve the SCANS outcomes. The high school programs yet to be developed will require a foundation of vocational/occupational/career exploratory education in middle level schools vastly different from what exists today. Well-conceived middle level exploratory programs could effectively address young adolescents' concerns about the future and finding their places in it.

To help youth develop awareness of their need to develop employability skills will require that schools/communities either reallocate finances or seek additional funding for those purposes. Holt (1993, p. 393) noted that schools, like the business sector, must recognize that "the pursuit of quality may cause profits to fail in the short term, but quality pays off in the end." "The contention that high tech skills will be the key to employability is being rethought in view of the growing need for the employable population at large to develop some technology literacy." Weisman (1993, p. 360) concludes that "researchers once wedded to the idea that jobs will require increasingly higher skills are hedging their bet." This supports an earlier contention of Beane, Toepfer, and Alessi (1986, p. 368):

> All students need some technology education and to develop an awareness of how technology will increasingly impact on our culture and lives. This low-technology education needs to become a general education concern.

It now appears this will also impact students' employability as well. In addition, developing a competitive workforce will also require better interfacing and integration of academic and vocational learning (Kolde, 1991). Gray (1993, p. 372) correctly noted that "despite all the rhetoric about equality, high schools teach elitism, not egalitarianism." As to the perception of vocational education, Aring (1993, p. 399) stated that "vocational education in the U.S. tends not to be seen as a viable pre-employment system." The need for comprehensive high schools which overcome the current separation of academic and vocational learning is increasing. Stern, Dayton, and Weissberg (1989) documented the cost benefits of dropout prevention when high school programs interface academic and vocational preparation.

The notion that academic high schools are primarily for college-bound youth must be rethought, as all students need to develop some technological literacy for employability. Academically oriented students will need some vocational learning experiences which heretofore have been provided at vocational high schools and vocational-technical education centers.

In like manner, extended proficiency in language arts, mathematics, science, and computer/information processing is becoming essential to achieve literacy in those areas for employability. Grubb (1992) described how comprehensive high schools organized as schools-within-schools have integrated academic and vocational learning. Known as academies, these occupationally focused high schools are organized into career clusters in which teachers coordinate topics they teach by remaining with groups of students for two or three years. Grubb (1992, pp. 40-41) reported that these academy programs have achieved the following:

- brought coherence to the curriculum;
- improved teaching and achievement in all subjects;
- integrated academic and vocational education and enhanced reengagement of students in school;
- reduced the isolation of teachers and

the tracking and segregation of students;

● preserved options for all students in establishing two years of high school combined with two years of school after high school; and

● improved career guidance and counseling and provided a vision for business participation.

While this approach organizes schools-within-schools, smaller school districts that presently send some students to regional vocational or vocational-technical schools will face some difficulties. As receiving centers, those regional schools will either have to develop more comprehensive programs or blend their vocational/occupational/career education components with academic programs offered at the sending high schools. Such a substantive reorganization of American high schools merits serious consideration. Smaller schools and communities will need something of that sort to respond to the SCANS report's concerns.

Middle Level Education Position Issues

Its position between elementary and high school has led to the perception that the middle level school is primarily a *connection* from elementary to high school. This bridging notion was established in the earliest national reports (National Education Association 1907 & 1909; Baker, 1913). They recommended the establishment of junior high schools. Those reports envisioned the bridging from elementary to high school as a primary function of the junior high school. This connecting function, plus calling this new unit *junior high school*, combined to create the assumption that the middle level school should be a miniature, or junior edition, of the high school. As such, the junior high was not considered to be a separate entity with an "educational life of its own"! Recognition of the need for junior high to establish its own educational identity developed, subsequently.

As a result, middle level schools had to resist efforts to push elementary concerns up and high school concerns down into

their domain. The latter has perennially distracted attempts of middle level schools to focus on young adolescent developmental and learning needs. In the 1940s, the need for the junior high schools to develop such an identity achieved greater recognition. Gruhn and Douglass (1947) emphasized that junior high schools had to establish a free-standing, educational identity based on their functions to meet the specific educational needs of young adolescents. The middle school movement has subsequently moved that agenda forward. While middle level schools should be primarily concerned with their central functions for young adolescents, the bridging function is a legitimate concern. I have previously noted (1986) how middle level school programs play a vital role in articulating the district-wide learning experience for students.

Hodgkinson (1990) predicted that most types of work at which Americans will earn a living in the year 2005 will be initiated between now and then. In any event, the shift of requirements for employability will continue to change. As educators, we must prepare today's young adolescents to succeed in tomorrow's world, based on future needs that we can forecast. This has particular impact for the middle level school years.

As noted at the beginning of this piece, building on their childhood experiences, most people largely fashion their attitudes about learning, work, and their enduring adult values during early adolescence. Relatively few individuals substantially change those attributes in those areas after their middle level school years. The attitudes and outlook developed by young adolescents become increasingly critical to their becoming personally and economically self-sufficient in adulthood.

Moving high school vocational/occupational/career educational experiences down into the middle level only violates developmental and learning needs of young adolescents. No purpose is served by imposing learning challenges designed for a more mature population on younger students. Instead, middle level educators need to identify vocational/occupational/career-oriented learning experiences that are developmentally and intellectually appropriate for young adolescents. Two questions must be addressed in planning those programs for young adolescents:

1. Can, and should, middle level schools assume responsibility for vocational/occupational/career education?

2. Can, and should, middle level schools provide vocational/occupational/career exploration to help students become aware of their need to develop employability skills?

With regard to the first question, vocational preparation has never been a central goal of middle level education, and contemporary societal shifts provide no reason to change that. As for the second question, I recommend that middle level schools focus their vocational/occupational/career education programs on providing exploratory experiences. Such background and awareness would improve the foundation needed for more effective vocational preparatory experiences at high school and postsecondary levels.

Lifelong Learning and School-to-Work Issues

Today's students will face adult life in a society where upwardly mobile employment opportunities require more advanced skills. The twenty-first century may well become known as "the learning century" as one's capacity for lifelong learning becomes a requisite for employability. Increasing numbers of professionals and members of the general workforce will have to learn news skills as emerging occupations and career opportunities replace former ones. Middle level exploratory programs need to help students understand that their personal economic self-sufficiency will substantially depend on their ability to learn new employability skills.

Although always desirable, a "love of learning" was not a necessity in earlier times when factual recall largely dominated what students were supposed to learn. In earlier times, students completing or dropping out of school were welcomed by a world of work in need of non- and semi-skilled labor. Neither one's capacity for retraining, intellectual development, nor academic achievement were critical qualifications for securing a job as they are now.

Job security, paid medical and hospitalization care, vacations, and retirement plans were benefits of employment for nonskilled workers in the "blue collar" working-class era. Then, entering workers could maintain and increase their standards and levels of living, which allowed them to marry, raise children, and send their children to postsecondary schools. However, today's students will become adults in a society in which non- and semi-skilled job opportunities leading to higher personal and economic quality of life will continue to diminish.

Many fields already require more frequent job as well as career shifts. As existing jobs and positions are replaced by new ones, workers will increasingly have to develop skills for retraining. Students need to understand that continued learning of skills will be an entry to personal satisfaction and better quality of life. For that reason, schools must develop a continuum that helps youth develop capacities for continued learning. The National Alliance of Business report (1987, p. 5) cited earlier also noted that

● more than one million youth drop out of school each year and drop-out rates in urban schools are close to fifty percent, and that

● one of every four ninth graders will drop out of school each year.

Those dropout figures have not decreased since 1988. I am convinced that improved middle level vocational/occupational/career exploratory programs could substantially lower those statistics. Dropping out must be recognized as a systemwide, rather than a high school, problem. Often, the journey to dropping out begins with inappropriate learning challenges in the middle and even the elementary school levels. Those experiences for some individuals may be either too difficult or too simple.

Dropping out is the final action of what normally is a slowly building school-leaving syndrome. Many students who drop out could not find sufficient connections between their school experiences and the problems in their lives. This often leads to "learned helplessness," a terminal behavior, fostered by a student's decreasing self-esteem and confused self-concept as a learner. Those who leave school believing they are less capable than they really are will probably face diminished possibilities for achieving personal economic sufficiency. Yet school experiences that nurture a person's interests can positively influence poor affect (Beane, 1990). Many young adolescents who see little value in school could benefit greatly through middle level exploratory experiences that connect them with potential employment and career interests.

Revising the Middle Level Curriculum

The following ought to be emphasized in revisioning middle level vocational/occupational/career exploratory educational programs:

- Identify teaching and learning approaches especially appropriate for providing middle level exploratory vocational/occupational/career learning experiences.
- Develop middle level teaching and learning approaches particularly suited for vocational/occupational/career exploration.
- Identify how extra-class activities and other experiences available in middle level school programs can provide additional vocational/occupational/career exploration opportunities.

Young people's learning experiences must help them gain an awareness of the employability skills needed to achieve personal economic self-sufficiency. To be most effective, those experiences should be integrated with learning in other middle level content areas. (For example, social studies courses might study contemporary American and world economic issues and relate them to local conditions; industrial arts/

technology courses could address the changing world of work, relating it to local conditions). The focus of units will require teams that combine staff from academic and exploratory areas. This has great potential for integrating learning around student interests related to vocational/occupational/career area issues.

Stemmer, Brown, and Smith (1992) discussed some successful vocational/occupational/career exploratory approaches developed in Michigan middle schools. Those programs provide experiences that help students develop an awareness of employability needs and a portfolio of rudimentary employability skills. Business representatives, parents, and school personnel involve themselves by helping students gain perspective, confidence, and success in these initial efforts.

Beginning with vocational/occupational/career exploration, students identify their own needs to develop personal, academic, and teamwork skills. Business representatives, parents, and school personnel monitor these behaviors while working with students. Students have as one goal developing a portfolio that documents their progress in those areas. Teachers have reported that students in these programs demonstrate increased motivation and interest in other school work and even increased self-esteem. In some situations, businesses have reviewed student portfolios and given each student individual feedback.

Stemmer, Brown, and Smith (1992) reported that the portfolio project is not merely an improved sorting system but that it encourages students to recognize their successes. They also show progress in looking for opportunities to fill gaps in their skills and gain confidence in preparing for work. Some districts have used an employability skills guide that lets parents help their young adolescents learn to plan for accomplishing schoolwork and chores within a given amount of time.

I have modified and increased the skills listed by Stemmer, Brown, and Smith (1992, p. 33) to provide outcomes that middle level schools can use to develop vocational exploratory experiences that help students develop awareness of the importance of these skill areas and to gain personal growth through developing those skills.

Academic skills (Defined as those skills that provide the basic foundation for a person necessary to get, keep, and progress on a job):

• Understand spoken language and speak using the language in which business is conducted.

• Write in the language in which business is conducted.

• Understand and solve problems involving basic arithmetic and know how to apply the results.

• Use library and research skills.

• Access and use specialized knowledge when necessary (e.g., the sciences or skilled trades) to get a job done.

• Think and act logically by developing the attitudes and behaviors required to get, keep, and progress on the job.

Personal skills (Those skills related to developing the attitudes and behaviors required to get, keep, and progress on a job):

• Identify personal, job-related interests, options, and opportunities.

• Demonstrate personal values and ethics valued in the workplace (e.g., honesty, fairness, and respect for others).

• Develop tentative career plans.

• Attend school/work on time each day.

• Meet school/work deadlines.

• Exercise a sense of responsibility.

• Demonstrate self-control.

• Pay attention to details.

• Show pride in one's work.

• Be enthusiastic about things to be done.

• Follow written or verbal directions.

• Learn to work without supervision.

• Learn new skills and ways of doing things.

• Identify and suggest new ways of doing things.

Teamwork skills (Those skills needed to work with others on a job):

• Identify with the goals, norms, values, and customs of a group.

• Know the group's rules and values.

• Actively participate in the group.

• Listen to other group members and communicate with all group members.

• Use a team approach to identify problems and devise solutions for getting a job done.

• Show willingness to compromise, if necessary, to accomplish the goal.

• Exercise "give and take" to achieve group goals.

• Function in changing work settings and in changing groups.

• Determine when to act as a leader and when to be a follower, depending on what is necessary to get a job done.

• Show sensitivity to the needs of women and ethnic and racial minorities in the group (and outside it).

• Be loyal to a group.

Students would progress in particular areas in terms of their personal experiences and abilities. They could pace themselves to work on specific skills as their readiness allows and their interests emerge. Experiences that help young adolescents develop the attributes described above will lay a foundation for their pursuit of entry-level skills such as those mentioned in the SCANS report in high school.

Young adolescents typically want to know why they must learn certain things. Effective middle level vocational/occupational/career exploratory programs relate students' "here-and-now" concerns to possible employability concerns. Hands-on and applied exploratory learning experiences provide an excellent means for such experiences. Hollifield (1992) described how revitalized apprenticeships can provide avenues for young adolescents to identify and explore vocational/occupational/career interests. Raizen (1992) further suggests the use of apprenticeship *early* in a student's school experiences to develop understandings about the world of work–not just as part of the school-to-work transition.

Actual hardware and equipment in cutting-edge technologies have long been too costly for schools to purchase and update.

Instead, middle level vocational/occupational/career exploratory programs could use computer simulations that provide situational learning for students to explore evolving, state-of-the-art innovations. Well-defined apprenticeships, community service projects, and computer simulations can help middle level students understand the changing world of work and the employability skills they will need to develop in becoming lifelong learners.

Increasing numbers of young adolescents are growing up in families and in communities in which their siblings, parents, guardians, and neighbors seldom have employment. In both urban and rural communities, there are families that have been on welfare for several generations. Youth from such circumstances do not understand the work ethic, employability, or life with regular employment. It would help to provide middle level school exploratory experiences for these young adolescents in which they "shadow" and study work. Observing and later interviewing people who work in different jobs and careers could help them to understand economic self-sufficiency and to discover how employability relates to upward mobility and improved quality of life.

Because of the possibilities in the coming technocracy, it may be that, regardless of the skills they gain, increasing numbers of people will not be employed in the sense of what we considered "work" in the industrial society. The passing of the "industrial society work ethic" poses serious challenges to schools. In any circumstances, people's psychological wellness requires that they feel they have worth, dignity, and something to contribute as citizens. Shadowing of volunteerism and participation in school community service projects that address real local community needs can benefit middle level students. (It also appears that our existing welfare system will move in that direction as well.) Regardless of how conditions may change, middle level schools must consider the implications that those changes will have for exploratory learning by young adolescents.

Another Reflection on the Past

The first vocational high schools in the United States developed shortly before 1920. The first identification of vocational education as a major high school goal occurred when "vocation" was listed as one of the seven *Cardinal Principles of Secondary Education* (Commission on the Reorganization of Secondary Education, 1918). Two decades later, *Purposes of Education in American Democracy* cited economic efficiency as one of four major purposes of secondary schools (Educational Policies Commission, 1938). Six years later, that commission identified salable skills as 1 of the 10 imperative needs of youth in Education for All American Youth (Educational Policies, 1944).

Education for work and vocation have been high school functions, but the middle level education literature has not endorsed vocational/occupational/career education as a major purpose at that level. Therefore, exploratory education remains the most appropriate focus for vocational/occupational/career learning at the middle level. Appropriately developed experiences can help young adolescents to define potential vocational/occupational/career educational interests, become aware of changing employability skill demands, and develop attitudes and understandings about work and employability as a foundation for developing advanced skills in high school. Districts must give sufficient priority to developing programs at both levels and to providing adequate time for them during the school day. The high school cannot dictate a school/community's middle level vocational/occupational/career exploratory programs. Programs at the two levels should be developed in cooperation with one another.

We must approach this issue carefully and thoughtfully. It would be inappropriate and probably disastrous for middle level schools to take on any responsibility for providing young adolescents with specific vocational skills. We would do well to consider the concerns the author of the first text on the junior high school expressed about vocational preparation more than 70 years ago (Briggs, 1920, p.38):

> The objections to the conception that would make junior high school a trade-training institution are four: first, that it is undemocratic t make an early segregation of pupils on the ł sis of future vocations, thus prematurely s ping the common education that make common understandings and integratic ond, that because of the social stigma tached to the vocational curricula, or rathei . the positive social distinction associated with the academic, it is difficult to secure registration for vocational training by many students most in need of it; third, that it is impossible to foretell with anything like accuracy, at the age of 12 to 14 what specific trade a pupil will or should follow; and finally, that the concrete work and novelty of trade courses attract and send prematurely to wage earning many pupils who can and should have extended education, either academic or technical.

Briggs made an additional powerful statement we need to consider in making certain that middle level vocational/occupational/career education does not abandon an exploratory focus.

> The junior high proposes not so much to save time for each pupil by earlier beginning of specific preparation for his [or her] chosen or destined work in life as it does to spend two or three years in assuming that differentiation is made as intelligently as possible. In other words, it proposes to explore by means of material in itself worthwhile, the interests, aptitudes, and capacities of the pupils, and at the same time, to reveal by material otherwise justifiable, the possibilities of the major fields, both intellectual and academic. (1920, pp. 41-42)

That still holds true for developing best vocational/occupational/career education practices at the middle level. Rapidly occurring changes in social, economic, and political life are shaping serious challenges to our democratic way of life. American youth will have to deal with the intertwined di-

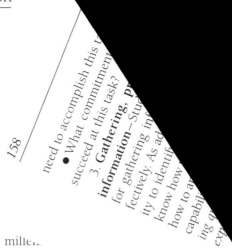

need to accomplish this t
• What commitment
succeed at this task?
3. **Gathering, p**
information—Stu
for gathering in
fectively. As ad
ity to identif
know how
how to a
capabil
ing q
ex

millei.

Guidelines .
Needed Areaɔ

Areas of skill today's studenɪɔ include the following (Toepfer, 1995):

1. **Developing a vision**—Students need to develop the skills necessary for building a vision, communicating that vision, and making that vision a reality. As adults they must be able to identify attributes that changing conditions will require for their continued employability. *Guiding questions for developing student learning experiences*:

• What does/will the vision look like?

• Do I/we want to accomplish it?

• What do I/we need to do to complete or accomplish it?

• How will I/we determine whether or not it has been accomplished?

2. **Building an awareness of self**—Students need to develop skills to identify their strengths and weaknesses, and to improve areas where they are weak. As adults, they will need to know how to use their strengths to develop skills that changing conditions will require for continued employability. *Guiding questions for developing student learning experiences*:

• What does this task require of me/us?

• How does the task relate to my/our responsibilities?

• What strengths do I/we bring to the task?

• What areas of weaknesses or deficiency do I/we need to improve to accomplish the task?

• What skills or information do I/we

...sk?

...must be made to

...ocessing, and using
...ents must develop skills
...ormation and using it ef-
...ults, they will need the abil-
... what information they need,
...o access and obtain it, and know
...alyze it to maintain their personal
...ty for continued employability. *Guid-*
...estions for developing student learning
...riences:

● What types of information do I/we
need to know?

● How will I/we find and access it?

● What technological or manual skills
will I/we use to process that information?

● Are there new processes I/we have to
learn?

● If so, how will I/we learn them?

4. **Developing decision-making skills—**
Students must develop skills and strategies
necessary for making informed decisions.
As adults, they will need to determine what
skills and attributes they need to develop
for continued employability. *Guiding ques-*
tions for developing student learning experi-
ences:

● What issue(s) must be decided?

● What decision(s) must be made?

● Who will be involved in planning and
making the decisions?

● What additional decision-making procedures may need to be investigated or
learned?

● Should alternative decisions be made?

5. **Developing communication skills—**
Students must develop and improve their
written and oral communication skills. As
adults, they will need to interact effectively
with colleagues in the workplace. They will
need to communicate with others to determine what they need to learn and develop
to remain qualified for continued employability. *Guiding questions for developing stu-*
dents' learning experiences:

● What must be known?

● Who (what individuals or groups)
needs to know it?

● How do I/we communicate that information (written, oral formats)?

● Have I/we received all of the necessary
information to move ahead?

● If not, what additional information is
needed to do so?

Conclusion

Best school practices will better meet student employability skill needs by first attending to the needs of young adolescents
to define and explore their vocational/oc-
cupational/career interests and then, initiating and developing employability skills of
maturing adolescents and young adults in
high school. Improving the national
economy is critically important, but it
should not directly drive middle level and
high school programs. We can best serve
both our economy and our youth by encouraging development of vocational/occupa-
tional/career education practice that is responsive and appropriate to the developmental capacities of middle level and high
school students.

References

America 2000. (1991). Washington, DC: Superintendent of Documents, U.S. Government Printing Office.

Aring, M. (1993). What the "V" word is costing
America's economy. *Kappan, 74,* (5): 396-404.

Beane, J. (1990). *Affect in the curriculum: Toward de-*
mocracy, dignity and diversity. New York: Teachers
College Press, Columbia University.

Beane, J., Toepfer, C. F., Jr., & Alessi, S., Jr. (1986).
Curriculum planning and development. Boston, MA:
Allyn & Bacon.

Briggs, T. (1920). *The junior high school.* Boston, MA:
Houghton-Mifflin.

Commission on the Reorganization of Secondary Education. (1918). *Cardinal principles of education.* Bulletin 1918, no. 35. Washington, DC: U.S. Office of
Education.

Duckworth, E. (1984). What teachers know best: The
best knowledge base. In H. Howe, II (Ed.). *Sympo-*
sium on the year of the reports: Response from the
educational community. *Harvard Educational Review,*
54, (1): 15-19.

Educational Policies Commission. (1944). *Education*
for all American youth. Washington, DC: National
Education Association.

Educational Policies Commission. (1938). *The purposes*
of education in American society. Washington, DC:

National Education Association.

Goals 2000. (1993). Washington, DC: Superintendent of Documents, U.S. Government Printing Office.

Gray, K. (1993). Why we will lose: Taylorism in American high schools. *Kappan, 74*, (5): 370-374.

Grubb, W. (1992). Giving high schools an educational focus. *Educational Leadership, 49*, (6): 36-43.

Gruhn, W., & Douglass, H. (1947). *The modern junior high school*. New York: The Ronald Press.

Hodgkinson, H. (March 1990). The demographics of school reform: A look at the children. *Demographics of Education Newsletter*. Washington, DC: Institute for Educational Leadership, Inc.

Hodgkinson, H. (1989). *The same client: Demographics of education and service delivery systems*. Washington, DC: Institute for Educational Leadership.

Hollifield, J. (1992). Learning to work: R&D preview. *Council for Educational Development and Research* (Washington, DC), 6, (2): 4-5.

Holt, M. (1993). The educational consequences of Edward Deming. *Kappan, 74*, (5), 382-388.

Turning points: Preparing American youth for the twenty-first century Washington, DC: Carnegie Commission on Adolescent Development.

Johnston, J. H., Arth, A., Lounsbury, J., & Toepfer, C., Jr. *An agenda for excellence at the middle level*. Reston, VA: National Association of Secondary School Principals Council on Middle Level Education.

Kolde, R. (1991). Integrated learning for a competitive workforce. *Kappan, 72*, (6): 453-457.

A nation at risk: The imperative for educational reform. (1983). Washington, DC: U.S. Office of Education.

National Alliance of Business. (September 20, 1987). *Employment in the year 2000*, 10 pp. (A Supplement to the *New York Times Magazine*.) (Copies available from Marketing Dept., National Alliance of Business, 10151 5th St. NW, Washington, DC, 20005.)

National Education Association. (1909). Report of the progress of the committee on the culture elements and the economy of time in education. *Journal of Proceedings and Addresses at the Forty-Eighth Annual Meeting*. Chicago: University of Chicago Press.

National Education Association. (1907). Report of the progress of the equal division of time between the district and the high school. *Journal of Proceedings and Addresses at the Forty-Sixth Annual Meeting*. Chicago: University of Chicago Press.

National goals of education. (1990). Washington, DC: U.S. Department of Education.

Raizen, S. (1992). *Reforming education for work: A cognitive science perspective*. Macomb, IL: National Center for Research in Vocational Education Materials Distribution Center, Western Illinois University.

Report of the Committee on the National Council of Education on economy of time in education. (1913). U.S. Bureau of Education Bulletin 1913, no. 38. Washington, DC: U.S. Government Printing Office.

Secretary's Commission on Achieving Necessary Skills (SCANS). (1991). *What work requires of schools–A SCANS Report for America 2000*. Washington, DC: U.S. Department of Labor.

Stemmer, P., Brown, B., & Smith, C. (1992). The employability skills portfolio. *Educational Leadership, 49*, (6), 32-35.

Stern, D., Dayton, C., Paik, I., & Weissberg, A. (Winter, 1989). Benefits and costs of dropout prevention in a high school combining academic and vocational education. *Educational Evaluation and Policy Analysis, 11*, 405-416.

Toepfer, C. F., Jr. (1995). Learning to lead by developing relationships. In *Experiencing leadership–Helping middle level students through change*. Reston, VA: Future Business Leaders of America.

Toepfer, C. F., Jr. (January, 1994). Vocational/career/occupational education at the middle level: What is appropriate for young adolescents? *Middle School Journal, 25* (3), 59-65.

Toepfer, C., Jr. (1992). Middle school curriculum: Defining the elusive. In J. Irvin (Ed.) *Transforming middle level education: Perspectives and possibilities*. Boston: Allyn & Bacon, 1992.

Toepfer, C. F., Jr. (1986). Middle level transition and articulation issues. *Middle School Journal, 18*, (10), 9-11.

Weisman, J. (1993). Skills in the schools: Now it's business's turn. *Kappan, 74* (5) 367-369.

Wirth, A. (1992). *Education and work for the year 2000: Choices we face*. San Francisco: Jossey-Bass.

16

Basic Academic and Vocational Skills Required of Employees with Only a High School Diploma

By Kenneth S. Volk and Henry A. Peel

Research sponsored by the Eastern North Carolina Consortium for Assistance and Research in Education

THERE has been a great deal of discussion in recent years about the need to prepare young people for the challenges they will face in a technology-based global economy. To meet this challenge, schools must help students master the necessary reading, writing, and math skills required for employment. Students must be confident in their ability to communicate, critically think, and work in group situations. Given these highly technical times, students must also have an understanding of technological innovations, and issues affecting their lives. In essence, schools must prepare students to live knowledgeably and contribute productively in this complex environment.

Despite calls for an educated workforce, in North Carolina there remains a sizable number of individuals that do not receive post-high-school education or training. According to the *Statistical Profile of North Carolina Public Schools* (North Carolina State Board of Education, 1985), nearly 20 percent of the high school graduates do not pursue further education through commu-

nity colleges, universities, or the military.

For consensus to be determined on the need for employees' basic skills and the lack of post-high-school education being obtained by many in North Carolina, there are several critical issues that need to be examined. First, how many people are hired with only a high school education by the major manufacturing firms in North Carolina? Second, what are the projected trends? That is, will employers likely continue to hire high school graduates at the current rate, or will openings for high school graduates increase or decrease? Third, and the primary focus of this study, what types of skills do employers require of high school graduates?

Through an examination of these issues, necessary high school competencies can be prioritized, community colleges can better determine recruitment strategies, and employers can identify areas where additional training is needed.

Provided here are the results of a study conducted to address questions related to job opportunities available for high-school-degreed employees, as well as the necessary skills these employees must have to be successful. A survey of manufacturers in North Carolina was used to determine basic academic and vocational skills required of employees with only a high school diploma.

The Survey

In generating the Survey of Basic Academic and Vocational Skills, necessary skills required for an educated and employable citizenry were reviewed through the policy and position papers issued by a number of government, manufacturing, and educational organizations (Carnevale, 1991; National Center for Education and the Economy, 1991; North Carolina Department of Economic & Community Development, 1992; Secretary's Commission on Achieving Necessary Skills, 1991; William T. Grant Foundation on Work, Family and Citizenship, 1988). From the list of competencies identified, an instrument was designed to determine the importance of the academic and vocational skills required of those employees with only a high school diploma.

This six-page instrument was designed to have a manufacturing firm representative indicate the specific skills required of high-school-graduated employees. Additional information about the firms' hiring practices and employee characteristics was also solicited.

Respondents were asked to rate skills as *absolutely required, desired but not required,* or *not required* from a high school graduate in their firm. Company representatives were also given the opportunity to provide additional comments on high school graduation requirements.

Manufacturers with more than 500 employees, identified through the *Directory of North Carolina Manufacturing Firms,* were mailed surveys. Each survey was addressed to the representative identified in the *Directory*—most often the company president or plant manager. Approximately one month after the initial mailing, a follow-up mailing was conducted for those not responding to the first mailing.

From the 289 firms identified and sent surveys, 129 responded. This represented a 45 percent response rate. For data analysis, the manufacturing firms were categorized by the number of employees at their location and their type of manufacturing operation. Table 1 shows the sample sizes and respondents by establishment size.

Survey Respondents

Information regarding the range of employee numbers at each particular firm's location was provided in the *Directory*. These ranges were used to determine employee totals. Using the high and low ranges, it was estimated that between 98,000 and 165,000 North Carolina employees were directly represented in this study. (See Table 1.)

When representatives were asked the number of people the company employs in North Carolina, the total number of employees represented in this study greatly increased. From the responses, it was indicated that more than 250,000 individuals are employed throughout North Carolina by these firms and were indirectly represented in the study.

According to the Standard Industrial Classification (SIC) System used in the *Directory*, 13 broad groups of manufacturers participated in the study. Since the survey was mailed to all manufacturing firms in North Carolina identified in the *1992 Directory* as employing 500 or more at their particular location, no attempt was made to control for manufacturing type.

Table 2 provides a summary of the manufacturing groups participating in this

TABLE 1
Respondents by
Establishment Size

Number of Employees	Number of Firms Responding	Percentage of Total Firms
500-999	91	70.5
1,000-2,499	28	21.7
2,500+	10	07.8
Total 129		

study. Of the 129 respondents, more than 15 types of manufacturing firms were represented. The textile and apparel group represented nearly a third of all manufacturing firms. Electronic and machinery companies, combined with textile manufacturers represented over 50 percent of the firms responding.

Profile of Employees

The *Survey of Basic Academic and Vocational Skills* requested information from employers concerning the number of current employees and anticipated hirees with only a high school diploma. The purpose of collecting these data was to establish the availability of jobs in manufacturing firms which require only a high school education.

As indicated in Table 3, more than 69 percent of the employees from these manufacturing firms are hired with only a high school diploma. The employers also reported there exists a large number of jobs that could be done by high school graduates. According to these firms, nearly three-quarters of the jobs could be done by someone with only a high school diploma.

There was a high percentage of high school graduates hired in 1993 by these manufacturing firms. This number compares well with the number of jobs that can be done with a high school diploma.

TABLE 2
Respondents by
Manufacturing Type

Manufacturing Type	Number Responding	Percentage of Total
Textile & Apparel	39	30.2
Electronic & Electrical Equipment	17	13.1
Machinery & Computer Equipment	10	7.8
Food	8	6.2
Furniture	8	6.2
Chemical Products	7	5.4
Rubber & Plastic Products	7	5.4
Transportation Equipment	7	5.4
Lumber & Paper	6	4.7
Measuring & Analyzing Instruments	5	3.9
Printing & Publishing	5	3.9
Tobacco	3	2.3
Stone, Clay & Glass Products	3	2.3

More than half the firms felt their percentage of new hirees requiring only a high school diploma will remain unchanged in the future. Only 13 percent indicated an increase, while 30 percent indicated a decrease.

Also requested in the survey were skill levels needed from employees with high school degrees. Statements regarding skills or competencies were generated from a review of current reports on education. These skill statements addressed not only academic concerns; issues regarding personal attitudes and conduct were included as well.

The following material summarizes the results of this portion of the survey. Numbers in the bar graphs indicate the mean response for each item.

Reading, Writing, and Math Skills

Nine categories were used to group the skill statements for the survey. Category headings were generally patterned after an earlier study conducted by Northern Illinois University which only broadly defined these skill areas (Northern Illinois University, 1991). (We wish to acknowledge the help and suggestions provided by the staff at the Northern Illinois University's Center for Governmental Studies, as well as their encouragement to build upon their earlier study.)

TABLE 3
Employee Profiles

Characteristics	Average Response
Percentage of people employed with only a high school diploma:	69%
Percentage of jobs that could be done by someone with only a high school diploma:	73%
Percentage of people hired in the past year with only a high school diploma:	72%

	Percentage of Total
Future number of employees expected to be hired with only a high school diploma will:	
Increase	13%
Decrease	30%
Remain the Same	57%

Employers agreed that basic math and reading skills were absolutely required for high school graduates to successfully enter the workforce. (See Figure 1.) Graduates should be able to perform the simple mathematical functions of addition, subtraction, multiplication, and division. Almost equally important was an understanding of common job-related words.

Generally, high school graduates who are seeking employment need to be proficient

While half of the respondents desire this skill, less than 20 percent require it.

Understanding principles of geometry was, in fact, as important to employers as algebra. An interesting finding from this study was that more employers desired skills in elementary statistics than either algebra or geometry.

Writing skills were viewed as being less important than reading and math, with employers generally desiring these skills, but not requiring them.

Communication Skills

A great deal of consensus was found among employers related to communication skills needed for high school graduates. As shown in Figure 2, there were few employers who did not require graduates to be able to give or follow clear directions. All but two survey respondents required or desired these general listening and speaking skills. The expectation is that high school graduates who go directly to work, must be able to follow procedural instructions and speak clearly.

Listening skills and the skills necessary to give clear directions were viewed as being equally important. More than 70 percent of the respondents considered these skills to be absolutely required of high school graduates.

FIGURE 1

Reading, writing and math skills

High school graduates should have the basic skills necessary to:

Skill Not Required	Skill Desired, But Not Necessary	Skill Absolutely Required
0	1	2

perform simple mathematical functions (+, -, *, /)
1.90

understand common job-related words
1.89

read the local newspaper
1.73

read instruments such as gauges and meters
1.62

write simple memoranda
1.48

read technical manuals
1.36

estimate time, weight, and speed measurements
1.26

understand elementary statistics
1.16

read blueprints
0.95

perform algebraic equations
0.88

understand geometric principles
0.86

write a technical report
0.85

---

in reading at a level comparable to reading the local newspaper. Seventy-six percent of those surveyed absolutely require this level of reading to be successful on the job.

There is less agreement among employers concerning required mastery level of skills beyond basic reading and math. For instance, few employers require high school-degreed employees to understand algebra.

FIGURE 2

Communication skills

High school graduates should have the basic skills necessary to:

Skill Not Required	Skill Desired, But Not Necessary	Skill Absolutely Required
0	1	2

follow procedural instructions
1.91

speak in clear sentences
1.81

listen to formal presentations
1.71

give clear directions
1.71

sketch and dimension an object in multiview
0.45

understand and/or speak another language
0.30

While communication skills encompass more than just listening and speaking, there was little indication that employers required such skills as representing information graphically. Less than 7 percent absolutely required their employees to have the ability to sketch objects in multiview.

While most employers did not require high school graduates to speak or understand another language, one-fourth of the employers required or desired these skills.

Critical Thinking Skills

Critical thinking skills were generally viewed as being absolutely required or desired by respondents. As shown in Figure 3, three of the four statements were rated on the average above 1.58, indicating their importance. Generally, employers desired problem solvers and independent thinkers. The remaining area of critical thinking, the ability to formulate a hypothesis, received less support.

FIGURE 3
Critical thinking skills

High school graduates should have
the basic skills necessary to:

Skill Not Required	Skill Desired, But Not Necessary	Skill Absolutely Required
0	1	2

understand problem-solving processes
1.74
troubleshoot problems
1.68
make decisions independently
1.58
formulate a hypothesis
1.05

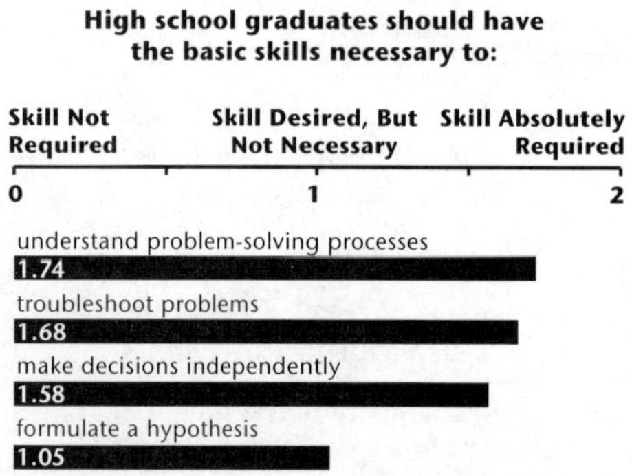

Every employer surveyed required or desired that high school graduate employees demonstrate the ability to solve problems. This item was one of only two statements on the survey that every employer supported to at least some degree. Of the 129 respondents, 96 required and 33 desired this skill.

Also important for high school graduates is the ability to troubleshoot problems and make decisions on their own. More than half of the survey respondents absolutely required that employees have these skills. Only one respondent in each of these areas did not at least desire this skill.

There was little consensus among employers on the need for graduates to form hypotheses in the workplace. One-fourth of the respondents absolutely required, one-half desired, and one-fourth did not require this skill.

Group Interaction Skills

As Figure 4 indicates, all eight skill statements listed in the Group Interaction Skills category received strong support from employers. In fact, of the nine skill categories on the survey, "high school graduates needing group interaction skills" was marked the highest. With the exception of only three areas—recognizing cultural diversity, recognizing equality of sexes, and participating in group discussions—more than 100 of the 129 respondents indicated all of these skills were absolutely required of high school graduates.

Respondents especially want graduates who can work well with supervisors, team members, and colleagues. All three of these statements were rated on the average above

FIGURE 4
Group interaction skills

High school graduates should have
the basic skills necessary to:

Skill Not Required	Skill Desired, But Not Necessary	Skill Absolutely Required
0	1	2

work well with supervisors
1.95
work as a member of a team
1.94
work well with colleagues
1.93
respect others' opinions
1.85
be willing to ask questions
1.81
participate in group discussions
1.74
recognize equality of the sexes
1.72
recognize cultural and ethnic diversity
1.64

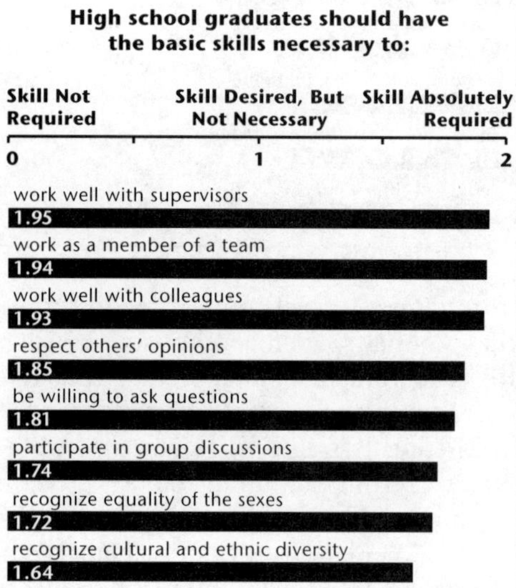

1.90, indicating how extremely important it is for high school graduates to possess the ability to get along with others in the workplace.

High school graduates having the ability to work as team members was absolutely required by 94 percent of employers. This skill goes beyond having to work well with supervisors and colleagues. Workers must be able to work together as a team in order to solve problems in the organizational environment.

Tied closely with working well with others and participating as a team member is respecting others' opinions. This statement received a 1.85 average rating, indicating its importance.

Two other areas, while receiving slightly lower ratings, were still viewed as being very important. These skills, seemingly related, are the willingness to ask questions and participate in group discussions.

Finally, while there was some disagreement of the importance to recognize cultural and ethnic diversity and the equality of the sexes, both areas received strong endorsements.

Personal Development Skills

There was again a great deal of consensus among employers on the need for high school graduates to enter the workforce with well-defined personal development skills. Figure 5 shows the relative strength of this category.

High school graduates should exhibit self-esteem to be successful in today's manufacturing world. As was the case for graduates having basic problem-solving skills under the Critical Thinking Skills category (Figure 3), every employer required or desired that employees exhibit self-esteem.

Respondents want high school graduates who set goals and work towards advancement. Employers also expect high school graduates to recognize career options. Finally, skills related to further education and training were considered important. Over 98 percent of the employees absolutely required or desired all five skills in this category.

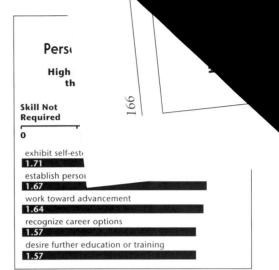

Emphasizing the importance of this category, it is noted that the category of Personal Development Skills was rated as the third-most-important category, when average group responses were compared. (See Figure 10 for comparisons of categories.)

Computer Skills

Computer skills were the least important category of skills required of high school graduates. This skill category ranked the lowest of all nine categories. (See Figure 10 for a comparison of categories.)

As Figure 6 indicates, the only skill receiving a high endorsement was the ability to operate a computer keyboard. Even in this case, only 46 percent of respondents absolutely required this skill of its high-school-graduated employees.

Understanding software for word processing was rarely required but often desired. Only 13 percent of respondents absolutely required this skill, while 68 percent desired it. Nineteen percent did not require this skill at all.

All other skills listed in this category were rarely absolutely required. With the exception of keyboarding operations and word processing, no computer skill listed was absolutely required by more than 15 of the 129 respondents (12 percent).

Equally as important, over 30 percent did not require any of these five skills for

FIGURE 6
Computer skills

**High school graduates should have
the basic skills necessary to:**

Skill Not Required	Skill Desired, But Not Necessary	Skill Absolutely Required
0	1	2

operate a computer keyboard
1.42

operate word-processing software
0.95

understand DOS commands
0.79

operate spreadsheet software
0.78

operate database software
0.72

operate desktop-publishing software
0.60

operate computer-aided drafting software
0.60

high school graduates to enter their manufacturing firms. For instance, even the skill and ability to understand DOS commands was not required by 33 percent of employers. Computer-aided drafting skills were not required by 54 percent.

Technological System Skills

Employers responding to this survey were mixed on the importance of high school graduates needing to understand technology systems. While more than 50 percent absolutely required high-school-degreed employees to have the ability to select proper tools or equipment for a given task and follow written directions to assemble equipment, less than 30 percent required graduates to calibrate instrumentation or know how technological systems operate.

As indicated in Figure 7, the skills necessary to select the proper tools or equipment received an average rating of 1.73, suggesting its importance. Following written directions, closely related to the skills of following procedural instruction in the Communication Skills category (Figure 2), received a rather strong endorsement.

Knowing how technological systems operate with such features as the inputs, processes, and outputs of manufacturing and communication technology was absolutely required by only 30 percent of the respondents. However, it was desired by 55 percent. Calibrating instrumentation was the only skill listed on the survey that received a 1.00 rating, indicating the neutrality of employers desiring this skill.

Leadership Skills

Most employers required or desired graduates to have leadership abilities. There was a great deal of consensus among respondents that graduates should enter the workforce with general skills and abilities to lead others. Regardless of whether high school graduates begin in leadership positions, demonstrating leadership skills was viewed as important to employers.

Figure 8 shows the relative importance of individuals being able to negotiate and resolve conflicts. Over 96 percent thought this skill was absolutely required or desired. This skill compared favorably with the skills listed under the Group Interaction Skills category. (See Figure 4).

While more than half of those surveyed absolutely required graduates to be able to negotiate and resolve conflicts, it was less important for high school graduates to be able to motivate others. Only 36 percent absolutely required this skill.

Improving organizational effectiveness was considered a valuable skill for high-school-graduated employees to possess.

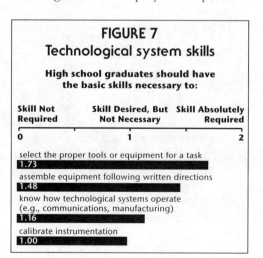

FIGURE 7
Technological system skills

**High school graduates should have
the basic skills necessary to:**

Skill Not Required	Skill Desired, But Not Necessary	Skill Absolutely Required
0	1	2

select the proper tools or equipment for a task
1.73

assemble equipment following written directions
1.48

know how technological systems operate
(e.g., communications, manufacturing)
1.16

calibrate instrumentation
1.00

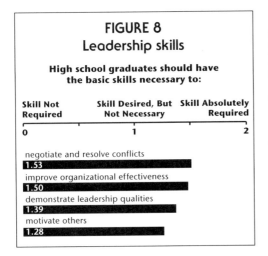

FIGURE 8
Leadership skills

High school graduates should have the basic skills necessary to:

Skill Not Required	Skill Desired, But Not Necessary	Skill Absolutely Required
0	1	2

negotiate and resolve conflicts
1.53
improve organizational effectiveness
1.50
demonstrate leadership qualities
1.39
motivate others
1.28

More than 50 percent of respondents absolutely required that degreed employees participate in such productivity-related matters. Generally, employers are looking for those individuals who have the skills necessary to lead the organization. This skill was desired by 97 percent of respondents.

Employability skills were the second-highest-rated skill category in this survey. (See Figure 10 for a comparison of categories.) With the exception of participating in community and civic activities, there was general agreement on the desirability of all skills in this area.

A further indication of the importance of the particular skills in this category was that maintaining quality standards and regular work habits were the two skills from throughout the entire survey that were most often rated by respondents as being absolutely required. (See Figure 9.) Of the 129 employers, 125 marked these areas as absolutely required of high school graduates.

Employers also want high school graduates who are punctual and take pride in their work. More than 93 percent (120 of the 129 respondents) absolutely required these skills. Of these four top-rated items, only 1 respondent per item did not support the skill as being required or desired. For example, of the 129 respondents, 124 absolutely required, 4 desired, and 1 did not require that employees demonstrate punctuality.

While less important, it was expected that high school graduates practice a healthy lifestyle and have knowledge of the company. Again, many employers (more than 70 percent) absolutely required that graduates demonstrate these skills.

The least important area required in this category was for employees to participate in community and civic activities. Still, more than 93 percent at least desired this participation.

Group Comparison

A comparison was made between the nine categories of skills to gauge their relative importance. Using responses to skill statements in each area, the average for the categories was determined. Figure 10 shows the results of the comparison.

Group interaction skills was the most important skill area high-school-graduated employees must have. This category included such skills as working well with colleagues and supervisors, working as a team member, and respecting others' opinions.

The second-most-important skill area identified by employers was employability skills. High school graduates should have skills necessary to maintain quality standards, maintain regular work habits, and

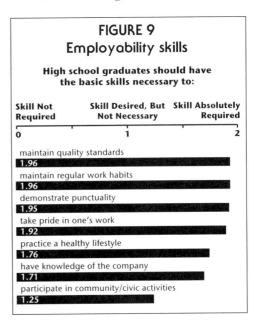

FIGURE 9
Employability skills

High school graduates should have the basic skills necessary to:

Skill Not Required	Skill Desired, But Not Necessary	Skill Absolutely Required
0	1	2

maintain quality standards
1.96
maintain regular work habits
1.96
demonstrate punctuality
1.95
take pride in one's work
1.92
practice a healthy lifestyle
1.76
have knowledge of the company
1.71
participate in community/civic activities
1.25

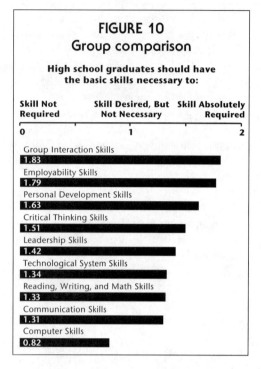

FIGURE 10
Group comparison

**High school graduates should have
the basic skills necessary to:**

Skill Not Required	Skill Desired, But Not Necessary	Skill Absolutely Required
0	1	2

Group Interaction Skills
1.83
Employability Skills
1.79
Personal Development Skills
1.63
Critical Thinking Skills
1.51
Leadership Skills
1.42
Technological System Skills
1.34
Reading, Writing, and Math Skills
1.33
Communication Skills
1.31
Computer Skills
0.82

and ability to sketch objects in multiview are not considered. Computer skills were indicated as being less important than all others. Although there was a need for basic keyboarding skills, little indication was given for other areas such as spreadsheets, data bases, and computer-aided drafting.

A general observation made from these comparisons was that skills relating to affective domains—that is, the attitudes, personalities, and emotions of the employees—were rated generally higher than those categories dealing with technical or academic concerns.

Conclusion

Documents such as *America's Choice, High Skills or Low Wages!*, The SCANS report, and *America and the New Economy* have identified educational standards and workplace skills. These documents described in great detail the state of the American economy and the changes being made in the workforce.

North Carolina's workforce is a reflection of the type and amount of education its citizens receive. With nearly 20 percent of high school graduates not continuing further

take pride in their work.

Personal development skills was the third-most-important skill area. This category included exhibiting self-esteem, establishing personal goals, and desiring further education.

Basic reading, writing, and math skills were viewed as being less important to employers than most other skill categories. These basic academic skills ranked seventh of the nine categories examined. It was interesting to note that skill statements relating to statistics, algebra, and geometry were rated below 1.00 for this category. (See Figure 1.)

Communications skills rank around third, when the need for foreign language

COMMENTS FROM INDUSTRY

"We look for people who are competent in various areas, more than just academic grades."–C. Kelly Ange, Westinghouse Electric

"The employee who is able to understand directions and communicate ideas can make major contributions in the workplace."–Linda W. Tatum, Greensboro News & Record

"Problem-solving skills is an area that deserves emphasis in the high school curriculum."–James Harris, Jr., Kelly Springfield Tire Company

"The ability to interact effectively in a team-oriented environment is essential."–Harold M. McLeod, Jr., Burlington Industries

"We need math, communication, and realistic goal-setting skills from our prospective employees. If they own these qualities, we can help them with the more technical skills."–Daniel L. Grimsley, Black & Decker

education through community colleges, universities, or military service, the skills they receive from their terminal program is of paramount importance. This point, coupled with the more than 12 percent high school dropout rate, places even greater significance on the high school experience.

Employers, on the other hand, are left with a pool of individuals who may, or may not have the necessary skills for the types of positions available. This study was designed to clarify the necessary skills employers desired of high school graduates. The focus group for the study was manufacturing firms in North Carolina employing more than 500 individuals at their particular locations.

Results indicate that high-school-graduated employees will remain a commodity in the future. That is, most firms will remain constant or increase the number of jobs requiring a high school diploma. Further results indicate that these graduates may need different skills from what is currently being suggested. What have been traditionally perceived as the skills necessary for high school graduates to be successful in the workplace was not born out.

Reading, writing, and math skills, while important, were not given the priority that would be expected. Conversely, group interaction skills received an overwhelming endorsement. Generally, the affective domain was emphasized by employers.

Educators, policy makers, and the public are therefore recommended to consider these findings when setting educational priorities, procedures and improvement strategies for the future.

References

Carnevale, A. (1991). *America and the new economy.* Alexandria, VA: American Society for Training and Development.

National Center for Education and the Economy. (1991). *America's choice: High skills or low wages.* Washington, DC: Author.

North Carolina Department of Economic and Community Development. (1992). *Directory of North Carolina manufacturing firms.* Raleigh, NC: Author.

North Carolina State Board of Education. (1985). *Statistical profile of North Carolina public schools.* Raleigh, NC: Author.

Northern Illinois University, Center for Governmental Studies. (1991). *Building public-private partnerships to improve vocational education in Illinois.* DeKalb, IL: Author.

Secretary's Commission on Achieving Necessary Skills. (1991). *What work requires of schools: A SCANS report for America 2000.* Washington, DC: U.S. Department of Labor.

William T. Grant Foundation on Work, Family, and Citizenship. (1988). *The forgotten half: Non-college youth in America.* Washington, DC: Author.

17

Apprenticeships and Community Colleges: Linkages in America's Defense

By Jeffrey A. Cantor

Reprinted with permission from *Journal of Industrial Teacher Education*, Vol. 31, No. 3, Spring 1994.

A CONCERN of the U.S. Navy and the American maritime ship-building industries is to identify more effective and appropriate means for attracting, training, and educating a workforce. This concern is underscored by changing demographics, fewer available workers, and severe literacy problems among Americans (Johnston & Packer, 1987). At the same time, increasing technical requirements are mandating an equivalent of two years of post-high-school education and training for the majority of workers (Eurich, 1990). A training process that has seen renewed interest is apprenticeship—cooperatively sponsored by employers (and organized labor) and community colleges (Cantor, 1987). This article reports on a study of initiatives in the U.S. Navy and maritime industries to see what works and why and to propose methods and processes to foster better working relationships between defense and high-tech industries and community colleges.

Need

Research conducted by the U.S. Navy's Office of Civilian Personnel Management indicates a serious shortage of skilled workers in the American workforce for the next decade (U.S. Department of the Navy, Office of Civilian Personnel Management, 1989). Findings also indicate significant changes in the characteristics of the available labor pool, including increases in average worker age, percentage of immigrants in the labor pool, and the numbers of women and minorities entering the workforce (MacKenzie, 1983). Pessimism also exists about the ability of our education system to provide workforce entrants with adequate mathematics and English language skills to support defense-related technical work (U.S. Department of the Navy, 1989). Apprenticeship is desirable, given the difficulty of recruiting, training, and often remediating a workforce according to Department of Defense, Office of Personnel Management, and Government Accounting Office findings (U.S. Department of the

Navy, 1989). All of these issues underscore the need for community colleges to support worker training and education more effectively and proactively. This study was undertaken to determine what both the federal and private sectors are presently doing in apprenticeship training and how more effective apprenticeship-community college dual enrollments can happen.

Specific objectives posed for this study were the following:

1. To identify apprenticeship programs that successfully link the U.S. Navy and maritime employers and job training with the community college.

2. To identify the factors that promote successful interorganizational partnerships.

3. To develop recommendations and guidelines to promote partnerships through apprenticeships between Navy and maritime employers and the community college.

Definition of Apprenticeship

The term *cooperative apprenticeship*, as I have defined it for this article, is a form of structured workplace training in which (a) employers and labor unions join with community colleges to provide formal instruction in which a structured work-based experience is an integral part of the instruction, (b) an apprentice agrees to work for the employer for a specified period of time, (c) the employer agrees to provide structured and formal training in a specific field or trade over a defined period of time, and (d) the employer provides continued journeyman-level employment after the training is successfully completed (MacKenzie, 1983). In turn, the community college agrees to (a) provide related technical and general classroom and laboratory instruction to complement the structured workplace training, (b) provide supportive technical assistance in the forms of course/program design and development and instructor training, (c) provide assistance with trainee recruitment, screening, and testing, and (d) award credit for the structured workplace training.

This work-based experience might be termed *cooperative apprenticeship* or, alternatively, *cooperative education,* or *internship.* In any event, it is a structured apprenticeship experience (Cantor, 1988).

Apprentices on Campus

Dual enrollment of apprentices in community colleges is not new. What is new is a move toward an apprentice earning associate degree credit (Cantor, 1988). This concept is now attracting national policy attention (Starr, Maurice, Merz, & Zahniser, 1980). This article looks at programs sponsored by (a) the U.S. Navy's shipyards, (b) other federal maritime agencies, and (c) commercial shipbuilding and dry-dock firms. In these cases, either college credit or full associate degree programs were initiated by the employers cooperatively with community colleges to meet current and future needs for well-trained and educated workers.

The Maritime Apprentice

Apprenticeship as a formal method of training dates as far back in history as the Babylonian Code of Hammurabi. Apprenticeship training in the United States dates back to pre-American-Revolution days (MacKenzie, 1983). The U.S. Navy apprenticeship is the oldest continually operating program of this type in the United States. Apprenticeship has a long tradition in the U.S. Navy's civilian workforce training. The Navy's first "apprentice boy" was hired in the Washington Navy Yard in 1810. The first formal U.S. Navy apprentice school opened at Mare Island Navy Yard in 1858, under the administration of David Farragut. Yet, apprenticeship remains one of the most vital forms of training for today's civilian defense worker, especially in high-technology areas (Cantor, 1986). Today, all eight naval shipyards (Portsmouth, New Hampshire; Philadelphia, Pennsylvania; Norfolk, Virginia; Long Beach, California; Mare Island, California; Puget Sound, Washington; and Pearl Harbor, Hawaii) operate some form of apprentice training. Other Navy activities, including naval air rework facilities, also use apprenticeship.

Not to be overlooked are some very long-standing and prestigious apprenticeship training programs operating at private sector yards, such as Newport News Shipbuilding and Drydock Company; Norfolk Shipbuilding and Drydock; NASSCO, San Diego; Ingalls; Bath Iron Works; and Avondale Shipyards (Cantor, 1986).

Methodology
The Case Study Method

A case study research process was chosen for this study, systematically identifying and reviewing factors influencing successful maritime industry-community college collaboration and linkages. The case study was drawn around a hypothesized model developed from a literature review as well as my past work in collaboration and linkage. The case study method permitted the phenomenon of interorganizational collaboration (for achieving linkage) to be studied in context, thereby highlighting what works and why and how other schools and communities can join together to achieve like results (Yin, 1989).

The model initially describes the several necessary organizational members—a community-technical college, employers, (and labor organizations, if applicable), governmental and/or quasi-governmental agencies, and sometimes a not-for-profit educational foundation. It then describes the roles and responsibilities of each organizational member—as well as the quid pro quo realized from participation to each member. The model also describes the interorganizational communications medium that acts as a catalyst for efficient linkage—in this case a not-for-profit educational foundation to which each member will belong to participate. This legal entity provides the formal structure through which the member organizations can transact business and establish written agreements.

How and why organizations collaborate. In order to test the hypothesized model, instrumentation (questionnaires and interview checklists/protocols) were devel-

oped based on organizational collaboration and communication theory. The literature on collaboration indicates that it is the key to successful organizational, hence apprenticeship, partnerships. Organizations collaborate for a number of reasons (Cantor, 1990; Banathy, Haveman, Madsen, & Oakley, 1978):

1. They derive mutual exchanges from each other.

2. Their access to external funds is increased.

3. They are given mandates.

4. They develop a formal agreement.

5. They assist each other in mediating conflicts.

Each of these areas was analyzed based upon data collected.

Data collection. I conducted all data collection. Data were collected from each program studied. Each shipyard program constituted a case and involved on-site review and analysis of programs and interorganizational agreements (written apprenticeship program standards; on-the-job training (OJT) documents; agreements of employment/indenture; formal curricula) including in-depth interviews with both Navy and maritime shipyard program operators and community college personnel in each of the colleges serving the particular programs. Interviews with apprentices were also conducted.

Findings
Background: U.S. Navy Programs

The U.S. Navy's eight naval shipyards (NSYs) each operate apprenticeship training programs for new technical workers. These programs provide training in approximately 43 different trade areas, depending on each shipyard's needs. NSY apprenticeship program sizes vary from 38 trainees at Long Beach NSY in 1992 to 661 at Norfolk NSY. In total, in 1992 there were 2,651 apprentices in the eight yards. This represents approximately 10 percent of the total NSY worker population—a goal that the U.S. Navy strives to maintain in order to ensure a continual supply of trained manpower.

Private-sector yards exceed these Navy apprentice numbers significantly.

Apprentice-trained journeymen form a majority of each shipyard's workforces. The apprenticeship programs are important to these shipyards not only because they are a source of skilled workmen but also because apprentice-trained journeymen provide the pool from which supervisors and managers are drawn. Some 87 percent of the naval shipyard superintendents (heads of the major shop and trade groups) are former apprentices. This system of internal advancement provides shipyards with dedicated upper-level management, skilled in the nuts and bolts of ship construction and repair. It sets naval shipyards apart from other industrial organizations which tend to employ managers without the same hands-on experience or pride of product. Herein lies a principal reason for sponsoring higher educational opportunities through coordination with local community colleges for these defense workers.

The NSY Apprenticeship Program

For some years, naval shipyards have been almost completely in the repair, as opposed to the ship-building, business. Despite recent modernization and automation in the industry, effective and safe ship repairs remain dependent upon the knowledge and abilities of large numbers of highly skilled craftspeople. There are no assembly lines in ship repair. Craftspeople work independently at nonrepetitive tasks and must apply analytical abilities and initiative, as well as judgment, to accomplish their work. Good reading skills are required for interpretation of job orders, technical manuals, and specifications; mathematics supports a variety of work-related calculations.

Apprenticeship training in all trades is designed as a four-year program. However, recent dialogue among the yards, the U.S. Naval Sea Systems Command, and the Navy's Office of Personnel Management indicates a desire to shorten this to three years for some trades, where appropriate, so as to reduce costs and facilitate worker entry into journeyman ranks. Private-sector yards' programs vary in length—from two to four years.

Availability of local community college services, worker population characteristics, and potential pools of labor varies among the eight Naval shipyards. Many of these variations apply to private yards as well. Apprenticeship training programs are administered locally to ensure that programs meet local needs and requirements. Each yard's apprentice training coordinators matches its apprentice-related training requirements to the local community college program offerings. Hands-on training and related classroom instruction take place in the shipyard. College instructors work on site in the yard. Some of the programs use college facilities for portions of the shop instruction or for additional classroom space.

Dual enrollment variations. Encouragement is given to the apprentice by the government to complete an associate degree while in the apprentice training. Each of the NSYs has worked with its local college to make this feasible for the apprentice. Several different program designs have been used. These include (a) college-level credit granted for apprenticeship hands-on work, as well as classroom trades theory work, such as exists at Long Beach and Norfolk NSYs, (b) cooperative education apprenticeships with a community college, as done at Norfolk, Charleston, and Pearl Harbor NSYs, and (c) high school preapprenticeship programs, such as at Norfolk and Charleston NSYs.

Most of the NSYs now front-load their regular apprentice programs; the community college provides the apprentice with the required related trade and general education and training during the first year of the apprenticeship. Those trainees not academically prepared to handle this work would be identified early on and terminated from the program or provided remediation.

Cooperative education programs, another variation for apprentice recruitment, are gaining popularity among the NSYs. In operation, the college and the NSY work together to recruit trainees from high schools or the general college community. The trainees initially attend the college's existing technical education programs for the first two semesters, at their own expense. The student serves as an apprentice during the summers in the NSY. Upon evaluation by the NSY, acceptance into the apprentice program, and completion of the first year of college, the student becomes an apprentice. The second year of college is then attended part time and paid for by the NSY. In the Trident Technical College coop program, completers enter the third year of the Charleston NSY apprenticeship. In many instances the enrollment of these workers in the college provides for a major portion of the college's enrollment.

Table 1 summarizes the NSY programs. In most cases the NSYs have contractual relationships with a local community college to provide the related trades theory, general education, written and verbal skills, and math and science necessary to carry out their duties.

The college role. *College participation also varies from program to program.* (See Table 2.) For instance, Trident Technical College in Charleston is a leader in cooperative education. The NSY and other Navy programs contribute a large population of students to the college—half of all cooperative education students are Navy workers at Trident. Trident is motivated by a full-time equivalent (FTE) enrollment of 120 a year.

Trident recognizes the value of the hands-on activity portion of the apprenticeship and

TABLE 1—NSY Apprenticeship Programs

Naval Shipyards	Active Apprenticed Trades	Participating Community Colleges	Cooperative Program Option Available	Current Number of Apprenticeships	Percentage Down From 1985	Cost Per Apprenticeship to NSY	Credit for On-the-Job Training
Pearl[a]	7	Honolulu Com. College	Yes	180	10	—	No
Mare Island[b]	28	Solerno College	No	421	55	None/Free	No
Puget Sound[c]	41	Olympic College	No	550	28	$100,000	Yes
Long Beach[d]	4	Long Beach City College	No	38	80	None 8 Theory 4/sem/OJT	Yes
Philadelphia[e]	32	Springgarden Univ.	Yes	371	65	$1,000	Yes 12
Charleston[f]	20	Trident	Yes	180 (40 coop)	60	$3,000	40-50qh
Portsmouth[g]	30	Hesser College	No	250	50	—	Yes
Norfolk[h]	10	Tidewater Com. College	Yes	661	50	$572	Yes 21.5 cr

[a]NSY Pearl Harbor working on a coop program which will provide 50% of its opportunities in future. Currently there are 80 coop students who work two summers in Yard while attending college. Coop students upon satisfaction graduated with degree, then enter the NSY apprenticeship program without any entrance examination.

[b]NSY Puget Sound uses a three-week on-the-job followed by one-week in-classroom model. Additional humanities credits offered after hours via Olympic College will qualify apprentice for the Associate in Technical Arts degree. Thirty percent of these entrants come in with an associate degree and another 10% have a bachelor's degree.

[c]NSY Mare Island is currently working with the Solerno County business community and the Vallejo Unified School district toward starting a coop program in the summer of 1993. They had one in the 1970s. Solerno has a coordinator and administrative support at NSY.

[d]NSY Long Beach currently has its program on hold. Yard is downsizing.

[e]NSY Philadelphia's program closing down as yard is scheduled to close. Springgarden College awards 12 credits for work in yard. Coop program is under development which will provide 1-2 years toward apprenticeship.

[f]For coop student associate degree from Trident coop program, enter into three-year apprenticeship at NSY. NSY Charleston is employing coop as a means of entry. Student pays for coop program.

[g]NSY Portsmouth is currently in bid process for new college support. Articulation agreement with NHVTC provides for college credit for apprenticeship work. 1,600 workers out of current 8,000 in yard were apprentices.

[h]NSY Norfolk's preapprenticeship program is operating also, junior/senior high school students work summers, then go to Tidewater Community College for two semesters, then go to work in yard. Their 3rd and 4th semester at Tidewater Community College is then paid for by NSY. In regular apprenticeship program, academics are front-loaded to maximize best apprentices going on. Eighteen percent of entrants already have an associate degree.

grants credit for apprenticeship. An associate degree in technology is offered for apprentices. Trident participates actively with the NSY employer and has a full-time coordinator and a Shipyard Advisory Committee that provides guidance to the program. The program was initially developed under a Federal Title VIII cooperative education grant.

Tidewater Community College (TCC) in Norfolk, VA, is another leader in apprenticeship program support. Tidewater generates about 250 FTE a year from these programs and is developing an associate degree program similar to Trident's Associate Degree in Technology. TCC provides several methods of instructional delivery for the NSYs, including preapprenticeship, cooperative education, and on-site related trades instruc-

TABLE 2—Community College Involvement

Community College	Cooperative Arranged With	Specialized Certificate or Degree	Shipyard On-site Coordinator	Number of Instructors	Full-Time Equivalent Year	Cooperative Program	Recruit and Counsel Assistance	Remedial Work Provided	Financial Assistance
Tidewater Community College	NSY-Norfolk NAVAIR Norfolk	Engineering Technology Certificate (in program)	Yes	8	250	Yes	Yes	Yes	Yes
Thomas Nelson Community College	Newsport News Shipbuilding NAVAIR	Engineering Technology Certificate	Yes			Yes	Yes	Yes	Yes
Maine Maritime Academy	Bath Iron Works	Associate in Ship Design	Yes	12			Yes	Yes	N/A
San Diego Community College	NASSCO	No	No			No	Yes	Yes	Yes
Ann Arundel Community College	Curtis Bay C.G.	No	No			In Work		Yes	Yes
Jackson County Community College	Ingalls Shipyard								
Trident Technical Community College	Charleston NSY Other Naval Facilities	Associate in Technology	Yes		120	Yes	Yes	Yes	Yes
Honolulu Community College	Pearl Harbor NSY	Associate in Applied Arts	Yes			Yes	Yes	Yes	N/A
Olympic Community College	Puget Sound NSY	Associate in Technical Arts	Yes	8	153	No	Yes	NSY Provided	N/A
Solerno Community	Mare Island NSY	Associate in Shipbuilding	Yes	3		No	Yes	Yes	N/A

tion. The on-site program equates to 43 college credits and an engineering technology certificate. The additional courses requisite to an associate degree are offered at the NSY and at the private sector firms in the area (e.g., NORSHIPCO) as after-hours courses.

Student personnel and recruitment. All the community colleges assist in recruiting students for cooperative apprenticeships. Most of the colleges also provide remedial and basic academic skills learning opportunities at the NSY for apprentices.

Finances. NSY apprenticeship training costs are borne by the government. All of the colleges report that they counsel students about Pell grants (GSL) and other sources of funds for any portion of the training program that they must personally pay. In California, the program is essentially underwritten by the state as a result of its very low tuition status. Programs operating in Maryland are cosponsored by the state division of continuing education using Perkins and other federal monies. For instance, Avondale Shipyard uses Job Training Partnership Act (JTPA) and Perkins funding. Programs sponsored by unions are also eligible for joint-training trust fund monies. The Tidewater maritime industry formed a nonprofit educational foundation to fund its training programs.

Other support. Naval shipyards provide on-site classroom space for the college at all of the yards. In turn, the colleges make lab space available for specialized instruction. Such arrangements become mutually profitable.

Other Federal Apprenticeship Programs

U.S. Navy-NAVAIR rework facilities. NAVAIR operates a four-year cooperative apprenticeship program in several trade areas in cooperation with Tidewater Community College. Students accepted into the program complete the first year as full-time engineering students at the college. Summer is spent at a Navy facility working as an apprentice. Upon satisfactory completion of the first year of the program and acceptance into the yard, the student becomes an apprentice and works under the supervision of a master technician for three more years. College work then continues on a part-time basis.

Curtis Bay Coast Guard facility. A four-year apprenticeship program is also sponsored by Curtis Bay. Anne Arundel Community College provides on-site related instruction to accompany this program. Some of the related instruction can be applied toward college credit.

Not unlike their federal counterparts, private sector yards conduct similar programs using community colleges to provide both related trades instruction and college degree credit. In many instances, the enroll-

TABLE 3—Private Sector Programs

Shipyard	Number of Trades	Participating Community College	Number of Aprenticeships	Degree/ Certificate	Credits Awarded	Funds
Ingalls	13	Jackson County Community College	1,000	B.S.	45	Perkins/JTPA
Avondale	2	Delgato Community College	60	—	15	Perkins/JTPA
Norfolk Shipbuilding	17	Tidewater Community College	—	Engineering Technology Certificate	45	Full Paid
Newport News Shipbuilding	20	Thomas Nelson Community College	712	Engineering Technology Certificate	30	Full Paid
NASSCO	1	San Diego Community College	10	Machine Shop Certificate	24	Full Paid
Bath	5	Marine Maritime Academy	200	Associate in Ship Design	60	Full Paid

ment of these workers into the colleges provides for a major portion of the local college's enrollment statistics. Table 3 presents the private sector programs.

Norfolk Shipbuilding's apprenticeship program is three years in length and is offered in 17 different trade areas. Like each of the other corporate programs discussed here, Norfolk Shipbuilding pays the full cost of an apprentice's training. TCC provides the related trades instruction on site at the shipyard and complements the program with the general education necessary for successful job performance in the chosen trade. Many of the firm's top management personnel have come from apprentice ranks. TCC awards an engineering technology certificate for program completion and an associate degree upon completion of several additional general education courses.

A well-recognized preapprenticeship program providing entree into Norfolk Shipbuilding's program, the Tidewater Maritime Training Institute (TMTI), is conducted by the Tidewater Maritime Trades Foundation. TMTI is a nonprofit educational foundation whose members are the area shipyards. TMTI has been in operation since 1982 and has successfully provided preapprenticeship training for almost two dozen Tidewater area shipbuilding firms. The foundation is also a medium for collective business development for the area shipyards. TMTI trainees are taken into the Norfolk shipbuilding apprenticeship program with credit for 18 months of the three-year program.

The Newport News Shipbuilding and Drydock Company operates a prestigious four-year apprenticeship program in 20 trade areas. Thomas Nelson Community College provides on-site related trades theory classes, advanced technical training, and general education courses to complement the program. All costs, including college-related course costs, are borne by the firm for the apprenticeship training; additional college general education costs are reimbursed by the firm upon successful completion of the college work toward an associate degree. College work follows the apprenticeship training after hours at the firm. Newport News also allows the college to use company classrooms for other instruction in addition to apprenticeship-related instruction. It's noteworthy that the apprenticeship itself is creditable toward a degree. Apprentice program completers receive a TNCC engineering technology certificate; upon completion of the additional college courses, the student can earn an Associate Degree in Science in a technology area. About 20 percent of the apprentices complete the college degree.

The Bath Iron Works program is somewhat different in method of delivery. Its close liaison with the Maine Maritime Academy (MMA) provides an opportunity for a Bath apprentice in any of five different marine design areas to earn an associate degree after completion of 8,000 hours of instruction as part of the apprenticeship with the company. Trade and related education instructors are faculty who work on site at Bath Iron Works. MMA and Bath Iron Works jointly developed the program and operate it. Program options include electrical, heating/ventilation/air conditioning (HVAC), hull, piping, and structural specializations. About 15 credits of the college curriculum are awarded for the technical hands-on portion of the apprenticeship.

NASSCO's four-year apprenticeship program is supported by San Diego Community College. NASSCO's apprentices attend college-related instruction courses together with apprentices from a number of other firms in the area. Courses are taught on NASSCO's site or at other area firms. They earn three units of college credit per semester over eight semesters, attending classes two nights a week after work hours. However, to complete an associate degree, they must complete additional arts and science courses on their own, after the apprenticeship period is completed.

Ingalls Shipyards, Pasgagula, Mississippi, has operated an apprenticeship program in 13 trades since the 1950s. For the last five years, it has cooperated with Jackson

County College. Their programs are traditional four-year apprenticeships with the exception of welding, which is a two-year program. The community college awards credit for the full program; however, the apprentice must complete 15 credits of general education independently of the firm's program in order to complete the associate degree. Ingalls reports that about 30 percent of the apprentices complete the degree. State Perkins funding via the community college pays for instructors and facilities and equipment to operate the program.

Avondale Shipyards operates a small apprenticeship program with the support of Del-gato Junior College. Again, state Perkins monies fund the salaries of instructors. In some instances JTPA funds have also been used.

Conclusions and Recommendations
Toward Solution

Apprenticeship can be more than a training tool or system. It can be a mechanism for bringing together, in a planned and co-hesive manner, the human and capital resources within an industry to solve human resource and training needs. As an added benefit, it acts as a catalyst to foster partnerships for training and economic development. (See Figure 1.)

Collaboration is the key to successful apprenticeship dual enrollment. How can employers and colleges collaborate? Findings indicate that collaboration occurs when (a) all parties concerned are able to derive mutual exchanges from each other (i.e., quid pro quo), (b) all parties are able to access external funding collectively that they individually could not obtain, (c) the parties have conflicting goals and collaboration allows for a mediation of these conflicts in a socially approved manner, and/or (d) all parties formally agree on a contract stipulating specific roles and responsibilities to collaborate.

Partnerships Derive Mutual Exchanges

The Navy and maritime industries collaborate with community colleges to reap mutual benefits that cannot be achieved

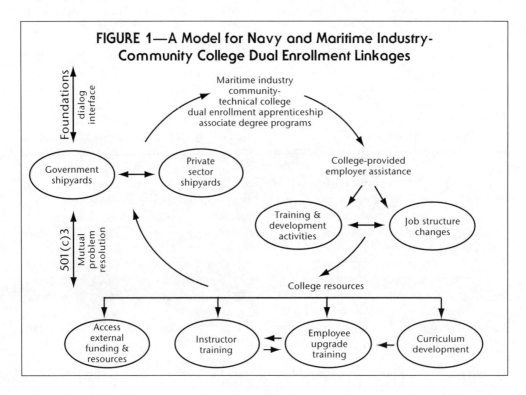

FIGURE 1—A Model for Navy and Maritime Industry-Community College Dual Enrollment Linkages

TABLE 4—Benefits of Mutual Exchanges

Program Development	Commercial firms, government, and colleges cooperate for program development.
Trainee Recruitment and Screening	Students are recruited jointly by firms or goverment and colleges.
Instructor Recruitment and Training	Instructors are identified by industry and trained by colleges.
Facility Development	Firms and government provide facilities for OJT and classrooms for related instruction.
Equipment Procurement	Firms and government provide equipment to college for training.
Related Education	Community colleges provide remedial education for students and shipyard employees.
Community College on-site Programs	Colleges operate on-site training and course delivery.
Quality Control	Maritime firm representatives sit on college advisory committee. Competency-based tests are used to measure student progress.

individually. Table 4 displays those mutual benefits. Employers benefit from the community colleges' course and program development assistance and from specialized instructional services such as remedial education for their workers. In many cases, they also benefit from the on-site administrative support provided by the college to operate the day-to-day program. Employers also benefit from college-assisted recruitment of new trainees, especially minorities and women. Such recruitment has not always been successful when done directly by the employer.

The college in turn benefits from the large numbers of dual-enrolled apprentices. These additional FTE's off-campus provide very desirable revenues without space constraints on the college. Colleges are also able to better meet their instructional commitments and institutional goals through employer-supplied facilities and equipment.

Of paramount concern to the college is the ability to identify and train employer staff as adjunct instructors who often possess unique technical skills. College faculty in turn benefit from the association with these craftsmen, enabling them to maintain or develop state-of-the-art skills.

Accessing External Funds

Training programs require significant costs, which are often not readily available in times of tight budgets. Often, training paybacks are long in coming and not easily measurable by an employer. Identification

and use of training program funding is not a simple matter. New legislation such as the Perkins Act of 1990 and the Community College Act do provide funding opportunities for apprenticeships. Employers have successfully accessed these kinds of monies as a result of partnerships with community colleges.

Many of the private sector yards use Perkins and JTPA monies to fund instructors and instructional equipment. However, more dialogue is needed between shipyard apprenticeship coordinators, especially in government yards, and community college personnel to explore funding opportunities. These revenue sources make it more desirable for the Navy and the maritime industry and the community college to cooperate for apprenticeship training.

The training trust fund concept also continues to be used as a mechanism for jointly funding apprenticeship programs and projects and complements dual enrollments with the community college. Employers sometimes use joint apprenticeship trust funds to support apprentice training.

The use of a nonprofit educational foundation also is a catalyst for exchange of ideas and resources as administrated by the TMTI in Norfolk. The commercial shipyards are able to share business development ideas and resources, lobby for policy changes, pursue international business opportunities, and train entry-level workers collectively. Perkins, JTPA, and now Youth Apprenticeship Act monies can be accessed by employ-

ers and colleges through the nonprofit educational foundation.

Formal Contracts

The U.S. Navy has very formal arrangements for the programs reviewed. It serves
as a model for other programs. The federal
government uses the competitive bidding
process to secure these services. Programs
also have standard forms for written agreements for credit award, faculty use, instructor compensation, and so on. Formal agreements are important for program continuity and for mutual understanding of roles
and responsibilities. They provide for clear
communications to institutionalize cooperative programs.

Apprentice registration (indenture) is
another kind of formal agreement most used
by the private sector. By registering the apprentice with a state department of labor,
the employer is able to access additional
department of labor funding (through the
Joint Apprenticeship Council) to offset some
of the training costs.

Partnerships Can Mediate Conflicts

Apprenticeship has traditionally provided
a mechanism for organized labor and employers to control and monitor employee
training and development jointly. In recent
years, it has also provided a way to control,
to some degree, technological changes in
the workplace through a phase-in process
with employee retirement and replacement.
The apprenticeship serves as a mechanism
for using the community college as a training resource and source of technical advice
and consultation. However, partners must
alleviate barriers through communication.
The use of a program coordinating and advisory committee, such as exists at Tidewater and Trident Community Colleges, does
so, and the operation of a joint industry
board by NASSCO and San Diego Community College has proved successful in this
regard. The Maryland community colleges
also cite examples of technology upgrade
training via dual-enrollment apprenticeships. As a training ground for tomorrow's

leaders and business people, apprentice
participation on these committees also allows the potential leader experience in mediation and problem-solution formulation.

In Closing

Dual enrollment of apprentices in associate degree programs is a practice that
should be promoted. Suggestions for further use by business and colleges include
the following:

● *Establish working relationships to provide
state-of-the-art training opportunities.* Where
good programs and active college program
advisory committees already exist, consider
use of apprenticeship as a means to deliver
the hands-on portion of the basic skills/
laboratory training. Ensure that all organizations and parties come away with defi-
nite benefits for participation (e. g., access
to new trainees, literacy courses, entry-level
employees when and where needed or business development technical assistance for
firms; OJT for students to industry standards and in facilities which are state-of-the-
art, adjunct instructors with up-to-date experiences for colleges; learn-and-earn opportunities for students; and reduced unemployment, entry-level labor forces with
up-to-date and needed skills, and firms with
a workforce ready to meet economic demands—all requisites for economic development—for the community).

● *Establish written agreements specifying
each organization's roles and responsibilities.*
Written agreements facilitate good communications. These agreements should provide
specific responsibilities, tasks, and timelines
for the firm, the college, and the trainee to
complete. All parties should agree upon
their roles and responsibilities. A specific
point of contact should be designated for
each organizational participant.

● *Firms should consider negotiating apprenticeship as a mechanism for training with their
labor unions.* Apprenticeship makes good
sense for organized labor. Apprenticeship
guarantees organized labor's involvement in
training and employment. The college can
involve organized labor in providing the re-

lated classroom training, as well as the technical guidance to make apprenticeship happen. Organized labor should be represented on the program advisory committee. Colleges should not forget how union-accessed funding can be handled to facilitate program development. Establish a joint apprenticeship council (JAC) training trust fund to support the concept. Operate the program cooperatively. Discuss with your state's JAC and the firm or industry how to access more resources (including funding) for the training program as a result of a bona fide apprenticeship program.

● *Identify and list the various kinds of resources each of the firms, unions, and community colleges can bring to an arrangement.* These can include the firm's master craftsmen as adjunct instructors; training facilities and equipment; program funding; and recruitment, screening, and apprentice testing and certification services—all valuable contributions to a joint relationship.

References

Banathy, B., Haveman, J. E., Madsen, M., & Oakley, G. (1978). *A model, case study, and implementation guide for the linkage of vocational education programs in public postsecondary institutions and business, industry, and labor: A monograph.* San Francisco: Far West Laboratory for Educational Research And Development.

Cantor, J. A. (1986, June). The Job Training Act and shipbuilding: A model partnership. *Personnel Journal, 118-125.*

Cantor, J. A. (1987). A systems approach to instructional development in technical education. *The Journal of Studies in Technical Careers, IX* (2), 155-166.

Cantor, J. A. (1988, February). *Apprentice program and community-technical college linkages: A model for success.* Paper presentation at the Eastern Educational Research Association at the Eleventh Annual Conference, Miami, FL.

Cantor, J. A. (1990). Job training and economic development initiatives: A study of potentially useful companions. *Educational Evaluation and Policy Analysis 12* (2),121-138.

Eurich, N. P. (1990). *The learning industry: Education for adult workers.* Princeton, NJ: The Carnegie Foundation for the Advancement of Teaching.

Johnston, W. B., & Packer, A. H. (1987). *Workforce 2000: Work and workers for the 21st century.* Indianapolis: Hudson Institute.

MacKenzie, J. R. (1983). *Education and training in labor unions 1982 report.* Washington, DC: U.S. Department of Health, Education, and Welfare.

Starr, H., Maurice, C., Merz, H., & Zahniser, G. (1980). *Coordination in vocational education planning—barriers and facilitators.* Columbus: Ohio State University, National Center for Research in Vocational Education.

U.S. Department of the Navy, Office of Civilian Personnel Management. (1989). *Department of the Navy Task Force report.* Washington, DC: Author.

Yin, R. K. (1989). *Case study research: Design and method.* Beverly Hills, CA: Sage.

18

Youth Apprenticeship in the United States: Transmission or Transformation of the German Apprenticeship System

By Nevin R. Frantz, Jr.
Reprinted with permission from *Journal of Industrial Teacher Education*, Vol. 31, No. 3, Spring 1994.

THE economic competitiveness of the United States in a global marketplace has created a concern for preparing high-skilled and high-wage jobs for Americans (Commission on the Skills of the American Workforce, 1990). According to a report by Finegold (1993), the United States is failing to provide most of its population with the needed craft and technical skills, unlike Japan and Germany. Other concerns are being voiced that many American youth, especially minorities, are having great difficulty in making a successful transition from school to work (William T. Grant Foundation Commission on Work, Family, and Citizenship, 1992). According to a study using data from the National Longitudinal Survey on Youth, Osterman (1992) concluded that "roughly one-third of all high school graduates and somewhat more high school dropouts, fail to find stable employment by the time they are 30."

In an effort to address these issues, American policy makers have begun to ex-amine workforce preparation in other nations (Glover, 1986; Council of Chief State School Officers, 1992; Lynch, 1993). A surge of interest in apprenticeship programs has occurred, and, in particular, the German dual system of workforce preparation has emerged as a leading model for Americans to emulate (Hamilton, 1990; Marshall & Tucker, 1992).

The German Apprenticeship System

The German approach to workforce preparation begins in the elementary and secondary schools. All children attend the primary school, or *Grundschule,* from the age of 6 until the age of 10 or 11. At this time, the student's record is reviewed and a decision is made between the teacher and parents about attendance at one of three schools. The most academically successful enroll in the *Gymnasium*, which is preparation for university entrance, the middle group attend the *Realschule*, which continues their general education until age 16, and the remaining students attend *Hauptschule* until age 15. In some *landers*, or states, of Germany a comprehensive school, or *Gesamtschule*, has also been introduced in an attempt to avoid early streaming of students. But its popularity varies from *land* to *land*, and the *land* retains most of the authority for public schooling in the country. Physically or mentally handicapped children attend special schools called *Sonderschule* (Romer, 1987).

For those students completing the *Realschule*, opportunities are available for them to attend a technical school (*Fachschule*) or a specialized upper secondary school offering vocational training or to enter an apprenticeship program. Students finishing the *Hauptschule* complete their education under the dual system in which they go to a vocational school (*Berufsschule*) part time and receive technical training at an industry or business in an apprentice program. All young people who do not attend a full-time school must attend a part-time vocational school and employment training program until the age of 18. Approximately two-thirds of the German youth participate in the dual system and about one-fourth enter higher education with the remainder entering the labor force as unskilled workers (Romer, 1987).

During the latter part of students' secondary school program, they are given an opportunity in most schools to begin selecting an apprentice training program from among some 375 state-recognized occupations. The students are brought to a nearby career information center which is part of the Federal Institute for Employment. In the center, career information is available to students in various forms, such as print materials, slides, tapes, and computer information systems. The information provides students with knowledge about work requirements, skills needed, and compensation. The Federal Board for Vocational Education is responsible for providing the career information and keeping it current. In this approach, the government cooperates with the *lander* and public schools in providing the career information and counseling services for work-bound youth (Federal Minister for Education and Science, 1992).

The apprenticeship program is conducted in Germany as a cooperative venture of social partnership between business and industry chambers, public vocational schools, and various companies, both large and small. The curriculum for each formal occupational training program is developed at the federal level with committees representing the crafts, unions, and educational system establishing the requirements for each program. The approved programs provide a national standard that each company and school must follow in the dual system of schooling.

When a young person enters an apprentice program, a contract or training agreement is prepared which specifies the content, duration, length of working day, holidays, and payment. Most of the training programs require a two-and-a-half to three-and-a-half-year time period. After approval by the local chamber, the apprentice begins training at the company while attending vocational school one or two days a week, or in longer periods of time, between the training site and the school depending upon the agreement. As the apprenticeship progresses, there are both written and performance examinations at various times, and increasingly more time and responsibility is given in the workplace. Upon completion of the program, a final examination with hands-on components is given, and successful apprentices are then journeymen in their particular crafts or occupations.

The instruction for the company-based apprenticeship program is given by a person employed by the business called a *meister*, or master. These individuals are qualified to act as *meister* through years of work experience and successfully completing the *meister's* examination for their occupations. In large company training programs such as Mercedes-Benz, the *meister* is a full-time position, while in small businesses it might be the owner or manager of the business. The training is provided by the company with no federal or *lander* subsidies other than a tax reduction for the cost of operating the training program. Most of the apprenticeship training is done in small concerns or businesses.

Transfer of the German Apprenticeship System

The feasibility of transferring the German dual system of workforce preparation to America has been discussed by a number of scholars and experts (Kazis, 1993; Rosenbaum, 1992; Batt, 1993; Ostermann, 1992). A leading advocate of adapting the German approach for American youth is Hamilton (1990). His proposal would take advantage of the existing vocational cooperative education structures and build upon them with a four-year program that provides a high school degree, an associate degree, and certification of high-level skills. Others, such as Bailey (1993), have discussed some obstacles that may interfere with the strength of the adoption process in the United States. He cites three broad problems that threaten the move toward youth apprenticeship. These are (a) the extent to which employers are willing to participate, (b) the quality and nature of learning that will take place on the job, and (c) the issues of equity and social stratification found in the workplace.

In a memorandum on youth transition, Barton (1993) enumerated 10 environmental elements that impact on the adoption of a system for school-to-work transitions. Although Barton expressed concerns about the complexity of the issue and the formidable conditions that need changing, he is convinced "that the key to the 'system' is a collaborative approach between the school and the employers," which is a common characteristic of our competitors. Finegold (1993) concluded that "it is neither desirable nor feasible for the United States to create a national, German-style apprenticeship system" (p. 4). He advocated that the Clinton administration use a targeted approach for key economic regions that would

involve all the main actors, set clear high standards, and share costs equitably.

Rosenbaum (1993) prepared five core principles essential for effective school-work programs: (a) use work-based learning methods that build on school learning and are connected to schools, (b) build upon work experiences, (c) develop cognitive as well as practical skills using experience-based teaching methods, (d) have school-work linkages that reward learning and effort with good jobs, and (e) develop credentialing procedures that identify clear standards and certify attainment. The principles offered by Rosenbaum are important to consider in any school-to-work transition program for the United States. He addresses several of the concerns expressed by Barton, Bailey, and Finegold and provides a framework for the complexities inherent in any collaborative relationship between schools and employers. Vocational educators can embrace the principle of developing cognitive and practical skills that lead to credentialing based upon clear standards. Employers should also be supportive of school-to-work linkages that certify attainment of standards and, hopefully, would use this in rewarding students with good jobs and suitable compensation.

Issues to Consider for Vocational Education

In the discussion of workforce preparation in the United States using the German apprenticeship model, it appears that several advocates assume a qualified position of support for the approach. The major issues of concern appear to be the level of collaboration and partnerships needed between schools and employers, the kind and quality of work-based education and training, and the potential for further social stratification in schools and the workplace. These concerns should be taken into consideration in the development and implementation of any federal-state partnerships in workforce preparation. An analysis of the discussion and recommendations made by authorities on apprenticeship programs in the United

States brings to light at least four issues or considerations that vocational educators should contemplate in developing an American version of the German youth apprenticeship program.

Students graduating from high school should have the skills and knowledge needed for the workplace as well as continuing their education. The proposals for youth apprenticeship programs advocated in most reports and embraced by the Clinton administration are targeted for the forgotten half, who are defined as those not planning to attend a four-year college or university. Although it is crucial that education for this group be strengthened, this policy perpetuates the bifurcation of youth into two groups and could intensify the sorting and tracking process now practiced in most schools. The adoption of an apprenticeship model for only those students who are non-college-bound could result in the same stigma of vocational education as a program for those who cannot succeed academically. Approximately one-half of the high school graduates in this country continue on to higher education, and only half of those students complete a baccalaureate degree. Some type of work preparation would be of value to those who do begin but do not complete a baccalaureate degree program.

It is important for policy makers at the federal and state levels to recognize the demographic reality of the youth cohort aged 18 to 22. Over three-fourths of the nation's high school graduates—rather than just the forgotten half—could benefit from having occupational skills and a smoother transition into the workplace. We need better options for high school students to consider than merely choosing between going to work and going to college. Policy makers should provide a coherent approach to serving the majority of students with the capability to obtain employment as well as enter, without remediation, and complete a two-year postsecondary program. A distinctive feature of American society is the flexibility and opportunity to continue a for-

mal higher educational program while in Germany the apprenticeship program is the primary route of opportunity for over 60 percent of German youth. This cultural difference between the two societies should be recognized and dealt with accordingly rather than simply attempting to emulate the German system in the United States.

The development of apprentice programs will be dependent upon business and education cooperation at local levels rather than a state or national system of apprenticeship programs. The development and utilization of an apprenticeship program in this nation will be dependent upon the commitment of business and education leaders at local levels rather than on a national and state system of social partnerships that characterizes the German approach to workforce preparation. The tradition of community support and control of public schools in the United States is a major difference between the European and American structure of educational policy and practice. The geographic and demographic diversity of the United States will allow local initiatives for workforce preparation to occur between education and business. There is a surge of interest in business-education partnerships across the country, and this trend will probably continue and could be enhanced with improved school-to-work transitions for high school graduates. Furthermore, there do not appear to be on the horizon any incentives for the private sector to assume complete responsibility for the initial preparation of workforce entrants. Several initiatives sponsored by the Clinton administration (United States General Accounting Office, 1992) would have provided the financial means for business and industry to move more aggressively into sponsorship of apprenticeship training programs. However, these initiatives were not embraced by Congress, and it does not appear likely that apprenticeship training will occur on a widespread basis under corporate sponsorship as is the case with large and small firms in Germany. There is no compelling interest on the part of corporate leaders to assume financial responsibility for apprenticeship training in this nation. Federal funding will be available to states and local school divisions to support school-to-work initiatives, but there is concern that these funds will supplant existing federal support for vocational education rather than supplement appropriations for any new initiatives such as apprenticeship programs. Therefore, it will be incumbent on vocational education leaders at the local level to take the lead in developing partnerships that focus on workplace transitions for high school students.

A national system of standards for occupational certification will take effect in the future. Of all the initiatives on school-to-work transition programs, the one most likely to have national impact is the development of standards for entry into key occupations. There is widespread support politically for educational accountability, and the adoption of national standards by various professional groups for subjects such as mathematics and history is already in process. The National Assessment of Educational Progress is another example of examinations already being used in several states in determining the acquisition of basic subjects by high school students. Various industrial and business organizations such as the automotive industry have already adopted and are using standards for hiring auto mechanics, among others. The U.S. Department of Labor and the Department of Education have jointly funded several projects for occupational standards in areas such as electronics and construction.

These efforts are underway, and it behooves vocational educators to be involved in the process if work preparation programs are to be kept current. The curriculum development centers sponsored by individual states as well as consortia such as the Vocational-Technical Education Consortium of States will need to utilize these standards in revising or developing contemporary curriculum information and content. The certification of teachers will take on new meaning, and organizations such as the National

Occupational Competency Testing Institute (NOCTI) will need to develop new examinations for certifying occupational competencies of teachers and students.

It will be imperative that teacher preparation programs and state licensing of vocational education teachers include requirements that transcend the work experience criteria and certify teachers on the basis of knowledge and skill needed for occupational competence (Duenk, 1990). State departments of education will have to agree upon a common occupational teacher certification approach if national standards are to have meaning across state boundaries. The implications for preservice and inservice vocational teacher education programs are enormous in preparing occupationally competent teachers and will require a concerted cooperative effort between state departments of education, teacher preparation institutions, and local school divisions. Federal funding will be necessary for the implementation of standards as well as teacher preparation. Recent budget reductions in state-supported vocational teacher preparation institutions are reducing the number of programs nationwide. Federal policy makers must recognize this fact if vocational technical education programs are to remain a vital component in providing well-qualified teachers for the occupational preparation of students.

There will continue to be a demand for high school graduates to have mastered higher levels of communication, computational, and scientific skills and knowledge than is currently the case. The global economy is forcing business and industry to adopt new strategies in their efforts to remain competitive in a multinational environment. These strategies include the use of new technologies in the production and distribution of goods and services, employment of part-time workers, outsourcing to independent contractors, shifting low-skill production to lower-wage-rate geographical areas within and outside the country, and reducing and reorganizing the workforce within the corporate structure (Reich, 1991).

Many companies are restructuring their organizations into high-performance work organizations. Under this approach, each employee is given more direct responsibility and empowered to make decisions as part of a team of workers that produce a product or service (Carnevale, 1991). The high-performance work team requires individuals to obtain and use information and solve problems in a continuous manner that requires highly motivated and educated workers. Flexibility is also needed to move workers to new assignments, particularly in the increasing number of client-driven, customized, high-quality service and product delivery organizations. The front-line worker is now expected to process information and make decisions that a supervisor or middle manager used to make. These changing conditions mandate that employees have the basic skills and knowledge to function successfully and immediately in initial jobs as well as provide a base for further retraining as economic and technological changes impact on the workplace (Congress of the United States, Office of Technology Assessment, 1990).

These expectations are driving educational reform efforts in many states and public school systems across the nation. Most states have adopted higher graduation requirements, are moving toward eliminating multiple sections of basic skill courses and are requiring more students to master the same level of achievement. The integration of these basic skills with content in vocational education courses is also becoming more widespread as a function of the Perkins Act requirements and efforts such as the Southern Regional Educational Board programs in the southeastern region of the nation (Bottoms, Presson, & Johnson, 1992).

The impact of the movement will require vocational education teachers who have a conceptual understanding of the principles underlying the basic skills and subject teachers who have a working knowledge of how the skills and knowledge taught in their classrooms are applied in the workplace. It is highly unlikely that preservice teacher education programs will be able to address this challenge in the four-year time period allocated for the typical baccalaureate degree program. The strategy that appears to be most likely for success is one in which a commitment is made by the central office administration and building principal to mount a total school effort and involve all teachers in the planning and conduct of an integrated, interdisciplinary approach. However, it is important that future public school teachers and administrators be aware of the need and acquire some fundamental knowledge of strategies that are available to use in site-specific situations where they will be employed in the future. Vocational teacher educators could play an invaluable role in providing this knowledge and developing positive attitudes toward integrating vocational and basic skill subjects in the preservice preparation of administrators and subject matter teachers. In-service programs planned and organized by local school divisions with the cooperation and support of state departments of education and teacher educators would be the most viable route for successful implementation of an integrated approach to students acquiring basic skills needed for workforce preparation, as well as those who plan to continue their education.

Implications for Vocational Education

The realization that economic prosperity and the social welfare of this nation is dependent upon the preparation of a highly skilled workforce is becoming more evident each day. The priority given by the federal administration in supporting effective school-to-work transitions is a welcome response to the challenge of improving workforce preparation programs in the United States. The development and utilization of occupational standards has the potential for recognizing and rewarding students who complete a formal education and training program. The use of an apprenticeship approach that requires close cooperation and coordination between schools and industry could benefit many high school students who now flounder in the labor market system of today.

As the discussions on workforce preparation for youth and adults move from policy decisions to practice, vocational educators should remain vigilant in their appraisal and support of these initiatives. The focus of school-to-work transitions on only those students who do not continue their formal education will continue to exacerbate the problem of sorting high school youth into two groups and will continue to promote social bifurcation in the American society. All students would benefit from having some type of occupational preparation and real work experience before graduation from high school, regardless of their future career plans.

The development and utilization of occupational standards is a worthy effort but must have widespread support by industry and must serve as a prerequisite for employment for higher-entry-wage positions, if there is to be an incentive for students to remain in school, complete a formal occupational preparation program, and successfully master the requirements for certification. There must be tangible, visible rewards if the demand for higher standards and accountability is to be recognized and accepted by students and their parents. The success of an apprenticeship program in this country will also be dependent upon the leadership and initiative of local communities working together in cooperative ventures. The potential exists for a transformation of the German apprenticeship system at the local level in America rather than a direct transmission of the German approach at a national level. Leadership from the vocational education community should be an integral part of the process of improving the transition of students from school to success in the workplace through further education and training.

References

Bailey, T. (1993). Can youth apprenticeship thrive in the United States? *Educational Researcher, 22* (3), 4-10.

Barton, P. E. (1993). A memorandum on the youth transition. In P. E. Barton (Ed.), *Improving the transition from school to work in the United States.* Washington, DC: American Youth Policy Forum.

Batt, R. (1993). *A national policy for workplace training: Lessons from state and local experiments.* Washington, DC: Economic Policy Institute.

Bottoms, G., Presson, A., & Johnson, M. (1992). *Making high schools work through integration of academic and vocational education.* Atlanta: Southern Regional Education Board.

Carnevale, A. P. (1991). *America and the new economy.* San Francisco: Jossey-Bass.

Commission on the Skills of the American Workforce. (1990). *America's choice: High skills or low wages.* Rochester, NY: National Center on Education and the Economy.

Congress of The United States, Office of Technology Assessment. (1990). *Worker training competing in the new international economy.* Washington, DC: Author.

Council of Chief State School Officers. (1992). *European lessons from school and the workplace.* Washington, DC: Author.

Duenk, L. G. (1990). The certification of trade and industrial teachers in the United States, District of Columbia, Puerto Rico, and the Virgin Islands. *Journal of Vocational Education Research, 15* (3), 41-63.

Federal Minister for Education and Science. (1992). *Vocational training in the dual system in the Federal Republic of Germany.* Bonn, Germany: Author.

Finegold, D. (1993). *Making apprenticeships work.* Rand Issue Paper 1. Santa Monica, CA: Rand Institute on Education and Training.

Glover, F. M. (1986). *Apprenticeship lessons from abroad.* Columbus: The Ohio State University, National Center for Research in Vocational Education.

Hamilton, S. F. (1990). *Apprenticeship for adulthood: Preparing youth for the future.* New York: The Free Press.

Kazis, R. (1993). *Improving the transition from school to work in the United States.* Washington, DC: American Youth Policy Forum.

Lynch, L. M. (1993). *Strategies for workplace training: Lessons from abroad.* Washington, DC: Economic Policy Institute.

Marshall, R., & Tucker, M. (1992). *Thinking for a living: Education and the wealth of nations.* New York: Basic Books.

Osterman, P. (1992, February). *Is there a problem with the youth labor market and if so, how should we fix it?* Unpublished manuscript. Sloan School of Management, Massachusetts Institute of Technology.

Reich, R. B. (1991). *The work of nations.* New York: Knopf.

Romer, K. (1987). *Facts about Germany: The Federal Republic of Germany.* Gutersloh, Germany: Bertelsmann Lexicon Verlag.

Rosenbaum, J. E. (1992). *Apprenticeship learning: Prin-*

ciples for connecting schools and workplaces in youth apprenticeship in America: Guidelines for building an effective system. Washington, DC: W. T. Grant Foundation Commission on Work, Family, and Citizenship.

United States General Accounting Office. (1992). *Tran-* *sition series: Labor issues.* Washington, DC: Author.

William T. Grant Foundation Commission on Work, Family and Citizenship.(1992). *Youth apprenticeship in America: Guidelines for building an effective system.* Washington, DC: Author.

19

Postsecondary Technical Education: The Proprietary Sector

By Albert J. Pautler, Sterne Roufa, and John Thompson

Reprinted with permission from *Journal of Studies in Technical Careers*, Vol. X, No. 1, Winter 1988.

EACH year, thousands of recent high school graduates face the task of selecting some form of a postsecondary technical education program. In addition, many adults, due to changes in the economy, workplace, or career desires, consider returning to school for technical job training.

These two groups, recent high school graduates and adults returning to school, are making decisive career choices concerning technical training that will affect their future lives. However, the theme of this article is not concerned with the process of career decision making or the selection of a career area for further study and training. It is assumed that the person has arrived at a decision in regard to an area of study that will be followed and a site at which to pursue that study. The area of study may be information systems, electronics, or any other of the myriad of fields for which training is available under the rubric of technical education

Postsecondary technical training is available in most areas of the country in public or private community colleges; public or private four-year universities; private for-profit trade, technical, and business schools; and correspondence home study courses. In addition, the military is a source of technical training in a variety of areas of specialization.

Our system of free business enterprise allows for the creation of entrepreneurs who are willing to take risks in developing technical training programs that in many cases duplicate existing programs in publicly supported community colleges. These entrepreneurs, be they small or large, are willing to challenge the public community colleges in competing for the same students.

Background

Jung (1980, p. 1) noted that "proprietary schools have provided a significant portion of vocational training in America since the Colonial period." Since 1965, students attending for-profit vocational training schools have been eligible for student loans. Under the Higher Education Act, Title IV of 1972, these same students became eligible for basic educational grants, direct student loans, and other features of the Act. The United States Congress thought the 1972 Education Amendments mandated that representatives from proprietary schools should take part in federally funded efforts to coordinate planning for postsecondary education (Jung, 1980).

Proprietary schools have been able to

work with veterans who were eligible under the G.I. Bill and to assist them in learning vocational skills. In more recent years, these same schools could enter into agreements to provide training for individuals or groups under the Comprehensive Employment and Training Act (CETA) and the Job Training Partnership Act (JTPA). Also, these schools can contract with local educational agencies to provide vocational training under the Vocational Education Act.

Many proprietary technical schools are well-established organizations operating in many cases in close proximity to the public community college. In some locations, a duplication of programs may exist between these two institutions. When this situation occurs, consumers of educational services are given a choice among two or more program operators. Usually, the tuition is lower at public community colleges since public funds are used to support the college. But the length of programs is usually shorter in the private postsecondary schools. Liberal studies are usually required in the public institutions but are optional in most proprietary schools.

Number of Schools and Students

Hebert and Coyne (1980), in *A Guide to Private Trade and Technical Schools: Getting Skilled* indicated that in 1978 there were approximately 1,500 public postsecondary schools with vocational programs and 4,800 private vocational schools (accredited and nonaccredited). At the time, 53 percent of the men students and 67 percent of the women students were enrolled in private postsecondary schools. The remaining were enrolled in the public schools.

Moore (1986), in *Career Training*, published by the National Association of Trade and Technical Schools (NATTS), stated the following:

The National Center for Education Statistics (NCES, 1982) estimated that there are 6,013 private postsecondary vocational schools in the country, accounting for two-thirds of all schools that offer postsecondary vocational training and enrolling an estimated 1.2 million students, 72 percent of all postsecondary vocational students. (p. 25)

It is not surprising that there are so many more private than public schools since many such schools are rather small and specialized in their curriculum. What is surprising is that these private schools have 72 percent of all postsecondary vocational students, leaving the balance in public schools.

Swanson (1982), in the *Yearbook of the National Society for the Study of Education* reported that "there are 1,955 public (enrollment 712,150) and 7,382 (enrollment 991,805) postsecondary schools, many of which offer advanced levels of instruction in vocational subjects" (p. 30).

The National Center for Education Statistics publishes a yearly statistical report entitled *The Condition of Education*. The 1983 edition presented the following data, taken from the various state plans for vocational education, concerning providers of vocational education. It reported that "there were 1,118 two-year institutions of higher education; 811 public noncollegiate postsecondary institutions; and 6,766 private noncollegiate postsecondary institutions" (p. 139). Enrollment in these schools was "4,423,000 in the two-year institutions of higher education; 741,000 in public noncollegiate postsecondary schools; and 989,000 in private noncollegiate postsecondary schools" (p. 141). The 1985 edition of *The Condition of Education* reported that "3.7 million persons were enrolled in some type of postsecondary vocational education program. . . . About 55 percent were women" (p. 90).

An increase in private noncollegiate postsecondary schools, along with an increased student enrollment, has taken place since 1980. What are some of the factors that may have accounted for this growth in private noncollegiate postsecondary schools?

Large Corporate Private Schools

Several large corporations are very much involved in the increase in private trade and

technical schools. Some of the most successful schools are backed by big money. The
largest chain of schools is the National Education Corporation (NEC), which is based
in California. In addition to National Education, ITT, Bell and Howell, and Control
Data each owns a chain of private trade and
technical schools.

The *National Education Corporation's
Annual Report* (1985) indicated that 42 campuses were in operation at the time. "NEC
earnings increased 4 percent in 1985 to a
little over $12 million" (p. 2). In July 1986,
the NEC opened its Brown Institute Campus in Minneapolis, the largest "super
school" ever built by the company. Its *Interim Report* (1986) stated, "To alleviate over-
crowding, expanded facilities are currently
planned for Louisville, Houston, Dallas, and
Chicago" (p. 5).

Sensing a serious lack of study skills,
math skills, and reading skills on the part
of applicants for their programs, the National Education Corporation developed a
fundamental study skills program. Available
at all NEC education centers, these programs have yielded dramatic results, according to company claims. The company intended to market these materials to industry and public education. They also predict
an increase in enrollment at their centers.

The *Value Line* (1985), an investment
survey publication, reported that NEC
courses run from six months to two years,
with most averaging 18 months. The cost
for these courses varies from $3,500 to
$8,500. The survey stated, "Though one-
third of the students drop out over the term
of the course, nearly 90 percent of the remaining two-thirds graduate and are placed
in jobs for which they have been trained"
(p. 473). No additional mention was made
regarding the one-third who dropped out.

Another large chain of schools is that
operated by DeVry Inc., a Bell and Howell
Company. DeVry includes a network of technical institutes with nine campuses in the
United States and two in Canada. Their specializations are electronics engineering technology and computer information systems.

DeVry was established in 1931 by Dr.
Herman DeVry and in 1967 merged with
Bell and Howell. In the fall of 1985, DeVry
had "an enrollment of over 29,000 including both day and evening students" (*DeVry
Academic Catalog*, 1986, p. 1). The schools
offer diploma, associate degree, and bachelor of science degree programs. In addition, a Master of Project Management program was opened in 1985 at DeVry's Chicago institute.

The *DeVry Annual Report for 1985* is interesting reading for those in technical education. DeVry increased its marketing expenses by $3 million in an attempt to coun-
teract high school students' reduced interest in engineering and computer-related
studies. Since student enrollment did not
increase, the result was higher expenditures
and reduced earnings. DeVry began development of two new curricula to enhance
its position with its traditional market. These
two areas are a bachelor of science in business operations and another in telecommu-
nications management. DeVry plans to aggressively market these programs. "The direct cost of student enrollment and marketing increased 13 percent in 1985 from the
previous year for a total of $28.8 million. . . .
This was based on a total revenue of $148
million for 1985 compared to $146 during
1984"(p.1).

Vocational educators may want to obtain
annual reports from these major corporate
sponsors of private trade and technical
schools. Forecasts generated from these operators of for-profit vocational schools may
serve as indicators for strategic planning for
public school operators and managers.

Small or Single-Purpose
Proprietary Schools

The previous section described some of
the large corporations that are in the business of providing vocational instruction on
a for-profit basis at the postsecondary level.
For the most part, proprietary vocational
schools are small or single-purpose schools.
It may be of interest to look at the situation
in one's own state rather than that for the na-

tion as a whole. *Proprietary Vocational Schools: Ensuring Quality Standards to Protect Student Interests* (Kadamus, 1986) described what is happening in New York State. In 1984-1985 New York State's vocational proprietary schools reported serving 150,000 adults in nondegree occupational education programs. These accounted for 62 percent of the adults who were pursuing nondegree occupational education in the states.

> To give an indication of how rapidly the proprietary school sector has expanded, nondegree occupational education enrollment in all sectors combined increased by about 20 percent from 1979-1980 to 1984-1985. During those same six years, proprietary school enrollment increased by 38 percent, almost double the rate of total nondegree adult enrollment in the state as a whole, and twice the rate of adult enrollments in secondary and postsecondary institutions. (p. 10)

Prior to 1976, there were only 28 registered business schools in New York. By November 1985, there were 124 registered business schools, representing a 343 percent increase in just eight years. "The number of curricula to be approved by the Education Department jumped from 681 before 1976 to more than 2,000 in 1985" (p. 10).

In the mid-1970s, the majority of proprietary schools were locally owned and operated. Most school operators were knowledgeable about the community and the educational needs of potential students.

> As the economy changed to more service jobs and the potential market of students grew, as did the availability of student aid, national chains of proprietary schools sprung up and many adopted open enrollment, multistart occupational programs—particularly the registered business school programs. (Kadamus, 1986, p. 11)

New York is also experiencing a growth in proprietary schools that do business in the state but have corporate headquarters elsewhere. National corporations are setting policies and procedures for these schools. Most operate on a year-round basis with multistate occupational programs. The experience in New York may or may not be representative of what is happening in other states. But its example suggests that comparable study in other states may be merited.

Selection of a School

The selection of a school by students can be a complicated process. While it is not the intent of this paper to treat school selection in depth, the following limited review of the literature is drawn from Marecki's research (1985) in examining college choice, student characteristics, external influences, college characteristics, career choice, and school image.

College Choice

One must assume that the choice of a college or other postsecondary institution would follow after the individual makes a career decision. This would also seem to be a safe assumption for the individual selecting a career program in a proprietary school in that proprietary institutions provide training in the specific skills necessary for specific employment.

The assumption, for the purpose of this paper, is that the individual has decided to continue his or her education at the postsecondary level and has made an occupational or career-field decision. Career fields of choice might be: automotive mechanic, broadcasting technician, computer service technician, dental laboratory technician, or others.

Kotler (1976) conceived of career selection as a funnel-like process viewed as a series of steps that the individual goes through leading to a final choice. The process begins with a decision to go to some type of postsecondary education and ends with a particular choice of institutions and program (Tierney, 1980). A later reexamination may conclude that the choice of career or institution has been unwise. The student may then drop out or switch career fields.

Proprietary School Students

A limited amount of research was found relating to student selection of proprietary institutions. A few studies reported characteristics and influences of students who choose to attend proprietary institutions. Hoyt (1968) suggested that proprietary students are highly motivated and desire to acquire specific occupational skills. Braden, Harris, and Krishan (1970) restated this in a study of some 3,000 graduates of private vocational schools. They found that students were mainly interested in gaining occupational skills and had limited interest in taking courses not related to employment goals. According to Marecki (1985), proprietary schools are seen as vehicles designed for quick access to employment. This finding was also supported previously by Shoemaker (1973) and Trivet (1974). Successful job placement is seen as a significant variable (Bender, 1973; Shoemaker, 1973; Trivet, 1974).

Jung (1980) described proprietary school students:

A major distinguishable characteristic of proprietary school students 1977 survey of students in noncollegiate postsecondary schools with occupational programs indicated that 77 percent of private school students selected schools because they had favorable placement records. The comparable figure for public vocational schools was 53 percent. Twenty-one percent indicated their choice was based primarily on the shorter length of the program, as compared to 16 percent of public vocational students. . . . While fewer than 25 percent had a vocational program in high school, more than 90 percent had worked full or part time before enrolling in their current program. (p. 17)

The following statements about proprietary school students appear to be safe assumptions:

● They are highly motivated and have a desire to acquire specific occupational skills (Hoyt, 1968).

● Their main interest is to gain an occupational skill, with little interest in taking courses not directly related to employment

(Braden, Harris, & Krishan, 1970; Hebert & Coyne, 1980).

● They desire quick access into the job market (Jung, 1980; Shoemaker, 1977; Wilms, 1974).

● They view immediate job placement after completion of training as being of major importance (Bender, 1973; Jung, 1980; Shoemaker, 1973; Trivet, 1974).

They are generally older, married, from lower socioeconomic backgrounds, and need financial aid (Anderson & Barnes, 1979; Christian, 1975; Wilms, 1974).

● The majority of business students are women (Juhlin, 1976).

In addition, Marecki (1985) observed:

Overall then, it can be seen that Juhlin's study and the study by the National Center for Educational Statistics are quite consistent with the literature. This seems to indicate that through the course of the years, the goals and the types of students enrolling in proprietary institutions have not changed greatly. It appears what was true in 1968 is true in 1983. (p. 62)

Implications and Prospects for the Future

Several things have occurred since we started writing and completed this article. Within western New York in a three-month period, three proprietary schools had been forced to close. One was a very successful trade and technical school, which at one time was graduating 600 students per year. It was forced to close due to low enrollment and cash flow problems. The other two were specialized schools: one in electronics and the other in business subjects. These closings created a stir in the media since students were enrolled and at various phases of completion, had paid their tuition in advance, and were not notified of the closing. Immediately, the State Education Department was called to investigate the situation to see what might be done to assist the students. At this point, the students appear to be the losers.

Jung suggested that competition for students will become more intense in the next decade. This competition will be between proprietary schools and public schools, such as community colleges. Likewise, competition will exist among schools of the same genre. He predicted an increase in the need for both types of schools to do more marketing of their programs. Such marketing by public institutions is frequently a problem due to restrictions to the budget for that purpose. Proprietary schools, on the other hand, are and need to be aggressive in their marketing efforts. Many such schools include marketing professionals as part of their admissions staff. Proprietary schools realize that they must attract students for their programs to survive.

The proprietary model includes four staffing categories: (a) marketing or admissions, (b) financial aid, (c) instructional, and (d) placement. This model is similar to that for a traditional educational institution. Students must first be encouraged to learn about and register for programs, and then the institution must provide the instructional staff and encouragement for students to complete the programs. To do so, of course, includes remedial instruction as needed. Lastly, provision for aggressive placement is essential. The model thus represents entrance, training, and successful exit.

Jung (1980) stated that "Proprietary schools will probably remain as successful but unlauded providers of postsecondary occupational training" (p. 28). Kadamus (1986), writing about what has taken place in New York, reported a 38 percent enrollment increase in the proprietary schools between 1979 and 1985. This rate of increase is about double that for the total increase in nondegree adult enrollment in the state. These trends, plus the expansion of national chains operating proprietary schools, seem to forecast the further development of this form of postsecondary vocational training.

The recent reform movement in vocational education taking place in the United States may create two possible situations that will influence proprietary school developments. Secondary school students who might ordinarily take vocational education in high school may not be able to do so due to increasing academic requirements. This change, in turn, may create a greater need for postsecondary vocational programs. A related possibility is one in which more students drop out of high school—due again to the increased academic requirements. Proprietary schools may view this situation as an opportunity to provide special vocational training while simultaneously offering remedial basic education. The remedial materials that the National Education Corporation is developing and marketing is such an illustration.

It would seem that the various states will try to protect the interest of the potential consumers of nonprofit education. The Federal Trade Commission continues to watch the over-zealous marketing efforts of some private trade schools. Private trade and business school associations and accreditation agencies will look out for the interests of the school owners while attempting to maintain educational standards. Agencies that regulate proprietary schools must do all in their power to protect the rights of the consumers who, in this case, are the students who attend these schools.

Kadamus (1986) mentioned the following concerns regarding the control of proprietary schools:

- violation of entry requirements,
- illegitimate recruitment practices,
- failure to meet established standards of quality,
- limiting the nonvocational component of the JTPA eligibility programs,
- institutional failure to maintain required records,
- failure to offer programs in approved form, and
- creative accounting masking financial instability.

These are some of the major implications and prospects for the future regarding proprietary schools. Whether students attend a public institution or a for-profit school, their protection is a major concern. Choosing a career, as well as choosing a public or private school, involves a certain amount of risk.

Educators at public institutions should be aware of what is happening in the private sector schools. Educators in private institutions should similarly be aware of what is happening in the public sector. Competition is good for both, as long as the consumers of the educational services are not hurt in the process.

References

Anderson, M., & Barnes, T. (1979). *Proprietary education: Alternatives for public policy and financial support. Part II.* (Final report). Carbondale, IL: Southern Illinois University.

Bender, L. (1973). Community college should adopt competitive free market initiatives. *Community College Review, 3,* 14-22.

Braden, P., Harris, J., & Krishan, K. (1970). *Occupational training information systems.* (Final report). Stillwater, OK: Oklahoma State University.

Christian, C. (1975). *Analysis of a pilot survey of proprietary schools.* Los Angeles, CA: Higher Education Research Institute.

DeVry Institute of Technology. (1986). *1986 academic catalog.* Chicago: DeVry Institute of Technology.

Hebert, T., & Coyne, J. (1980). *Getting skilled.* New York: Dutton.

Hoyt, K. (1980). SOS: A call to action. *American Vocational Journal, 43* (3), 41-43.

Juhlin, L. (1976). *Characteristics of students enrolled in resident proprietary schools in Illinois.* Research report for proprietary education; alternatives for public policy and financial support. Carbondale, IL: Southern Illinois University.

Jung, S. (1980). *Proprietary vocational education.* Columbus, OH: National Center for Research in Vocational Education.

Kadamus, J. (1986). *Proprietary vocational schools: Ensuring quality standards to protect student interests.*

Albany, NY: New York State Education Department.

Kotler, P. (1976). *Applying marketing theory to college admissions: A role for marketing in college admissions.* Albany, NY: New York State Education Department.

Marecki, T. (1985). *A comparison of selected student characteristics and external influences: Public community college and a two year (degree-granting) proprietary institution.* Unpublished doctoral dissertation, State University of New York at Buffalo.

Moore, R. (1986). Seizing the policy initiative through research: The Virginia case. *Career Training, 3,* 25-31.

National Center for Education Statistics. (1983). *The Condition of Education.* Washington, DC: U.S. Government Printing Office.

National Center for Education Statistics. (1985). *The condition of education.* Washington, DC: U.S. Government Printing Office.

National Education Corporation. (1985). *National Education Corporation annual report.* Newport Beach, CA: Author.

National Education Corporation. (1986). *National Education Corporation 2nd quarter interim report.* Newport Beach, CA. Author.

Shoemaker, E. (1973). Community colleges: The challenge of proprietary schools. *Change, 5,* 71-72.

Swanson, G. (1982). *Vocational education patterns in the United States in education and work. Eighty-first yearbook of the National Society for the Study of Education.* Chicago: The University of Chicago Press.

Tierney, M. (1980). Student matriculation decision and financial aid. *Review of Higher Education, 3,* 14-25.

Trivett, D. (1974). *Proprietary schools and postsecondary education.* Washington, DC: Government Printing Office.

Value Line. (1986, November 15). Stock highlight: National education corporation. *The Value Line investment survey.* New York: Author.

Wilms, W. (1974). *Public and proprietary vocational training: A study of effectiveness.* Berkeley: University of California.

20

Best Practices for Work-Based Learning in Community Colleges

By Lee Melnik and Charles R. Doty

THIS chapter describes exemplary community college work-based learning programs and provides sources for obtaining ideas and information for planning, implementing, and improving such programs. (Note that here the term *community college* includes technical colleges and institutes, as well as junior colleges.) Research on the value of work-based learning reinforces the worth of these programs. Researchers have discovered evidence that learning through the work process provides an effective method for acquiring work-related knowledge. In contrast, what is learned in classrooms does not always transfer to actual work environments (Stern, 1991). In addition to research, administrators have learned from experience that cooperative education students are more likely to complete their studies, to graduate from college with lower school-related debt, and to find a permanent position. Cooperative programs also often engage women, minorities, and disabled students in undergraduate work experiences (Bonas, 1995, p. 61).

To accomplish our goals, we will provide a brief description of the search methodology and criteria for selection of programs, definitions of terms and types of programs, and sources available on the Internet. Program planners must now master use of the Internet to obtain up-to-date information via E-mail, list serves, and home pages. Finally, we provide a few conclusions.

Search and Criteria for Selection of Programs

The search for sources and programs entailed an extensive review of the literature, including contacting national sources such as the National Society for Experiential Education and state departments of education. One of the surprising findings was that some programs are well known more due to good public relations than to exemplary practices. However, we did find many exemplary work-based programs in community colleges. They have in common these attributes:

- staff members who commit themselves to student success and quality programs,
- employers who commit themselves to participating in the programs to help improve the quality of workers,
- faculty who commit themselves to work-based learning as an integral component of any academic curriculum,
- policies that pay attention to the components of the school-to-work initiative, and
- involved professionals who commit themselves to lifelong learning.

Definition of Terms

These definitions come from the National Society for Experiential Education (NSEE) and other sources.

Appprenticeship—An intermediate stage of education that combines school and work; apprentices acquire specific work-related skills both on the job and in school. Programs were traditionally offered in trades associated with unions. However, a new emphasis has been initiated that expands into services such as computer programmer, veterinary technician, chef, and paramedic. Apprenticeship programs in community colleges normally involve a three-way partnership between a company, relevant trade union, and college. The training function normally is conducted in college facilities by college faculty. The faculty receives an outline of the course from the employer/union training advisory board and prepares a curriculum for review. Apprentices generally work full time for a period of months, then study full time for another period of months. Most programs linked with two-year colleges allow trainees to earn a certificate of completion as well as an associate's degree (Inger, 1995). For those planning career-oriented programs with apprenticeship, contact: Bureau of Apprenticeship and Training, U.S. Department of Labor, Frances Perkins Building, 200 Constitution Avenue NW, Washington, DC 20210; telephone: 202-219-5943.

Career development—An experiential learning process that helps learners understand their past experiences and use this understanding to choose new experiences. In this process, learners achieve greater insight into their own interests, values, aptitude scores, and abilities. They can build on these insights as they further develop their knowledge and skills and make more informed career choices (National Society for Experiential Education [NSEE], 1995).

Career academies—Specialized schools in which students receive a focused education (e.g., math, science, arts, technology) that emphasizes simulation of the work environment and applied academic instruction in broad occupational areas. Students experience job-shadowing in their early years, mentoring in their junior year, and paid summer work the summer after their junior year that might continue during their senior year (National Alliance of Business, 1994, p. 8).

Clinical experience—Worksite learning associated with preparation for a credential in a professional field such as health care, law, or education (Bragg & Hamm, 1995, p. 4).

Cooperative apprenticeship—Gives a worker access to employer-sponsored postsecondary school degree-earning technical education. In turn, these cooperative ventures are designed to promote local economic development initiatives by preparing workers for existing jobs, when and where needed by employers. This can also be termed cooperative education or internship (Cantor, 1992).

Cooperative education—An academic program that enables college students to enter employer-paid work experiences in business, industry, government, and human services as part of their education. Students have opportunities to apply academic theory to real work situations, acquire career experience, enhance personal growth, and earn an income to help defray college expenses (NSEE, 1995). More than two-thirds of two-year colleges offer cooperative education or work experience and approximately one institution in six offers the classroom component of apprenticeship training. Cooperative education and apprenticeship do not involve large numbers of students at the postsecondary level, accounting for only 2.25 percent and 1.39 percent of two-year college enrollment, respectively (Inger, 1995). Consequently, great potential exists for increasing cooperative and apprenticeship education. The president of Brookdale Community College notes, "Co-op is one of the most valuable tools for students preparing for the real world, partly because that world is changing faster than the academic faculty can adapt. Building connections between the workplace will ultimately benefit students and employers" (P. Burnham, interview, 1995).

Independent study—A student works independently with an instructor but does not attend class. Instead, the student works on written and field assignments and is awarded academic credit after meeting criteria set by an institution (NSEE, 1995).

Internship—Any carefully monitored work or service experience in which an individual has intentional learning goals and reflects actively on what he or she is learning throughout the experience. Ordinarily, internships are taken as part of a formal academic curriculum (NSEE, 1995). Internships and cooperative education were previously distinguished from one another because internship was not necessarily a paid experience. More and more institutions are administering both from one academic unit as the lines between these become blurred. Both are monitored experiences that are part of a formal academic curriculum. Both have intentional learning goals, which are the premise of each experience respectively.

Mentoring—A situation in which an experienced professional works supportively one on one with a student. This strategy can apply to all work-based learning situations. As described in the *Royal Bank Letter* (1995), education, for the most-part, tells people about things using paper and words. Mentoring shows people how to do things in actual situations. The learning theory for mentoring follows the notion that much of what is studied through reading or another secondhand means is forgotten, while things learned by practice are not easily forgotten. The image of a mentor is that of a loyal, wise, and helpful friend—a teacher, protector, and guide who uses experience to show how to overcome difficulties and avoid dangers. A mentor uses psychology to encourage the student to make the most of abilities and personalities. A mentor must not consider mentoring as a peripheral task; it is an integral part of the job. A mentor must guard against playing favorites, trying to produce a clone of him- or herself, over protecting, or trying to run the student's personal life. A mentor must take into account the student's abilities and weaknesses. A good

mentor has high standards and demands the student's best possible performance.

Occupational education—This type of education prepares the student for a specific job, as does vocational education. The terms *occupational* education and *career* education have been used by community college educators to escape the stigma of the term *vocational* education, though all have as their purpose job-specific education. (Note that career education also has another meaning, as established in the career education initiative in the 1970s. There it had more of a vocational guidance slant, giving students information about careers in all disciplines, plus testing on their interests, aptitudes, and abilities, to allow them to make more informed career decisions.)

Practicum—An academic class in which a real-life problem is given for students to study. Students receive a problem, then collect data from local, state, and national sources, and conduct on-site visits and interviews of key agencies and people to collect information and data. They then prepare a paper that states a logical conclusion, based on information collected.

School-based learning—The integration of academic and occupational curricula.

School-to-work transition—A program that integrates on-the-job learning with school-based instruction that bridges high school and postsecondary schooling and results in both an academic credential and a certification of work skills mastery.

Service learning—A carefully monitored service experience in which a student has intentional learning goals and reflects actively on what he or she is learning throughout the experience. Service-learning programs emphasize the accomplishment of tasks that address community issues. They include features that foster participants' learning about larger social issues and an understanding of the reciprocal learning and service that can occur between students and community members (NSEE, 1995).

Tech prep—A school-to-school transition program that incorporates applied academics (math, physics, and communication) at the secondary level and promotes articulation agreements between secondary schools and postsecondary institutions. (National Alliance of Business, citing Osterman & Iannozzi (1993), 1994, p. 7). Tech prep emphasizes academic preparation rather than work experience (Doty, 1995).

Work-based learning– The incorporation of work experience, workplace mentoring, and industry-specific skills into a sequential program of skill mastery and job training (School to Work Opportunity Act of 1994, Sec. 1).

After examining best practices in work-based programs in community colleges, we have concluded that they can provide a framework for establishing similar programs in other colleges. The programs seem to fall under industry-based and college-based categories. Industry-based programs were found in automotive, construction, maritime, food, and entertainment. College-based include cooperative education, internships, practicum, service learning, and tech prep. As a source of further information, colleges discussed in this chapter are listed in the references and resources section at the end of this chapter.

Industry-Based Programs

In industry-based programs, the employer controls training content and receives instructional assistance and other needed support from the college. Assistance can come in the form of (1) instructors and instructor development, (2) trainee screening and/or recruitment, (3) remediation of a trainee's basic skills, (4) shared facilities, (5) shared or donated equipment, (6) college credit granted for the related education and training or hands-on portion of the apprenticeship, (7) technical consultation and assistance in business or technical matters, and (8) access to external sources of program funding (Cantor, 1992). Descriptions of several industry-based programs follow.

The Automotive Industry

In the 1970s, leaders in the automotive industry recognized that the rapidly changing automotive technology was creating a need for more technically skilled mechanics to repair and maintain cars. At that time, technicians were rapidly replacing mechanics. The National Automobile Dealer's Association (NADA) quickly moved to work with community colleges to design and implement automotive technician apprenticeship programs. Since the 1980s, manufacturer-specific programs have been established in community colleges throughout the U.S. These programs have as a common mission upgrading the competency and professional level of the incoming dealership technician (Toyota Corporation, T-Ten Program). Toward this goal, all programs include the following components:

A manufacturer-oriented curriculum. Manufacturers outline competencies that students must achieve to successfully complete the program.

Program quality control. Most manufacturers want program certification by the National Automotive Technology Education Foundation (NATEF). This requires that a college meet rigorous standards and pass an on-site review in nine subject areas.

A cooperative format. All programs require cooperative education so that students alternate classroom learning and on-the-job paid work experience with participating dealers and businesses. The work experience is supervised by master-level technicians and often involves rotation throughout the dealership.

College credit for workplace experience. Students receive college credit for their co-op experiences. This can represent from 6 to 12 credits toward an associate's degree.

Quality facilities. A college's facilities must meet industry standards before industry will agree to sponsor a program.

Industry resources and incentives. Manufacturers provide colleges with training materials, equipment (including new model vehicles), training, and development for college faculty and ongoing technical support. Student incentives include paid work experiences, tools, and some tuition reimbursement. Some manufacturers pay for students to take certification exams.

Associate degree. All programs include general academic course work, business management courses, and automotive-related courses. All programs lead to an associate's degree in automotive service.

Manufacturers who have developed such high technology training include General Motors Corporation (GM ASEP Program), Toyota Corporation (T-Ten Program), Ford Motor Corporation (FORD ASSET Program), Chrysler Motor Corporation (PROCAP Program), Nissan Motor Corporation (PROCAP Program), and the Recreational Vehicle Industry Association.

A typical associate's degree curriculum is shown in Table 1.

The National Automotive Association of College Automotive Teachers (NACAT) estimates that there are more than 500 programs in the U.S. and Canada (Cantor, 1992). Many community colleges have partnered with more than one manufacturer. Some exemplary college automotive programs include Shoreline Community College, Seattle, which operates GM-ASEP, T-Ten, and Honda programs; Monroe Community College, Rochester, New York, with a generic NADA program, plus Toyota, GM, and Nissan programs; Brookdale Community College, Lincroft, New Jersey, with T-Ten and GM-ASEP programs; and El Camino College in Via Torrance, California, which offers Nissan, Toyota, GM, Ford, Chrysler, and Honda programs that lead to associate degrees and certificates.

Although these programs have produced many associate degree automotive technicians, more work must be done. Manufacturers do not always provide enough incentives to dealers to encourage them to participate. Therefore, students may have difficulty locating sponsoring dealers who will offer them paid employment on an alternating basis for the duration of the program. Still, the opportunity for students to work on donated state-of-the-art equipment and vehicles— provided by manufacturers to college programs—has afforded students a

---

TABLE 1
Typical Automotive Associate Degree Curriculum

First Semester	General Education Courses Automotive Courses
Second Semester	Cooperative Education Work Experience
Third Semester	General Education Courses Automotive Courses
Fourth Semester	Co-op Work Experience
Fifth Semester	General Education Courses Automotive Courses
Sixth Semester	Cooperative Education Work Experience

---

luxury of learning in technologically advanced facilities that could not be maintained by college funding alone.

The Construction Industry

In the late 1970s, two construction industries sponsoring apprenticeships saw a need to promote completion of an associate degree as a required part of their apprenticeship training. The International Brotherhood of Electrical Workers (IBEW), Local No. 3, viewed this as a means to meet both union and industry needs–higher education would boost members' commitment to the union, improve their technical skills training, improve the union's public image, and create better career mobility for its members. The International Union of Operating Engineers (IUOE), heavy equipment operators in the construction industry, supported this dual-enrollment program (enrollment in registered apprenticeship training and a community college). It provided a way for operating engineers to keep up with rapid changes in the trades and to achieve better-trained management personnel in the future (Canton, 1992).

Each state that participates has a coordinating committee that oversees the programs and discusses common problems and solutions. Technical subjects tend to be taught by local union journeymen. The community colleges provide labor, business, and general education courses, and they award college credit for work-based learning experiences. Often, there are competency tests associated with this work. IBEW Local No. 3 worked with the Harry Van Arsdale School of Labor Studies to provide a fully accredited labor studies program. IUOE, on the other hand, encouraged local unions to establish a dialogue with its community college for dual-enrollment opportunities. A national model curriculum was drafted to serve as a baseline. A national program director provides direction and advice (Cantor, 1992).

The number of college credits granted for on-the-job training differs among colleges. Each year, unions sponsor approximately 2,500 students to participate in these dual-enrollment programs. All programs boast of college-paid instructors. Community colleges that participate include Fox Valley Community College in Wisconsin, Allegheny Community College in Pennsylvania, Central Arizona College, Catonsville Community College in Maryland, and Community College of Rhode Island.

The Maritime Industry

The American maritime shipbuilding and repair industry realized, as a result of the Workforce 2000 research conducted by the Navy's Office of Civilian Personnel Management, that it would experience a serious shortage of trained workers. In an attempt to meet the recruitment, training, and remediation needs of the future workforce, both federal and private sector yards are working to establish community college linkages and to develop dual-enrollment apprenticeship programs with them. Dual-enrollment programs are not new. What is new is the move toward an apprentice earning associate degree credit (Cantor, 1992).

That 87 percent of naval shipyard superintendents are former apprentices and that people in the maritime industry believe strongly in internal advancement are the primary reasons for the maritime industry's support of higher education for workers and dual-enrollment apprenticeship relation-

ships with community colleges. This potential career ladder for workers makes the field more attractive to potential workers and, therefore, facilitates recruitment efforts. Because ship repair is not assembly-line work, each worker must be a craftsperson and have strong skills in working independently, reading, and mathematics.

Apprenticeship training in the maritime industry ranges from two- to four-year programs. The U.S. Navy's shipyard works with the local community college to match apprentice-related training with the college's programs. Cooperative education programs provide a good framework. Students begin by taking two semesters of college-level technical course work and then co-op in the summer. After completing the first year, the students become apprentices and co-op on a parallel basis, both working and attending school part time.

Some exemplary programs were found at Trident Technical College, Charleston, South Carolina, where maritime apprentices earn an associate in technology degree. Half of all cooperative education students at Trident are Navy workers. Tidewater Community College in Norfolk, Virginia, generates approximately 250 FTE (full-time enrollment equivalent) students from its maritime program and has developed an associate degree program umbrella for these students. Anne Arundel Community College coordinates the program with the Curtis Bay Coast Guard Facility, which is a four-year program. In addition to other instruction, the college provides on-site related instruction that may be applied toward college credit. Other community colleges offering maritime programs are San Diego City College, Thomas Nelson Community College in Virginia, and Jackson County Community College in Michigan.

The Food Industry

Recently, the New Jersey Food Council approached the New Jersey Council of County Colleges to help establish a statewide community college curriculum that would prepare people to work in manufacturing and distribution in the food industry. Seven community colleges (Bergen, Brookdale, Essex, Gloucester, Middlesex, Morris, and Union) established a committee which included academic administrators, faculty, work-based learning administrators, N J Council of County Colleges, and members of the New Jersey Food Council to develop a curriculum, based on industry needs. This curriculum will include a work-based-learning component and will culminate in an associate degree.

The motives of the food industry were very much the same as those of other business and labor organizations that developed associate degree programs and community college partnerships. These were to increase the professionalism of workers; to meet the growing need for more-educated people; to create a more professional image for workers in the food industry, therefore making the field more attractive; to provide greater career mobility for workers; and to create a partnership between education and industry to facilitate lifelong learning opportunities in the industry.

The Entertainment Industry

The Disney World College Program provides an example of a co-op/internship program that participates with both community colleges and four-year schools. It is cited as an exemplary model for community college work-based learning. The program's outlook is reflected in its brochure:

> Get ready to roll up your sleeves and go to work, because one of the key elements of the Walt Disney World resort is the ability to interact with our guests in various roles. Whether you're greeting guests at park entrances or lending support in restaurant operations, you'll have the opportunity to work in a position that will enhance your experience, both on-property and on your resume. . . . You'll work in one assignment for at least 30 hours a week (for one semester), and, best of all, you get paid for it. . . . One of the most exciting aspects of our college program is the ability to work side by side with the people who operate and manage America's

> number one entertainment and hospitality company. . . . You'll have the ability to gain incredible working knowledge through your seminar instructors on a weekly basis. Each of our weekly sessions will revolve around Theme Park Management and Resort Management, Managing and Communicating, and Human Resources Management. . . . You'll also participate in independent learning assignments designed to give you a firsthand look at the company. . . .

Each year, Walt Disney World recruits 3,000 students from the U.S. and elsewhere because it cannot fully staff the park with recruits from Orlando and the surrounding area. Disney College Program recruiters make two recruiting trips during the year to participating colleges to recruit students for fall, spring, or summer semester. The selection process is competitive, so students must know how to interview professionally. Those who are accepted take a semester from college to participate in this living, learning, and working program for which they receive college credit or college recognition. Each student must be approved by his or her college to participate.

This program is unique for community college students because it gives them an opportunity to live away from home for a semester. Unlike their four-year-college counterparts, community college students usually find this a new experience. Living with college students from all over the world provides an opportunity for independent living in a multicultural environment. To further the opportunity for personal, academic and professional growth, students work in paid jobs related to their major and attend three days of Disney orientation and three hours of business seminars per week. Volunteer and other career-related experiences are available to the students. Participants can also choose to spend a semester at a Disney College Program abroad. Once students have successfully completed their Disney College program experience, they can apply for an advanced internship opportunity.

Other Business/Industry and Community College Relationships

Advisory councils are mandated for all community college vocational/career programs. These employer-academic councils create a permanent partnership between the colleges and business and industry. Their mission is to ensure that curricula remain current and that program graduates meet the human resources needs of local businesses by having mastered state-of-the-art technology and business skills as well as workplace skills.

Recently, some community colleges have begun to guarantee that graduates will have these necessary skills or the colleges will provide free further education to bring them up to the guaranteed skill level. This community college contract with business and industry and commitment to using employers as teachers through work-based learning experiences creates a partnership to provide well-trained workers for the future.

College-Based Programs

College work-based programs are designed to partner with business/industry to serve a multitude of students and a diverse group of businesses, industries, and agencies. These programs include, but are not limited to cooperative education, internship, practicum, service learning, and tech prep. These programs exist in 97 percent of all community colleges (American Association of Community Colleges, 1995) and differ from industry-based programs because the collegiate programs are required or elective components of vocational and liberal arts curricula, usually involving many different employers for each curriculum. For example, technology students could participate in a work-based learning experience with a small local engineering firm, with a government agency, or with a large communications corporation. These choices are made jointly with the employer, student, faculty, and work-based learning administrator. Work experiences can be part of a particular course requirement or a unique credit-bearing course that is an elective or required offering within a specific curriculum. Students can participate in one or more experiences while earning their associate degree.

A typical student attending college with multiple work-based-learning programs might complete a service-learning experience as a component of a general education course taken freshman year. This might involve volunteering at a social service agency. Subsequent to that experience, the student, who is majoring in, for example, communications media, might spend a semester completing a cooperative education experience at a major TV network and co-op an additional semester at a local cable TV station. As a result, the student will have completed three work-based-learning experiences while completing an associate degree program. The student graduates with a well-developed resume, substantial experience in a career field with a diversified group of employers, and a clear understanding of career options in the field of communications. Because the majority (80 percent) of community college students do work while attending college, experiential programs provide students with opportunities to work in their field of study rather in a job that is not career related.

Profiles of the efforts of selected colleges follow.

LaGuardia Community College

When LaGuardia Community College was established in 1971, its first president established a culture of innovation and experimentation that, faculty and administrators report, has persisted to this day. In part, this culture represented an effort to develop a particular niche at a time when several community colleges were being established in New York. The spirit of innovation was also a vision of what a community college might be. . . .Over the years, there have been two major sources of innovation. From its inception, LaGuardia has been a mandatory co-op college, in which all full-time students are required to enroll in cooperative education. (The only other community colleges, to the authors' knowledge, to have mandatory co-op are Cincinnati Technical College and the Ohio College of Applied Science, also in Cincinnati.) The rationales for co-op were and remain those commonly associated with cooperative education: the opportunity to learn in different ways, to connect school-based learning to its applications, to explore occupational alternatives, and to earn money while in school. (Grubb & Badway, 1995, p. 3, citing Gabelnick, MacGregor, Matthews, & Smith, 1990, Spring)

Every full-time day student at LaGuardia is required to enroll in three 12-week internships or co-op placements which vary from 15 to 40 hours per week, depending on the co-op employer's and the student's schedule. Students earn 9 credits toward graduation for these experiences. Excluded from this credit requirement are students enrolled in curricula that do not have a co-op requirement because the programs have practicums. The program is administered by co-op faculty who advise, place, evaluate, and grade co-op students. These faculty also teach a co-op preparation course.

More than 16,000 students have graduated since 1973. Recently, LaGuardia Community College was awarded a school-to-work implementation grant for its Queens School-to-Work Opportunities Initiative. This initiative includes a consortia of K-8 and 9-12 schools, as well as LaGuardia and Queensborough community colleges. The foundation of this initiative is the strong co-op program at LaGuardia and the community partnerships that have been established.

Cincinnati State Technical and Community College

Cincinnati Technical College requires students enrolled in business and engineering to co-op, while Allied Health programs all have some version of clinical or work experience. Co-op programs started at Cincinnati in the late 1960s. Typically, a student goes to school for a 10- or 13-week term. He or she then works with an employer for the same amount of time, repeating this cycle two to six times. Approximately 20 percent of the college's full-time en-

rolled students participate in co-op. (The national average at other colleges is closer to 10 percent.) The magnitude of co-op at Cincinnati (and Sinclair) Community College is reflected in the statistic that one-third to two-fifths of new hires at the sub-baccalaureate level in the country came from co-op programs (Grubb & Villeneuve, 1995, p. 3).

Employers in Cincinnati are virtually unanimous in their support of co-op, because of the duration and quality of the program. In the words of some employers:

We tell co-op students we're not hiring you because we're nice people and we're good corporate citizens and all of that. We're hiring you because we want people coming out of this program to become future employees. And we want work done in the interim. They come in and they do productive work. And the biggest thing is that it's a tremendous recruiting tool and it's probably the best that you've got because you're not going, well I think they'll be a hard worker, or I think they'll be able to learn and adjust. You know, because they've been there. As long as the experiences they get as a co-op are close enough to what they're going to be doing. So my dream is never to have to hire anybody anymore. My dream is to go out and help the schools recruit students so they can put them in our co-op program, and when they get out we hire them full time. But that's exactly what I would like to see happen. (Grubb & Villeneuve, 1995, pp. 9-10)

Cincinnati's program is unique in that its benefits do not have to be explained to faculty, employers, or administrators. The program is so well established that everyone has long experience with co-op and it is now embedded in their culture. Grubb and Villeneuve (1995, pp. 25-26) attribute program popularity and persistence to four primary factors:

● The state of Ohio supports co-op through state aid, because students are enrolled at the college during their work cycles.

● The community college co-op coordinators, funded through state aid, provide the "glue" that holds the co-op program to-gether.

● The fact that co-op is required means that students accept it as routine.

● The employer community's support rests on the long history of co-op, since many workers and managers where them-selves co-op students.

Cincinnati State's 1995 brochure reveals this philosophy regarding co-op:

> The primary mission of Cincinnati State Tech-nical and Community College is to prepare stu-dents for immediate employment and advance-ment in technical and mid-management ca-reers. The college's faculty and staff believe that this preparation is best accomplished when classroom and laboratory instruction is com-bined with practical, hands-on experiences in a "real" work environment, or cooperative edu-cation, as it is called.

Brookdale Community College

Brookdale Community College in Lincroft, Jew Jersey, started its co-op pro-gram in 1973 using federal Title VIII money. The initial program was in engineering. Through the use of additional Title VIII and college funds, the program has become fully institutionalized and now offers co-op and internships in all majors, except allied health, which includes clinical work expe-riences. The president, administration, and board of trustees support this program by including co-op and work-based learning in the mission. The program is guided by a co-op steering committee that includes faculty from all programs, the dean of student de-velopment, the dean of academic services, the director of counseling, the registrar, and the co-op staff. All members of this com-mittee take pride in and ownership of the program.

The program is administered by career services, which also includes service learn-ing, international education, and placement. These programs are coordinated in function and provide a career-development program in which students are encouraged to par-ticipate. All work-based learning and place-ment programs are coordinated with the college student data base, each other, and other college offices that have employer contact. The data base allows program pro-fessionals to record and view student and employer profiles, including all activities the college has with each student and em-ployer, to provide student counseling and service.

Both cooperative education, which is awarded no credit but is recorded on each student's transcript, and internship, for which credit is given, are administered by the director of cooperative education. Through the availability of both credit (in-ternship) and noncredit work-based learn-ing experience, students can enhance their academic instruction with experiential learning almost as soon as they enter Brookdale. Service learning is offered as part of most liberal education courses and is combined with co-op in some programs, such as criminal justice. It is not unusual for students who participate to graduate with five or six work-based learning experi-ences. The co-op program has also been articulated with a number of secondary schools in the county to allow tech prep students and school-to-work students to enroll in co-op the summer before entering Brookdale. Brookdale also sponsors a GM ASEP and Toyota-Ten program. Brookdale Community College advertises itself as "a co-op college."

More than 500 students per year partici-pate in Brookdale's co-op program which has relationships with more than 1,000 employers. More than 450 students com-plete service learning projects. These work-based learning programs are run as busi-nesses for business, in the spirit of serving the college and the business community.

Brookdale strives to involve students in experiences that will allow them to live away from home for a semester. Work-based learning programs that include a living ex-perience are highly promoted and are popu-lar with students. These programs include Walt Disney World's College Program (co-op), as well as programs with the Student

Conservation Association and International Education/Service Learning.

Central Piedmont Community College

Central Piedmont Community College (CPCC), Charlotte, North Carolina, has an enrollment of 62,000 students. Co-op is offered in 52 curriculum areas. In 1994, 767 students participated in co-op with 82 percent being hired in a related field after graduation. The college offers both the GM ASEP and T-Ten programs, as well as the North Carolina Department of Labor Pre-Apprenticeship Program, the North Carolina State Government Internship Program, and the Disney World College Program, to name a few special partnerships.

What is particularly unique about Central Piedmont's program is the tech prep work-based program. Through this program, and the relationship that CPCC has with area high schools, students are strongly encouraged to participate in work-based learning experiences such as co-op, career internships, youth apprenticeships, job shadowing, or comparable experience through the Explorer Scouts. CPCC is also involved in an adult apprenticeship program, Catalyst Charlotte, that involves the Charlotte Chamber of Commerce and local employers. Students enroll in classes that teach job-specific skills and involve themselves in work-based learning experiences 24 hours a week.

Recently, a new youth apprenticeship program has been implemented in four local high schools. Participants enroll in the tech prep curriculum and are involved in work-based learning experiences after school that are related to their course of study. The goal of all these programs is to provide students with a natural progression from the high school to the community college work experience, often with the same employer. Together, high schools and CPCC are working to improve the quality of work experiences at both levels. They have also developed the CPCC/High School Work-Based Learning Collaboration with the purpose of developing professional relationships, shared resources, and professional development activities. Their cooperative efforts continue in planning, evaluation, and improvement of programs to serve both youth and adults, as well as the economic needs of the area.

Miami-Dade Community College, Kendall Campus

Miami-Dade Community College, Kendall Campus, has an annual enrollment of 19,000 students. In addition to its traditional co-op program, Miami-Dade offers three unique work-based learning programs:

Transition Cooperative Education is directed toward "undecided" students (i.e., students who have not decided on a college major). In this program, students research career fields that best fit their interests. They receive career counseling before conducting their research. Students are assisted by co-op transition coordinators, who are full-time faculty counselors. Students also plan an academic program, based on their research, and explore the local job market. Three elective credits are awarded for this experience. This experience is suggested for undecided students as good preparation for entering the cooperative education program.

Operation Student Concern (OSC) is an interesting integration of co-op and service learning. OSC has two goals. First, to serve the community by fulfilling community needs for volunteers. Second, to give students an opportunity to gain work experience in areas of career interest. The Student Activities Office supervises the program and faculty supervise the students.

Career-Type Volunteer Work Experiences is a program administered by the Cooperative Education Office. Students may work 6-8 hours per week with professionals in their career field, under a carefully designed volunteer program, and they earn 3 elective credits through cooperative education. This program is a solution to the long debate over whether to involve students in unpaid work-based learning experiences.

For those who feel that the value of the experience should not be forfeited due to lack of compensation, this program provides an excellent model.

Collin Community College

Collin Community College, Plano, Texas, initially funded outreach programs in 1990, through its co-op program with the use of Carl Perkins funding. This money was used to develop a relationship between the college and district high schools in a project called SEE (Students with Education and Experience). The program goal was to use the community college as a resource for building a bridge to connect high school students with postsecondary education. From this program, the college began to analyze specific program models for helping at-risk students to acquire safety nets through the development of self-management and employability skills. The Summer Career College is one resulting idea.

In the beginning, the concern was to develop a quality program, not to work with large numbers of students. The goal was to build a career development system that would perpetuate itself and strengthen the connection between the community college and the high schools by using available resources in the high schools, community college, and community. The motivation for this program is the need of employers across the country for better, more productive workers and the community's need for better citizens. The key for this program is to teach personal and employability skills, while involving students in work-based learning experiences.

The college's Cooperative Work Experience Division offers programs and services to Collin County high school students through SEE. Staff liaison is available to

• assist students who may be at risk of leaving the educational system through presentations about careers, personal development, and co-op, and to work with developing goals for college.

• assist teachers and counselors in using the resources of the co-op program, as well as other college resources.

• provide information to all types of students about cooperative work experience.

Types of services offered include life/work skills seminars; orientation programs for students, parents, and teachers; coordination of the career development ladder with students, including planning for and arranging work experiences and ongoing education; coordination of students' bridging from high school to college through individual counseling, assessment, and mentoring; and working with parents to help them understand College Work Experience and other college programs. Many of the students who participate in SEE enroll in the co-op program their first semester in college.

Community College of Rhode Island

The Community College of Rhode Island (CCRI) has an enrollment of 18,000 students on campuses in Warwick, Lincoln, and Providence. The college has committed itself to the school-to-work initiative and, as a result, has implemented an exemplary program called Career Pathways. According to *The Career Pathways Resource Guide for Educators*:

> Career Pathways is a partnership between representatives of the nine career and technical centers in Rhode Island and the Cooperative Education Program at the Community College of Rhode Island. Through Career Pathways, students can become a part of the national school-to-work initiative. Here's how: Work-based and school-based learning are seamlessly integrated through Community College of Rhode Island's Career Pathways Program. The primary outcome of the program is an employable, technically competent CCRI graduate who possesses the necessary workplace readiness skills which will serve them well in whatever they decide to do, whether it be to enter the workforce, continue their education, or enter the military. (1995, p. 3)

At the secondary level, students are involved in a workplace readiness curriculum that was recently developed by representatives of the state's career and technical centers, the college, and business leaders. There are career exploration activities including job shadowing, guest speakers, job clubs, and job expos. Through articulation with CCRI's co-op program, secondary-level students involve themselves in productive, sequential employment in their field of study at the college. Also, at the post-secondary level, students participate in a seminar that focuses on self-discovery, occupational/job analysis, communication styles, and career development. Credit is awarded for successful completion of the cooperative work experience and related academic requirement. Businesses get involved through participation in a speakers bureau, allowing mentoring and/or job shadowing for Career Pathways students, permitting students to tour their businesses, providing internships, or providing paid work experiences for CCRI students (Community College of Rhode Island, 1995, p.3).

The curriculum for this program was developed with the following career clusters: industrial/engineering, health/human services, business management/office technology, environmental resources and communication arts. The curriculum includes skill description, grade span, generic activities, and assessments. The program is funded by the U.S. Department of Education and is an exemplary model of school-based and work-based learning, and of the school-to-work initiative.

Table 2—Internet Sources

School to Work Initiative: S2WTP: majordomo@cccins.cccneb.edu [Central Community College, Nebraska]

School to Work Initiative: SWTNET: majordomo@conf.edc.org

School to Work Clearinghouse: e-mail: brownjea@msu.edu or 517-353-4403; also http://www.educ.msu.edu/mccte/ [Michigan Center for Career and Technical Education Home Page]

http://vocserve.berkeley.edu/CenterFocus/cf7.html or vocservc.berkeley.edu [National Center for Research in Vocational Education]

http://www.gse.ucla.edu/ERIC/eric.html [ERIC Clearinghouse for Community Colleges, telephone: 800-8328256]

http://www.aacc.nche.edu [American Association of Community Colleges Home Page]

http://www.utexas.edu/world/comcol.html [Web U.S. Community Colleges]

http://www.yahoo.com/Education/Community Colleges [Community Colleges Web Directory]

http://www.sp.utoledo.edu/twoyrcol.html [U.S. Two-Year Colleges, send e-mail to dsolarek@baddog.sp.utoledo.edu or arioux@baddog.sp.utoledo.edu for information on University of Toledo Community & Technical College Home Page]

http://www.accc.ca [Association of Canadian Community Colleges]

http://www2.infoseek.com/NS/Titles?qt=technical+colleges [For a search listing 100 leading technical colleges in the U.S. and other countries.]

http://www.ctc.edu/cgi-bin/findmail [Search Community & Technical College E-mail Directory]

http://ncrve-oss.ed.uiuc.edu[University of Illinois Office of Student Services; links to other home pages, e.g., National Center for Research in Vocational Education, the Office of Educational Research and Information]

http://goucher.edu/announce/cdo/cardev.htm [Goucher College career development office. Created in 1921 to provide transition from school to work.]

For a list and links to GOPHERS: gopher.faytech.cc.nc.us and select "Community College Gophers". A collection of school-to-work transition links is located at cccins.ccc.neb.edu.

CAPSNET: This list is specific to issues in two- and four-year institutions of higher education that relate to cooperative education and placement. To subscribe, send E-mail to: LISTSERV@UAIVM.UA.EDU. In the body of the message, put SUBSCRIBE CAPSNET Yourfirstname Yourlastname (e.g. SUB CAPSNET Leo Charette)

The Internet as a Resource

Anyone currently planning work-based programs must learn to access and use information on the Internet. Table 2 provides a list of excellent sources.

We also recommend searching with NETSCAPE and NETSEARCH using the descriptors "community colleges" and "technical colleges." Our searches immediately produced lists of 100 colleges with brief descriptions and Internet addresses.

Conclusions

Community colleges that require work-based learning as an integral part of education produce many students who graduate with useful, real-world skills. Even their students who do not graduate are more satisfied and successful in work than those from colleges that adhere to academic classroom instruction alone.

Work-based education will be a significant factor in motivating and helping faculty to keep up to date in their disciplines. It can also give them a realistic view of the purpose of education, which is not only to prepare a person for another level of education but for success in whatever the person chooses to pursue. As Wellsfry (c1994, p. 2) wrote for the National Council for Occupational Education, "the demographics of today's students and the dynamics of the changing labor market make student intent a critical variable. If placement statistics or graduation rates are examined without looking at the intent of students enrolled . . . the results will be severely distorted."

References and Resources

Acting as a mentor. (1995, July/August). *Royal Bank Letter,* 76 (4). [Published by Royal Bank of Canada, P. O. Box 6001, Montreal, P.Q., H3C 3A9, Canada.]

Allegheny Community College, Cumberland, MD 21502; 301-724-7700, ext. 202.

American Association of Community Colleges, One Dupont Circle, NW, Suite 410, Washington, DC 20036-1176; phone: 202-728-0200, ext. 216; fax: 202-833-2467; Internet homepage: www.aacc.nche.edu.

Anne Arundel Community College, Arnold, MD 21012-1895; 410-541-2240.

Bonas, J. E. (1995). Invited commentary: Cooperative education and federal government: Future direc-

tions? *Journal of Studies in Technical Careers,* XV(2), 59-62. [Special edition on Issues in Cooperative Education. Members of NCOE receive the *Journal,* or contact Southern Illinois University, College of Technical Careers, Carbondale, Ill. 62901-6604.]

Bragg, D. D., & Hamm, R. R. (1995, Fall). Work-based learning in two-year colleges: An American tradition. *Centerwork,* 6 (3), p. 4.

Bragg, D. D., & Hamm, R. E. (1996). *Linking college and work: Two-year college work-based learning policies and programs.* Berkeley, CA: National Center for Research in Vocational Education.

Brookdale Community College, Newman Springs Rd., Lincroft, NJ 07738; 908-224-2570.

Burnham, P. (1995, November 1). [Interview with president, Brookdale Community College, Lincroft, NJ.]

Cantonsville Community College, Baltimore, MD 21228-5381; 410-455-4304.

Cantor, J. A. (1992). Apprenticeship and community colleges: Collaboration for tomorrow's workforce. Bronx, NY: City University of New York. (ERIC Document Reproduction Service No. ED 347 384)

Cantor, J. A. (1992, March). Apprenticeship 2000: A model for community college collaboration with business and industry. Results of a national study involving three industries. Paper presented at the Annual Meeting of the Educational Research Association, Hilton Head, NC.

Central Arizona College, Coolidge, AZ 85228-9779; 604-426-4260.

Central Piedmont Community College, Cooperative Education Program, Kratt-Room 121, P. O. Box 35009, Charlotte, NC 28235; phone: 704-342-6217; fax: 704-342-6201.

Chrysler Corporation (PROCAP Program), 12000 Chrysler Dr., Highland Park, MI 48288; 313-956-5741.

Cincinnati State Technical and Community College, 3520 Central Parkway, Cincinnati, OH 45223; 513-569-1767.

Colin County Community College, Plano, TX; 214-8815735 or 214-548-6730.

Community College of Rhode Island, Cooperative Education, 1762 Louisquisset Pike, Lincoln, RI 02865-4585; 401-455-6011 or 401-333-7254 (co-op). [Produced *The Career Pathways Resource Guide for Educators,* 1995.]

Doty, C. R. (1995). *Tech-prep articulation: Is this an answer for the forgotten half?* New Brunswick, NJ: Rutgers University. (ERIC Document Reproduction Service No. ED 375 247)

El Camino College, 16007 Crenshaw Blvd., Torrance, CA 90506-0001; 310-660-3418.

Employment & Training Administration, Bureau of Apprenticeship and Training, 200 Constitution Ave., NW, Room N-4649, Washington, DC 20210; 202-219-5921.

ERIC Clearinghouse for Community Colleges Internet

home page: www.gse.ucla.edu/ERIC/eric.html

Ford Motor Corporation (Ford Asset Program), The American Road, Dearborn, MI 48121-1877; phone 313-322-3000; fax: 313-845-0570.

Fox Valley Technical College, Appleton, WI 54913-2277; phone: 414-735-5715; www.foxvalley.tech.wi.us

Gabelnick, F., MacGregor, J., Matthews, R., & Smith, B. (1990, Spring). Creating connections among students, faculty, and disciplines. In R. Young (Ed.), *New directions for teaching and learning*, No. 41. San Francisco, CA: Jossey-Bass Publishers.

General Motors Corporation (GM ASEP Program), 3044 W. Grand Blvd., Detroit, MI 48202-3091; phone 313-556-5000; fax: 313-556-5108.

Grubb, W. N., & Badway, N. (1995, June). Linking school-based and work-based learning: The implications of LaGuardia's co-op seminars for school-to-work programs. Paper prepared for the Office of Technology Assessment, U.S. Congress, by the National Center for Research in Vocational Education, Berkeley, CA.

Grubb, W. N., & Villeneuve, J. C. (1995, May). Cooperative education in Cincinnati: Implications for school-to-work programs in the U.S. Paper prepared for the Office of Technology Assessment, U.S. Congress via the National Center for Research in Vocational Education, Berkeley, CA.

Inger, I. (1995, January). School-to-work programs in postsecondary education. *CenterFocus*, (7). Berkeley, CA: National Center for Research in Vocational Education. (http://vocserve.berkeley.edu/CenterFocus/cf7.html)

International Brotherhood of Electrical Workers (ICEW), 1125 15th St. NW, Washington, DC 20005; phone 202-833-7000; fax: 202-467-6316.

International Union of Operating Engineers (IUOE), 1125 17th St. NW, Washington, DC 20036; phone 202-429-9100.

Issues in cooperative education. (1995). *Journal of Studies in Technical Careers, XV* (2).

Jackson County Community College, Jackson, MI; 517-787-0800.

La Guardia Community College, City University of New York, 31-10 Thompson Ave., Long Island City, NY 11101; 718-482-7200.

Lankard, B. A. (1990). Employability: The fifth basic skill. *ERIC Digest No. 104.* Columbus, Ohio: Center on Education and Training for Employment.

Miami-Dade Community College, Cooperative Education, 11011 S. W. 104th Street, Miami, FL 33176-3393; 305-237-2360.

Monroe Community College, Rochester, NY 14623.

National Alliance for Business. (1994, May). *How school-to-work works for business.* Washington, DC: Author. [1201 New York Ave., NW, Suite 700, Washington, DC 20005-3917; 202-289-2972.]

National Automobile Dealers' Association, 8400 West Park Drive, McLean, VA 22102; 703-821-7000.

National Automotive Technicians Education Foundation, 13505 Dulles Technology Drive, Herndon, VA 22071-3415; 703-713-0100.

National Council on Occupational Education (NCOE), 1161 Francisco Rd., Columbus, OH 43220; 614-451-3577; fax: 614-538-1914; or contact AACC 202-728-0200, ext. 216; fax: 202-833-2467. [Produces *Journal of Studies in Technical Careers* and *WorkPlace.*]

National Society for Experiential Education (NSEE). (1995). Membership brochure. [NSEE, 3509 Haworth Dr., Suite 207, Raleigh, NC 27609-7229; phone 919-787-3263; fax: 919-787-3381.]

New Jersey Council of County Colleges, 330 W. State St., Trenton, NJ; phone: 609-392-3434; fax: 609-392-8158.

New Jersey Food Council, 30 West LaFayette St., Trenton, NJ 08608; 609-392-8899.

Nissan Motor Corporation USA (PRO CAP Program), P. O. Box 191, Gardena, CA 90248; 310-532-3111.

North American Council of Automotive Teachers (formerly National Automotive Association of College Automotive Teachers), 11956 Bernaroo Plaza Dr., Dept. 436, San Diego, CA 92128-9713; 619-487-8126.

Peterson's two-year colleges. (1996). Princeton, NJ: Peterson's Guides, Inc. [202 Carnegie Center, P. O. Box 2123, Princeton, NJ 08543-2123; 609-243-9111; also see U.S. two-year colleges on the Internet for a comprehensive listing of two-year colleges: www.sp.utoledo.edu/tworcol.html]

Recreational Vehicle Industry Association, 1896 Preston White Dr., P. O. Box 2999, Reston, VA 22090; 703-6206003.

U.S. General Accounting Office. (1993, September). *Transition from school to work: States are developing new strategies for preparing students for jobs.* (GAO/HRD-93-139). Washington, DC: Human Resources Division. [Available from 202-512-7224.]

U.S. General Accounting Office. (1993, August 16). (GAO/HRD-93-89). *Vocational education: Status in two-year colleges in 1990-91 and early signs of change.* Washington, DC: Human Resources Division. [Available from 202-512-7224.]

San Diego City College, San Diego, CA 92111-4998; 619-627-2689.

School to Work Opportunity Act of 1994 [P.L. 103-239], HR/2884/S1361. *Legislative fact sheet.* Washington, DC: U.S. Department of Education and U.S. Department of Labor.

Shoreline Community College, Seattle, WA 98133-5696; 206-546-4581.

Stern, D. (1991, March). *Options in high schools and two-year colleges.* Washington, DC: U.S. Department of Education, Office of Vocational and Adult Education.

Stern, D. (1992). School-to-work programs and services in secondary schools and two-year public postsecondary institutions. Paper prepared for the National Assessment of Vocational Education. Berkeley: University of California at Berkeley, School of Education.

Stern, D., Finkelstein, N., Stone, J., Latting, J., & Dornsife, C. (1995). *School-to-work: Research on programs in the United States*. Bristol, PA: Falmer Press.

Taylor, J. E., Montague, E. K., & Michaels, E. R. (1972, January). An occupational clustering system and curriculum implications for the comprehensive career education model. Alexandria, VA: Human Resources Research Organization. (ERIC Document Reproduction Services No. ED 061 427)

Thomas Nelson Community College, Hampton, VA 23670; 804-825-2800.

Tidewater Community College, Portsmouth, VA; 804-484-2121.

Toyota Corporation (T-Ten Program), Toyota Motor Sales, U.S.A., Inc., 19001 S. Western Ave., #S-201, Torrance, CA 90509-2991; 1-800-441-5141.

Trident Technical College, Charleston, SC, 29401; 803-572-6000.

Walt Disney World's College Program (Co-op), P.O. Box 10090, Lake Buena Vista, FL 32830-0090; 800-722-2930.

Wellsfry, N. (Chair, NCOE Accountability Task Force). (c1994). *Accountability in community colleges: Balancing the perceptions with reality*. Columbus, OH: National Council for Occupational Education.

21

Essential Information for Community College Faculty

By Lee Melnik and Charles R. Doty

A RECENT report on the school-to-work transition stated:

> Many youth are ill prepared for work when they leave high school, often with long-term negative consequences. For example, about 30 percent of youth aged 16 to 24 lack the skills for entry-level employment, and 50 percent of adults in their late twenties have not found a steady job. This situation may be explained in part by poor academic preparation, limited career guidance, inadequate workplace experiences, and other impediments to efficient school to work transitions. (U.S. General Accounting Office, 1993, September, p. 1)

The only hope for these young people—especially those from middle- and low-income families—is excellent, low-cost work-based education provided by public community colleges, especially for middle- to low-income people. As stated by a vice president of a major community college that emphasizes career studies, "There are many new faculty who do not know the history and principles of community colleges. They really need professional development beyond their classroom interests in order to contribute to the future development of these institutions." We heard similar statements from several people throughout the nation as we prepared the preceding chapter of this book. Faculty need to know the environment shaping students who are coming to community colleges so they can adjust curricula for students' needs. Because of the restructuring of public education, eliminating most practical arts curricula, students now come to college with little knowledge of tools, materials, and machinery, as well as work skills—mental or physical. For example, we know of students in an agricultural technology program at a community college who lack basic knowledge such as when to change oil or when to inflate tires. In this chapter, we describe the restructuring of American public education, including relevant theories and attitudes; government intervention; and the current final stage of restructuring. We follow this with a brief explanation of the history and role of community colleges, plus vital statistics concerning community colleges. Community college faculty need to understand why community colleges have the curricular offerings and public services that they do. They need to know why money is spent on particular offerings and services. They need knowledge of statistics concerning community colleges to plan for the future. Finally, we draw some conclusions concerning the community college role.

Restructuring American Public Education

Theories and Attitudes

Since 1980, the American public education system, prekindergarten through twelfth grade, has been restructured by Congress with the goal of educating people who can compete effectively in a global economy. This would result in maintaining or reestablishing American status as the leader in the world economy. The restructuring has produced a curriculum that is college preparatory—general education and vocational education have virtually been eliminated in "comprehensive" high schools. The comprehensive high school, the great American experiment, has been evaluated as a failure for integrating citizens and providing an adequate education. Comprehensive high schools are being dismantled and replaced by college preparatory high schools and magnet schools with special emphases such as arts, math, science, high technology, and vocational studies for special populations. In addition, we now see changes occurring in which vertical articulation of secondary schools with postsecondary education takes place through computer networking, exchange of faculty, and instruction on postsecondary campuses with problem solving as the key instructional strategy. This restructuring of public schools reflects a restructuring of American society.

In this restructuring, the varying theories and attitudes of politicians, educators, business and industrial leaders, and parents have been argued continuously, both logically and emotionally. Among these theories are those of William Bennett, former U.S. Secretary of Education, who proposed that a classical education should be taught in K-12, with preparation for work taking place after high school graduation. This theory holds that education, at any level, is for preparing a person to enjoy life (i.e., liberal arts education). Education should not

have any career focus. Persons wanting education for work should seek knowledge somewhere else. Bennett's theory is basically what has been implemented in today's K-12 public schools, although we do see attempts to implement varying forms of education for work preparation.

Educators who control public education seem to have been happy to implement Bennett's theory. However, the academic teachers and guidance counselors who teach every day and who aim to help each individual student are in conflict. They now have to work with all students, some of whom do not want to go to college or are not capable of higher learning. Problems with motivation and discipline often result. Educators in practical arts have been totally frustrated because those students having the lowest ability and least self-discipline are routinely dumped into their programs. They have also in some cases seen their programs virtually eliminated from the curriculum. As one high school guidance counselor stated, "I had to place several students in a foreign language class, due to state graduation requirements, who could not pass sixth-grade English. Eliminating practical education makes no sense."

Business and industrial leaders have been quick to label public education a failure. Emerging from this population is the theory of marketing. That is, offer education for which there is a demand. This can result in the elimination of tenure and implementation of a short-term curriculum, especially in work preparation programs. Instructors would be employed on an "as needed" basis. In some cases, there have been business-education partnerships. Yet, business and industrial leaders often experience frustration when they try to communicate with educators. Their frustration arises from the differing theories of education. Educators show concern for the fulfillment of the individual, with what seems little regard for work skills, while business and industrial leaders are concerned with hiring large numbers of people who have flexible work skills. They also do not seem to know that most educators have never had full-time work experience in profit and loss businesses—experience that is a necessary attribute of a competent teacher in most disciplines and a necessary component for communication between these two groups.

Parents feel frustrated because they do not know that restructuring has occurred. Most parents want the best education for their children. Because of constant publicity by educators in postsecondary institutions and government, most parents want their children to attend a four-year college or university. Unfortunately, much of the publicity concerning college is based on statistics that are not explained properly. The public is, in effect, misled.

Students must face the facts described by R. J. Coley of the Educational Policy Information Center, Education Testing Service, who wrote:

> Education, more and more, has become key to a productive and satisfying life. Gone are the days when a lack of education didn't hurt one's chances for finding good, steady work. Opportunities are expanding for those with higher-level skills and abilities and withering for those without such skills. Yet, many of our citizens are not acquiring the skills or training needed to participate in this changing workplace. In 1993, about 381,000 students dropped out of high school. (1995, p.2)

Coley writes that students face these additional facts:

> U.S. secondary schools generally direct most of their resources toward preparing students for college. However, our analysis of . . . data showed that few youth—about 15 percent of incoming high school freshmen—complete a four-year degree within six years of the end of that group's high school graduation. This reflects the fact that roughly 20 percent of incoming freshmen drop out before [high school] graduation, and only about 1 in 5 of the remaining students ends up with a four-year college degree within six years of high school graduation. (p. 5)

We should also express our observations that there are enormous enrollments in two- and four-year colleges and universities in English, social studies, history, psychology, political science, and elementary teacher education. Many students seem incapable of selecting curricula other than ones to which they have been exposed previously.

Government Intervention

The U.S. Congress, almost from the birth of the nation, has continually initiated through its funding programs the integration of work education into the public school curriculum. There have been some notable successes and some massive failures. All the initiatives, though, have too often failed due to the basic theory that education should primarily lead to pure learning and another stage of education. Work-related programs have always had third-class status because of the predominant purist theory. For example, secondary-level guidance counselors have generally evolved their work role to that of college guidance counseling. At two- and four-year college and university levels, occupational instructors rarely achieve full professorships. Congress can only continue to initiate programs and hope that some day educators' attitudes will change.

We noted with interest the February 1995 issue of *Reader's Digest*, which reported that the people of Iceland make much of their limited resources. The keys to their success are discussed in this way:

> Iceland also benefits from cultural advantages: a strong work ethic, respect for practical education, a powerful sense of national identity. "This is not primarily about economics," says Thordur Fridjonsson, director of the National Economic Institute. "It's about attitude." (Notes from All Over, p. 191)

Also, Congress must consider the effect of what is called "seed money"—initial money invested to fund programs, with the expectation that once in operation, the programs will continue. This expectation is erroneous. As Delker found when studying the discontinuation of cooperative education programs in two-year colleges, "While external grants had provided the seed money which made possible the start-up of co-op at each institution, these grants also encouraged dependency on outside sources for help" (1988, p. 184). Once government funding was withdrawn, most of the programs were eliminated. Regarding cooperative education, J. E. Bonas states, "For 1995, the coop community again finds itself defending the Title VIII program against elimination. . . . [T]here seems to be less interest this year in Title VIII at the White House and on Capitol Hill" (p. 60). We believe that educators, especially prekindergarten through twelfth grades, who have little experience in business and industry and whose main purpose is preparing students for the next stage of education, will not support work programs. These educators do not realize that Congress is providing seed money to initiate programs to prevent or solve some social and economical illness.

One of the latest interventions is P.L. 103-239, the School-to-Work Opportunities Act (STWOA) of 1994. Its goal was to create a system that would increase the skill level of America's workforce and prepare students for rewarding careers and economic security. It is intended as an initiative, rather than a program, that "establishes a national framework for the development and expansion of programs that integrate academic and practical education" (*Congressional Record*, 1994, p. 27). The components of this initiative include career information and advising, beginning in elementary school; high academic standards for all; work-based learning; and connections between school-based and work-based learning. The community colleges, with their accessibility, low tuition, and focus on vocational education have become the linchpin for this initiative.

Congress authorized $100 million for fiscal year 1994 and $300 million for fiscal year 1995 to implement STWOA. Local area partnerships were established for implemen-

tation. These partnerships include community colleges, four-year colleges, vocational and technical school, local community and business agencies, business and industry, and social service agencies. Workforce investment boards (WIBS) were established at the county level to coordinate and administer all programs.

Foderaro (1995) summarized five advantages community colleges offer to the school-to-work initiative. First, current initiatives appear to serve only students outside colleges' potential enrollment, but community colleges are in a position to offer educational programs that students and parents desire. Parents fear tracking of their children. Linking new school-to-work initiatives to established postsecondary programs will demonstrate to parents that there are many options. Second, community colleges account for 40 percent of all postsecondary co-op programs. These programs can be used as an avenue for implementing school-to-work transition. Third, co-op faculty have worked to build credibility among parents and employers. For employers, co-op provides cost-effective recruitment and training of potential full-time employees. Fourth, community colleges have shown versatility in serving both younger students and adults returning to school. Fifth, mandated advisory boards including business leaders and educators design career programs to meet local business and industry. The college programs, when well designed, fulfill the key components specified in STWOA: initiating school-based and work-based learning, integrating academic and vocational learning, and connecting activities between school and work.

Transition from School to Work

The last stage of the restructuring of American public schools is that of developing curricula for helping students successfully make the transition from school to work. In this phase, the goal that instruction should exist in kindergarten through twelfth grades to prepare students for specific-job entry-level employment on graduation has virtually been dropped. What has replaced that goal is that of teaching generic work knowledge and skills, such as interacting cooperatively with others, linking learning to work, and developing career planning skills, without the expense of business and industrial standard tools, machinery, materials, and supplies. In addition, less expensive programs are being started or more fully used, such as apprenticeship, cooperative education, career guidance, internships, and school-business partnerships. The goal of reform for these systems of workforce preparation is based on 10 guidelines in the *National Assessment of Vocational Education: Final Report to Congress*:

● Include all non-college-bound and some college-bound students.

● Prepare students for careers rather than jobs.

● Broaden the curriculum framework from occupations to industries or other more inclusive constructs.

● Emphasize the development of cognitive skills, broad technical skills, and understanding of industries at the secondary level.

● Emphasize the use of applications to teach underlying principles (e.g., how electricity works) before teaching occupational procedures (e.g., steps in repairing an air conditioner).

● Use work experience, including jobs students find for themselves, to increase understanding of issues such as how the labor market functions and what skills and personal qualities the workplace requires.

● Prepare most students for some form of postsecondary education (e.g., two-year college, technical college, four-year college) and additional training.

● Defer much, but not all, occupation-specific training to the postsecondary level.

● Be competency-based; be geared to high external standards; be assessed by valid, reliable methods; and lead to portable certification.

● Allow for other essential courses, such as core academics (Boesel & McFarland, 1994, pp. 54-55).

History and Role of Community Colleges

Bennett and Boesel and McFarland recommend that most of occupational-specific education be placed in postsecondary institutions. This recommendation rests on the assumption that community colleges are the best sites for such education because of accessibility and low cost. The Carnegie Commission in the late 1960s identified the basic principles for these institutions. One held that they be located so that 90 percent of the population lived within commuting distance. In addition, funding for these institutions is based on county, state, and federal monies. This triple source of funding has enabled the institutions to offer occupational education more inexpensively than private trade/technical schools, four-year colleges, and universities. Therefore, the majority of students can afford the tuition and fees, a national average of $1,392 per year, and travel to community colleges. Nationally, student enrollment in these institutions increased 10 percent per year from 1991 to 1993, when a drop occurred due to birth cycles, a slightly improving economy, and a tuition imposed by California for four-year graduates returning to community colleges to learn how to earn a living. This enrollment results directly from the restructuring of primary and secondary education in America, the college's offering of occupation-specific education, and the reduced incomes of American families.

The role of community colleges is evident when one searches the National Newspaper Index and finds titles such as "Community Colleges Guarantee Graduates Skills" (*New York Times*, September 21, 1994), "Opening Doors to Success" (*The Washington Post*, October 11, 1993), "Retooling American Workers: Community Colleges Are Now a Key to Corporate Retraining Efforts" (*Business Week*, September 27, 1993), and "Community Colleges: In These Economically Tight Times, Growing Numbers of Young People Are Taking a Second Look at Two-Year Institutions. They Like

What They See" (*U.S. News & World Report*, October 4, 1993).

This role began to form in 1892 when William R. Harper, president of the University of Chicago, created two divisions of the University. In 1896, the divisions were called "senior" and "junior," and from this the term *junior college* arose. Junior colleges had the role of transfer education until the mid-1930s, when local communities began to demand curricula for agriculture, oil production, and similar fields. In 1947, President Truman charged a President's Commission on Higher Education that suggested the name *community college*. This commission was followed in 1948 by the Carnegie Commission on Higher Education publishing *Open Door Colleges*. The commission created 12 guiding principles that have generally been achieved:

1. Community colleges should be within commuting distance of all persons, except in sparsely populated areas.

2. The commission favors comprehensive colleges rather than more specialized colleges.

3. Community colleges should remain community colleges because they have an important role that should not be abandoned.

4. Full transfer rights to four-year colleges and universities should be established.

5. Occupational programs should receive the fullest status and support within the colleges.

6. The commission supports open access for all high school graduates and other qualified individuals.

7. Tuition should be low-cost or free.

8. The colleges should provide occupational and personal guidance.

9. The colleges should function as cultural centers.

10. Optimum college size would be 2,000 to 5,000 students.

11. A local advisory board should govern each college.

12. Financing should be equitably shared by federal, state, and local sources (Doty, 1993, pp. 73-74).

The evolution of the field has been reflected in the evolution of the titles of its professional association and journal: 1921–American Association of Junior Colleges; 1972–American Association of Community and Junior Colleges; 1978–the Association journal title changed to *Community, Technical, and Junior College*; finally, 1992–American Association of Community Colleges (AACC) (with "colleges" referring to community, technical, and junior) and the journal title changed to *Community College Journal*. Within the AACC is the affiliate National Council for Occupational Education. The council publishes the *Journal of Studies in Technical Careers* and *Workplace*. All involved in work-based learning programs can benefit from membership in these organizations. In addition, the League for Innovation in the Community College has given priority to workforce development in its 1996 national conference titled Workforce 2000. The league is a nonprofit educational consortium of leading community colleges organized to stimulate innovation in community colleges.

Vital Statistics on Community Colleges

The 1995 Peterson's Guides, Inc., statistics indicate that more than 7,500 institutions of higher education offer awards, certificates, and diplomas that require two or fewer years of study. There are 240 career programs accredited by six accrediting groups and 31 agencies that accredit specific programs (Peterson's Education Center home page, 1995).

Of the 7,500 institutions, there are approximately 1,024 two-year publicly supported colleges. More than 90 percent of the U.S. population lives within an hour's drive of a campus. The 1,024 institutions have an enrollment of 5.3 million credit students and an estimated 5 million noncredit students. Credit students comprise 47 percent of all U.S. undergraduates and 49 percent of all first-time freshmen. The average age is 29. Approximately 46.7 percent of all minorities enrolled in higher education attend community colleges. Sixty-three percent of all students enroll part time and 37 percent full time (12 or more semester credits). Fifty-eight percent are female. The average annual tuition and fees ($1,392) are about one-tenth those of most four-year colleges and universities. Enrollment ranges from 200 to 100,000 students. Approximately 200,000 associate degrees are awarded each year. There are 254,000 faculty, 53.4 percent being part time, with 11,819 administrators (American Association of Community Colleges home page, October 1, 1995; ERIC Clearinghouse for Community Colleges home page, November 28, 1995).

Partnerships in workforce training for business and industry can be found in 97 percent of community/technical colleges. Approximately 65 percent of nurses and allied health care professionals are educated by community colleges, with education provided for 7 of the top 10 "hot jobs" identified by the Bureau of Labor Statistics for the next century (American Association of Community Colleges home page, October 1, 1995).

In the latest survey by Cohen for the UCLA Center for the Study of Community Colleges, 22.6 percent of all community college students nationwide who began in 1987 and completed at least four college credit courses transferred to a four-year state college or university by 1991. Cohen stated that community colleges remain the only avenue for many students for entry into a four-year college or university (ERIC Clearinghouse for Community Colleges home page, November 28, 1995).

To summarize the data, 20 percent of students drop out before graduating from high school. Of the 80 percent left, 49 percent begin their college studies in community colleges. Of these 49 percent, 22.6 percent transfer to four-year colleges or universities. Only 15 percent of all entering high school freshmen complete a four-year degree within six years of high school graduation. These percentages mean that millions of students depend on effective and efficient education in public community colleges for their sur-

vival in the global economy. According to the National Center for Educational Statistics (1995) there were 46.6 million children in kindergarten through the twelfth grade in school year 1993-1994. Unless community colleges provide excellent, low-cost education, millions of these children who cannot afford public and private four-year colleges and universities will be undereducated.

Conclusions

Due to the national policy to greatly reduce or eliminate specific-job education in secondary education, the community college system is the best avenue for many students, especially those from families with low and middle incomes. This conclusion rests on the fact that community colleges can offer quality education at a much lower cost than private schools or public four-year colleges and universities. Community colleges are more accessible to most students and the cost for attending a community college is about one-tenth that of a four-year institution.

Because community colleges have adhered to the original principles of the Carnegie Commission, curricular offerings are more closely aligned with local economies and occupational education has equal status with other studies, although there is still resistance by some faculty who view transfer education as the prime goal of community college education. However, the statistics on student activity—only 22.7 percent of community college students transferring, the vast majority of students enrolled in career programs, and many students with baccalaureate degrees entering community colleges for occupational education—refute the transfer function as the main goal of community colleges.

References and Resources

American Association of Community Colleges, One Dupont Circle, NW, Suite 410, Washington, DC 20036-1176; 202-728-0200, ext. 216; fax 202-833-2467; Internet home page: www.aacc.nche.edu

Boesel, D., & McFarland, L. (1994, July). *National assessment of vocational education: Final report to Congress, Volume I: Summary and recommendations.*

Washington, DC: Office of Educational Research and Improvement. (ERIC Document Reproduction Service No. ED 371 191)

Bonas, J. E. (1995). Invited commentary: Cooperative education and federal government: Future directions? *Journal of Studies in Technical Careers, XV*(2), 59-62. [For information on the journal, contact Southern Illinois University, College of Technical Careers, Carbondale, IL 62901-6604.]

Coley, R. J. (1995). *Dreams deferred: High school dropouts in the United States*. Princeton, NJ: Policy Information Center, Educational Testing Service.

Congressional Record. (1994, May 21). School to work system. In *Youth Policy, 15 & 16*, p. 27.

Delker, D. L. (1988, May). *A comparative case study to determine the relationship between critical change factors and the discontinuation of cooperative education programs*. Unpublished doctoral dissertation, Rutgers-The State University of New Jersey.

Doty, C. R. (1993). Postsecondary occupational education. In A. J. Pautler, Jr., (Ed.), *Vocational education in the 1990s: Major issues* (pp. 71-97). Ann Arbor, MI: Prakken Publications.

Employment & Training Administration, Bureau of Apprenticeship and Training, 200 Constitution Ave., NW, Room N-4649, Washington, DC 20210; (202) 219-5921.

ERIC Clearinghouse for Community Colleges home page: www.gse.ucla.edu/ERIC/eric.html

Foderero, A. (1993, November 16). Summary of the advantages community colleges offer to the school-to-work initiative. Paper presented for New Jersey Council of County Colleges.

Human Resources Division. (1993, September). *Transition from school to work: States are developing new strategies to prepare students for jobs*. Washington, DC: U.S. General Accounting Office.

Issues in cooperative education. (1995). *Journal of Studies in Technical Careers, XV* (2).

League for Innovation in the Community College, 26522 LaAlameda, Suite 370, Mission Viejo, CA 92691; 714-367-2884; fax: 714-367-2885.

Mason, R. E., Furtado, L. T., & Husted, S. W. (1989). *Cooperative occupational education* (4th ed.). Danville, IL: Interstate Printers and Publishers.

National Alliance for Business. (1994, May). *How school-to-work works for business*. Washington, DC.[National Alliance for Business, 1201 New York Ave., NW, Suite 700, Washington, DC 20005-3917; 202-289-2972]

National Center for Educational Statistics. (1995, October). *Announcement: Schools and staffing in the United States: Selected data for public and private schools, 1993-94 released*. NCES 95191a. Washington, DC: Office of Educational Research and Improvement, U.S. Department of Education.

National Council on Occupational Education, 1161 Francisco Rd., Columbus, OH 43220; 614-451-3577; fax 614-538-1914, or contact AACC 202-728-0200,

ext. 216; fax: 202-833-2467. [Produces *Journal of Studies in Technical Careers* and *Workplace*.]

National Society for Experiential Education. (1995). Membership brochure. [National Society for Experiential Education, 3509 Haworth Dr., Suite 207, Raleigh, NC 27609-7229; 919-787-3263; fax; 919-787-3381]

Notes from all over. (1995, February). *Reader's Digest*.

Peterson's Education Center, home page: http://www.petersons.com

Peterson's two-year colleges. (1996). Princeton, NJ: Peterson's Guides, Inc. [202 Carnegie Center, P. O. Box 2123, Princeton, NJ 08543-2123; 609-243-9111; also see U.S. two-year colleges on the Internet for a comprehensive listing of two year colleges: www.sp.utoledo.edu/tworcol.html]

Proposed principles for new legislation. (1995, April/May). *Centerwork, 6* (1).

School to Work Opportunity Act of 1993 [P.L. 103-239], HR/2884/S1361. *Legislative fact sheet*. Washington, DC: U.S. Department of Education and U.S. Department of Labor.

Stern, D. (1991, March). *Options in high schools and two-year colleges*. Washington, DC: U.S. Department of Education, Office of Vocational and Adult Education.

Stern, D. (1992). School-to-work programs and services in secondary schools and two-year public postsecondary institutions. Paper prepared for the National Assessment of Vocational Education. Berkeley: University of California at Berkeley, School of Education.

Stern, D., Finkelstein, N., Stone, J., Latting, J., & Dornsife, C. (1995). *School-to-work: Research on programs in the United States*. Bristol, PA: Falmer Press.

Taylor, J. E., Montague, E. K., & Michaels, E. R. (1972, January). *An occupational clustering system and curriculum implications for the comprehensive career education model*. Alexandria, VA: Human Resources Research Organization. (ERIC Document Reproduction Services No. ED 061 427)

U.S. General Accounting Office. (1993, September). *Transition from school to work: States are developing new strategies to prepare students for jobs*. Washington, DC: Human Resources Division. [Available from 202-512-7224; GAO/HRD-93-139]

U.S. General Accounting Office. (1993, August 16). *Vocational education: Status in 2-year colleges in 1990-91 and early signs of change*. Washington, DC: Human Resources Division. [Available from 202-512-7224; GAO/HRD-93-89]

Wellsfry, N. (Chair, NCOE Accountability Task Force). (c1994). *Accountability in community colleges: Balancing the perceptions with reality*. Columbus, OH: National Council for Occupational Education.

Youth Policy Institute. *Creating a successful comprehensive school-to-work system, 15-16*(12 & 1). [Youth Policy Institute, 1221 Massachusetts Ave., NW, Suite B, Washington, DC, 20005-5333; 202-638-2144]